THINKING

An Introduction to its Experimental Psychology

***

GEORGE HUMPHREY

Director of the Institute of Experimental Psychology
and Professor of Psychology in the
University of Oxford

SCIENCE EDITIONS, 1963
JOHN WILEY & SONS, INC., NEW YORK

Originally published by
METHUEN & CO., LTD.

TO MY WIFE

PREFACE

THIS BOOK WAS begun in 1934 at the suggestion of Professor F. C. Bartlett.[1] The first draft was practically finished when war broke out, and for various reasons the book had to be laid aside for nearly ten years. The whole manuscript has now been revised and a good deal of it rewritten.

Those who have read the manuscript in duplicated form at various stages have made many suggestions about its content. Some, for instance, have urged that the section on the Würzburgers, which now occupies three chapters, should be deleted or at least shortened. Others have been equally urgent that these chapters should be left intact. With the exception of some pruning where the argument seemed to have become diffuse, the Würzburg chapters have been left substantially as they were originally written, and for the following reasons. The contribution of this group still stands in its own right as the most massive, sustained, and acute experimental attack on the problem of thought. It is true that the vocabulary, and behind it the general theory, employed by these men is now out of date, and that for this reason their work often seems arid and devoid of significance for modern psychology. But actually they were concerned with a set of general problems that are still very much alive to-day. Of these, the most important can thus be stated: *Can organic response be reduced without remainder to response strictly correlated with individual receptors?* The problem has a long history and is still being debated. At the present time, for example, Hull and his pupils are maintaining a theory of behaviour built on the foundations laid by Pavlov, and which maintains that behaviour can be explained in terms of fundamentally unchanged motor response to specific receptoral stimulation.[2] The controversy concerning "imageless thought" debated the same problem, couched, however, in terms of experience. The Würzburgers were concerned with the question whether Experience can be built up out of experiences referable to particular sense modalities. The problem is the same, though the co-ordinates have been changed. In the same way, the Würzburg workers found it

---

[1] Now Sir Frederic Bartlett.

[2] The controversy over the "continuity theory" of learning sprang of course from the original theory. For a simple statement, both of Meaning as treated in terms of the referential function and of much of the material collected in this book, see G. Humphrey, 1948, *Directed Thinking* (Dodd Mead).

PREFACE

necessary to postulate the "Determining Tendencies" and the "Task" to supplement their version of Associationism, which is fundamentally a peripheral hypothesis. The modern counterpart is the "Motive", which has been extensively investigated during the past twenty years, and which sprang out of exactly the same difficulty as theirs.

Thus, in addition to its intrinsic merit, the work of the Würzburgers gives a kind of preview of work which is central for modern experimental thinking. No apology should be necessary for treating it in some detail. It may be added that the original sources of both the Würzburgers' work and that of their successor, Selz, are becoming increasingly difficult to obtain.

Another point of criticism has been the treatment of meaning which, in the original writing, was described by the use of the term "referential function." This appeared to be at least a neutral term, stating the facts if it did not illuminate them. However, it now seems fairly clear that many of the difficulties that have surrounded the concept of meaning grew up at a time when psychologists had almost forgotten that a human being is a biological system living in a biological environment. When thinking man is considered strictly together with his environment, the problem of meaning largely dissolves into a set of problems familiar to the modern experimentalist as well as to the analytic psychologists of the last generation. That is, there is no psychological problem of meaning *per se*. With any philosophical problems that the term meaning may engender, this book does not concern itself.[3]

In general, the book is intended to give a critical treatment of experimental work that has already been done. It can of course make no pretence to be exhaustive. There are, no doubt, important researches that have been missed, and it is obvious that whole areas have been left uncovered. It has been urged, for instance, that the book must include chapters on the psychoanalytic theory of thinking, on pathological thinking, on the comparative psychology of thinking, and on children's thinking. But what has been written is already long enough. As it is, the present lag in publishing has made it impossible to include several important researches which should have been treated in a publication dated 1951. Chief of these is Professor Piaget's stimulating though difficult volume, *The Psychology of Intelligence*, the French edition of which escaped the writer's notice. By its nature, the treatment of the material included was almost necessarily historical, especially in the first third of the book. This

---

[3] See Humphrey, *British Journal of Psychology*, 43, 3 and 4, 1951 (in the press), for a fuller treatment than that given in this book.

has meant that the earlier work must be described in the language of its time; that is to say, in terms which, because of their implications, often offend a modern psychologist. Since for reasons already given the work was too important to be left out, the alternative would have been to attempt a translation into those more biological terms which would have been more acceptable to the writer and the modern reader alike. This would necessarily have involved a certain dishonesty.

If this strictly introductory volume serves to help those who are planning psychological research into the all-important subject of the intellectual processes of human beings, its purpose will have been fulfilled.

It is a pleasure to acknowledge the help of the many, on both sides of the Atlantic, who have critically read various chapters. I think in particular of Professors D. O. Hebb, Martyn Estall, and Gregory Vlastos, all of them at one time my colleagues. Professor R. B. MacLeod read the whole manuscript through with a class, and suggested that I really must do something about *Meaning*. On this continent, also, I am grateful to Professor R. C. Oldfield, and to my present colleague, Mr. O. L. Zangwill. Mr. Zangwill's often disconcerting criticisms have been of special value. I wish to thank also the staff of the Institute of Experimental Psychology, who have patiently endured what must at one time have seemed an interminable task. And finally, in my own family, I am most of all grateful to my wife, from whom the book has stolen many hours that rightly belonged to her.

GEORGE HUMPHREY.

Magdalen College,
    Oxford.
August 1951

CONTENTS

CHAPTER I

ASSOCIATION

"NO DOUBT THERE is a sense in which it is true to say that experiment in psychology is 'at least as old as Aristotle'; but certainly it can claim no great age as a method of *systematic* exploration of human reactions."[1] These words, with which Bartlett begins his study of remembering, form a singularly appropriate introduction to an account of the experimental psychology of thinking also. For the method of observation, though not of systematic observation, was used in the analysis of thinking at least as early as Aristotle's time; and, indeed, the conclusions reached by that remarkable mind may today be read with profit by every student of psychological science. Further, the doctrine of association, with which an account of the experimental psychology of thinking logically begins, was originally the product of the same worker, though he did not use it in any systematic way in his general account of thought. On the other hand, in spite of the early work of Aristotle, it has not been until comparatively lately in the history of experimental psychology that the process of thinking has been subjected to that systematic observation which is demanded by the experimental method; and although the doctrine of association in particular has long been of primary importance in the theory of thought, nevertheless, if we can believe the ancient dates, its experimental investigation had to wait for twenty-two hundred years after Aristotle's death.[2]

The term association, or mental association, is a general name often used in psychology to express the conditions under which mental events, whether of experience or behaviour, arise; it is also "the name of a principle of explanation put forward by an important group of thinkers to account generally for the facts of mental life."[3] The great vitality of the theory is shown by the fact that in every age

[1] Bartlett, 1932, p. 1.

[2] According to tradition, Aristotle was born in 384 B.C. and died at about sixty-three years old. Galton's investigation of associative reaction times by means of the stop-watch was published in the second volume of *Brain* in 1879.

[3] J. C. Robertson, 1878. The first part of the statement is modified from Robertson's to suit modern terminology.

it has risen superior to the psychological fashion of the moment, and has, in fact, been progressively reformulated to suit the fashion of the day. In Aristotle's time it was the fashion to speak of "processes", and it was consequently in terms of processes that the first quasi-systematic theory of association was couched. "Recollection occurs", Aristotle says, "because processes naturally follow each other in an orderly manner."[4] It is in this passage that the doctrine of association by Contiguity, Similarity, and Contrast was first laid down, although there has been considerable discussion as to the exact meaning of the text. Aristotle's statement was elaborated and annotated by his successors both in classical and scholastic times. The reader who is interested in this aspect of the history of the doctrine, and in its development from the age of scholasticism to the rise of modern philosophy, is referred to Hamilton's edition of *Reid's Works*.[5]

The beginning of the school known as the British Associationists is certainly to be found in Thomas Hobbes, who clearly enunciated what is known as the *Principle of Contiguity*. "The *cause* of the *coherence* or consequence of one conception to another is their first *coherence* or consequence at that *time* when they are produced by sense: as for example, from St. Andrew the mind runneth to St. Peter, because their names are read together; from St. Peter to a *stone* for the same cause; from *stone* to *foundation*, because we see them together; and for the same cause from *foundation* to *church*, and from church to *people*, and from people to *tumult*: and according to this example the mind may run almost from anything to anything."[6] According to this principle, if two mental events have occurred at the same time, then if one occurs in the future the other will be reinstated. Other principles of association were added, or, as some would prefer it, rediscovered, by later members of the school of the British Associationists. According to the principle of Association by *Similarity*, a mental event will reinstate another one *like* it; according to that of *Contrast*, one which is its opposite. Other principles were at various times proposed, and the question of the number of the principles of association and their relative importance was debated for more than a century. Hume, for example, in 1739 laid down three principles, namely resemblance, contiguity in time or place, cause or effect; while ten years later Hartley maintained that

---

[4] Aristotle, *De Memoria*, 451; trans. J. A. Smith.
[5] Notes D** and D***.
[6] Hobbes, *Humane Nature, or the Fundamental Elements of Policie*, Chapter IV, section 2. Reprinted from Rand, 1912, p. 157.

one principle was sufficient to explain all instances of association, namely that of contiguity. In 1829, James Mill agreed with Hartley and made an express attempt to reduce the principles of Similarity and Contrast to one fundamental law of contiguity. "Our ideas spring up or exist in the order in which the sensations existed of which they are the copies"[7]; while in 1855 Spencer reduces all association to the single principle of similarity. Thirty-five years later we find William James writing at the beginning of the period of "Physiological Psychology". A trained physiologist, he was an immediate forerunner of what was to be called the "stimulus-response" psychology. It is not therefore surprising to find him rejecting Locke's term, "association of ideas", which was, as a matter of fact, almost the only contribution which Locke made to the subject; instead, James proposed a formulation in terms of the more fashionable language of the day.

"*Association*, so far as the word stands for an *effect, is* between THINGS THOUGHT OF—*it is* THINGS, *not ideas, which are associated in the mind.* We ought to talk of the association of *objects*, not of the association of *ideas*."[8] And again, "Let us assume as the basis of all our subsequent reasoning this law: When two elementary brain processes have been active together or in immediate succession, one of them, on reoccurring, tends to propagate its excitement into the other."[9] That is to say, in place of ideas we have a step towards what even then in Russia, at least, was beginning to be known as an "objective statement".[10] James reduces all association to the one fundamental process. "The whole body of the associationist psychology remains standing after you have translated 'ideas' into 'objects' on the one hand, and 'brain-processes' on the other; and the analysis of faculties and operations is as conclusive in these terms as in those traditionally used."[11]

The progress towards objectivity of statement had its culmination in the behaviourist school, where the term association was replaced by that of "conditioned reflex". The physiologist Pavlov had, in fact, in 1903 explicitly set himself to study what had hitherto been called associative or psychic events by a method which had as its aim to ignore absolutely the possible subjective condition of the

---

[7] James Mill, 1869, Vol. I, chapter on "Association of Ideas", p. 56.
[8] James, 1890, Vol. I, p. 554. Italics and capitals as in original.
[9] Ibid., p. 566.
[10] See Bechterew, 1926, p. vi, footnote. In 1866 Ssetchenoff published his *Reflexes of the Brain*, with an objective programme.
[11] James, 1890, Vol. I, p. 604.

object of experimentation. Instead, his purpose was to ascertain exactly the external conditions under which these events took place.[12 and 13] Hence the name conditioned reflex, which has won favour over the term "associative reflex" proposed by Pavlov's rival savant, Bechterew.

And again: "During the two and one-half centuries since the beginning of the English association movement there has been a slow but fairly constant tendency for associationism to stress more and more the aspect of physical reaction. This has reached its logical limit in the behaviouristic psychology of America, which, despite its migration to another continent, and its general repudiation by present-day English psychologists, is a genuine and perfectly natural evolution of English associationism."[14] This statement from one of America's foremost behaviourists clearly exhibits the continuity existing between present and past associationism.

Pavlov's list of "conditions" is intended to correspond with what had earlier been called the "laws of association". In the knowledge of the writer, it is the latest attempt at a complete statement of the conditions under which association arises. Once more we find Contiguity laid down as fundamental. "The fundamental requisite is that any external stimulus, which is to become the signal in a conditioned reflex, must overlap in point of time with the action of an unconditioned stimulus . . . a first and most essential requisite for the formation of a new conditioned reflex lies in a coincidence in time of the action of any previously neutral stimulus with some definite unconditioned stimulus. . . ."[15] Other conditions are that the conditioned stimulus shall begin to operate before the unconditioned; this has since been found to be unnecessary. The animal under experiment must be alert and healthy. These would probably have been accepted by an "associationist" of the old school, such as Hartley, who had, as a matter of fact, anticipated the objective psychologists by a hundred and fifty years in extending association so as to include motor associations. Pavlov's last condition, however, is probably contrary to the spirit of the associational psychology. "Successful transformation", he says, "of the unconditioned stimulus for one reflex into the conditioned stimulus for another reflex can

---

[12 and 13] Pavlov, 1926, p. 24. Thorndike published his *Animal Intelligence* in 1918; it is avowedly associational and primarily interested in "what animals do" though it does admit as a secondary question "what they feel".

[14] Hull, 1934, p. 382.

[15] Pavlov, 1927, p. 26.

be brought about only when the former reflex is physiologically weaker and biologically of less importance than the latter."[16]

With this statement of conditions for association should be joined two other passages. "Three hundred years ago Descartes evolved the idea of the reflex. Starting from the assumption that animals behaved simply as machines, he regarded every activity of the organism as a *necessary* reaction to some external stimulus, the connection between stimulus and response being made through a definite nervous path: and this connection, he stated, was the fundamental purpose of the nervous structures in the animal body. . . . In the eighteenth, nineteenth, and twentieth centuries the conception of the reflex was used to the full by physiologists." He goes on to say that the more complex unlearned activities may be treated in the same way, and are properly termed reflexes. "Instincts and reflexes are alike the inevitable responses of the organism to internal and external stimuli, and therefore we have no need to call them by two different terms. Reflex has the better claim of the two, in that it has been used from the very beginning with a strictly scientific connotation."

With the Cartesian reflex he compares the conditioned reflex, which is initiated by a *signalling stimulus*. By means of such a reflex the animal is enabled to respond to stimuli which only *signal* the approach of the first class of stimuli. "This evidently makes the machine-like responsive activities of the organism still more precise, and adds to it qualities of yet higher perfection. The fundamental and the most general function of the hemispheres is that of reacting to signals presented by innumerable stimuli of interchangeable signification."[17] This fundamental function may, he says, be of the same nature as the simpler Cartesian reflex. "In our general survey we characterized a reflex as a necessary reaction following upon a strictly definite stimulus under strictly defined conditions. Such a definition holds perfectly true also for signalization; the only difference is that the type of the effective reaction to signals depends upon a greater number of conditions. But this does not make signalization differ fundamentally from the better-known reflexes in any respect. . . ." And, finally, it is only the " preconceptions of the human mind [that] stand in the way of any admission that the highest physiological activity of the hemispheres is rigidly determined."[18]

[16] Pavlov, 1927, p. 30.
[17] These quotations are taken *passim* from Pavlov, 1927, Lecture 1.
[18] Ibid., p. 32.

On the basis of this scheme the behaviourist psychology has attempted to "account generally for the facts of mental life". Here the unconditioned reflex takes the place of the sensation, while the conditioned reflex and its elaborations takes the place of associationally derived elaborations of the sensation. The point is illustrated by the following passages from the founder of Behaviourism.

"The relationship, theoretically, between the simplest cases of the conditioned responses we have studied and the more complicated, integrated, spaced, and timed habit responses we are considering seems to me to be quite simple. It is the relationship apparently of part to whole—that is, the conditioned reflex is the unit out of which the whole habit is formed. In other words, when a complicated habit is completely analysed, each unit of the habit is a conditioned reflex." We may add that by a complicated habit Watson means the most complicated habits that exist—"Isn't typewriting, piano playing and every other special act of skill resolvable or analysable into just such a set of units?"[19] When such habits are not explicit or observable, but implicit, then according to Watson we are justified in speaking of "thinking", and such thinking is mainly effected by means of the muscular fields of the larynx and throat. By thinking in general, the behaviourist understands "all implicit language activity and other activity substitutable for language activity",[20] and according to the general behavourist scheme such language activity or such other substitutable activity is the product of conditioned reflexes, like every other acquisition. That is to say, Watson's system reduces all psychological activities, from the simplest to the most complex, including the activity of thinking, to the original reflexes and conditioned reflexes based upon them.

Thus in the Pavlovian system, and the perhaps more fully elaborated behaviourist system based upon it, we have an attempt to account objectively for all psychological facts in terms of the primary interaction of organism and environment together with the mechanism of association. It may readily be seen that this description is an atomistic one. It attempts to explain complex activities as collocations of elementary activities, conditioned and unconditioned, that are generically unaltered by the fact of collocation. It is, further, avowedly mechanistic. Pavlov's account is professedly an extension of the rigidly mechanical Cartesian reflex. Its fundamental psychological activity, from which the most complex operations may be

[19] Watson, 1925, p. 157.   [20] Idem, 1920, p. 89.

derived, is a process consequent upon the primary stimulation of a receptor, namely the reflex process.

With appropriate translation of terms, these statements are true of the older associational theory. That theory has had a long history, and it has been seen to have suffered many modifications during that history. But it is fair to say that the classical theory of association was atomistic, mechanistic, and sensationalistic; that is to say, it derived its ultimate datum from a psychological process consequent upon the stimulation of a sense organ. The objective psychologist cannot of course consistently use the term sense organ, but he means the same thing.[21] It is true that certain of the later associationists attempt to introduce principles of combination of the mental elements other than the purely mechanical one. Thus John Stuart Mill rejects the principle which his father, James Mill, had laid down, and according to which the sole function of association is to bind together experiences which are essentially unchanged by the process of combination. Instead, Mill the younger postulated a kind of combination which changes that which is combined, producing a doctrine of "mental chemistry" in place of the older "mental mechanics". But this is really an admission that the classical theory has failed to explain the facts.[22]

To sum up, it may be said that the associational theory, where it stands by its own principles, represents all mental events, simple or complex, as collocations of generically unchanged elements resulting from the elementary stimulation of the organism. "Carried to its full extent, this conception might fairly be called that of psychical atomism; for on the whole in its two fundamental features it presents a strong resemblance to the physical doctrine of atoms: in the first place the elements are simple and retain throughout their original character; and in the second place the combination which occurs among them is represented as being of the general nature called mechanical."[23] This statement, written by a great analytical psychologist at the beginning of the century, is equally true today of the modern objective associationism. So that, of both forms of the hypothesis, objective and subjective, it may be said as Adamson said of Herbart's

[21] According to Bühler, quoted by Frenkel (1931, p. 193), the four characteristics of the Association Psychology are subjectivism, atomism, sensualism, and mechanism. These he says are axioms of the system.
[22] See the admirable statement in Adamson, 1903, Vol. II, p. 171. Adamson points out that the same thing is true of Herbart's treatment of feeling.
[23] Adamson, ibid., p. 167.

system and of the classical Associationism: "It is peculiar to both that the higher products, the more concrete forms of mental life, should be regarded as mechanically resulting from the grouping together of elementary parts."[24]

Pre-experimental Criticism of the Associational Psychology

If the vitality of the associational hypothesis is attested by the fact that it has survived, in a changed form, the changes of psychological fashion, it is equally well attested by the fact of the vigorous criticisms which have been consistently directed against it for the last sixty years. In briefly stating some of these criticisms, there will of necessity be a certain repetition of what has already been said.

In 1883 Bradley criticized the hypothesis on several heads. First of all, he claims, an atomistic theory cannot account for the facts of mental life. Association means chance-conjunction, and it is true that in our mental history we do find that ideas are conjoined by the merest accident. The elements which are thus represented as associated are particular images. But there is no evidence for the statement that the reproduction of a particular image ever takes place without change. "There is nothing we know which can warrant the belief that a particular fact can survive its moment, or that, when it is past, it can ever live again. We know it is true in our actual experience that reproduction presents us with particular images; but to assert that these *are* the perished originals is to demand a miracle to support our false beliefs. We have absolutely no kind of warrant in experience for our assurance that what comes into the mind by Association is the particular as we had it. For the particular fact is made particular by an elaborate context and a detailed content. And this is *not* the context or content which comes back. What is recalled has not only got different relations; itself is different. It has lost some features and some clothing of its qualities, and it has acquired some new ones. If then there is a resurrection, assuredly what rises must be the ghost and not the individual."[25] The rest of Bradley's argument in this chapter is perhaps a piece of special metaphysical pleading, and the interested reader is referred to the original. The general criticism that reproduction does not normally take place is independent of Bradley's philosophical argument, and is stressed throughout the chapter. "Without respect for the past,

[24] Adamson, loc. cit., p. 171.
[25] Bradley, 1883, reprinted anastatically 1912, p. 306. See also James, 1890, Vol. I, p. 231. Hartley would have allowed that it is the ghost alone that rises.

such images (i.e. so-called reproductions) vary freely within a certain limit."[26] James put Bradley's point thus:

"*A permanently existing 'idea' or 'Vorstellung' which makes its appearance before the footlights of consciousness at periodical intervals is as mythological an entity as the Jack of Spades.*"[27] Bradley further criticized associationism as not having accounted for the fact that thought is "controlled by the object"; that is, the object of thought.[28] That is to say, what is today called "directive thinking" cannot be explained as a fortuitous concourse of sensational elements; some other principle is necessary to explain the directiveness. The same point had already been made in somewhat different terms by Adamson, who pointed out the importance of motive in the process of thinking.[29] These two criticisms are typical of the objection which has continually been raised against the atomistic character of associationism. Mental life is directed, purposive, motivated, and cannot be explained as being governed by the chance clashing of elements derived haphazardly from without. We shall see the Würzburg group, years after Adamson's paper, insisting that motive, which they called determining tendency or Task, must be brought into the picture.[30] We shall see also Selz launching a polemic against what he called the "diffuse theory of reproduction", which is the classical associatory theory,[31] and supplementing it with the notion of motivation. Conformably with the temper of the times in which they lived, both Selz and the Würzburgers carried out an extensive programme of experiment.

The two criticisms thus far considered are then briefly to the effect that there is no reproduction or reinstatement such as the hypothesis demands; and secondly that to explain the process of thought some kind of extra-associational direction must be postulated.

The first criticism was in a way accepted by certain of the dynasty of British Associationists. Mention has already been made of John Stuart Mill's use of the chemical analogy to explain mental events. "The laws of the phenomena of mind are sometimes analogous to mechanical, but sometimes also to chemical laws. When many impressions or ideas are operating in the mind together, there sometimes takes place a process of a similar kind to chemical combination. When impressions have been so often experienced in conjunction that each of them calls up readily and instantaneously

[26] Bradley, 1883, p. 302.
[27] James, 1890, Vol. I, p. 236.
[28] Bradley, 1887.
[29] Adamson, 1884.
[30] See Chapter III.
[31] Selz, 1922, Introduction; 1924.

the ideas of the whole group, those ideas sometimes *melt and coalesce* into one another, and appear not several ideas but one." In this single composite idea the components are not necessarily perceivable. The principle of combination is that of "*mental chemistry* in which it is proper to say that the simple ideas generate, rather than that they compose the complex ones". It has already been pointed out, that this is a departure from the strict associational hypothesis, a confession that the general principle is inadequate. For it implies that the wholes which come into being when the elements are brought together have properties which do not belong to the elements, and which are therefore not explained as primary sensation plus revived sensation. If sensation plus revival of sensation is not adequate to account for these new properties, one is entitled to ask on what principle they come into being. To use the words "mental chemistry" or "engendered" is not sufficient. Whether or not Mill's descriptions are good psychology, they are certainly not associationism. The modern reader will of course recognize that Mill's "mental chemistry" stands in close relation to the account given by an almost truculently anti-associational group of today—the Gestalt psychologists.

In fact, part of Stout's criticism of the associational hypothesis is that it completely fails to recognize the apprehension of a *form* of combination as a distinct psychical element. "The presented whole is for them simply the sum of its presented components.[32] On the contrary, Stout maintained that mental elements must be changed when they enter into new combinations, very much as the Gestalt psychologists claim.

A particular instance in which the associational psychology has considered it necessary to bring in some further principle is to be found, according to many critics, in the apprehension of relations.[33] "The association psychology, in its strictest form, has always found the explanation of these relational elements a hopeless problem. [He is speaking of the primitive relationships of coexistence and succession.] Indeed, criticism of it has generally consisted in drawing attention to these; and the counter theory has too often been rapidly developed by finding an explanation of them in some non-sensuous relating synthetic activity of the mind or ego or self."[34] As the point has often been made, the fact that experiences occur in

---

[32] Stout, 1902, Vol. II, p. 48.   [33] See Adamson, loc. cit., p. 171.
[34] Ibid., p. 174.

certain relations, must not be confused with the experience of those relations. Of two musical notes that are successively experienced, one may be louder than the other. It does not follow that it will be experienced as louder than the other. In fact, if the two notes are separated by a long enough interval of time, it is almost certain that the relationship will not be experienced. It is improbable that if the notes emitted by Big Ben were to be changed at noon to a note a semitone higher, the alteration would be perceived by more than a small fraction of the surrounding population; and it is still more improbable that if there were any listeners on the wireless who heard the clock striking at noon and one o'clock respectively, more than an infinitesimal proportion would notice that there had been any change. The stimuli would have been different at twelve and one, and correspondingly the experience at one o'clock would be of a note a semitone higher. But the experience of the relationship would not necessarily be present. The existence of relations as experienced has then always proved a difficulty to the associational psychology, which has often had recourse to some extra-associational theory to explain them. In James' words, the fact that *two ideas* are given in a certain relation does not give *the idea* of that relation. "Somehow, out of 'ideas', each separate, each ignorant of its mates, but sticking together and calling each other up according to certain laws, all the higher forms of consciousness were to be explained, and among them the consciousness of our own personal identity. . . . Two ideas, one of 'A' succeeded by another of 'B', were transmuted into a third idea of '*B after A*'. . . . Two similar ideas stood for an *idea of similarity*."[35]

Very closely allied is the criticism that while the "ideas" with which associationism deals are disconnected, discrete, atomic; on the other hand, Experience, and particularly that kind of experience which is ordinarily called thinking, is close fitting and continuous. This criticism is implicit in such writers as Bradley and Adamson.[36] The unity of experience as it actually exists cannot, say the critics, be provided on the associational scheme. "Consciousness . . . does not appear to itself chopped up in bits. . . . It is nothing jointed; it flows. A 'river' or a 'stream' are the metaphors by which it is most naturally described."[37] And in a later terminology, the experimentalist Bühler states—though in a different context—"A glance at the

---

[35] James, ibid., p. 353.   [36] See, e.g., Adamson, op. cit., p. 183.
[37] James, op. cit., p. 239.

protocols will tell us; anything so fragmentary, so sporadic, so thoroughly at the mercy of chance when it enters consciousness as the image in our thought experiences, cannot be regarded as the carriers of the close-fitting and continuous thought content."[38]

There is a final criticism which, although historically it belongs earlier, has been deferred to the end of the list. It is couched in terms which are least familiar to the psychologist of today. It originates from, or was at least first published by, Bradley, and attacks the sensualistic aspect of associationism. The conventional doctrine of association, says Bradley, represents ideas as revived copies of sensory data. Now such sensory data are and must be particulars. We have seen that particulars cannot be repeated. What happens in association is that there is something common to the original (particular) impression and the associated (particular) experience. "Association", he says, "marries only universals." And in any case thought proper is not of particulars, it is rather of general validity. Therefore association cannot explain thinking. The reader may perhaps be reminded that the answer is not valid that the particulars brought by association *stand for* generalities; for the very process by which the particular images are thus caused to stand for something else is extra-associational. Further, it may be noticed that under the particulars of which Bradley speaks, verbal images should be included. The mere silent repetition of the words of a syllogism is not the process of thinking the syllogism, unless the process of *standing for* is present. Such a process might occur in a person ignorant of the language in which the syllogism is couched. And if this process is added, once again we have gone beyond the associational scheme proper.

Summary of Pre-experimental Criticism of Associationism

It was stated that associationism has three aspects. It is sensationalist, mechanical, atomistic. The criticisms that were directed against the original theory may be listed under these three heads.

Against the *sensationalism* of the theory it was urged that the events of which the higher mental processes are comprised are not the primary sense data in an unchanged form, since there is no evidence that mental processes are thus reinstated. Further, sense data or presentations are particular, while thinking is general.

Against the *mechanical* aspect of the theory it was urged that

[38] Bühler, 1907, p. 317.

thinking is directive, purposive, controlled, and can therefore not be described as the blindly mechanical interplay of purposeless elements.

Against the *atomic* aspect of the theory the first two objections hold good also. That is to say, to put these statements in somewhat different words, there is no unchanging mental atom; and if there were the delicate adaptations of directive thinking could not be explained as the product of its mechanical combinations. Further, it was also objected that mental life is continuous, not analysable into atoms. In particular, the theory cannot account for the fact that we are conscious of relations between the primary data, which experience is not explainable on the theory that the mind *is* the clash of unchanging, discrete atoms of experience.

The general charge was then brought that in order to explain the facts of the thought process various other principles must be added. Such a principle was slipped into the system by John Stuart Mill, who was not justified in calling the new system by the old name.

Warren's comments on this point are worth quoting. "First of all . . . the associationists included under the term *association* two or three rather distinct operations. Simultaneous association and successive association operate in different ways; the former is a *union*, the latter a change of *passage* from one experience to another. Furthermore, the *transformation* or mental chemistry which occurs in simultaneous association seems to be still another sort of operation." To group these three operations under a single name, association, "is a verbal simplification scarcely justified by the facts with which we are dealing. . . . Again the phenomena of *attention* and *discrimination* do not seem to be accounted for under the associationist's treatment. These phenomena appear to involve distinctive operations upon the elementary data."[39]

The fact that this passage comes from an avowed associationist makes it doubly interesting. Warren concludes: "A complete interpretation of experience would appear to involve at least discrimination, two synthetic processes, and transformation, in addition to the original sensibility and revival, and possibly also a focalizing factor."

Earlier Experimental Work on Association

The advent of the experimental method coincided with a certain decline in the importance of classical association psychology. This

[39] Warren, 1921, p. 306.

was due partly to a reaction which came from such sources as the Scotch faculty psychology, which stressed the broad division of the mind into groups of operations such as feeling, knowing, and willing; partly to the even more important opposition of a group of analytical psychologists, including Stout, Ward, and Adamson. In addition, the experimental examination of association developed its own set of problems, which diverted attention from the more ambitious programme of the associationists.[40]

Since the experimental work of this period which covered the last twenty years of the last century did not concern itself directly with the problem of thought, its discussion is not germane to the purpose of this book. Wundt, in fact, maintained stoutly that thought processes could not be investigated experimentally. His own theory postulated an "apperceptive" process, which was of a higher order than association. The stream of thought was of an "apperceptive-associative" nature, and association played a fundamental, though by no means an exclusive, part. Little is heard today of Wundt's Apperception, although Boring refers to it as a "colossal achievement".[41]

As a classical experiment on association, involving the "higher" processes though not the highest, should be mentioned the work of Ebbinghaus on Memory.[42] Ebbinghaus introduced the method of the nonsense syllable, by which he hoped to bring it about that the significance of material to be memorized should be the same for everybody. This he did not accomplish, since nonsense syllables breed their own set of meanings even more individual and certainly more bizarre than ordinary words used as stimuli. Ebbinghaus did, however, succeed in throwing a great flood of light on the process of memory. His work is typical of the more modest objectives which experimental psychology was begining to set itself when the somewhat grandiose announcements of the associationists were beginning to be suspected. His aim was simplification both of stimulus and response, and he could hardly perhaps be blamed for not seeing that such simplification was easier to advocate than to achieve.[43] The nonsense-syllable investigations are of particular interest as apparently refuting the contention of those, such as Bradley and James,

[40] See Warren, 1921, p. 213.
[41] See Boring, 1929. Wundt, 1902–3, Vol. III, section on "Association".
[42] Ebbinghaus, 1885.
[43] For an acute evaluation and criticism of Ebbinghaus's work, see Bartlett, loc. cit., p. 2.

who had maintained that mental events, or ideas, are not reinstated. If a subject learns the series TOB-VID-RUD and later says these syllables, is he not reinstating the original mental process?

First with reference to the "ideas" in terms of which the classical association psychology was conceived. For a long time it was believed that an "idea" or an image necessarily precedes speech. With the disappearance of the idea-motor theory this belief evaporated, though not before it was able to influence the theory of aphasia in the wrong direction. Modern theory and modern experiment alike have now dissipated the hypothesis.[44] With the precedent idea eliminated, we are left with the asserted identity of the speech-reactions when the subjects learn and when they repeat the syllables TOB-VID-RUD. If they do not say the words aloud, repeating them in a whisper or silently, then it is clear that the repetition is not simply a reinstatement of the original psychological process. We are then left with the case where the subject says the words aloud when learning them, and repeats them aloud.

Are the psychological processes involved in the two cases *identical*? It would be a bold man who would assert that they are. Bradley's original argument applies here. The words are said in entirely different contexts in the two cases. In the one case they are being said for the purpose of retention; in the other case for the purpose of saying what has been learned. In the knowledge of the writer, no objective records have been taken for the purpose of ascertaining whether the speech-behaviour in the two cases is identical. It is very improbable that they would be found to be so. Common observation is able to detect differences in tone, pitch, accent, and so on between the original time of learning and the repetition, and even between repetitions. There will, of course, be *something* [45] in common between the syllables as learned and the syllables as repeated. Otherwise we should not say that the syllables were learned. But that which is in common *is not the total psychic activity, including the speech behaviour and the speech experience. It is rather a general experience and a general behaviour, which is exactly that which is common to different repetitions of these syllables.* In explaining how it is that we can preserve a constant core in the changing contexts of successive experiences or successive activities, recourse must be had to some principle that is not association in the ordinary sense of the term. Aristotle said that we "see the universal in the particular".

[44] See Chapter VIII on "Thought and Language".
[45] See the footnote in Ebbinghaus' *Grundzüge*, 1913, pp. 634–5.

Bradley epigrammatically states that "Association marries only universals", and this is what he has in mind. Apologies are perhaps due at this point to the reader who is interested primarily in experimental psychology for introducing what will no doubt appear to many as a rather fine-drawn distinction. The fact is that in the non-sense-syllable method we have a limiting case, which perhaps may be made to approximate closely to sheer reproduction, but never succeeds entirely. If Bradley's argument seems to split hairs when it is applied to Ebbinghaus' technique, it is because the hairs are there.

In ordinary life, memory is not the identical reinstatement of previous experience or behaviour. The closer the psychologist approaches such absolute reinstatement, the less valuable his work is in the analysis of the working mind. If he were able to reach it, his work would be completely valueless in the analysis of everyday experience and conduct, because he would have eliminated one of the most striking characteristics of such everyday psychic activity, namely the fact of variation.[46] By the use of his peculiar and valuable technique, Ebbinghaus did bring into relief the identical factors in the memorial process, but his results cannot be taken as an argument that the process of thought involves identical reproduction from the past.

The same tendency to think in terms of associational reinstatement is evident as late as 1913 in Meumann's *Psychology of Learning*.[47] The generation that had passed since the experimental work of Ebbinghaus had begun to make fairly explicit the criticism that memory, or association, do not reinstate or reproduce. So that on page eight of the work cited we find Meumann saying "everyday experience no less than psychological investigation shows us that memory also transforms ideas" as well as reinstates them. But the trend of a fundamentally associational bias was too strong, for after this purely lip service to the conventional criticism we find him speaking of dispositions to a subsequent *revival* of ideas, and of the conditions of *reproduction* in the narrower sense.[48] Apologies have already been tendered to the experimentalists for the analytical nature of this discussion. The apology is coupled with the antici-

---

[46] Certain readers may ask whether the above statement does not preclude altogether the scientific treatment of memory. It does not. Bartlett is able to give an excellent account of memory without the postulate of reinstatement. He calls it an imaginative reconstruction, and the thesis of the book is that changes occur from repetition to repetition.

[47] English translation, New York, 1913.

[48] O.C., p. 15. See also Ebbinghaus, *passim*.

patory statement that exactly the same point will come out in the discussion of that bulwark of behaviourist psychology—the conditioned reflex.

Further than this theoretical point, the early experimental work on association has contributed little that is of interest in a discussion of the psychology of thinking.

The Conditioned-reflex Theory

The conditioned-reflex theory is the product of an aggressively experimental age. It may fairly be said that it, rather than the work of such psychologists as Ebbinghaus, is the typical form of associationism in such an age. One should therefore expect to find the same criticisms developing from the experimental side, and being subject to experimental verification, as had developed in connection with the earlier non-experimental theory. To some extent, at least, this is so.

Before showing this in detail, certain implications of the conditioned-reflex theory must be made plain. The theory in its popular form implies that behaviour is analysable into unit conditioned reflexes, each one of which is the result of the elementary stimulation of a sense organ. This implies that each unit of behaviour is generically unaffected by the presence of the others; it further implies that the situation to which reaction is made can be considered as composed of elements the effect of each of which on the organism is unaltered by the presence of the other elements. That is to say, a situation is, so to speak, an arithmetical or linear sum of stimuli, meaning by this a sum such that the elements, in this case stimulating agencies or energies, are unaltered by the fact that they are here combined with other stimuli. In another place I have examined the concept of the linear summation of stimuli, and found it inadequate to explain the facts.[49] Certain points may, however, be mentioned here.

The implication that stimuli may be linearly summated is accepted by representative objective psychologists, at least when writing in the earlier period of behaviourism. Thus Watson says: "A situation is of course, upon final analysis, analysable into a complex group of stimuli. . . . Stimuli must be added to or subtracted from."[50] "A stimulus appears to be connected of necessity with a definite response, as cause with effect. It seems obvious that the whole activity of the

---

[49] Humphrey, 1933, Chapter IX.   [50] Watson, 1924, pp. 8, 10.

organism should conform to definite laws."[51] The latter passage from Pavlov connects the idea of lawfulness in the body with that of definite *stimuli* followed by definite responses. Stimuli are later equated with "physical or chemical agencies—waves of sound, light, and the like".[52] The general implication is clear. Stimuli, both unconditioned ones and those which by association have acquired new responses,[53] may be treated by the methods of physical science, and summated to form a situation. That is to say, they may be combined in the manner suggested by physical science on the assumption that the fact of such combination has in itself no specific effect of its own on the organism.

The psychological criticism is that an energy-change must be distinguished from a stimulus. In order to see how this is so we must contrast the series of energy-changes, "waves of sound, light, and the like" with the series of responses which each such energy-change may be supposed to bring about when it occurs separately upon the same constant background.[54] Then there is no guarantee that the rules by which physical science finds that it can express the combination of such energy-changes, such as simple addition of light energies, will hold good also for the combination of the corresponding responses. Twice as much light energy will not produce twice as intense a response. But this is really the postulate underlying Watson's statement that "stimuli can be added to or subtracted from". As a matter of fact, what physical science describes as the addition of a given quantity of energy to that which is already present may completely transform the reaction, that is to say, the stimulus-value of stimuli already present, as any man may observe who increases over a certain limit the energy with which he pats the baby's cheek. This is the same as to say that while energy-changes may be linearly additive,[55] stimuli are not necessarily so. For the combination of energy-changes may, and indeed regularly does, change the stimulus-value of that which is combined. *The objective theory of association identifies energy-change with stimulus-value.* At least, it does so in its programme. For example, that most able psychologist, E. B. Holt,[56] maintains that stimuli are normally "algebraically additive", by which he means what we have called linearly additive; and quotes the physiologist Magnus to that effect. In spite of the weighty support

[51] Pavlov, 1927, p. 7.   [52] Ibid., p. 14.   [53] Ibid., p. 394.
[54] This statement, of course, involves an over-simplification.
[55] And there is reason to believe that they are not always so!
[56] Holt, E. B., 1931, p. 71.

of Professor Holt, it seems to be certain that no psychologist consistently adheres to the theory. The fact of colour-contrast alone provides an obvious exception. Pavlov himself provides another, when he maintains that "there is no summation of the individual reflex effect of each single component" in a specific case.[57]

The *programmes* of Watson and of Pavlov are atomistic in exactly the sense that they postulate the linear addition of stimuli; though the men are too good scientists to follow the programme to its logical conclusion. It may be added that the postulate of linear addition of stimuli is the same as the "constancy hypothesis", which the Gestalt group have so persistently attacked.[58] Bradley's criticism of the classical theory of association is really a criticism of the "constancy hypothesis", and it proceeds on lines very similar to those of the Gestalt group.

To return to the criticisms which experimental results have caused to be levelled against the conditioned-reflex theory. Parallel with the sensational, mechanical, and atomic aspects of the older theory, the conditioned-reflex hypothesis of mental life may be said to have three corresponding aspects. They may be called sensory,[59] mechanical, and atomic respectively. Criticism has been directed against the hypothesis on each of these three heads. The atomic aspect has already been dealt with.

Concerning the sensory aspect Lashley has stated: "The performance of the habit cannot be ascribed to the functioning of stereotyped paths from sensory to effector cells. This characteristic of the stimulus has been emphasized by Driesch, Bergson, Wertheimer, Koffka, Goldstein, and many others, and although we need not accept the anti-physiological conclusions which have sometimes been based upon it, we must recognize the problem as a serious one for psychological and neurological theory."[60] This is a direct negation, by an experimentalist on strictly experimental grounds, of the proposition that the highest adaptive behaviour is analysable into elements each of which is the unchanged product of sensory stimulation. That is to say, it is the denial of the sensationalistic counterpart of the conditioned-reflex hypothesis. It is, incidentally, a denial of the

[57] Holt, 1931, p. 71; Pavlov, 1927, p. 144.

[58] See Koffka, 1935, index, and *passim*. Many have claimed that the constancy hypothesis is a straw man.

[59] Had it not been for the example of Dr. Lashley, I should not have dared to use this term in connection with the conditioned-reflex theory. See Lashley, 1934, p. 476.

[60] Lashley, ibid.

hypothesis of the linear addition of stimuli. It is derived, as one might expect of its author, primarily from neurological considerations.

The sensory aspect of the conditioned-reflex hypothesis is also contradicted by quantitative examination of the character of conditioned response. Bradley maintained that there was no evidence that mental processes are reinstated. Quantitative examination of conditioned responses shows that there is no reinstatement of the original responses to receptoral stimulation. Such reinstatement is demanded by the hypothesis. Pavlov, in fact, speaks of the conditioned stimulus as the *substitute* for the unconditioned one, implying reinstatement of the unconditioned response.[61] The nervous impulse is *diverted* from one physiological path to another.[62] Hull has collected the results of eight quantitative studies for which he has calculated the proportion which the extent of conditioned bears to unconditioned response. In seven of these studies the proportion varies from 33 per cent. to 68 per cent. That is to say, conditioned response is from one- to two-thirds as extensive as unconditioned response. In the eighth study, that of Wendt on the knee jerk, the proportion is 129 per cent.; conditioned exceeds unconditioned response by 29 per cent. In the same way, examination of Pavlov's results shows conditioned salivation to be much smaller in extent than unconditioned salivation.[63] These results may be summarized by saying that they afford a translation in objective terms of Bradley's statement "without respect for the past such images [i.e. so-called reproductions] vary freely within certain limits." In another context I have shown that there is considerable evidence that the conditioned reflex is an entirely new response, built up by the interaction of two cerebral centres of activity, each centre being altered in the process.[64] The best example is given by Hilgard's work on the wink reflex, where by careful timing the conditioned blink appears as a supernumerary reaction in addition to the unconditioned reaction, the new response appearing on the record as a small hump preceding the sharp rise denoting the unconditioned reaction. Thus the more exact measurement made possible by objective registration makes possible an objective confirmation of Bradley's criticism that the original mental event is not reinstated in association.

[61] According to Pavlov, writing in 1913, the conditioned stimuli are "*Stellvertreter der beständigen Reize*"; 1926, p. 195.

[62] Idem, 1926, p. 30.

[63] On page 425 of Pavlov, 1927, is quoted the title of a paper dealing with "Relative Magnitudes of Conditioned and Unconditioned Salivary Reflexes".

[64] Humphrey, 1933, pp. 212–14; Hilgard, 1931.

The mechanical aspect of the associational hypothesis has likewise found its critics on the objective side. Adamson stressed the importance of motives in thinking. Bradley objected to the "mechanism of ideas"; thought he said is controlled by the object. These criticisms grew out of analytical considerations. Arguing from experimental results, Lashley states: "The facts are those which are held to characterize behaviour as purposive rather than mechanical and, although we need not admit the finalistic implications of 'purpose', we must recognize that a definite type of neurological problem is involved and that the behaviour does not have the commonly admitted properties of the reflex."[65] The facts to which he refers concern the behaviour of animals in the maze and of chimpanzees trained to open boxes, where it is shown that such behaviour cannot be explained as due to fixed neural paths, but may vary in the mechanism used to attain the end result. The argument is based on the plasticity of objectively observed behaviour; behaviour towards an end is not stereotyped, according to the statement, but may vary; such variation must then be, in Bradley's terms, "controlled by the object", or by the end to be attained. Such control by the object is of course the correlative of the fact of variation; it is not sheer behavioural chaos of which Lashley is speaking, but, on the contrary, variation of behaviour within the limits set by the attainment of the end result.[66]

One of the most interesting of the modern experimental attacks on the principle of association was made in 1922 by Kurt Lewin. It is directed against the older, subjective associationism, but its discussion belongs with Lashley's statement just quoted. According to Lewin, association cannot serve as the cause of a mental event. In his words: "The experimental investigation of habit formation [association] has shown that the couplings caused by habit never supply as such the motor of a mental event; . . . Rather in all cases certain mental *energies* originating, as a rule, in the pressure of will or needs, i.e. mental systems *under stress* are the necessary conditions of mental events."[67] For example, nonsense syllables were repeated in pairs three hundred times over a period of twenty days. Instructions were then given: "As usual, read softly the syllables

---

[65] Lashley, op. cit., p. 477.

[66] Reference will be made to the objective fact of variation in behaviour at several points of this book.

[67] Lewin, 1926, p. 311, Koffka's translation. Lewin's experiments were anticipated by May, 1917, and largely confirmed by Freeman, 1930.

presented, but beyond this make no attempt to do anything; at the same time, do not prevent yourself from doing anything." This was intended as a neutral instruction. None of the twelve associated syllables were repeated when these instructions were given. Later, on the same day, seventeen other control syllables were presented with the instruction: "Name the next syllable you learned", with the result that fourteen correct reactions followed.[68] As the result of this and other experiments, Lewin concludes that the law of association, as it is ordinarily stated, has left out of account the conditions under which associations are formed. The laboratory experiments are all made on determined, that is to say motivated, association. Motive is necessary not only for reproduction but for the formation of the associatory bond. Once more, this is fundamentally the criticism of Adamson, when he states: ". . . the question what determines the train of thought, what causes us to think as we say of something else, is really the question what causes attention to include this or that at the moment. The motives are infinitely numerous. . . ."[69]

Lewin's experiments would then lead to the conclusion, which is that of Bradley and Adamson, that the *blind and mechanical interplay of associations cannot account for the facts of mental life.* An additional extra-associational principle, which we may call motivation, must be assumed to operate.[70] Exactly the same point was made by Leeper, in certain experiments on rats. Twenty-three animals were trained in a simple maze, one arm of which led to food, the other to water. The motivation was alternated irregularly from day to day, by keeping the animals without food or water for twenty-two and a half and twenty-two hours respectively. "An accuracy of over 90 per cent. on first trials was achieved at the end of eighteen days of training with five trials daily." First trials were plotted because the experimenter was interested in ascertaining whether the animal would turn to the right or left, as the case may be, because it was thirsty or hungry, and apart from the fact that on an immediately preceding trial it had found food or drink by turning in one direction

[68] Idem, 1922, p. 230 (apparently results from one subject).

[69] Adamson, 1884. In commenting on this passage Bain said: "Far more serious ground of difference of opinion [i.e. than Wundt's apperception] is the treatment of Association as almost exclusively an affair of motives." Bain, 1887, p. 181.

[70] It is not here maintained that this is the only extra-associational principle that must be postulated, but only that these three workers agreed that what may be called motive is necessary.

or another. "This set of experiments permits an unequivocal answer to the question of whether motivation can exercise a directive function in relation to the utilization of habits. ... The present study shows that motives . . . may serve as differentiating or selective agents to determine which of several responses will be employed."[71] This study is of capital importance in modern comparative psychology. It confirms, on an entirely objective basis, the anti-mechanical criticisms raised against the associational theory. It exhibits a situation in which some principle other than the clash of associations must be invoked to explain behaviour; the extra-associational principle is termed motivation, and the distinction is clearly laid down between habit or association and its utilization. It is noteworthy that Leeper's experiment was worked out without reference to the earlier criticisms of the same nature. It is particularly interesting, too, that with appropriate change of terminology Leeper's statement is almost exactly the same as that of the Würzburg psychologists Ach and Watt, who, it will later be shown, likewise invoked an extra-associative principle, which they called the *determining tendency* or *Aufgabe* respectively, and which acted as a differential agent to determine which of several responses may be employed. Leeper, however, disagrees with Lewin, in that he claims that, for learning proper or acquisition, motivation is not as important as is commonly believed.

To return to the conditioned reflex, it may readily be seen that motivation is here also important and, in certain cases, indispensable. The animal must be hungry if the salivary reflex is used as the basis. Some unconditioned reflexes, says Pavlov, may display a temporary weakness when used in the process of conditioning. "In the hungry animal food naturally brings about a powerful unconditioned reflex, and the conditioned reflex develops quickly. But in a dog which has not long been fed the unconditioned stimulus has only a small effect, and alimentary conditioned reflexes are either not formed at all or are established very slowly."[72] That is to say, the hunger motive is a necessary, extra-associational condition for the establishment of the salivary reflex. There seem, however, to be cases of conditioning where the motivation appears at least to be unnecessary. Such, for example, is exhibited by the admirable study of Wendt on the conditioning of the knee jerk. Wendt used as conditioned stimulus a blow on the tendon of the left knee, and as unconditional stimulus

[71] Leeper, 1935.   [72] Pavlov, 1927, pp. 31–2.

a similar blow on the right knee.[73] Thus stimulation of the left knee was associated with reaction of the right leg. It is hard to bring this experiment under the rubric of motivation. It seems, therefore, that for certain of the objective experiments motivation is necessary for association, while for others motivation is unnecessary. It will be remembered that Leeper maintained that "learning [acquisition] takes place which is not dependent on motivational satisfaction or punishment, but which is dependent merely upon the perceptual reaction to the situation". The relation of association as objectively registered to motivation must still be considered obscure. It does, however, seem to have been sufficiently demonstrated that motivation is sometimes necessary, sometimes not, for the establishment of conditioned reflexes; and that for the operation of conditioned reflexes it is sometimes though apparently not always necessary to invoke the concept of motivation to explain the facts.

It has been seen that the classical theory of association was criticized on the ground that we actually have experience of relations, and that this experience cannot be explained by the presence in consciousness of atomistic ideas. Here again experiment designed to test the reflex conditioned-reflex hypothesis has found itself confronted with the same difficulty. According to Lashley (1934), we react to patterns, ratios, or gradients of excitation to relations; and this fact is impossible of explanation by a hypothesis which postulated a one-to-one correspondence between stimulus and response.

"The theory of the reflex was evolved to account for the most unintelligent of behaviour, the activities of the 'spinal' animal. . . . More recently . . . it has been promulgated by the Russian objective school as an adequate basis for explanation of all behaviour. . . . The chief difficulty is in its implication of a point-to-point correspondence in the relations of receptors, nerve cells, and effectors. Not that this is always expressed; but the comprehensibility and explanatory value of the reflex-arc hypothesis lies in just this definiteness of connections, which permits the tracing of nerve impulses over predetermined paths. Omit this element of restricted paths and the theory becomes nothing more than an assertion of uniformity in the sequence of stimulus and response." First among the facts which give difficulty to existing theories is, according to this worker, "the determination of reactions by patterns or ratios of excitation imposed upon varying anatomical elements". What determines

[73] Wendt, 1930. The importance of extra-associational factors of a motivational type in conditioning has also been stressed by Razran, 1936, 1939.

reaction is the existence of a specific gradient of excitation. Such a cortical gradient, releasing a specific response, may be established by events at the sensory level which vary very widely among themselves. The only stipulation is that they must all be cast in the same pattern. An admirable illustration is to be found in Köhler's well-known experiment with hens and chimpanzees. It will be remembered that the animals were trained to choose the lighter of two greys; that is to say, grey "A" was chosen, where grey "A" is lighter than grey "B". The animal was then confronted with grey "C" and grey "A", where "C" is lighter than "A". Under these circumstances, "C" was chosen and "A" now rejected in a significant number of trials. This result illustrates Lashley's general thesis that response is to an excitatory gradient rather than to a topographically or quantitatively determined impact of energy upon the receptor. Its explanation upon conditioned-reflex lines is grotesquely ponderous.

A final criticism of the conditioned-reflex doctrine, as generally stated, has come from Professor Lashley, who suggests, first of all, that generalization is one of the primitive basic functions of organized nervous tissue. Further, he claims to have shown experimentally that association is established in rats to "aspects" of a situation, such as " larger size", rather than to detailed, particular features. Thus, again, a chimpanzee will tend to respond to a "lighter grey" which it has never seen before. A rat will associate food with a *larger* figure to which it has been trained, whether it is a larger *triangle* or *circle*. This is in essence Bradley's doctrine that "association marries only universals". Professor Lashley has been severely criticized on this point; but his work does seem to be a remarkable confirmation of earlier, analytical criticism (Lashley, 1942; Lashley and Wade, 1946).[74]

Bringing these results together, it can be seen that the newer form

[74] The objection has been raised by some of my philosophical friends that Bradley does not mean the same as Lashley. In answer, it may be pointed out that Bradley himself apparently thought he did! Speaking of a dog which has had a fight at a certain place, Bradley asks what the dog will do the next day if he finds a differently appearing dog in the same place. "Size, blackness, and roughness are the typical ideas which will certainly operate ... from the outset universals are used. From the first beginnings of intelligence it is the type which operates and not the image. . . . In the sense of not using the particular as particular . . . and of holding true always and valid everywhere what has ever and anywhere once been experienced, the earliest and the latest intelligence are the same from one end to the other of the scale of life" (Bradley, 1912, pp. 36–8). My attention was drawn to this quotation from Bradley by Professor Blanshard's book (1939, p. 92). For the latest and one of the thoroughgoing criticisms of Lashley's point of view, see Grice, 1948.

of the associational hypothesis has found itself confronted with much the same methodological and other difficulties as the older form of the same hypothesis met in the latter part of the nineteenth century. This is the more striking in that the correspondence seems in most cases at least to be unwitting on the part of the writers. One is encouraged to believe that the difficulties are real ones, inherent in the nature of an associational psychology of whatever kind; rather than in a particular method of psychology, whether analytic, introspective or experimental-objective. If a list were made of the criticisms with their sponsors on either side of the line, it would be something as follows.

Arguments Against Associationism

Analytically derived criticism against the classical hypothesis:

Experimentally derived criticism mainly against the conditioned reflex hypothesis:

(1) *Reproduction of images does not occur.*
Bradley, 1883: "What is recalled has lost some features and acquired others."
James, 1890. Dawes Hicks, 1938.

(1) *Reproduction of response does not occur.* Conditioned responses are not quantitatively equal to unconditioned ones nor qualitatively identical with them.

(2) *Thinking is directed; the clash of associations cannot explain this.*
Adamson, 1884: "Thinking is motivated."
Bradley, 1887: "Thinking is controlled by the object of thought."
Würzburg, 1904–5: "We must postulate determining tendencies [*Aufgabe*], in addition to Association."

(2) *The clash of stereotyped habits cannot account for behaviour.*
Lashley, 1934: "Behaviour is purposive rather than mechanical."
Leeper, 1935: "We must distinguish habit from the utilization of habit."
Lewin, 1922: "Habits are not productive of action, but are the directive channels through which motives work."

(3) *Mental elements are changed when they enter into new combinations. Thus mental life cannot be built up of sensations and essentially unchanged sensory elements as reproduced by association.*
Bradley, 1883.
Stout, 1902: "The form of combination is a distinct psychic element."

(3) *The nature of a mental event is determined by the configuration.*

Gestalt, 1920. Cf. Köhler, 1941.

ARGUMENTS AGAINST ASSOCIATIONISM (*cont.*)

(4) *We are conscious of relations. This is unexplained by the presence of isolated ideas.*
Adamson, 1903.
James, 1890: "The idea of 'A' followed by the idea of 'B' is transmuted into the idea of 'A-after-B'."

(4) *We react to relations. This is unexplained by the doctrine of isolated stimuli.*
Lashley, 1929.

(5) *Thought is general; sensation and image are fundamentally particular.*
Bradley, 1883: "Association marries only Universals" (not particulars, as the classical theory demands).

(5) *Association is to generalized aspects of stimuli.*

Lashley, 1942.

To the analytical psychologist the table may be read as a justification of the experimental method. The experimentalist may read it as a justification of the analytical method. Criticisms originally of an analytical character are seen to become concrete by the powerful technique of objective registration. Bradley claims that we cannot revive a mental experience. Conditioned response technique enables us to measure response and associated response. Adamson states that thinking is motivated; Leeper is able to show that motive is able to decide whether a rat will utilize a habit which turns the animal to the right or the left, and so on. Certain changes in the phrasing of the criticisms have been introduced, in order to exhibit the essential similarity of the thought on either side of the column. This is particularly true of the right-hand column. The writer believes, however, that the fundamental thought has been preserved.

The reader will miss the name of Freud in this table. His name should probably appear on the right-hand side, under (2), together with that of Lewin. Freud's general thesis is that all mental events are motivated by the "wish"; although he apparently allows certain exceptions, as when, in his later work, he postulates a tendency towards reinstatement of the past on associatory lines. It is ironical that while at least the popular conception of Freud's work is that it has an associational basis, the whole of the system really rests on the explicitly anti-associational postulate that wish or motive determines action and thought. "Free association", for example, is not properly called "free", according to psycho-analytic theory. It is determined or motivated by a "complex", and is, indeed, used as an indicator of the complex. Similarly "day-dreaming" is claimed psycho-analytically to be motivated by egoistic wishes.[75]

Summary and Conclusions

(1) The classical theory of association came to its climax in the middle of the nineteenth century as a hypothesis claiming (*a*) to account for the way in which mental events followed each other, and (*b*) to explain the whole of mental life.

(2) An experimental and behaviouristic form of the hypothesis is to be found in the conditioned reflex theory, which correspondingly claimed to account for the occurrence of response and at the same time to explain the whole of behaviour.

(3) The classical theory was criticized on the ground that experiences are not reproduced; that thought is directed; that mental elements are changed when they enter into new combinations; that we are conscious of relations, which would not be possible if mental life were made up of isolated ideas; that image and sensation are in themselves particular, while thought is general.

(4) The modern objective form of the theory has been criticized by experimentalists on grounds that are strikingly parallel.

It is probable that experiment has not said the last word on the question of association. That association of itself, without the use of the concept of motive, can account for all the facts of mental life now appears to be excessively improbable. That motive, in the sense in which the term is used by Lewin, can account for all mental facts, seems to the writer also to be doubtful. The final judgment waits for experimental decision.

It may be said that the history of the psychology of thinking consists largely of an unsuccessful revolt against the doctrine of association. This statement is excellently illustrated by the Würzburg work, an account of which follows in the next three chapters.

NOTES

(1) In the foregoing it has been argued that the conditioned reflex is the modern form of the classical theory of association. The following differences between the two should, however, be borne in mind.

(*a*) The formation of the conditioned reflex involves a change in the responses concerned, in that the original response to the unconditioned stimulus disappears.

[75] Varendonck, 1921.

(*b*) One of the stimuli to be conditioned must ordinarily, at least, precede the other.

(*c*) Conditioned stimuli may, according to Pavlov, be arranged in a hierarchy of potency. This may possibly have a parallel in the principle of *vividness*, adopted by later writers.

(*d*) According to Pavlov, a repeated conditioned reflex gradually disappears. This is contrary to Associational theory, particularly as expounded by e.g. Hume.

However, in that both *hypotheses* are atomistic and analytic in nature, depend on a reproductive theory in their original form, and, likewise, in the original form are motiveless, the parallel, which is made also by such writers as Hull, may be allowed to stand. It is difficult in each case to separate the original theory, as proposed by enthusiasts, from the additions made necessary by further thought and experimentation, as by Hull (1943).

(2) At the outset of this book the word motive has been used where many psychologists would have preferred "set". This is because I am wholly convinced by J. J. Gibson that the word "set" has been used to mean so many things that it is now a psychological danger. (Gibson, J. J., 1941. See also note appended to Chapter II.)

THE WORK OF THE WÜRZBURG GROUP

IMAGELESS THOUGHT

The Rise and Fall of the Bewusstseinslage

The work of the Würzburg school was conducted within the framework of the "presentational" psychology, which postulated that we perceive the world, and also react to it, through the medium of presentations, i.e. perceptions and images. Mental life thus becomes very close to a manipulation of such presentations; in order that voluntary movement may take place, a "presentation of movement" (idea of movement) must first occur. Much of the difficulty for a modern reader comes from this framework. The outdated psychological theory does not, however, detract from the fundamental novelty of the experiments and the power of the thought behind them, or their importance for modern psychology. The unnecessary problems raised by the "presentations" give an instance of what happens when "thought" is analytically divorced from its context of action.

1901.   Mayer and Orth. Investigation of association. Attempted to classify association psychologically as opposed to logically.
   Result. Certain mental events cannot be classified under any of the accepted categories. These unknowns were named "*Bewusstseinslage*" (Bsl.), which had no sensory content.

1901.   Marbe. Attempted to find a psychological criterion of judgment. He could not do so, but verified the existence of Mayer and Orth's Bsl.

1905.   Ach. Investigation of the Will, which turned out to be also an Investigation of Thinking.
   Method. Introspection of reaction experiment.
   Result. The non-sensual thought, the Bsl. is directed towards an object. It is the imagelesss *knowing that* . . . (*Bewusstheit*).

1906.   Messer. Paper entitled: "An experimental investigation into the Psychology of Thought".
   Method. Associations, free and constrained, to various stimuli. Judgments to be made concerning various objects, etc.
   Results. Various. The Bsl. is identified with thought. It is thought of a relatively unformulated kind. A large part of thought is unconscious. "Meaning" is described in terms of Bsl. The term Bsl. has outlived its usefulness. We had better replace it by the current term Thoughts (*Gedanken*).

1907–8. Bühler. Investigated thought by using difficult problems.
   Result. Thought is a new "Mental category". The Bsl. is the "turning-point" of thought. During the activity of thinking, the

meaning is represented in conscious experience but usually not in sensory terms.

IN THE WORK of the Würzburg group we have the first systematic experimental investigation into the psychology of thought. At the beginning of the twentieth century the experimental method had accomplished much for psychology. The fifth edition of Wundt's *Grundzüge* appeared in 1902–3, and although it contains much that is of a theoretical nature, yet the whole work is predominantly experimental in tone. The results achieved were indeed imposing; nevertheless, they had stopped short of the most important problem of all. Wundt, in fact, definitely believed that the higher mental processes were not amenable to direct experimentation. It is true that experimental work had been done on certain slightly more complex activities, such as the comparison of lifted weights and the judgments therein involved. More important, Ebbinghaus had, in 1885, published his highly significant investigation of memory. Yet until the advent of the Würzburg group experimental psychology had not come to grips with the problem of the higher mental processes. Once in the laboratory, thought has stayed there. No psychologist now seriously questions the applicability of the experimental method to the psychology of thinking.

Now the investigations to be described raised a number of questions which belong primarily to the spheres of analytical psychology and philosophy. With these questions we shall not primarily concern ourselves, except in so far as their discussion is necessary for adequate exposition of the experimental results. Not that experimental psychology can ultimately dispense with the two disciplines in question. On the contrary, there is at the present time no branch of inquiry in greater need of a rigorous examination of its categories and postulates. But we have now reached the stage where such examination is out of keeping in a study whose purpose is primarily to discuss the experimental psychology of thought. With this proviso, it may be said that the achievement of the Würzburg group may roughly be classified under two headings, involving what may be called the matter and the mechanism of thinking respectively. Under each heading radical innovations were proposed. Direct experimental contradiction was given to the Aristotelian dogma that thought is impossible without images.[1] Descartes had maintained the existence of pure

---

[1] "We cannot think without imagery, for the same thing occurs in thinking as is found in the construction of geometrical figures. There, though we do not employ as a supplementary requirement of our proof a determinateness in the

intellection as contrasted with thinking in imaginal terms. Stout had urged the reality of imageless thought. Beginning with an almost incidental observation that there are mental processes without imaginal content, the Würzburgers gradually developed a doctrine which, in its final form, maintained that the very warp and woof of our thinking consists of psychic processes containing no trace of any sensory or imaginal content. For the mechanism of thinking there was adopted a modified form of associationism, whereby " reproductive tendencies" were guided—favoured and impeded—by a previously accepted task, or *Aufgabe*.[2] Behind the whole movement, the source of its power, stood Külpe, philosopher, student of æsthetics, pupil of Wundt in experimental psychology. While it is true that the work of Würzburg was actually performed by a band of exceptionally able experimenters, yet it must not be forgotten that it was Külpe who, with others, sat many hours as their expert subject. When in 1909 Külpe went to take a famous chair at Bonn, and at the same time was beginning to interest himself in other things, the movement died.[3]

Chronologically the movement began with a paper of Mayer and Orth, published in 1901, and characteristically intended to bring into the laboratory a subject which had long been the battleground of logicians. At the outset the writers refer to previous publications in which they have pointed out that the conventional classification of Associations is a logical one, and that it is not based upon the psychological peculiarities of the associations classified. In the present paper, entitled "A Qualitative Investigation of Associations", it is proposed to establish such a psychological classification by means of a strictly controlled procedure of introspection.

The method was that of free association of a verbal stimulus. After the signal "ready" had been given, the observer called the stimulus word. The subject was instructed to report everything that went on

size of the triangle, yet when we draw it we make it of a determinate size. Similarly in thinking also, though we do not think of the size, yet we present the object visually to ourselves as a quantum, though we do not think of its quantum."— Aristotle, *De Memoria*, II, 453*a* (trans. Loukas, slightly modified). It is clear that here as elsewhere he distinguishes thought from the image used by thought.

[2] The German *Aufgabe* is translated as "task" rather than "problem" (Titchener). Watt, in his English writings, uses the term "task". The word "problem" has misleading implications. It tends to insinuate the theory that "all thinking is directed towards the solution of a problem"—a statement to which no specific objection need be made, but which was not in the minds of the Würzburgers. Bühler, who was chronologically the last of the group, largely departed from the associationist point of view as an explanation of thinking.

[3] For a brief account of this remarkable man, see Boring, *History of Experimental Psychology*, pp. 386 *et seq.*

in his consciousness until he gave his response. Reaction time was measured with a stop-watch. Four observers were used, including, it should be noted, both Orth and Mayer, the writers of the paper. In all, 1,224 associations were evoked.

In the course of the process of classification, which has not proved to be of any particular importance, an interesting fact emerged. After exluding perceptions, images, and acts of will, the authors state:

"In addition to these two classes of conscious events we must set up also a third group of facts of consciousness, one that has not been sufficiently stressed in psychology up to the present day. In the course of our experiments we were, again and again, involuntarily brought up against the fact of the existence of this third group. The subjects frequently reported that they experienced certain events of consciousness which they could quite clearly designate neither as definite images nor yet as volitions. For example, the subject Mayer made the observation that, in reference to the auditory stimulus-word "metre" a peculiar event of consciousness intervened which could not be characterized more exactly, and which was succeeded by the spoken response "trochee". In other cases, the subjects could give a closer account of these psychic facts. For example, Orth observed that the stimulus word "mustard" released such a peculiar event of consciousness, which he thought he could characterize as "Memory of a common figure of speech". Thereafter the reaction "grain" (*Korn*) followed. In all such cases, the subject could, nevertheless, not detect the slightest trace of the presence in consciousness of "presentations"[4] (*Vorstellungen*) by which they specified the psychic fact more exactly in their reports. "All these events of consciousness, in spite of their obviously, often totally, different quality, we class together under the name *Bewusstseinslagen*—states of consciousness. The replies of the observers show that these states of consciousness are sometimes marked by feeling, but are, however, sometimes without any feeling tone."[5] These special states were not of such frequent occurrence as images (Mayer & Orth, 1901, p. 6).

Later in the same year appeared a monograph by Marbe. Once

---

[4] Ward's *Psychological Principles*, 1933, has been followed in translating *Vorstellung* by *presentation*. Ward includes under presentation "sensations, percepts, images, intuitions, concepts, notions". According to the Law of Association, the presentation tended to reproduce others with which it had been "in the mind". This "reproductive tendency" will frequently be referred to in this and the succeeding chapter.

[5] The translation of the word *Bewusstseinslage* has caused considerable confusion. Since Titchener called it "an almost untranslatable word meaning some-

more the experimental method was to be used to settle an ancient problem of logic. This time it was the logical judgment upon which the young science was to pronounce. The judgment, said the logicians, is the unit of thought. Thus: "The true unit of thought, the simplest complete act of thought or piece of thinking, is the Judgment or Proposition between which, where a distinction is intended, it is that the proposition is the expression in words of a judgment" (Joseph, 1916, p. 14). If, however, the logicians were asked what is the nature of this elementary act of thinking, they gave very different answers. Wundt's *Logic* contained, on about a single page of print, seven definitions, none of which were accepted by Wundt himself. It would not be difficult to find a dozen others. Such a state of affairs would never do. Psychology must find out what a Judgment *is*. This it must do by rejecting the haphazard methods by which confusion has been reached, and which consisted in a more or less casual observation of the writer's mental processes by the writer himself. Instead, a strict experimental procedure must be used. A number of observers must be caused to make judgments under standard, controllable conditions, and a careful record made of what takes place in their consciousness. Thus we shall find out what a judgment really is.

Now, there are facts of our experience which are not judgments. Our problem is then to find what further experiences must be added to make a judgment. By the word *Judgment* is provisionally understood an event of consciousness to which the predicate true or false

thing like posture or attitude of consciousness" (1909, p. 100), "conscious attitude" it has remained. This is clearly wrong, since the English word "attitude" ordinarily implied direction, both in its non-technical and still more in its psychologically technical use. It is important to realize that the term was originally used by the Würzburgers in a purely neutral sense. The *Bewusstseinslage* was an event of consciousness that was not an act of will, was not an image or a perception, and which could not be further analysed. The term was recommended by Marbe (Orth, 1903, pp. 69–70). It is not very felicitous. Orth remarks that it is ambiguous, since it may also mean the total state of consciousness at a given moment—a cross-section of consciousness. For this, however, he says we have the word "*Bewusstsein*". "The *Bsl.* observed by us and Marbe", he adds, "are of very varying character, and have only this in common, that they represent psychological facts which were not exactly capable of further analysis." Flournoy's term "intellection" does not seem to fit the case, nor Larguier's "conception", though both were apparently employed by Descartes in a similar connection (Bovet, p. 15). After reading the literature through several times, the writer finds himself naturally using the term "states of consciousness". It is neutral, and seems to correspond best with what the earlier workers had in mind. In what follows, the abbreviation Bsl. will be used when possible, as in the German texts.

can be meaningfully applied. Not only words, but also perceived gestures, may pass over into judgment, as when, for example, we answer a question as to the location of a place by pointing with the index finger. In fact, all conscious events of any sort whatever can pass over to judgment,[6] including the Bsl. and feelings.

A series of varied though simple experiments followed. Weights of similar appearance had to be compared and the heavier reversed. Tones heard on a tuning-fork were whistled or sung. The lightest of three greys was to be fixated. Imaginary circles had to be compared, geometrical illustrations imaged, and so on. Simple questions were asked, to which the answer was given by a gesture. How large is an ell? The corresponding gesture is made with the two hands. How many are 7 minus 4? The arm is stretched out and three fingers extended. Other judgments are evoked that were expressible in a single word. 12 plus 3? $\frac{3}{3}$? Or the same kind of question might be answered by a proposition such as 8 plus 7 equals 15. Propositions were stated in internal speech. Finally, translations had to be made. "Homo cogitat." "*Der Mensch denkt*", answered Külpe, the subject. "The translation followed by pure association," he reported.

One feels that Marbe has kept his promise to base his conclusions on a large number of different experiences under varied conditions. The conclusion is the same throughout. The same sentence is repeated time after time with endless variations; like a refrain, as Bovet remarks. "There are no concomitant events", says Marbe, "of which it could be said that they lend to judgment its character." That is to say, there is no psychological criterion of Judgment, and Judgment is the unit of thought. But judgments exist. Therefore, there must be other, non-psychological factors which raise experiences to the rank of judgments. Into the investigation of these we shall, however, not follow him.

This first peep which a properly controlled introspection afforded into the working of the thought process gave the early workers something of a shock. No psychological criterion of Judgment, which is the very backbone of thought, and apparently an utterly familiar experience to everybody! Judgments, recognized as such, with nothing in consciousness to indicate why they are judgments! Apparently Marbe can hardly believe his ears, and has to repeat the astonishing fact to give himself confidence.

Thus the predominant note of Marbe's paper was negative, at

---

[6] *Alle Bewusstseinsvorgänge . . . zu Urteilen werden können*, p. 15.

least in the first part. He had failed to find the psychological criterion for which he was seeking. What he did find, however, was "certain obviously present facts of consciousness, whose content either escapes further characterization altogether, or proves accessible to such characterization only with difficulty. These experiences, which had already been discussed in the work of Mayer and Orth, may, like all other experiences, be affectively toned or otherwise, and will here also be designated as *Bewusstseinslagen*."

Orth's paper of 1903 confirmed the existence of the Bsl., and, more important, anticipated Ach in relating it to cognition.

Külpe later remarked on the noteworthy fact that one of the first results of the Würzburg investigation of thought was negative. The sole result had been the discovery that the conventional descriptive terms of experimental psychology were not adequate to account for the intellectual processes (Külpe, 1922, p. 309). Yet one can already discern positive achievement of a high order. For if the results were, at this stage, mainly negative, yet the method was obviously worth pursuing. Already one could see growing a faith in the efficacy of that systematic self-observation which was in large measure to constitute the programme of the school, and was technically developed by the later comers. To have subjected association and judgment to careful introspective examination, thereby making clear the necessity for new descriptive concepts and, as it turned out, improvement of technique—this was no mean achievement. One feels an enthusiasm already present.

On reading Marbe's study one is struck by an apparent naïveté. He explains the meaning of experiment in psychology. He tells his reader that in order to obtain quantitative results one must employ statistical devices—this fourteen years after Fechner's death! He states that observation of physical events, such as the intensity of light, comes within the purview of the psychologist. This naïveté is difficult to define, but is unmistakably present. Whether it was a personal characteristic, or whether Marbe conceived that such details were necessary in a work with the sub-title *An Introduction to Logic*, and perhaps intended partly for philosophers, is hard to say. Whatever the reason for these apologetics, they are very much absent from the later work. With Marbe, and to a certain extent with Mayer and Orth, one feels that the new movement is a little shy. With Watt, writing only three years later, it has grown up and lost the need for self-justification. With Bühler, after six years, it has become almost boisterous.

The ensuing papers fall naturally into two groups.[7] Those of Watt and Ach appeared successively in 1905. They dealt primarily with what we have called the mechanism of thought, although each of them made important contributions to the problem of the material of thinking. These two form a natural pair, and their full consideration will be deferred until later, although one part of Ach's work is described in this chapter. Following were the papers of Messer, 1906, and Bühler, 1907 and onwards. The work of these two men seems most naturally to articulate with that already considered. It will, therefore, be described next in order.

Messer's work seems to show a remarkable growth of sophistication in the psychology of thought, a growth which one suspects was the product of countless discussions, papers at seminaries, arguments in the small hours. One gains the impression that in these five years an idea had developed into a more or less homogeneous school. Watt's work had appeared. Ach's was published while Messer was preparing his results. Messer is able to write on the "Psychology of Thought" the longest of these long articles, filling 224 pages, of which perhaps a third are in small print.

The paper is entitled "Experimental Investigations into the Psychology of Thought". Its general purpose is announced as the exploration of the events that occur in consciousness during simple thought processes—a much more ambitious programme than Marbe's five years before, and, in fact, the most ambitious of the programmes yet undertaken.[8] The conventional, logical, division of conception (*Begriff*), judgment, and conclusion is accepted, though with a hint that the classification may be only provisional. The investigation of thought is beginning to find its psychological feet.

Messer proposed for himself a big task. As Titchener remarks (1909, p. 96), he hardly proved equal to it. He has given us no general account of thought, but a series of disconnected papers, which are, however, of great value. He should perhaps be considered as the systematist who at least in this paper did not quite systematize. If, however, one wishes to find introspective data on any particular

[7] See Titchener, 1909, pp. 118–19, for a brief statement.
[8] Watt's paper (1905) was called "Experimental Contributions to a Theory of Thought", and was stated to contain investigations into "so-called Association reactions". Ach's, in the same year, was primarily an inquiry into the activity of the will, and apparently contained an investigation of thought processes only as an afterthought, although the title was "On the Activity of the Will and on Thought".

point, such as the psychology of images or the Bsl., one naturally turns to his paper.

The Hipp Chronoscope was used, with Ach's card changer. Cards were shown to the subject, whose reactions were timed by means of a voice key and the chronoscope. There were six subjects, including Külpe, Dürr, and Watt. Fourteen different series of experiments were conducted, as follows:

(1) Free association to the word printed on the card.[9]

(2) A co-ordinate object to be named (e.g. stimulus, hand; response, foot).

(3) Co-ordinate idea (e.g. stimulus, cellar; response, vault).

(4) Any adjective to be chosen.

(5) The idea denoted by the stimulus was to be characterized (e.g. flood—"a great mass of water in movement", 7529 sigma).

(6) Remember a definite object which falls under the idea of the stimulus word, and make a report about it.

In series (7) to (11) two words, one printed over the other, were given as stimuli:

(7) Give a relation between the words.

(8) Give a relation between the objects signified.

(9) The names of famous men, artists, etc., to be compared objectively.

(10) Personal preference to be expressed between two famous men, things, states.

(11) A noun and an adjective given. A judgment to be made including them.

(12) Propositions were shown. A position to be taken concerning them.

(13) Objects or pictures. Free association.

(14) Give a report on the object or picture shown.

(12) to (14) were timed with a stop-watch.

The first part of the paper deals with matters with which we shall not concern ourselves in detail at present, although reference will later be made to certain of the sections. Suffice it to say that Messer devotes ten pages to a justification of the method of introspection as he uses it; twenty-two to a very interesting account of the general behaviour of the different observers during the different tasks; ten to an important discussion of imagery, and so on. On p. 93 there comes an important section on the Judgment, discussion of which will be deferred until Watt's paper is being considered. The term Bsl. was, says Messer, already familiar to his observers, and was frequently employed by them in their reports. For this reason, he says in

---

[9] Substantives of one and two syllables were used for the first six series. For series seven to eleven, longer words were used, up to four and five syllables.

a footnote, he has used the term as a provisional collective name for all experiences, "*Erlebnisse*"—the italics are his—different from the generally recognized classes of conscious contents, and not resolvable into them by analysis (p. 175).

It is in Messer's study that we first find an attempt to do anything more than proclaim that the Bsl. is unanalysable. If they cannot be analysed they can be classified, says Messer. He concentrates his attention on the Bsl. of meaning.

The first group consists of those which represent in consciousness the meaning of word-presentations. This group includes the Bsl. of understanding.

When we examine these Bsl. of the meaning of words, we find that they occupy an intermediate position between two other groups of facts of consciousness. When a word is presented to a subject, the meaning of the word may be immediately clear, and appear in consciousness as inseparably bound up with the presentation of the word. "The stimulus word comes and I am clear about the meaning" (p. 72). "Some kind of knowing of the meaning is present," says Messer (p. 176, note). In other cases, however, the meaning may differentiate itself from the reading of the word as a separate experience. This may happen for a number of reasons, such as the strangeness or ambiguity of the word. When it happens, the subject may know what the word means, but be unable to make any further report. That is to say, there is an unanalysable Bsl. of meaning attached to the presentation of the word.

Thus to the printed stimulus "horse-fly" Külpe's reaction was "dragon-fly" (826σ). His report was "the superordinate idea 'vermin' was clearly present as a Bsl". To the stimulus "ball" another subject reported: "Had to wait purposely for a determinate meaning of 'ball'; this came through the Bsl. *dancing place*".[10]

Finally, a definite image may be, so to speak, crystallized. Thus when the word "cellar" was given, with the task of naming a co-ordinate object, Dürr reported: "saw a house (schematic), with cellar and upper storeys. I wanted to name the upper part; the word did not come". This gives a ladder with three rungs. There is the word bringing its meaning directly with it; there is the word accompanied by a Bsl. of meaning; there is the word accompanied by an image of meaning.

---

[10] The discussion of the understanding of words and the representation of meaning in consciousness is treated in a separate section (pp. 71–93). Reference is made to it in the present discussion and elsewhere.

Thus Marbe's Bsl. was here found to be a transitional form between the presence in consciousness of a meaning immediately given with the stimulus, and its presence as an accessory image. One may say, perhaps, that it is something like an uncrystallized image.

The Bsl. of meaning hitherto considered are, so to speak, supernumerary to word-presentations. It is not, however, necessary that words should be present. Such states may exist with no verbal accompaniment at all. Here again these are transitional forms. Fragments of words[11] may be present, or the subject may know how the word sounds. Thus we have two varieties of Bsl. of meaning, those with and those without verbal accompaniment. Both varieties may be widened so as to include propositions and judgments. Messer gives a number of examples where they contained the meaning of complete propositions. One instance may be given. Dürr was given the stimulus word *Angle* and replied "*Corner*". He reported: "The tendency was towards the well-known proposition that the sum of the angles of a triangle equals two right angles (Bsl.); but it did not mature. A number of such thoughts may be united in an embryonic form into one experience" (pp. 177 to 180).

The content of such Bsl. may naturally be of very great variety, being coterminous with the content of thought. A full survey of them is impossible, and the task is, in any case, one for the logicians. A few varieties are specified, giving us a logical classification—a classification by content. There is that of reality, those of spatial and temporal relationships and peculiarities, those of causal connection and of suitability; there are ten of various logical relationships, such as likeness and co-ordination; another set gives a relationship between what is thought, as object or idea, and the subject. Such are those of familiarity, strangeness, and value. Two further groups are related to the task that is being fulfilled; they contain three and fourteen headings respectively, and include such categories as "suitability", which is said to be relatively objective, and, on the other hand, such states as that of doubt and confusion, which are said to be more subjective.

Further, Bsl. may be classified on an entirely different principle according as they are of a purely intellectual nature, or are affectively or volitionally characterized.[12] In this case we might speak of them as intellectual and affective. We should thus have a psychological

---

[11] Also reported by many others writers, e.g. Grünbaum, Fisher, and Ach.
[12] See also Marbe, 1901, pp. 11–12.

division into which, as a matter of fact, our logical classes easily fall.[13]

"With the 'conscious states' here treated, whether they are of a material or rather of a more formal nature, whether they can be rendered in a word or in one or more propositions, whether they be, finally, of a purely intellectual or of an affective nature—with all these manifold conscious states we find ourselves in the realm of experiences which B. Erdmann has designated as 'unformulated' (or 'intuitive') thought.

"Of course, in our actual thinking there is no clear line of demarcation between formulated and unformulated thought. . . . There are continuous intermediate stages and many kinds of transition between the two. One might regard as limiting cases on the one side a thought in fully formulated propositions with clear consciousness of meaning, and on the other a lightning reflection and recognition, with no trace of a word; the difference between the two would be even greater than that between the tedious and correct writing of a child who has just learned to write properly, and the rapid script of a practised shorthand writer. . . ." (p. 186).

In order to explain the facts of meaning, Messer has already made the assumption of an unconscious machinery underlying the conscious process of thought. There are apparently, he says, unconscious real processes which, under certain specified circumstances, occur in different intensities, exert a correspondingly different influence (*reflex*) on consciousness, and are represented in consciousness in different degrees of clearness. Thus are produced conscious effects varying from clear word-images to unanalysable Bsl. This same assumption explains the behaviour of the Bsl. in general. So that we find ourselves with "the hypothesis that the real psychic processes, which underlie the fully formulated thought, can run their course in manifold manner, abbreviated, intricately inter-penetrating, partaking more or less of the psychic energy" (p. 187), thus giving us all stages between fully formulated thought and the vaguest *Bewusstseinslage*.[14]

[13] Messer has slipped over into a general discussion of the *Bewusstseinslage*, from the particular case of the Bsl. of the meaning of words, without making explicit the relation of meaning to thought in general. He includes Ach's *Bewusstheit*, awareness, under the term Bsl.

[14] The notion that the *Bewusstseinslagen* were fundamental in the thought processes was evidently in the air. Thus Taylor states, in 1905, "More complicated structures of '*Bewusstseinslagen*' and word-images, which could not be described more closely, were designated as thought" (p. 235). In the same way Watt, speaking of the Bsl., says parenthetically, "Call it a thought" (1906).

He concludes the section with the following words: "The useful, provisional collective term *Bewusstseinslage* has then done its duty at this point, and it seems to us advisable to replace it by the current expression 'Thoughts' (*Gedanken*)." He adds in a footnote, "Further, it would best correspond to the usage of the language to call thoughts those conscious states alone whose content can only be fully formulated in one or more propositions; and by contrast to call those of the meaning of single words or phrases *Begriffe*, ideas" (p. 188).

This marks a real stage in the development of the theory of thought. The difficult problem of meaning and understanding has been examined, and a solution suggested, involving what we have called "unconscious machinery". The solution has been found applicable to the problem of thought in general, and in particular to that of the so-called *Bewusstseinslage*. At the same time the Bsl. have been rescued from the museum case where, as psychological curiosities, patently existing but unclassifiable, they had been jointly deposited by Mayer and Orth, and by Marbe. These states are now maintained to be of high functional importance in our thinking. They are, in fact, thoughts, though of a relatively unformulated kind.

The discussion has revealed an important feature of Messer's work, namely his insistence that the processes involved in thinking are not amenable to any clear-cut classification, but actually consist of experience-types merging one into the other with no clear line of demarcation. The Bsl. of meaning is half-way between the accessory image and the immediately given meaning. That without verbal imagery is likewise ushered in by transitional forms. In the same way, a "feeling of visual direction" may develop during an experiment into "presentations (*Vorstellungen*) of almost hallucinatory clearness" (p. 51,; cf. Titchener, p. 112). This last is, however, not usual. Generally, only one degree of clearness is present, different intermediate stages being reported by different observers.

By relating this Bsl. to "meaning" and to thought in general, Messer had prepared the way for Bühler. Quite apart from the rich introspective data, and the attempts, not always very happy, at classification, his was a very real contribution to the Würzburg theory.

Thus we take leave of the Bsl. as a specific subject of inquiry. What seems to have happened is that the new technique, and a new courage, perhaps, resulted in the discovery of something unclassifiable and purely negative. Later on, positive characteristics were discovered to belong to what had been discovered. The *terra incognita* was surveyed. This is the explanation which best fits in with Külpe's own account after the event.[15] Each of the investigators coming after Marbe bent the new discovery in the direction of his own enthusiasm. Watt called the Bsl. an "unnamed task". Orth investigated its relation with feeling. Messer, the systematist, tried to classify it, and found it coterminous with thought itself. Bühler, as we shall see, makes it the "consciousness of the turning-point " of his thought element. Aristotle's dogma, that thought is impossible without an image, had apparently broken down. Henceforward, if one was interested in a certain aspect of thought, one was now interested in imageless thought from the same aspect. This is, again, strikingly illustrated in Bühler's work.

Awareness.—In order to follow the development of the Würzburg doctrine as it concerns the material of thought, an aspect of Ach's work must now be considered. Ach's principal monograph appeared in 1905, a year before the publication of Messer's paper, but too late for Messer to do more than refer to it in footnotes (e.g. Messer, p. 11). Consideration of one of Ach's main theses has already been deferred to the next chapter, which deals with the mechanism of thinking. It is by his contribution to the latter problem that Ach is chiefly known. More important, however, in the opinion of the writer, is that part of his work which belongs to the present context, namely the experimental demonstration of the impalpable awareness of *knowing*.

Ach's primary object was the investigation of the will. His book is entitled *On the Activity of Will and on Thinking*. The preface states that the purpose of the monograph is a "treatment of the problem of the will upon an experimental basis". The problem of "willing" is, however, manifestly bound up with the whole problem of "thinking"; and thus it was that Ach found himself not only investigating "the Determination that fulfils itself in the adoption [*Anschluss*] of a purpose or an aim", but also discovered that it was "necessary to make a closer examination of other psychic processes, for example those which are connected with the presence of [the experience of] knowing and which are henceforward designated as Awarenesses". "In addition, there was adjoined a discussion of the process of 'determined abstraction', of attention and so on." Thus Ach was forced to add to the original title the words "and on Thinking". A legitimate

---

[15] Külpe says of the *Bewusstseinslage* that it was a "conception, obtruding itself through the observation of the facts, making possible a periphrasis rather than a description" (ibid., pp. 309–10).

alternative title, he says, might have been "On Determination and Thinking" (Ach, 1905, pp. v *et seq.*).

The basis of the investigation was the reaction experiment, which Ach varied in new and ingenious ways. His list of reactions follows.

A. *Reactions with Unique Stimulus-response Correlation*[16]

1. *Reactions with Simple Correlation.*—Stimulus and movement may remain the same; for example, there may be a simple reaction of the right index finger to a white card (*a*-method of Donders), or there may be different stimuli with a single response (recognitive reactions), or different stimuli (words, colours, etc.), with variable but adequate response, such as naming the stimulus.

2. *Reactions with Manifold Correlation.*—To each of three, four, or five stimuli is assigned a specific reaction (*b*-method of Donders).

3. *Conditional Reactions.*—Reaction follows only under certain conditions; for example, to red cards and to no others, reaction with the right index finger (*c*-method of Donders). Or the combination *ac* might be given, with reaction only if *a* stands to the right of *c*.

(4) *Associational Reactions.*—(*a*) Free association.

(*b*) Associations with special determination; e.g. the so-called judgment reaction, where the direction of judgment is determined by the previous setting of a task.[17] Or the name of a town may be given, with instructions to give the river on which it lies.

B. *Reactions without Definite Correlation*

This leaves much more to the subject; e.g. the stimulus or the response may not be predetermined; or neither the stimulus nor the response may be predetermined. For example, cards might be shown with either *rx* or *xr* printed, with the instructions, "To *x* react with the right thumb, to *r* react with the left thumb. Do not make more than one movement" (p. 163). Here, then, the subject chose to which of the letters he reacted.

For the purpose of closer examination of the experiences involved Ach divided the introspective period into:

(1) The fore-period, including the time between the signal and the appearance of the stimulus.

(2) The main period, including the actual experience to be investigated, i.e. from the perception of the stimulus to the giving of the response.

(3) The after-period.

The introspections were reinforced constantly by questions, to which Ach attaches great importance. These questions, he says, were not often included in the protocols (p. 18). The protocols were enormous enough as it was, and only a selection could be printed. It may, however, here be noted that the omission of the questions in the printed report constitutes a serious technical flaw; especially when we

---

[16] *Reaktionen mit eindeutiger Zuordnung*, ibid., p. 33.

[17] It is to be noted that Ach here uses the term *Aufgabe* in much the same way as Watt.

find Ach maintaining that one of their important functions is "the education of the subject in self-observation" (ibid.). In order to obtain real experimental certainty and control, these questions should have been fully standardized and fully reported. With the best will in the world, one feels that an unstandardized set of questions must result in leading questions. More will be said on this point later. This point was, of course, noticed by Ach (op. cit., p. 17); one has the impression that he is a little uneasy about it. The matter is discussed in the next chapter.

Samples of the instructions may be given. First, those which the subject received for the so-called sensorial reaction. "At 'now' the finger will be depressed; about three seconds later a white card will appear. As soon as you see the white card, let the finger go. Direct your attention towards the coming impression. Thereafter report what you have experienced." After practice, the subject was told merely "instructions as usual". The instructions were suitably modified for the "muscular" form of the reaction. A more complicated set of instructions ran: "Cards with two figures will appear. At the word 'now', you should undertake to perform an arithmetical operation; either divide, multiply, add, subtract, or else do nothing; and when you have finished say the syllable 'pe' into the voice-key" (p. 174). Early in the account of the experiments we find the term *Bewusstheit*, which has been translated by Titchener as "awareness".[18] When, for example, Ach is describing the sensorial series of reactions included in his "simple" reactions, he reports of subject "H", as follows: "The appropriate spot on the card changer is fixated and there is inner speech of the words: 'it will come now' or 'now it's coming', with the meaning that something (i.e. a white card) will enter there, at the point of fixation. At the same time sensations of tension, as sensory accompaniments of the concentration of attention, arise in the eyes, region of the brow, temples, sometimes also in the muscles of the face and in the shoulders, as well as a holding of the breath.[19] Sensations of tension in the hand or the finger were only exceptionally present. In spite of this, there was contained in the total state of tension the *knowing* (*Wissen*) that reaction should take place forthwith, without this being spoken internally or being represented

[18] Seeing that the word implies imageless knowing, the term is apparently not exact, though the translation is valid.

[19] The registration of tension-sensations in the eyes is evidence of the quality of the introspection. Such sensations have of course been fully confirmed by later observers. See, for example, Jacobson, E., 1929.

phenomenologically in any other way. Besides all this, there was present the awareness that in a short time that which was awaited—that is to say, the card—would come, and thus . . . there was also a temporal component" (p. 38). In the same way, on the next page: "the white card was present only as an awareness in the waiting-content; that is to say, the subject knew that the white card would appear over there, where he was fixating, without any palpable representation of this presentational content which related to the white card" (ibid., p. 39).[20]

It is impossible to list every context in which the term awareness is employed throughout the monograph. A representative selection of the passages will be given in order that the reader may have an idea of the kind of experimental evidence which Ach presents. In the description of the simple reactions, sensorial series, it is stated of subject "J": "On appearance of the card at the first trial a state of surprise and astonishment occurred, that is to say, the subject did not know what to do; then appeared the awareness that reaction should be made, after which the finger went up (611 ms). At the second trial after appearance [of the stimulus] there appeared the awareness that reaction should be made, and with it organic sensations were present in the head and in the right finger, after which movement followed (356 ms). At the third trial the finger rose immediately after the apprehension of the card; that is to say, without the aforesaid awareness (322 ms)."[21] The passage continues by stating that the awareness reappears if preparation has not been good, and at the same time latency may increase. Again, in the muscular series of simple reactions, it was reported of subject "H": "Between the fixation of the plate and the intentional sensations of movement a known relation was given, in the sense that reaction should take place to a change (that is, the appearance of the card) which had to do with the object of regard. A more exact analysis of this event was not possible. One can only say that there occurs an unequivocal 'knowing' that reaction should take place as quickly as possible, as soon as the familiar change comes on the plate. In this complex the most prominent place is taken by the sensation of tension in the hand, which represents the most expedited possible entrance of the movement to be carried out. In addition, it is also given that this movement shall take place in a very short time" (op. cit., pp. 49–50).

[20] The exigencies of the English language compel me thus to translate the words "*ohne dass dieser . . . Vorstellungsinhalt anschaulich repräsentiert war*".
[21] Loc. cit., pp. 45–6.

Again, in the same (muscular) series, it is stated of subject "L":
"With the fixation of the plate came the "knowing" that something
(i.e. card) will appear over there, uniquely determined (subject knows
that a card will appear, without the presence of any visual elements
or any kind of acoustic-kinæsthetic presentation-images) (ibid., p.
54).

In the account of reactions of recognition and discrimination
comes the following passage: "In the main period there develops
first the sensation of white or red, with which is bound up the
'knowing' that the subject must wait, the latter being not particularly prominent, however. It is given with the development of the
apprehension. Thereafter comes the awareness that the subject must
react, whereat the finger goes up. This 'knowing' is usually preceded
by a state of agreement or understanding. With increasing practice
the awareness that reaction should take place fell away, but in spite
of this the movement was characterized as willed, on account of its
known character" (pp. 81, 82). Later it is stated that practice diminishes the intensity both of sensations of tension and of the awareness.
"It was now a passive, indifferent state of waiting. The temporal
component . . . was no longer observable; . . . the expectation of the
coming impression might fall off so much in intensity that one could
no longer make certain that it was known to be present. With the
fixation of the plate and with very weak intentional sensations in the
reactive organ, there was present only the weakly impressed awareness that reaction should take place. Immediately after the carrying
out of the reaction, often no further report could be given of the
process of the reaction-event itself" (pp. 100–1).

Later, the awareness is equated with the will-impulse. In another
context it is equated with an act of the act-content antithesis. "The
two acts of understanding and of the awareness . . . followed very
closely as the result of practice. They could now no longer be
distinguished. The second act retreated more and more towards the
end of the experiments. Here too no 'distinction' could be noticed."
The awareness could admit of degrees of intensity (p. 94). And once
more, in the description of the reactions with double determination,
it is stated: "The waiting was in so far impalpable, as its content was
not further determined phenomenologically by inner speech, visual
pictures, etc.; but, nevertheless, the content corresponding to the
instruction that 'in accordance with instructions when a determinate
change takes place at the point of fixation, an unequivocally determined change in the behaviour of the subject is to follow'—this

content was present in an unequivocal, but not more closely describable manner. Accompanying it, diffuse sensations of tension in the head (neighbourhood of eyes and brows, upper jaws) were regularly perceived" (p. 127).

In summary of these and many other accounts given by his twelve subjects, Ach defines an awareness as follows: "We designate this presence of an impalpably given 'knowing' as an awareness."[22] It is uniquely given, but cannot be analysed further. The subject can immediately afterwards say what was present to him. In the after-period the total event just experienced persists by perseveration. It is present as in a nutshell, without obtrusion of details or palpable representation. Thus an account can be given to the experimenter. Normally, during the fore-period, when there has not been too much practice, the following complex-content is, for example, present simultaneously, as an awareness. (1) The coming stimulus (a white card), with a spatial determination, in so far as the subject knows that the uniquely determined change will take place at the point of fixation. (2) The subject is aware that thereafter must follow an unequivocally determined change on his side; that is to say, the reaction. (3) In addition there is a relation present between (1) and (2); there is awareness that the reaction must follow as soon as the stimulus appears. (4) There is a temporal component, in so far as the *knowing* is given, that the stimulus will appear within a certain known time. The subject knows, for example, that the stimulus will not come in a half-second, and will come within a minute. In addition to this immediately given content, "there are also the accompanying phenomena of sensory attention, such as sensations of tension in the upper part of the body, and in the optical sense organ as well as the visual perception (in our experiments with the closure plate of the card changer). At times some of the above-mentioned constituent parts of the awareness-complex come up in the form of images, particularly at the beginning of the fore-period or during the first experiments on any day. Individual capabilities play a large rôle here. But, nevertheless, there are an extraordinarily large number of experiments, in which, apart from the above-mentioned accompanying phenomena, the whole waiting-content appears only as 'knowing', and this presence of a knowing-content we designate as an awareness" (p. 211, 212).

The impalpably given content of the awareness is often elusive.

---

[22] *Wir bezeichnen dieses Gegenwärtigsein eines unanschaulich gegebenen Wissens als Bewusstheit*, p. 210.

Part of the experience is sometimes indicated by inner speech, such as "must come" or "corner, corner", or by rudiments of words, such as "add",[23] "folg",[24] and so on. This frequent occurrence of kinæsthetic or acoustic-kinæsthetic presentations, says Ach, may well be the reason for the widespread supposition that our thought "is always accomplished by inner speech or by adequate[25] visual, acoustic or other memory-images".

As against this supposition Ach points out that there are very complex contents in which the component parts are known in intricate, reciprocally related, manifolds, which have and indeed could have no adequate verbal representation. "If a phenomenologically constituent part is given, which as a relevant sign brings a meaning-content to expression, as, for example, "edge", then the correlative meaning is alone bound up with it, namely the expectation of the upper corner of the card, while the rest of the waiting-content that is simultaneously given has no such phenomenological representation, but is present in the total state of tension as awareness" (p. 215). In addition, there was recorded at times a "lightning-like momentary illumination of a complex-content, which can only be expressed verbally by several sentences, an event which because of its short-lived existence cannot possibly be given by inner speech" (ibid.). In these cases the meaning of the content is uniquely given, and the memory is clear and distinct, without any ascertainable sensational qualities. For instance, subject "C", in the fore-period of the reaction with double stimulus-response assignment, reported a visual memory picture of "O" with the lightning thought that it would be most practical to prepare for "O" alone, and in addition the awareness that perhaps only "E" will come. Ach maintains that it would be an abuse of terms to call such experiences "dark sensations" or memory pictures which are too weak to be identified. Often the palpable representation of a meaning-content is first given, as by inner speech, and thereafter the corresponding meaning-content as awareness without palpable representation. It has been seen that the awareness admits of degrees of intensity. For example, with practice, intensity gradually falls away.

Awareness of Meaning.—There are two main classes of awareness, those of meaning and of relation, with two transitional forms. The

[23] For "*addieren*".
[24] For "*folgen*" or "*folgender*" (p. 215).
[25] That is, images corresponding in every detail to that which they image; the phrase implies the correspondence theory of truth.

awareness of meaning is always accompanied by "a sensation as described above (i.e. a sensation of tension) or a visual, acoustic, kinæsthetic or other sensation, or a memory image" (p. 213). This is either simultaneous or it occurs immediately beforehand. In this way these sensations form the palpable conscious representation of the content impalpably present as a *knowing*. They are the signs of the meaning-content. It frequently came about that, for example, "after the appearance of a coloured card the sensation 'yellow' was present only in its optical quality. Not until after this did a 'knowing' appear, for example 'this is yellow'; and in fact this ingress followed clearly as a special act after the pure sensation was given. By this act the sensation was, so to speak, identified as the well-known colour yellow." A relation was thus established with previous experiences. This process Ach identifies with that of apperception.

Although the awareness is found in every subject, yet there are strong individual differences. Certain people incline to visual or kinæsthetic-acoustic illustration of the meaning-content. Ach claims that he personally has a distinct tendency to think in terms of *awarenesses*, which, he says, may be due to the fact that his attention has been especially directed to the analysis of this kind of thought. Physiologically Ach suggests that the awareness of meaning is due to the subexcitation of neural structures which, when fully excited, give a fully fledged image. One reads, for example, the written word "bell". Associated with this are a multitude of images, each with its correlative neural pattern. On reading the word, however, no one of these patterns need necessarily be excited to the pitch of producing an image outright. They may, nevertheless, be excited to the point of producing mental events which are related to the images concerned, but are not intense enough to be of imaginal quality. These together constitute the meaning of the original image, which thus serves as a focus with a halo of meaning correlated with subexcited patterns. These subexcited patterns are then the physiological correlate of the *knowing*. If a nonsense syllable such as "chuz" is read, there are no neural connections to such patterns of meaning. That is what we mean by saying it is a nonsense syllable. In the same way, the differences of intensity already noted in awareness may be explained by assuming that the effect of repetition is to make certain connections more readily accessible.

Certain facts should here be noted, some tending towards, others against this piece of theorizing. One's first impulse is to reject the notion altogether, on the ground that the "all or none law" of neural conduction would now make such subexcitation impossible. However, there do exist intensive variations both in images and in sensations of all kinds. Such differences are psychological facts, and it is the task of physiological psychology to explain them. Thus there is no *a priori* argument against the existence of degrees of intensity in awareness. But whether such difference may be correlated directly with differences in the degree of repetition is, of course, very doubtful. And it cannot be assumed that an image of a low degree of intensity may be equated with an imageless component of consciousness. To diminish the intensity of a conscious event belonging to a given sensory modality surely does not destroy the sensory modality. A weak smell, as perceived or imagined, is still of olfactory quality, and a slight sound of auditory quality. Ach's excursion into physiology surely proves the opposite of what he wished it to prove. A subexcited image still retains its imaginal character, and thus cannot be the explanation of imageless thought. Ach is able to cloud over the appearance of inconsistency by speaking of tendencies to reproduction. "We designate the awareness as a progressive function of such a state of excitation of reproductive tendencies" (p. 219). But his argument is throughout dependent on the implication of "presentations" of a specific sensory modality. If, for example, a connection only, or a bond, as Thorndike would put it, is excited, without the imaginal pattern (if that were possible), the hypothesis breaks down. The hypothesis demands the subexcitation of patterns, which when fully excited will give the presentation proper. It thus concerns experience belonging to a definite sensory modality, however slight the degree of its intensity.

Awareness of Determination.—The *awareness of determination* is defined through the fact that "the individual knows directly, as a characteristic experience, whether the given psychic occurrence is proceeding in the sense of a previously established determination or not" (p. 230). It may be called an awareness of agreement. It is not necessarily a special psychic act, but is rather a knowing contained in the course of such. The whole sequence of psychic processes is called a "willed" one—"The conscious experience of such an event is uniquely determined as regards its quality, and the individual can in every case immediately report whether the action was willed or not" (p. 230). This awareness of determination distinguishes such processes as free association, or æsthetic contemplation, from willed action or thought. It disappears or diminishes with practice, and the action becomes automatic. The activity of will is, accord-

ingly, immediately recognized while it is in progress by the characteristic awareness of determination (p. 232). A special form of it is
given in the awareness of a tendency. A tendency is designated on the
subject's part by such words as a search, an urge, and so on. One
subject spoke of a peculiar urge, which was designated as a need for
something to happen; there followed the visual image of the digit
that was intended. The awareness of tendency is transitional to the
events already discussed. I may feel the urge to lift my hand, either
with or without doing so. The first case would correspond to the
awareness of determination, the second to that of tendency. When the
urge is present without the action, I may, then, experience the
"awareness of tendency". Like other awarenesses, that of tendency is
of course impalpable, imageless. Nevertheless, when the subject is
asked he can say exactly what it is that he should or should not
do.

The awareness of determination proper is found whenever mental
events are occurring under the influence of the determining tendencies[26]—"whether these arise from a purpose, a suggestion, a command, the ordering of a task, or an instruction". According to Ach,
the awareness apparently differs in the several cases; in those occurring during "voluntary" actions, the "personality", the "ego", is
more prominent (p. 234). This is apparently an echo from Külpe.

The second main form of awareness is that of relation, where the
reference is backwards to a preceding content of consciousness (p.
235). "If, for example, we are set to receive a specified impression,
and another comes, this manifests itself in consciousness by an
awareness of surprise" (ibid.). Clearly such an event depends on
both the momentary state of consciousness and on that which interrupts it. Hence comes the term "awareness of relation". Instead of
surprise, there may be satisfaction if the later impression conforms
with the previous determination, or there may be confusion, with an
immediately appearing *knowing*, such as "I do not know what I
ought to do". The awareness of meaning refers then to a coming
event, that of relation to a past one; that of "determination" to the
directive process which unifies a past event (acceptance of purpose)
with a future one (conclusion of thought or action). The awareness of
determination, with its subdivision of tendency, thus stands between
those of meaning and relation. This awareness of relation Ach

[26] See the next chapter, on "The Mechanism of Thinking". Determining tendencies may be provisionally defined as directive influences in the thinking
processes.

identifies with the Bsl.[27] It may be accompanied by pleasant or unpleasant Affekt.

An excellent independent confirmation of Ach's experimentally
derived hypothesis of "awareness" is to be found in the letters of the
composer Mozart. The passage is worth quoting in its entirety.

"When I am," says Mozart, "as it were, completely myself, entirely alone and of good cheer—say travelling in a carriage or walking
after a good meal, or during the night when I cannot sleep, it is on
such occasions that my ideas flow best and most abundantly. When
and how they come I know not; nor can I force them. Those ideas
that please me I retain in memory, and am accustomed, as I have
been told, to hum them to myself. If I continue in this way, it soon
occurs to me how I may turn this or that morsel to good account, so
as to make a good dish of it, that is to say agreeably to the rules of
counterpoint, to the peculiarities of the various instruments, etc.

"All this fires my soul, and provided that I am not disturbed my
subject enlarges itself and becomes methodized and defined, and the
whole, though it be long, stands almost complete and finished in my
mind, so that I can survey it, like a fine picture or a beautiful statue—
at a glance. Nor do I hear in my imagination the parts successively,
but I hear them, as it were, all at once. What a delight this is, I cannot tell. All this inventing, this producing, takes place in a pleasing
lively dream. Still the actual hearing of the *tout ensemble* is, after all,
the best. What has been thus produced, I do not easily forget, and
this is perhaps the best gift I have my divine maker to thank for.
Everything is, as it were, already finished; and it rarely differs on
paper from what it was in my imagination."[28]

Here, vividly described, is the "presence of an impalpably given
knowing". For the *tout ensemble* of which the composer speaks
must be a fundamentally imageless experience; the psychological
process involved must be that which Ach calls *knowing*, even though
Mozart describes it as hearing. There was clearly no time to hear the
composition in an instant. In view of the criticisms raised by such
writers as Wundt, who claimed that the complex mental events involved in thinking could not be remembered with sufficient accuracy
for purposes of introspection, it is of interest to note that Mozart

[27] On the other hand, Ach quotes Marbe, in 1914, as claiming that "the
Bewusstheit forms a part of the general realm of the Bsl.". Ach says that Marbe's
claim is unjustified, because Marbe has explicitly excluded the *knowing* from
consciousness, and the *knowing* is the distinguishing mark of the awareness. See
Ach, *Analyse des Willens*, Berlin, 1935.

[28] Sitwell, O., *Life of Mozart*, London. Beethoven reports similar experiences.

claims that: "What has been thus produced, I do not easily forget. . . . Everything is, as it were, already finished, and it rarely differs on paper from what it was in my imagination." Considering what is known from other sources of the phenomenal musical memory possessed by Mozart, it is difficult to contradict the composer when he says that he was aware of the totality of his compositions "like a fine picture or a beautiful statue", and that he remembers later what he then experienced. The parallel is striking with the reports of Ach's subjects to whom was present "in a nutshell" a simultaneous, complex awareness of the stimulus of the reaction, of the relation between them, of the fact of the minimal time requirement, and of the approximate time when the stimulus was to appear.

Ach's awareness was a development of the Bsl. of preceding investigators; it assigned a function to the imageless processes of Marbe, and of Mayer and Orth, namely the function of *knowing*. The theory of this imageless-knowing process was still further developed by Bühler into the hypothesis that it *is* essentially the articulated thinking process. The discussion passes therefore to Bühler's work.

Before, however, leaving Ach, there are certain minor criticisms which should here be noted. First of all, there is the important question of scientific controls to which reference has already been made. This point will be raised in detail in the next chapter, when we come to consider the mechanism of thinking, and also in the succeeding chapter, which deals with the general criticism that has been directed against the method of the Würzburg school. Here it is sufficient to say that, judged by modern experimental standards, Ach's work is technically deficient, as is that of his predecessors at Würzburg. Nevertheless, and in spite of other technical flaws which can easily be demonstrated in the work of Ach, of Marbe, and of Mayer and Orth, these men seem to the writer to have proved their point on the question of the existence of imageless components of thinking.

There are minor inconsistencies to be noted. It is, for example, hard to find Ach's opinion as to whether the awareness is a psychic *act* or not in the terms of the act-content psychology. In one context he says that the imageless knowing is contained in the course of such an act (p. 230), in another context the awareness is equated with the act (p. 213). Whether it is meant that the awareness of determination, of which he is speaking in the first context, is contained in the course of a psychic act, while that of meaning is such an act, it is hard to say. And if so, difficult questions are involved as to the reason for this distinction. Again, it has been seen that Ach's physiological theory is probably untenable; but if psychologists are to be judged by their physiological theories, there are few, at least of Ach's generation, who would escape condemnation. Generations of physiological theorizing have taught psychologists to say as little as possible about the brain in their discussions of thinking. Again, there is some difficulty in deciding whether all awarenesses or only those of meaning have a palpable sign. In the footnote on p. 238 we are told that the sign is always present; though it is apparently not mentioned explicitly except in the account of the awareness of meaning. Further, the definition of the awareness on the same page contains no reference to it. Nor do the experimental results give data that would enable the point to be decided. This is a more serious omission, for on the point hangs the answer to the question as to whether Ach's experiments tend to the conclusion that thinking contains imageless *components*, or whether thinking may be entirely free from imaginal components. But these problems are raised only because Ach's work made it possible to raise them. They shrink into insignificance beside the massive solidity of his actual achievement. In spite of methodological errors, in spite of gaps in the presentation, the evidence which Ach has painstakingly amassed has placed the burden of proof squarely on the shoulders of those who maintain that the material of thought is of an exclusively sensory quality. There had been before this time theorists who had maintained the existence of imageless thought-processes. Ach gave overwhelming experimental confirmation of the fact that such processes do exist, in the form of the impalpable awareness or *knowing*. Bühler's work, next to be considered, did no more than complete the picture.

Imageless Thoughts.—A year later (1907) Bühler published a paper with the title "Facts and Problems in Relation to a Psychology of the Thought Processes. I. On Thoughts."[29] The problem he proposes to investigate is by far the most ambitious of all. It is no less than the fundamental question—What happens when people think?

One feels in Bühler a certain scorn of those who had gone before. Here, he says, we have the immensely complex act of thinking. It has been investigated—how? By inverting weights, singing tones, by "demonstrating the well-known mortality of Caius, by solving the problem 3×8" (p. 301). The real thought processes, he says, have

[29] *Tatsachen und Probleme zu einer Psychologie der Denkvorgänge. I. Ueber Gedanken.*

here been mechanized by repetition and have become unconscious. In order to investigate thought, we must investigate thought, not these elementary activities. Take a good aphorism from Nietzsche, such as "I explain to you your virtues from those of the future". I will guarantee that you think. Marbe was prejudiced by his preoccupation with Judgment. Messer had decided that he would find Ideas, Judgments, and Conclusions, and wished to examine these psychologically. For him, therefore, the question is already prejudged. But who knows whether psychological investigation will reveal these elements, or whether they are psychologically important? (p. 303). The true question for a psychologist is: "What is our actual experience when we think?"[30]

Seven subjects were used. The reports of two only were utilized, and those the most distinguished, namely Külpe and Dürr. For this is to be an investigation of thinking in its highest form. If these men cannot think, who can? A statement or question was put, always answerable by Yes or No. The subject was to answer, and then give the fullest possible report of his experience. Timing was done with a stop-watch. A selection of the questions follows, taken, all but the last, from his sample collection (p. 304):

When Eucken speaks of a world-historical (*welt-geschichtlichen*) apperception, do you know what he means?

Was the theorem of Pythagoras known in the Middle Ages?

Can you get to Berlin from here in seven hours?

Was Eucken right when he said: Even the limits of knowledge could not come to consciousness, unless Man somehow or other transcended them?

Do you consider the detailed presentation of Fichte's psychology a fruitful task?

Can you complete the sentence: The law of association states in its simplest form . . .?

Can we with our thought comprehend the nature of thought?

Can the atomic theory of physics ever be proved untrue by any discoveries?

Does monism really mean the negation of personality?

The smaller the woman's foot, the larger the bill for the shoes?

The first ten of these belonged to a group designed especially to throw light on the activity of knowing, and suggested by Ach's work (p. 310). The experimenter must adopt the most intimate and sympa-

---

[30] According to the definitions adopted in this book the problem-situations used in some of the earlier Würzburg work were certainly marginal.

thetic attitude towards the subject and his mental processes. The questions must be adapted to the interests and abilities of the subject.

On examining the protocols, many problems emerge. We must neglect them, and answer the problem: What are our experiences when we think, considered purely as modifications of consciousness and apart from their context? I.e. "*What are the constituent parts* [elements, *Bestandstücke*] *of our thought experiences?*"

The most obvious feature in the subject's reports, says Bühler, consists in sensory presentations of various modalities—auditory, kinæsthetic, and so on. Then come feelings. Then the peculiar stretches of consciousness described as doubt, astonishment, recollection, expectation, for which one can retain as a provisional designation the term *Bewusstseinslage* coined by Marbe. "It is exactly a consciousness of the process of thought, and particularly of the turning-points of this process in experience itself" (p. 315).

But this is not all. "The most important bits of experience are something that, in all the categories through which these formations can be defined, are not touched at all (I neglect for the time being the Bsl., whose position is peculiar). Something which before all shows no sensory quality, no sensory intensity. Something of which we may rightly predicate degree of clearness, degree of certainty, a vividness by means of which it arouses our psychic interest; which, however, in its content is quite differently determined from everything that is ultimately reducible to sensations; something for which it would be nonsense to try to determine whether it possessed a greater or less intensity, or even into what sensory qualities it could be resolved. These entities[31] are what the subjects, using Ach's term, have designated as awarenesses, or sometimes as knowing, or simply as 'the consciousness that', but most frequently and correctly as 'thoughts'. Thought, that is also the term proposed by Binet. We shall retain it as the most natural and the most suitable" (pp. 315–16)

The question now narrows itself to the following part questions: how does the function of carrying thought-content distribute itself between images and thoughts? and, secondly, what is the mutual relation of these two? The first problem is easily solved. "A glance at the protocols will tell us: anything so fragmentary, so sporadic, so thoroughly at the mercy of chance when it enters consciousness as the images in our thought experiences, cannot be regarded as the carrier of the close-fitting and continuous thought-content. . . . The thoughts

[31] *Stücke*. Titchener translates "items".

alone can be regarded as the real constituent parts of our thought-experiences" (p. 317).

That is to say, our thinking consists essentially of a specific conscious process which must be considered to constitute a fresh mental category. It is neither sensation nor feeling nor image, and may, in fact, exist without any trace of imagery. It has its own articulations, not those of logic. It definitely has reference to some object, namely that concerning which we are thinking.

Two reports follow, illustrating the imageless nature of such thought.

(Dürr) "Is this correct: 'The future is just as much a condition of the present as of the past'?" Answer: "No." (10 secs.) "First I thought: that sounds like something correct (without words). Then I made the attempt to represent it to myself. The thought came to me: Men are determined by thoughts of the future. Then, however, immediately the thought: *that the thought of the future should not be confounded with the future itself; that such confusions, however, constitute a frequent dodge in philosophical thought. (Of words or images there was throughout no trace.) Thereupon the answer: No.*"

Another protocol (Külpe). (Do you understand?) "When you think of purpose you must also think of chance and folly?" . . . "Yes." (11.5 secs.) "It was difficult and strange (*ungeläufig*) for me to bring purpose into contrast with the two others. That is to say, the thought darkly emerged, that the two others must be presupposed by purpose, in the same way as not-A is by A. Folly I succeeded, without more ado, in bringing into this scheme; with chance I did not succeed. Then I had the thought, *how, with Darwin, chance is considered as an explanation of purpose. (There were no images, not a trace of the word Darwin, this is the first time I have spoken the word. It was an immediate, quite clear Knowledge* (knowing).) Then I said with a measure of uncertainty for the second part: Yes. The task has a strong echo, it has not left me yet, because I am not yet finished with it." (pp. 318, 319. Bühler's italics.)

Such a thought is not the sum of a number of images. It is a true, unanalysable unity. Nor is it associated images which have not come into consciousness but are potentially capable of doing so. This latter is Wundt's view. The view is untenable, says Bühler, because thought is a fact, not a possibility nor a potentiality. In short, the thought of something is once again an irreducible fact of experience.

If we carry down to its lowest legitimate terms an analysis of what we experience while thinking, we come ultimately to the thought as thus understood. "We designate as thoughts the ultimate units of our thinking experiences" (pp. 324–9). The unit is such that it contains only dependent parts, not independent ones. That is to say, further analysis would destroy the essential properties of that which is being analysed—the thought experience.

Although the thought is a unit, yet it is not entirely homogeneous. By various means one may distinguish within it different features or "moments", which are then not independent parts but dependent items. Thus of the thought expressed by the words "perseverance is a daughter of strength, stubbornness a daughter of weakness, that is, of weakness of understanding", a subject remembered "there were two virtues, concerning which a contrasting statement was made". Here the two virtues, and the contrast between them, are distinguishable as different features or "moments" of the original thought, and so on (p. 333). The moments are embraced in a single thought-experience.

Types of Thought.—It is possible to give a rough classification of these thought-elements. A very frequent type of thought-experience is what may be termed "consciousness of a rule" (*Regelbewusstsein*).

Thus to the question "Can the atomic theory of physics ever be shown to be untenable by any discoveries?" Dürr answered "Yes", after nine seconds. As part of the report appeared the statement "there was contained [i.e. in the mental processes involved] a knowledge of how such questions are solved". To another problem his answer contained the statement: "I knew that such questions cannot be decided by reflection." Here the subject was conscious of a rule that was of general validity. One knows not only that one can solve the particular problem, together with the method of solution, but also the general principle involved. The "consciousness of a rule" is very easily remembered. It is one of the most frequently encountered types of thinking. It is not simply thinking about a rule. Rather it is thinking *of* a rule or *in the form of* a rule. Definite facts (*Gegenstände*, objects), which the logician designates as laws, are "adequately thought" (pp. 339–40). Such "thinking a rule" is of great importance in scientific thought. It is found, for example, when we prove a mathematical proposition or when we employ a mathematical function. An example of the latter is given when we think of decrease with the square of the distance. Here we "think the function", without reference to any particular quantity. Another frequent instance of the "consciousness of a rule" is to be found in the grammatical rules which come to consciousness when we are uncertain concerning our speech.

A second type of thought is characterized by the presence of the *consciousness of relation*. Such a relation may exist either between our thoughts or within a single thought as one of its moments. For example, a subject may say "it was a question of an alternative". Or "the thought contained 'a consequence' " or "an opposition", and so on. In specific cases it is often difficult to decide whether the relation forms a "moment" of a single thought, or whether it is a connecting-link between two thoughts. It is such *known* relations between thoughts that give continuity to the whole ramified experience of thinking. As in the case of the consciousness of rule, the relation is not simply meant but experienced.

Lastly, there is the type which Bühler calls "Intentions", where the act of meaning, rather than what is meant, is in the foreground. Thus a subject may make a rapid survey over a whole branch of knowledge. For instance, Külpe stated: "The picture (*Schilderung*) of the pre-Socratic philosophy, its relation to Socrates, how Plato fought against it, all this seemed to be included in the thought. . . . The thought did not come to formulation; in fact, I simply *thought* it." The same subject reported on another occasion: "I thought of the ancient scepticism (the word scepticism spoken internally); this included a great deal; the whole development in three phases was formally present".

The consciousness of rule, the consciousness of relation, and the intention have been termed types of thought. It would be more strictly true to call them "moments" or features of thought, which, by their greater or less prominence, give the thought a distinctive character. It is not asserted that they form the only types of thought or thought-moments. Nor can we say whether every thought contains them all. Every thought must, however, include an intention, and must refer to something meant.

The question now arises: how does this "something meant" appear in consciousness? The conventional answer is "by means of images". There are, indeed, instances where this occurs, but they are not the most important. There are, says Bühler, thoughts in which the object of thought is clearly defined in consciousness without any image, or even without any consciousness of rule or of relation. Subjects reporting these thoughts at first refer them to slight sensory elements, sensations of tension in the brow or the breast, and so on. Finally, however, they see that these sensations have nothing to do with the thoughts. We must conclude that thinking may contain an imageless modification of consciousness corresponding to the meaning of the thought. Whatever the meaning, it may appear in experience without an image. We may, in fact, "think" an object in the external world or an inference involving physical objects directly, without any "mental" intermediary. As Külpe said: "It struck me that one could think of the objects of the external world such as material bodies . . . in immediate fashion without having to form images of them."[32] This was of course the final rejection of presentationism, the fashionable hypothesis of the day, according to which one experiences not the world direct but the presentations engendered by it, or their reproductions. It is akin to the belief termed the " ideomotor" theory, and more specifically the belief that an "idea" had to precede speech. Bühler's later argument in this paper seems to a modern reader to present unnecessary complications. But the point that the meaning must have its effect on the conscious experience of thinking but need not be represented imaginally turned out to be of considerable importance. This will appear especially when Titchener's criticism is considered.

Bühler published two more papers which complete the picture. The first, to which reference has already been made, deals with the intermediate conscious processes between thoughts, which consist of "*knowing*", or *Wissen*, and which need not attain the dignity of thoughts. These processes may better be described as "known relations". The relations in question are between one thought and another, not between the meanings of the thoughts. They may be relations between thoughts and the *Aufgabe* or task. (See next chapter.) They serve to guarantee the unity of the thought process, thus giving it its teleological character, its direction towards an end. The "thread of the thought-process is the sum total of such intercalary processes. When they are absent we say we have lost the thread" (Bühler, 1908).

The third paper deals with the memory of thoughts. Here Bühler attempts to corroborate the independence of thoughts and their sensory accompaniment by demonstrating that thoughts and sensory processes do not follow the same laws. It is common knowledge that it is much easier to learn the sense of a passage of prose or poetry than to learn the exact words. The latter, says Bühler (and Külpe), is achieved by the association of sensory material. The former is an entirely different process. The difference is shown in a neat experiment where phrases were paired. Two of these pairs were:

> Increase of population in modern times:
> The future struggle between races.

and   Homer and the Bible;
> The unity of the human species.

[32] Quoted by Klein, 1938, pp. 368–9.

The instructions were to establish a connection in thought between the members of each pair. Twenty such pairs were read, after which the first member of each pair was given with the request that the subject should add the second. The average number of successes was between seventeen and eighteen, a far greater number than could be attained if nonsense syllables were used in the place of the phrases. The thought-connection between the two phrases is clearly a different thing from the association between sensory material, says Bühler. Occasionally a series of twenty pairs can be reproduced without error even on the next day. Sometimes the words are altered by the subject, showing once more that we have here not the sheer play of sensory association (Külpe). Thoughts are, in fact, to some extent independent of the particular verbal form in which they are cast. This was further demonstrated by reading a list of statements, some of them in the form of proverbs. Twenty such statements were given. Examples are:

When the calf is stolen, the farmer repairs the stall.

Where the fox has his store, he does not rob.

While the total series of twenty statements was being read, the subject was in ignorance of what was to follow. A further series was then read, with the instruction to say whether there had been anything in the first series like the statement now being read in the second, and to say how it was expressed. Examples of this second series are:

Even mice bite dead cats.

A clever thief keeps his nest clean.

A doctor and a peasant know more than a doctor alone.

Where there are doves, doves come.

One looks to the cask when the wine escapes into the cellar.

The subject could indicate with great certainty the corresponding sentence in the previous series. He might alter the words while retaining the sense. "Jokers" were inserted in both series; that is to say, sentences with no corresponding sentence in the other series. When the subject came to these, no memory was aroused. This recognition, not of the words but of the thought, was again surprisingly easy—too easy, says Bühler, for the mental processes involved were too much abbreviated to be properly observed.

Other experiments were made with proverbs, of which from fourteen to thirty were read to the subject. An example is: "Work has bitter roots, sweet fruits." After the whole series was read, single words from the proverbs were given, with the request to complete the proverb. A series of twenty to twenty-four proverbs took an

hour, together with the resulting introspections. The whole proverb
was in most cases given at once, though sometimes it was necessary
to add a second word to aid memory. Dürr completed twenty-seven
out of a series of thirty proverbs!

Thus, once again, writes Bühler, the thought is independent of
its sensory accompaniment. It is remembered in a way impossible for
sheer sensory material. He remarks that for such thought-repro-
duction to take place, it is necessary to make the subject *think*. Had
the sentence been of the nature of: "The table is an article of furniture", etc., where no thought is necessary, when the single words
"table" and so on were repeated, the subjects would "either have
forgotten nine-tenths of the sentences or else remembered them by
some memory system". The proverbs make them think, if only to a
slight extent, and the thought is remembered where sheer sensory
material would be forgotten (Bühler, 1908a).

Summary of Experimental Results on Imageless Thought

This completes the survey of the Würzburg experiments on imageless thought. Beginning with the negative observation that there are
processes that refused to be forced into a sensationalistic scheme, we
find Messer claiming somewhat prematurely that these processes are
"thoughts" of an unformulated type. Ach claimed, on the other
hand, to have discovered a kind of conscious event of which the
previously observed imageless states form a subdivision. By charac-
terizing what he had discovered as a *knowing* (*Wissen*), Ach had,
therefore, at the same time added a positive attribute to the hitherto
negatively defined "conscious state". Or, stated the other way round,
Ach had added a positive characteristic which was the class mark
of a more inclusive division. With Bühler, the original Bsl. has
almost dropped out, and indeed one feels that for consistency's sake
Bühler would have done better to leave it out altogether. He speaks
of it early in his first paper as occupying a peculiar position, and does
not appear to mention it for the rest of his hundred and sixty pages.
For him, the positive attribute added by Ach, namely the aspect of
awareness, has become a characteristic of something contained in
the only real thinking activity, namely the thought-element. At the
same time the thought-element retains the aspect of impalpableness,
of imagelessness, which so much struck the earlier workers in their
observations of simpler processes. This supersession of the original,
negative, idea of the *Bewusstseinslage* was clearly seen, some years
after Bühler's papers, by Külpe, who, in a passage already quoted,

speaks of the *Bewusstseinslage* as "the new idea, compelled by the observation of the facts, making possible a circumlocution rather than a description; it also was inadequate",[33] and had to be supplemented with the idea of *knowing*, before thought could be properly described.

APPENDIX

Bühler on Act and Content in Thinking

Bühler acknowledges his debt to Külpe in the development of his theory. It is indeed difficult fully to understand the text without references to Külpe's work. See, e.g., Külpe, 1922, especially the last lecture, and Chapter II, paragraph 13. I find myself compelled to differ from Titchener (p. 145) who quotes Bühler as saying "knowledge (*Wissen*) is a new manifold of modifications of our consciousness" (Bühler, p. 361), and adds "covering the variety of thoughts as the general term sensation covers the variety of sensations". I am obliged to believe that Titchener failed to see the point of Bühler's questions: "Fragen wir uns nun, wie die Bewusstseinsmodifikationen, die in unseren unanschaulichen Wasbestimmtheiten des Meinens vorliegen, funktionell zu bezeichnen sind? Wie werden wir dasjenige nennen, was sich zu ihnen eben so verhält wie etwa 'das Empfinden' zu 'den Empfindungen?'" I translate literally, "Do we ask ourselves now how the modifications of consciousness, which are at hand in our imageless, qualitative determinations of meaning, are to be functionally described? How shall we name that which is related to them as, for example, 'the act of sensing', is related to 'the sensations'?" This must mean, in the Külpe-Stumpf terminology, that we are to look not for a general term but for a *function* or a functional aspect. The point is made clear by Külpe in a passage where he is warning his lecture audience not to assume, from the existence of such word-pairs as "*Empfinden*" and "*die Empfindung*", that in *every* case there is a psychic function and a content corresponding to two words of a pair. "Although, for example," he says, "to sense, to image (ideate), to think, are correlative with sensation, image (idea), thought, yet we need not assume a sensation-, imaging-, and thought-function directed towards sensation-, image-, thought-contents. . . . We must make a particular examination, in specific cases, to discover whether there is such a thing as a function of sensing, imaging, thinking" (p. 131).

I have quoted the least favourable passage from Külpe, who has shortly before drawn a clear distinction on the one hand between "the act of perceiving, of remembering . . . of meaning, of thinking (in the narrower sense)", as functions, and a corresponding list of contents, viz. "the sense impressions, the memory- and imagination-pictures, the thoughts" (p. 130). The clue of Bühler's treatment of the whole problem is to be found in a passage where he distinguishes between the qualitative determinations of what is thought, which are "modifications of consciousness", and the relation of thought to its object. "We shall be able to distinguish in every thought the qualitative determinations (*Wasbestimmtheiten*) of what is

---

[33] The original lecture was published in 1912.

thought from the relation to the object" (p. 349). I.e. we must distinguish the meaning-datum present in the activity of thinking from that about which the thinker is thinking. Titchener has, it seems, not followed Bühler in making this distinction. He is thus unable to understand the demand for a "functional designation", and is led to bring against Bühler the charge of making the "stimulus error". This charge Titchener voices in his next paragraph (p. 145). We shall see later that the accusation depends on a misunderstanding of Bühler's real experimental achievement. The passage in Külpe coming between those quoted shows that he is uttering a warning against the very mistake which Titchener accuses Bühler of making. There is, says Külpe, an essential difference between an analysis of what is *meant* by a word and analysis of the state of affairs (*Tatbestand*) designated by a word. The latter kind of analysis alone is psychologically useful. That Titchener did not recognize what Bühler meant is the more strange in that he discussed the triple distinction, as made by Stout and Witasek, on p. 63 of the same book. One wonders whether it was this same misunderstanding that led to the Cornell series of experiments on thinking (see the next chapter).

CHAPTER III

THE WORK OF THE WÜRZBURG GROUP

THE MECHANISM OF THINKING

The First Experimental Attack on Association as producing Thought

(1) Watt, H. J., 1905: *Experimentelle Beiträge zu einer Theorie des Denkens*. An English abstract, "Experimental Contribution to a Theory of Thinking", is in the *J. Anat. and Physiol.*, 1905–6, Vol. 40, pp. 257–66. This summary by Watt is the only piece of the Würzburg literature originally written in English.

Method: Partially constrained association, e.g. name a whole to which an object signified belongs, name a part, etc. Introspections. Hipp chronoscope.

Object: To describe the effect of the task, as contrasted with that of the "stimulus" and the "reproductive tendencies" belonging to it.

Results: Using different tasks with the same stimuli:

(*a*) Imagery may change.

(*b*) Reaction time may change.

(*c*) On the principle that the quickest response for any one subject was most often repeated, and that this was likely to be the commonest response in a group of people (Marbe's "law"), Watt grouped together reproductive tendencies of the same intrinsic speed. Within these groups he found variation of task accompanied variation of reaction time.

(*d*) Hence we can distinguish *Association*, reproductive tendencies, from *Motive*, task.

(*e*) The task *ordinarily works unconsciously* (confirmed by Messer).

(*f*) *Both task and association* are necessary for thinking.

(2) Ach: *Method*, see last chapter. Also hypnosis.

Results: The determining tendencies must be postulated, which

(*a*) work unconsciously,

(*b*) proceed from the "aim-presentation",

(*c*) relate it to the "presentation of stimulus".

That is, Ach has related Watt's task intimately with "presentational" psychology. He has foreshadowed Selz's *Gesamtaufgabe*.

(*d*) Application to Abstraction.

(3) *Difficulty of Ach's Scheme:* He has interposed an unnecessary *tertium quid* between "purpose" or "motive" and thought or action. This he was forced to because he had to think in terms of presentations.

(4) *Difficulty of Watt's Scheme:* He has proposed the hypothesis that reproductive tendencies cannot function unless there is a motive present, and that both are necessary for (physical or mental) action. He cannot be consistent in this; e.g. in the reaction experiment, the stimulus (his own

example) has originally no reproductive tendencies attached to it. He was forced to his hypothesis because of the prevailing theory that the basis of thought was association.

THE DISCUSSION OF the Würzburg work has hitherto been confined to the qualitative aspect of the thought processes. To the question: What kind of mental event constitutes the process of thinking? it has been seen that the Würzburg answer was at first negative in the sense that it excluded imagery and imaginal processes, and, in its later development, positive, in that it maintained that the constitutive events of thinking were unique thought-processes, thoughts that are *sui generis*. It is now time to consider the correlative aspect of the question, namely by what principle do such thinking-events follow each other.

When the Würzburgers began their work, the conventional answer to the question was "by the laws of association". It is true that there were those who, repelled by the starkness of the associational scheme, which ultimately represented mental life as a fortuitous clash of elements, had attempted formulations which professed to do more justice to the real activity of the mind itself. Thus was born Wundt's doctrine of Apperception, the culmination of many theories carrying the same name. Wundt's doctrine was developed in the successive editions of his *Principles of Physiological Psychology* (first edition, 1874, sixth, 1908–11), and stressed the activity of the mind, as contrasted with the passivity of the process of association.[1] In the same way, Ward had attacked the doctrine of associationism or presentationism, as he preferred to call it.[2] Nevertheless, it is fair to say that in the early nineteen hundreds the conventional explanation of the mechanism of thought was couched in associational terms. Once more the Würzburg group developed a doctrine running counter to the conventional scheme, and once more we must look to Külpe for the ultimate source of the work. In 1893 Külpe had already stated[3] that reactions to the reaction-time experiments

---

[1] See Boring's *History of Experimental Psychology*, pp. 333–35, for a clear summary. See also Ward, 1918, pp. 308–11, for a history and criticism of the doctrine of Apperception.

[2] See his articles in the tenth (1902) and eleventh (1908) editions of the *Encyclopædia Britannica*. They were expanded and supplemented to form his *Psychological Principles*, 1918.

[3] *Grundriss der Psychologie*, Berlin, 1893, p. 422. This was pointed out by R. M. Ogden (1911, p. 185). The statement is actually repeated almost verbatim by Watt. "The *class*, i.e. sensorial or motor reaction, is not determined by the nature of the experiment after it has been made, but by the nature of the given

differed according to the preparation of the subject. This was the germ from which later sprang the work of Watt and Ach, whose contributions to the theory of thinking are here complementary although their experiments were independently conceived and executed. It has been seen that the associational theory had already been severely criticized on theoretical grounds. It was, however, as the result of elaborate experiment, of "systematic experimental self-observation", that these two men proposed, as a qualitatively different mechanism to account for the sequence of the thinking process, the Determining Tendencies (Ach) which spring from the Task (*Aufgabe*, Watt). The work of Watt will be considered first.

Experimental Demonstration of the Task

Watt used the method of partially constrained association which was two years later to be employed in the experiments of Messer already described. By means of Ach's newly devised card changer, printed words were shown on cards. According to the specified task (*Aufgabe*), the subject was to classify the object signified, to name an example of it, to name a whole to which it belonged, to name a part, to name another of the same class or another part of the same whole. Six subjects were employed, most of the work being done by four practised observers, who included Angell, Külpe, and Dürr. Fifteen words were allotted to each of the tasks, and in all over three thousand experiments were made. Time was registered by the Hipp chronoscope. Elaborate introspections were made after each word. These were recorded together with any remarks that the subject cared to make. Occasionally the experimenter questioned the subject on specific points. In addition, a series of experiments was made in which every observer was required to concentrate particular attention on one phase of the experience. For the purpose there were recognized four stages of the total process of association: that of the preparation[4] for the experiment, that of the appearance of the stimulus word, the search for the reaction word, when it occurred, and lastly the appearance of the reaction word (1905, p. 316). For example, the subject might be required to notice particularly what happened in consciousness before the stimulus word appeared. This was the method of fractionation, already mentioned in connection

---

preparation. Here we have the difference between what we call the task and the mere tendency to reproduction . . ." (1906, p. 262). The intimate connection between the Würzburg work and Külpe's thought is here well illustrated.
[4] The influence of Külpe's already quoted statement may perhaps here by seen.

with Ach's experiments. Watt claimed that the method made possible more careful and better introspection.

The experiences reported by the subject could be classified under three headings. (A) The subject followed, throughout the experiment, a single line which led directly to the spoken word. This was the most frequent type. (B) The subject might seek a word which he did not find. (C) He may have intended to say one word, but actually have said another[5] (1905, pp. 303, 321; 1906, p. 258). In each of these three classes Watt distinguished three subdivisions.

(i) The reaction word may follow directly upon the stimulus with no intermediate experience or none that was describable.

(ii) In a great many cases, visual imagery ("a visual representation") follows the stimulus. Thereupon, either directly or after a pause or a search, comes the reaction word.

(iii) Sometimes there appeared between stimulus and response a verbal image, or "some experiences which could only be described in conceptual terms and not analytically according to the content— call it a thought—appeared between the presentation of the word and the spoken reaction" (1906, p. 258). This last is of course the *Bewusstseinslage* of Marbe, and it so appears in the German text (p. 304). In a footnote Watt explains: "We understand provisionally by this term an experience which is not yet analysable more closely" (ibid.).

The main object of the paper is to describe the effect of the task; and to distinguish it and its influence from the "reproductive tendencies"—and their influence. The effect of the task may be seen by the uniform influence it exerts on the general nature of the thinking process. To take first the simple reproductions, where the subject followed a single line until the final response was given, the percentage of each of the three subdivisions was found to change regularly and similarly with each subject from one task to another. Thus when observer 1 was given the task "name a whole of", 76 per cent. of his responses occurred without intermediate step, 23 per cent. showed intermediate visual images, 2 per cent. verbal images or *Bewusstseinslagen*. When the same observer was given the task "name an example of", these figures were 68 per cent., 21 per cent., and 11 per cent. respectively.[6] Thus, says Watt, the nature of the task has an effect on the experiences of the subject. A subject who shows hardly any

[5] I follow here Watt's own English account in his abstract of 1906, which differs slightly in wording and arrangement from that of the paper of 1905.

[6] These figures are as given by Watt, 1905, p. 311.

visual imagery when asked to classify, may experience such imagery in 50 per cent. of his responses when he is asked to name a part. This same change of task may increase another subject's visual imagery from 50 per cent. to between 90 and 100 per cent. The duration of reaction is similarly influenced by the task.

We have hitherto been speaking of the simple "single-line" reactions. When we come to the complex reactions, where the subject follows more than one line or gives one word while intending to say another, here also we find reaction times varying with the task. The percentage occurrence of such complex reactions is, however, independent of it. This Watt explains as follows.

The occurrence of such complex reactions must depend on the number of associations or reproductive tendencies diverging from the stimulus in question. A stimulus with more reproductive tendencies attaching to it would be expected to give more cases where the subject pursued more than one line before giving his response. But the number of reproductive tendencies attaching to a stimulus depends on the stimulus and is independent of the task. Therefore it is natural to find that change in task does not change the number of complex reactions. Thus the experimental fact that the number of complex reactions is independent of the particular task shows once again that we must distinguish the influence of the task from that of the stimulus. This argument is put forward as embodying a probable hypothesis only.[7]

Watt attempts to separate the respective influences of the task and of the stimulus word upon the speed of the reactions in the following ingenious manner. Consider first the reactions of a single individual. Repetition, we know, diminishes reaction time. The more often an individual has made a given reaction, the shorter reaction time becomes, until the minimum time is reached. Now the associations that are more frequently experienced by one individual are likely to be those which he shares with other people. Consequently we are likely to find that, when the same response is made by different observers, the number of such different observers sharing the same response will vary directly with the speed of the response in question. The fastest responses would then be those given by the most subjects, and so on. Analysis of the experimental data shows this to be very generally true, with explainable exceptions. This gives a possible

[7] It will later be seen that Ach claims that a task, or what here comes to the same thing, the determining tendencies, may cause new associations to arise. If this contention is justified, it invalidates Watt's argument at this point.

method of eliminating the effect of repetition in an individual's reaction times.

Responses given by two or more persons are grouped together, and in each group the speed under different tasks is compared. It is found that within these groups of equally frequent responses, change of task has much the same effect as was found before when the general effect of task on duration was considered. That is to say, "the influence of the task is independent of the rapidity of the tendency of reproduction in itself". When that part of the speed which belongs, so to speak, to the stimulus word has been eliminated, it is found that the influence of the task in respect of speed of response is the same as before. So that, once again, the task is differentiated from the stimulus word (1906, p. 260). By a further analysis, he shows that "if other conditions remain the same, it is the individual strength or *rapidity* of the tendency to reproduction *which determines the reproduction*" (loc. cit., p. 261, original italics), and not any other factor such as arbitrary choice or selective attention. Different stimulus words, taken by themselves, have different sets of associations diverging from them. Any particular task, such as "name a part of", affects these equally, whatever their individual strength.

Thus he reaches the conception of a dual division of the factors affecting our mental life. There is the task in question, which has the same influence on all possible associatory reproductions. It acts by furthering certain reproductions and inhibiting others, and can only bring about a response if it has such previously existing associations to work upon. The task is generally repeated by the subject at the beginning of the series. Thus he may say "find a part", or "name an example", or exemplify the experiment to himself, in such terms as "animal—dog", and so on. Ordinarily, however, once the task is impressed responses are made without its repetition during the experiment, unless there is disturbance by the persistence or perseveration[8] of a former task, or for some other reason. In this case, the task will be repeated. The subject will "remind" himself that he is to "find a part", etc. Watt made the general statement, "The presentation becomes a task when it becomes constantly operative in the aforementioned manner; the task becomes a presentation or is

---

[8] Perseveration was first experimentally demonstrated by Müller and Pilzecker, *Experimentelle Beiträge Zur Lehre vom Gedächtnis*, Zts für Psych., Erg. Bd. I, 1900, p. 58. It was taken over by Watt from its associational context, and applied here to the other mental principle he is setting up, viz. the task. It is doubtful whether the transfer is theoretically justifiable, at least without more careful examination than Watt gives the matter.

known (*bewusst*) as such, when it is no longer operative or when it must again be brought into operation" (1905, p. 346). *The unconscious working of the task is one of the most striking features.* Thus a subject may report, to the stimulus word *copper* "consciousness of the meaning of the word 'lead' spoken involuntarily" (1905, p. 344). Only when the process of thinking is not running smoothly is the task brought to light in consciousness.

The task and the reproductive tendency may then be roughly demarcated in their function as follows: *the operation of both task and reproductive tendency are necessary for thinking. The essential material of the thinking process comes from the reproductive tendencies, which, according to the number of times the associations have been repeated, have acquired their own intrinsic speed. The actual speed of reproduction may, however, be affected by a task, which will favour some reproductions and repress others.* Thus to Watt thought is carried on by the fundamental machinery of association, with its own independent speed; the task directs the machinery, adding to, or in some cases possibly diminishing, the intrinsic speed of the fundamental mechanics on which it works.[9]

Application of the Concept of Task to Two Problems. Messer's Contribution

To illustrate this conception of the task it will not be out of place to show how Watt applied it to the solution of two psychological problems. The first concerns the old question of sensory and motor reaction types. It is well known that reaction times differ according as attention is directed ·to the stimulus or to the action to be performed. Into Watt's discussion we shall not enter except to say that he claimed that the subject is given a different task in the two cases. The distinction he says is, therefore, not physiological but psychological.

More important for our purposes is Watt's discussion of the Judgment which was adopted and characteristically elaborated by Messer. Watt points out that sheer association does not form a judgment.[10] Subjects refuse to recognize as judgments responses that were of the nature of free associations. Nobody, for example, would

[9] See 1906, p. 260.

[10] In the earlier paper of 1905, Watt quite clearly states this. In the later paper of 1906, he speaks of reproduction as being determined by the "overwhelming strength of the reproductive tendency", and thus conceivably against the influence of a task. The total context of the second passage implies, however, the contrast between free association and judgment.

claim that the ordinary association "man"–"woman" constitutes a judgment. Reproductions by themselves cannot then constitute judgment, but are "merely a succession of experiences under the one principle of association". It will be remembered that Marbe found no psychological criterion of judgment. He was right, says Watt, if attention is confined to what is experienced between the stimulus and the response. If, however, we look beyond these limits we see that what makes the difference between sheer association and judgment is the existence and the working of a task. Where there is a task operative, then there is judgment with reference to the task. Thus *copper–lead* as a sheer association would not be considered to constitute judgment; while if the accepted task was "find a co-ordinate object", and the stimulus word was *copper*, the same sequence would be accepted as a judgment with reference to the task in question.

This thesis that the task is a constitutive feature of judgment was, we have seen, confirmed and extended by Messer (1906, p. 93 *et seq.*), whose subjects very definitely refused to apply the term "Judgment" to a sheer association. Messer's analysis should be considered together with Watt's. A typical statement is "The judgment was experienced as something different from an association" (p. 95). Messer agrees that the task is of fundamental importance in judgment. Marbe's results are due, he says, to the fact that the tasks concerned have, by repetition, disappeared from consciousness because they have attained the status of self-evident presuppositions. This is the case with many of the tasks of everyday life, as, for example, the task that ordinary perception, thought, and speech shall so take place as to conform with reality.[11] Here we do not recognize the existence of a specific task. Yet a specific task must be present. In the same way we do not in ordinary circumstances recognize that a specific task is present when we make a judgment. Marbe's observers failed to take into consideration the question of the task, and for that reason they could find no criterion of judgment. In any case, the task had of course not been investigated when Marbe wrote, so that the observers did not know what to look for. However, Messer claimed that his own subjects were presented with so many different kinds of tasks that comparison and consequently self-observation was easier for them. Messer's general contention is that if judgment is compared, under proper conditions, with sheer association, it will be found that in the one case there is mental activity, act, function, while in the other there are only mental contents, data.

[11] One is curiously reminded of Freud's "reality principle" in thinking.

This he says is the real distinction as recognized by his own subjects in the judgments they made. Their judgment-experiences embraced first the stimulus and response words as perceived. These are data or content. In addition there was, however, the definite mental activity (act or function) of willing a specific judgment-relation between the two. There was gratifying agreement among the subjects that in judgment, "a relation between stimulus and reaction-presentation (*Vorstellungen*), which is characterized more closely as a predicative (or propositional) relation, must be willed (meant) or at least recognized" (p. 105). Like every other such mental act, according to the act-content psychology, the judgment refers to an object. The thinking activity is a *meaning* activity. When we pass a judgment we refer to something that is not the judgment itself, but is that concerning which we are judging. We judge *about* something. We do so because of a specific task which we have accepted, and it is this task which is so difficult to recognize, because it is so familiar. In this discussion we are keeping strictly to the territory of psychology, for this "intention", or "intentional relation to an object", is treated "solely as a characteristic aspect of conscious experience".

Watt then had claimed merely that the psychological criterion of judgment was the task. Messer expanded the thesis (1) by pointing out that the familiarity of the judgment-task ordinarily obscures the fact of its existence, and (ii) by equating the judgment-experience with the *act of judging* in the act-content antithesis.

For a general estimate of the work of the Würzburgers the reader is referred to the next chapter. On the specific point just discussed it seems better, however, to make certain criticisms *in situ*. The most cursory examination of Messer's general thesis reveals, in fact, many difficulties, which have been discussed in detail by Titchener.[12] They may be summarized by saying that if the act-content antithesis is to be used in the description of thinking careful distinction must be made between the "object" and the "content" of thinking. Thus Külpe[13] states: "Red is doubtless a content of the colour-sensation in which I experience it; the picture of a house is in the same way a content of the visual presentation in which the house is given to me. But the quartz-crystal of which I am thinking when I wish to represent to myself a case of hexagonal crystal formation, is not in the same way content of the thought by which I bring it to my con-

[12] On the whole, the present writer endorses what Titchener has to say concerning Messer's psychology of judgment.
[13] 1922, p. 320.

sciousness. Consequently there is no contradiction in the thinking of objects which are not thoughts, while in the sensing of a colour which is not the content of this sensation, there would certainly be a contradiction. Thinking can then be directed towards objects which are essentially different from thinking itself, and which, by being thought, do not become mere contents of thinking or mere thoughts."

That is to say we must, as did Bühler, distinguish between (1) the act or function of thinking, in Messer's case judging; (2) the (psychic) content of the act, including the terms of the judgment, and (3) the object of the judgment.[14] There is great difficulty in deciding what is the nature of the terms to be related in Messer's account of the judgment. Sometimes these must be facts of thought, sometimes objective facts. In the same way, there is difficulty in deciding what the judgment-relation is, whether it is a relation given by thought or a "relation between objects". As Bühler himself points out, Messer missed the further step of seeing that "the consciousness of the signification (of the terms related) must be regarded as something thought, as a thought *sui generis. . . . The predicative relation does not join two experiences as such but their objects,* that which was thought in them."[15] That is to say, one cannot get a judgment out of any manipulation of "presentations". There must be reference to the object of thought.

Summary and Criticism of the Würzburg Contribution to the Psychology of Judgment

The history and criticism of the Würzburg doctrine of the judgment may then be summarized. Marbe had attempted a psychological analysis of the process of judging. This was to contrast with previous analysis in that it was to use the experimental method of scientifically directed and controlled introspection to determine what actually happens in consciousness when a person undergoes the judging experience. Marbe was able to find no introspective criterion of judgment. He left the problem with the declaration that the criterion was physiological not psychological. Watt made the task into the criterion of judgment. Judgment is "a sequence of experiences whose procession from its first term, the stimulus, has been determined by

[14] Messer makes the distinction, but in this paper at least is apparently not consistent in its use. According to Boring (1929), Messer enlarged his formulation of the act-content antithesis in his book *Empfindung und Denken*, published two years later in 1908.

[15] *"Remarques sur les problèmes de la psychologie de la pensée"* in *Arch. de Psych.*, 6, 1907, p. 378. Italics by the present writer.

a psychological factor (that is, by the problem). As conscious experience, this psychological factor is itself past and gone, but it still
persists as an appreciable influence" (Watt, 1905, p. 416; Titchener's
translation). Actually, of course, Watt has not given a "psychological" criterion of judgment, any more than had Marbe. The fact
that there has been a certain experience in the past does not confer a
psychological (conscious) mark upon an experience at a later date.
The use of the term "appreciable influence" merely obscures the issue.
The critic is entitled to ask: is the task present in consciousness at
the time of judging or not? The answer must be the latter, in which
case no definition of judgment has been given in the terms Watt
proposed. Specifically the question may be asked: how can a past
task be "present" as a psychological[16] "influence" but not as a
conscious experience? The question is unanswerable for Watt's
psychology.

Finally, it might seem possible to amend Watt's analysis by adding
Ach's conception of awareness. Watt's statement concerning the relation
of the task to judgment would then read "as palpable, conscious experience, this psychological factor is itself past and gone, but it still persists as
an impalpable awareness". At first sight plausible, this emendation does
not, however, furnish a necessary and sufficient psychological criterion of
judgment. It still leaves judgment a process of the manipulation of mental
counters. The fact that one of these counters or a process involving them
is impalpable does not vitiate the criticism already made in connection
with Messer's work, namely that judgment does not solely concern experiences as such or their relation to a task. The emended statement would
also, as Titchener points out in another context, make the definition of
judgment too wide. Not every awareness of determination is a judgment-
awareness. If so, then the word "judgment" loses its meaning in a sea of
generality. Even the emended definition then leaves us with the original
problem: what kind of impalpable awareness of determination is an
awareness of judgment? Watt's criterion of judgment is not, and cannot
be made, valid, at least as a sufficient criterion. It has further been seen
that Messer accepted the "*Aufgabe*" criterion, and added an interpretation
in terms of the act-content psychology. This interpretation must be rejected on the same kind of grounds.

Out of the discussions of Watt and Messer two facts emerge which
do not indeed give a psychological criterion of judgment in the way
in which these men understood the term, but which are of value in
themselves. Judgment is more than association. This we knew
before; but examination of Messer's protocols convinces one that
his abundant introspective confirmation was very much worth while

---

[16] Using the term as equivalent to conscious, which is the point of the search
for a psychological criterion for judgment.

in confirmation. Secondly, judgment may be recognized by a practised observer as "willed" (Messer) or, in more modern terms, voluntarily motivated. Those who accept Ach's *Bewusstheit* may wish to go farther and claim that such willing need not necessarily be cast in imaginal terms. It may be an "impalpable awareness". This fact of motivation seems to lose something of its value if it be remembered that the tendency is today to believe that all mental life, even the so-called free association of ideas, is motivated.[17]

There seems little doubt that the relatively unsatisfactory outcome of the investigations which we have just been discussing is due to a confusion between two terms which have since been clearly distinguished, namely that between the proposition and the judgment. Since the publication of Husserl's *Logische Untersuchungen*,[18] modern logic has been at pains to insist that it deals with propositions which are objectively true or false, and, at a first analysis at least, irrespective of the activity of a thinker. Judgment is the mental activity of affirming belief in such propositions. Judgments are therefore primarily psychological, and the conditions of their arising may be investigated by psychological methods. Propositions are independent of psychological considerations, just as much and just as little as are mathematical formulations. In this respect of independence of psychological considerations logic is closely allied to mathematics; and indeed a great development in this direction is seen in modern symbolic logic. The general distinction between the judgment and the proposition is well brought out by Husserl in an extraordinarily able polemic against what he calls Psychologism in logic (loc. cit., p. 50 ff.). It deserves to be read for itself as a masterpiece of psychological exposition.

Granting this distinction,[19] it can readily be seen that the "objective" proposition cannot be derived from the act of believing or affirmation, which is the judgment. Nor can it be derived from any manipulation of mental presentations. Nor can a judgment that an "objective" proposition is true (that is to say, an affirmation of belief in such an objective proposition) be equated, as Messer thought it could, with the willing of a relation between presentations. Psychic

---

[17] See, e.g., Varendonck, *The Psychology of Day-dreams*, London, 1921.

[18] Husserl, Edmund: *Logische Untersuchungen*, Zweite Auflage, Halle, 1913. (The first edition was published in 1902, so that the Würzburgers could have read it, and indeed did so. The significance of the work for their problem seems, however, to have escaped them.)

[19] Which is now presupposed in textbooks of logic. See, e.g., Wolf, A., *Textbook of Logic*, London, 1930, § 1, p. 18.

activity is indeed present in judgment, but it is not adequate to describe judgment, any more than it is adequate to describe a mathematical formula. In each case, there must be an "objective" proposition which, independently of the thinker, relates its terms. Husserl's main endeavour was to free logic from the shackles of psychology. Equally he has succeeded in freeing psychology from the shackles of logic. The task for psychological research is now clearly demarcated, as it could hardly be in the time of the Würzburgers. It is to examine such problems as that of the nature and the conditions of the affirmation, on the part of individual thinkers, of "objectively independent propositions." Thus will a purely psychological research be unencumbered by the many epistemological difficulties which flock round the notion of the objective proposition, and which undeservedly confused Messer in his psychological inquiry.[20]

Watt and Messer on the Function of Task and Association in Thinking

To return to Watt and his chief contribution—the task. The properties of the task and its influence on thought were in the main confirmed by Messer. In general, Messer finds that the task *gradually disappears from consciousness*, and yet still functions. The usual course of events is for the task to be grasped attentively when the experimenter gives his instructions, and perhaps repeated several times. During the first experiments of a series the task is present in consciousness in a more or less definite form. As the series progresses it is no longer present, but the fact that it is still functioning is shown by the appearance of the appropriate responses. When the task is changed, it must again be brought into consciousness, and also when the nature of the stimulus demands careful attention. This is the case, for example, when objects or propositions are used as "stimuli". The fact that the task is not functioning properly is shown by the uncertainty of the subject, in which case the task is, as a rule, speci-

---

[20] Two quotations will illustrate the fundamental clarification of the important issue discussed on the last page and which modern logic has been able to effect. "Our use of the term proposition makes abstraction from the element or moment of belief." After a discussion of judgment, the same work proceeds "these are psychological matters with which we are not directly concerned" (Wolf, op. cit., pp. 40 and 44.) Compare with this the following quotation from a standard textbook of logic written in 1916. "The true unit of thought, the simplest complete act of thought, is the Judgment or Proposition: between which, where a distinction is intended, it is that a proposition is the expression in words of a judgment" (Joseph, H. W. B., *An Introduction to Logic*, Oxford, 1916, p. 14). Chapter VII of Joseph's textbook is entitled "Of the Proposition or Judgment", a heading which, I venture to say, would be impossible in a modern textbook.

fically recalled. Thus, even when the task has become unconscious, it can be recalled, and this recall serves to strengthen it (Messer, loc. cit., p. 209).

Since Watt claims that all thinking may be considered to be due to the interaction of the two principles, task and memory or reproductive tendencies, if the task finds no reproductions to hand, no reaction or thought can occur. On the other hand, the tendency to reproduction may be too strong for the task to operate. In this case it ("reproduced presentation") "forces its way out in spite of the task, when a wrong reaction takes place" (Watt, 1906, p. 261). The task can only overcome a limited amount of force, he says, a statement which is reminiscent of Herbart's mental dynamics.

Both Watt and Messer note that there may be a certain amount of interaction between the task and the reproductive tendencies. For instance, Messer shows that subjects may tend to specialize the task. Thus, in his first series, when his subjects were told to give any random word, the first that occurred to them, they often sought for a word that stood in some definite relation to the stimulus word. In fact, it was quite difficult to give a meaningless response. In these cases the subject often set himself a task which might spring naturally from the stimulus word. "I am 'set' to associate the co-ordinate idea," said Külpe on one such occasion (Messer, p. 23). So-called free association regularly shows the influence of "reproductive tendencies" in inducing such specialization of task. There are, of course, individual differences. Messer quotes Binet as noting the same fact of specialization of task in "free association". The same point has later been made by many experimentalists.

In the same way, Watt notes the reciprocal influence exerted by the task and the mental representations, the conscious correlates of the stimuli in question. A suitable stimulus, for example the spoken words of the experimenter, may introduce the task. When the latter has ceased to function properly, it may again come into consciousness. Here the further stimuli presented in the progress of the experiment have induced states of consciousness which have influenced the task, causing it to appear once more in consciousness. The reciprocal influence of task and stimulus word, in the narrower sense, will prove to be important when we later consider the work of Selz.

Thus we have experimentally exhibited for the first time a contrast between what may be called mechanical and non-mechanical factors in thinking. Watt's task is exactly a factor in thought which is not the sheer interplay of associative tendencies aroused by the stimulus.

Just what difference Watt imagined to exist between the task and the reproductive tendencies, it is difficult to say. In one context he protests against "the general tendency to interpret and schematically represent the task in the sense of sheer reproductive tendencies" (1905, p. 329). In another he speaks of "the task, which indeed is itself to be thought of as a greater and stronger reproduction-motive" (1905, p. 420; cf. 1906, p. 265). But the general burden of his experimental study is that the task must be distinguished from the reproductive tendencies belonging to the stimulus word. They cannot be interchanged, nor simply replaced one by the other. Watt's scheme is thus an emended associationalism. In addition to providing the fundamental material of the thinking process, the reproductive tendencies provide also a fundamental speed factor. As already quoted, p. 71, "the rapidity of a tendency to reproduction from one point to another in the stream of succeeding ideas is something by itself, independent of the task operating at the moment" (1906, p. 260). Each of these inherent properties of the reproductive tendencies, the qualitative and the temporal property, may be modified, as regards the ultimate effect on consciousness, by the task.

On this experimental foundation Watt erects a general hypothesis of thinking: "Thinking is accordingly the clash and mutual resultant of different groups of factors in a unifying consciousness. Of these factors that which we have called the task exercises a decisive influence on the relative sequence of the others and from many directions determines the manner of their appearance." The condition that a specific conscious experience shall arise is that the appropriate reproductive tendency shall meet with the appropriate task. The Bsl. is a task without a definite name.

To give one example only. I am asked to buy a copy of D. H. Lawrence's novel *Sons and Lovers* when I am in town. On my way I am completely unconscious of the task. I walk down the main shopping street and see a bookshop. The sight of the shop serves as a stimulus. From the correlative presentation diverge a number of reproductive tendencies and of these certain are favoured by the task, and conscious reproduction, memory, takes place. At the same time, the task comes into consciousness. "Oh yes, I was to buy a copy of *Sons and Lovers*." I pass, let us say a garage, but the sight does not remind me that garages sell motor oil. There is no task here. If, however, I stand at the window of the bookshop, and think "Oh yes, I was to buy a book. Let me see, it was by what do you call him?" Then I have a *Bewusstseinslage*, one of "doubt, with the cognate forms of uneasiness, difficulty, hesitation" (Titchener). I have a "task without a name"[21] as Watt called it. Anybody who has tied a knot in his handkerchief, in order to remember to do something, and has then forgotten what the knot was for, will feel that Watt's description of a Bsl. as a task without a name is sometimes justified!

In conformance with the practice already established for this chapter, general criticisms will be deferred to a later occasion. Specifically, however, it should be said at this point that Watt's account of the *Bewusstseinslage* is clearly inadequate. What Watt has done is first to dichotomize mental life into "task" and "reproductive tendency", and then to lay down the postulate that the experiences called Bsl. by the Würzburg school must belong on the "task" side of the dichotomy. There is hardly need to insist that such a postulate is unjustified. One need only mention the Bsl. of "*Memory* of a common figure of speech",[22] "*remembrance* of instructions", "*remembrance* of past conversations",[23] and "doubt" (*passim*) to make it abundantly clear that, even adopting the dichotomy, the Bsl. need not necessarily be of the nature of a task. As we have seen, the concept of the *Bewusstseinslage* was gradually found to be unworkable and was ultimately abandoned. One should then perhaps not take too seriously this enthusiastic attempt of Watt to explain it in terms of his own particular system.

The Determining Tendencies

Watt's conception was elaborated and fresh data on the whole problem were given by the complementary work of Ach. Ach attempts to make the method of the interaction of task and reproduction more specific. How does purpose bring about specific action? This is the question he asks. His answer is as follows.

There has been present in consciousness an "aim-presentation" (*Zielvorstellung*).[24] From part of the content[25] of this presentation proceed influences which carry with them a determination in the sense of, or according to the meaning of, the aim-presentation. When, in the laboratory, the stimulus is shown, these influences

[21] Here only part of the total conscious content is present as a Bsl. The whole task will take over the aspect of a Bsl. if on looking at the shop I am reminded "Oh yes, I am to do something or other".

[22] Chapter II, p. 33.

[23] Marbe, pp. 18, 87. Italics are the present writer's.

[24] The *Zielvorstellung* is first mentioned on p. 187, unless I have missed an earlier reference. The phrase was apparently regarded as self-explanatory, as I can discover no definition.

[25] *Eigenartiger Vorstellungsinhalt der Zielvorstellung*, p. 187.

work on the stimulus-presentation to form a (specific) purpose, and action takes place. These influences Ach calls the "Determining Tendencies". Instructions are, for example, to lift the right index finger if the letter E appears, the left if the letter O appears. Suppose that the letter E appears. From part of the content of the aim-presentation arising when the instructions are given, proceed influences which work on the stimulus-presentation of the letter E to form the specific purpose of lifting the right index finger and action follows.

Thus the specific purpose is formed by the establishment of relations between two psychic presentations, namely the "presentation of aim" and the "presentation of stimulus"[26]; when the stimulus actually appears, the latter of these is termed the "concrete stimulus presentation", to distinguish it from that which is present in the purpose as part of an awareness (Ach, 1905, p. 224).

The influence of the determining tendencies may be seen, says Ach, in a number of ways. When, for instance, the coloured card appears it may be seen not simply as coloured, but as "coloured according to instructions". Or a mental assent may be attached to the visual quality. "Yes, this is red." The process whereby this occurs is called "Apperceptive Fusion". It will be noted that there is no conscious representational experience directly correlated with these tendencies at the time when this fusion occurs. The influence of the same tendencies, says Ach, is evident in the attitude of surprise which is often experienced when an unexpected card appears. This happens, for example, when the subject is "set" to react to a white card, and a red one is shown instead; or when the subject had the purpose of dividing, and two figures appeared of which one cannot be divided by the other without leaving a remainder; here the influence of the (unconscious) determining tendencies is shown by their effect on the perception of the stimulus. Ach distinguishes, not very successfully, between apperceptive fusion and determined apperception. An example of the latter is to be found in the subject who carried a visual image of a "plus" sign when he was given the task of adding. The figures when they appeared fitted themselves into the visual scheme imagined, and the "determined presentation arose from this *apperceptive fusion*". To another subject stimulus-figures appeared distorted according to the task; when he had been told to add, the figures appeared to be pressed together, when he had been told to subtract they were pressed apart. All these effects Ach attributes to

[26] Or perhaps "object".

the influence of the unconscious determining tendencies. Such influences may even produce what Ach calls apperceptive substitution. When, for example, the task was to "find a rhyme for", and the subject had been thinking of a specific letter, the stimulus may be actually perceived with the first letter altered accordingly. Thus "mek" was perceived as "bek" by one person; the task was to "find a rhyme for", and the subject had been "thinking of" the letter "b". In all these cases, Ach argues, the effect upon consciousness of the stimulus is modified because of the existence of influences which spring from the "aim-presentation", but which have no direct and explicit conscious representation.

The existence of such determining tendencies, he claims further, is illustrated by many well-known experiments on hypnotic suggestion. In one of his own experiments (p. 188) a subject was told under hypnosis: "Two cards will later be shown to you, each with two figures on them. When you see the first, you will name the sum, when you see the second you will name the difference of the figures, etc." The subject was wakened up. "After a few minutes of trivial conversation, I held in front of him in my hand a card with the figures $\frac{6}{2}$. Immediately he said *eight*. When I showed him a second card with $\frac{4}{2}$, he immediately said *two*." On being questioned, he stated that he said eight "quite casually—I had the need to say eight", and so on. Control experiments were carried out. The hypnotic experiment is impressive evidence for Ach's unconsciously working, determining tendencies. It presents in a clear form a further argument for their existence. The argument is that it is necessary to postulate some psychic principle other than association pure and simple; for the same stimuli may cause different responses according to the particular purpose undertaken. If the figures $\frac{6}{2}$ are shown, the response may be either 8, 4 or 3 according as the subject has in mind to add, subtract or divide—the purpose, again, having had no representation in consciousness. Some selective influence between reproductive tendencies must be assumed. This he finds once more in the determining tendencies.

Association and perseveration[27] had already been postulated as mental mechanisms. Ach is then proposing to add the determining tendency as a third mechanism. According to his theory, it is these tendencies which give to thinking its ordered and purposeful character. Without them mental life would be a chaotic clash of associative

[27] The tendency towards persistence. See G. E. Müller and A. Pilzecker, *Zts. f. Psych. Ergänzungsbd*, 1, 1900, pp. 58 ff.

tendencies. The determining tendencies are the directive factor in thinking. They rule out irrelevancies. They prevent chance stimuli from distracting the course of the thinking-process. The rule is that they operate by favouring those reproductive tendencies which are in line with the purpose of the subject. On presentation of the stimulus, the aim may come to mind, though this is not usual; it apparently occurs when the purpose has not been intensively enough grounded. Determining tendencies may proceed, not only from an accepted purpose, but from a suggestion, a command, or a task, though Ach explicitly states that he is interested not so much in the problem of how they are established, as in the fact of their existence (p. 196).

That they are independent of the associative connections of the material presented, Ach claims to have shown by the fact[28] that by means of the determining tendencies fresh associative connections may be made. Thus the instructions were to find a nonsense rhyme to a nonsense syllable, or to give an alliterative response. For example, when "lep" was presented the response was "les", and these syllables were thereafter bound together associatively. This new association is formed by the subsumption of the two elements under a single common aim.

The final general statement of the book follows. It will be noticed that it stresses the unconscious nature of the determining tendencies. "Thus the qualitative determination of the determined presentation is here without doubt to be referred to influences which function in the unconscious, understanding by the unconscious simply that of which we are not conscious. These acts, which work in the unconscious, proceed from the meaning of the aim-presentation, are directed towards the coming object-presentation, and which bring with them a spontaneous appearance of the determined presentation, we designate determining tendencies" (Ach, 1905, p. 228).

The picture is completed by Ach in a work thirty years later.[29] Here once more it is explicitly stated that "the activity of the Determining Tendencies is brought to fulfilment **in the unconscious.** The determination . . . is effective without conscious memory of the Task" (op. cit., pp. 150–1). The aim appears in consciousness only under special circumstances and as a means of attaining the goal; "for example, on the occasion of diversion of the attention, of

---

[28] It will be remembered that this runs counter to Watt's belief.
[29] Ach, N., *Analyse des Willens*, Berlin, 1935. Reprinted from Abderhalden's *Handbuch d. biologischen Arbeitsmethoden*, Abt. VI, Teil E.

special difficulties, inhibitions, and so on, and also when false reactions have appeared, which come on the scene with the awareness of error". The determination knits the mental process into a functional whole, "whose parts", he says, "form a nexus, a structure; . . . the co-ordination of the parts, mutually and to the whole, is in functional dependence on the special properties of the determination".

So much for the primary function of the determining tendency. To the question as to its nature, Ach gives then no answer. We have seen that he was hardly interested in the problem. Thirty years after the original paper, he was inclined to think that no answer was possible at the present stage of psychological knowledge.[30] The determining tendencies remain like the atom, hypothetical agencies, known by their effects but apparently by their nature unobservable. We have noted that in his later work Ach is still quite explicit on the point that the determining tendencies operate in the unconscious, although the aim may at one time have been conscious (Ach, 1935, p. 150). It is important, of course, to distinguish between the original consciousness of the aim or purpose from that of the determining tendencies.

But although the determining tendency is not, as such, conscious, it is, nevertheless, not without effect upon consciousness. Such effect has already been found in the *Bewusstheit*, or awareness of determination. It has been seen that the *Bewusstheit* of determination is an intermediate form between the awareness of meaning and the awareness of relation. As an awareness, it is "the presence of an impalpably given *Knowing*" (*Wissen*). Ach's observers found that they were immediately aware, as a characteristic experience, whether or not a given psychic event conformed to a previously established determination. Where the train of events accords with a previous determination, it is characterized, because of its content, as "willed". "Such a train of psychic processes, which is to be referred to the influence of previous, determining tendencies, we designate as 'willed', or alternatively as a procedure which occurs with the agreement of the subject. The known experience of such an event is qualitatively uniquely determined, and the individual can in particular cases immediately report whether the procedure was willed or not" (Ach, 1905, p. 230). In this way one can distinguish between willed activities and such events as fantasy or reflection. With practice, the awareness of determination disappears, in

[30] Ach, 1935, p. 195.

greater or less time according to the nature of the purpose and the peculiarities of the subject. The awareness of determination has been described previously.

Application of the Determining Tendencies to the Problem of Abstraction

An important function of the determining tendencies should now be described, namely the *determination of abstraction*. According to Ach's scheme, repetition of any particular stimulus results in abstraction because the essential associations (reproductive tendencies) are repeated most often, and thus gain strength at the expense of inessential adventitious associations. Thus arises what he calls "associative abstraction", which is fundamental for conceptual thinking. In addition, he describes two other forms of abstraction. There is first *determined abstraction*, which is of two forms, simultaneous and successive.

Simultaneous determined abstraction was first described by Külpe. In response to a given task, Külpe's (1904) subject might for example describe a figure correctly, without conscious experience of the nature of the surrounding figures.[31] Ach's own subjects behaved in something the same way. A subject might carry the letter "s" in his head. When the stimulus "c s v z" appeared, "s" alone was perceived and the appropriate reaction made. The other letters were disregarded as the result of a process of abstraction. This process might be simplified. The mental repetition of the letter in question might be omitted, and there might be merely "intentional sensations of movement" in the appropriate finger. In either case, the abstraction was effected through the agency of the determining tendencies. The awareness of determination would have as its conscious token in the one case the verbo-motor image of the letter "s", in the other the kinæsthetic image of a finger movement. Closely allied is what is known as "concentration of attention".

In *successive determined abstraction*, the process of abstraction is directed towards conscious events which follow each other. Thus with the instructions to react as quickly as possible, the subject gradually abstracted from the quality of the stimulus as the series of reactions progressed. In general, this occurred whenever the instructions were sufficiently independent of the qualitative determination of the stimulus. The subject begins to react first to "something white", and then to a "change" pure and simple, apart from

[31] The experiment was repeated by Chapman, 1932.

spatial and other considerations. The transition came gradually (as indeed is the case in all experiments with abstraction). So strong is this tendency to abstraction that it is only by stringent repetition of the instructions or persistent watching of the stimulus that it can be avoided. Other instances of successive determined abstraction may be seen in the process whereby an intervening middle term may be gradually dropped. For example, a subject might begin a reaction series by mentally repeating the letter E when that letter appeared. Gradually this "acousticokinæsthetic presentation" disappeared, and reaction followed directly on the perception of the stimulus. The determined abstraction here operates in such a way that it "seeks as far as possible to eliminate all . . . intervening processes" (Ach, 1905, p. 242).

By the combination of these two forms of abstraction, associative and determined, the formation of general ideas is made possible. Suppose, for example, that reaction takes place to a "change", this being effected by means of the successive form of determined abstraction. This reaction may take place only when the change occurs under certain spatial conditions. Adventitious changes, such as irrelevant movements, will be eliminated as stimulus-factors by means of associative abstraction. In the same way, alterations in the quality of the motion will lose their psychological effect. Here both forms of abstraction are functioning, and Ach calls the process *Combined Associative-determined Abstraction*. By virtue of their associative function, the determining tendencies may cause a verbal sign to be attached to this psychic event[32]; and conversely, when the sign, e.g., "change" is given in consciousness, the correlative meaning is present in consciousness as a *Wissen*, a knowing, this being given by means of the subexcitation of reproductive tendencies.[33] Further repetition eliminates adventitious spatial determinations so that we are left with the sign "change", with a general, though delimited, meaning. Thus, through the combined influence of determined abstraction and associative abstraction, a general meaning has been attached to the word "change". This process bridges the gap between the concrete content of an awareness, which is already, from a psychological point of view, abstract, to ideas which are abstract in the narrower sense.

Thus Ach has distinguished three main processes of abstraction.

[32] It will be remembered that the determining tendencies may cause fresh associations to arise.

[33] See p. 50.

There is (*a*) associative abstraction, (*b*) determined abstraction, which may be either simultaneous or successive, (*c*) combined associative-determined abstraction.[34]

A child sees a bird flying in the street. The whole scene is psychologically registered, including houses, people, and so on. Later the same child sees a bird flying in another street. All the details with which each bird has been associated have left their mark on the nervous system, and appropriate reproductive tendencies have been formed. Of these reproductive tendencies the essential ones are reinforced, the inessentials—what Aristotle would call the "accidents"—remain relatively ineffective. When the child sees a bird on later occasions, the effective reproductive tendencies are subexcited, and the resultant in consciousness is a *Wissen*, a knowing, which is not present in terms of any specific sense modality, and is thereby to be contrasted with its explicitly visual sign, the bird as it presents itself to visual perception. Thus the bird as seen, the "visual presentation", is accompanied in consciousness by an impalpable halo of awareness of knowing, which is gradually sharpened and made more precise by repetition of essentials and dropping away of inessentials.[35] This again is the product of associative abstraction. It proceeds quite mechanically, and is not motivated, is independent of the action of determining tendencies.

With this mechanical process may be contrasted abstraction that is motivated, determined. Under social pressure, exerted by his teacher or otherwise, a child learns to read. At first he observes every detail of the complex situation before him, the position of the word on the page, the number of the page,[36] any individual peculiarity of the letters, and so on. With further experience, these irrelevant details gradually disappear from consciousness. Few of us who read a novel notice the number of the page which we happen to be reading. It is well known that reading takes place from the presence of strategically placed cues, that in what is called "proof-reader's error" we can actually misread words that are wrongly spelled (Ach's "determined

---

[34] These two methods of abstraction, both accepted by Ach, apparently embody the two hypotheses now in dispute in the discussions over the "Continuity Theory" (Lashley, 1942).

[35] It is difficult to see whether Ach believes that inessentials drop away by themselves, or whether their energy is sapped, so to speak, by drainage of energy towards essentials. On the last page but one of his earlier book (249), he speaks as though the latter were the case when concentration of attention occurs.

[36] The writer remembers a visitor to a class where he was learning to read asking "What page of the book tells you about so and so?" *With one accord*, it seemed to him then, the children answered "Page ten".

apperception"). The number of the page and the details of individually printed words are not present in consciousness because they are irrelevant to the aim in mind, which is to "read" the novel. Ach would say that the determining tendencies have eliminated the corresponding factors from consciousness. Since it is practice that has effected this result, such abstraction from all but a few relevant cues would be classed as successive. As Ach notes, it is difficult to avoid such abstraction, as anybody who has read proof can testify. As he finally points out, such abstraction, with the correlative concentration of attention which it entails, makes towards economy of action.

To illustrate the third form, combined associative-determined abstraction, let us take as a hypothetical example the way in which a new species of animal may be described. The child, having become familiar with birds in general, later, we may suppose, becomes an ornithologist. He is impelled by his scientific purpose to examine more closely the birds of a particular species, to which the name has been attached by the ordinary process of association. His idea of the birds of this species and his reaction towards them is now moulded by his general purpose. He notices certain members of the class with a particularly long bill. Still under the influence of the determining tendencies, he watches for this particular variety. "Long bill" becomes the sign for birds of this variety. His attention is abstracted from the rest of the bird's appearance, and is focused only on the bird's bill. Gradually the fact is borne upon him that the bird has a particular kind of song. A new variety is described, the "Long bill", the term being attached by determined association. In this process abstraction and determination are clearly very intimately related. It is hard to tell where associative reaction ends and determined abstraction begins. Finally the name "Long bill", whether seen in print, or repeated imaginally, serves as a palpable sign for the impalpable knowing (*Wissen*) that members of this variety have a long, slightly curving bill, a certain kind of song which changes to a deeper note as the summer wears on, that they lay four to six eggs with certain markings, and so on. These details, which have been attached to the sign "Long bill" by determined association, are not of course present imaginally whenever the name is read, heard, or imagined. Since they have in the past been observed together with the bird, reproductive tendencies corresponding to them are aroused when the bird is seen. The relevant reproductive tendencies have persisted, while irrelevant ones—such as the different details of the trees on which the bird has been sitting—have faded away. This happens, according to

Ach's theory, because the essential features have occurred more frequently in conjunction with the bird than inessential ones. When the word "Long bill" is heard or seen, the relevant reproductive tendencies are subexcited, such excitation being sufficient to produce an impalpable *Wissen* without coming to the point of imagery.[37]

By a devious path Ach has reached his experimental goal, which was the will. The subject is told to react in a more or less definite way to a stimulus which is to follow. When the stimulus appears, he forms a purpose to react to it. The whole course of events between the "ready" signal and the appearance of the stimulus is guided and unified by unconsciously working determining tendencies. When reaction follows, which occurs in accordance with these regulative, unconsciously working forces, the subject is impalpably aware of the conformity; he "agrees" with the response, recognizes that the procedure was "willed". In the interval between stimulus and response, there is present in consciousness an impalpable knowing of what is to come, embracing (*a*) the temporal and a qualitative determination of the stimulus, together with (*b*) what is to follow on the subject's own part, and (*c*) the relation between his reaction and the coming stimulus. This simultaneous, impalpable knowing is accompanied or immediately preceded by an imaginal or sensational sign. The combination is called an awareness.

Confusion of Ach's Exposition

This account has been presented as closely as possible to its original form in 1905. The exposition is poor. The argument is confused and repetitious. In particular, the general relation of experimental data to experimental result is disorderly to the point of chaos. Any faithful account of the monograph must inevitably reflect the confusion of the original presentation. To take examples: Apperceptive fusion is treated twice, on pp. 226 and the following, and on pp. 191 and the following: there is no apparent relation between the two treatments. The same sentence is repeated word for word in each of these two accounts (*Beim addieren . . . grösseren*, p. 227, lines three to five, and p. 192, lines eight to eleven). Again the main experimental results are described in chapters two and three. Chapter four is headed "The Determining Tendencies. The Awareness." Logically it should contain a discussion of the results of the main experiments just treated, and early in the chapter is to be found the statement that

[37] See Chapter IX for a fuller discussion of Abstraction, together with an account of Ach's later experiments.

the investigations described in the previous paragraphs make necessary the concept of the determining tendencies. This statement comes as a surprise to the reader; for the determining tendencies have apparently been mentioned in one previous context only (p. 119), and here almost incidentally in the course of a statement that the working of the will need not necessarily be "given as conscious experience" (ibid.). This seems to be the only mention of the determining tendencies as such during the whole course of the description of the original experiments, a description which covers a hundred and fifty pages.[38] Actually, therefore, the concept of the determining tendencies is not necessary for the description of the experiments. In view of his insistence on the strictly experimental nature of his inquiry Ach owes it to his readers to analyse the previous experimental data, and to show why they necessitate the conception of the D.T.'s. What he actually says is: "From the investigations described in the previous paragraphs it results that side by side with the associative and perseverative tendencies to reproduction we must place still other factors . . . the Determining Tendencies" (p. 187). The assumption of the existence of the determining tendencies may or may not be necessary for the adequate description of mental life. But the relation of this assumption to the previously described experiments has not been adequately shown. Again, after the statement that the determining tendencies are a necessary inference from experiments already conducted, there follows a description of further experiments, those on hypnosis, which illustrate the same tendencies. The resulting effect is one of further confusion, since once again it is here that the reader expects to find an analysis of experiments previously described, together with a demonstration that the D.T.'s follow as a necessary inference from them. Throughout the book, in fact, there is, at least in the matter of the determining tendency, *no clear expositional distinction between experimental data and description* on the one hand, and *deduction or hypothesis* on the other. This expositional confusion is further illustrated in section 13, p. 191, headed "On the Determining Tendencies". Here, at last, one feels, must come a conspectus of the previous experiments, showing how they necessitate the concept of the determining tendencies. It is once again disconcerting to find an account of an entirely fresh batch of experimentation, with no fresh heading, and proving a *special property* of the D.T.'s. This account of fresh experiments fills eleven

[38] There are, in contrast, many mentions of the word *Bewusstheit* in these pages.

out of the nineteen pages of section thirteen, which once more should logically contain deductions from the experiments previously described. These are, in a sense, trivialities. But they do illustrate the fact that Ach's exposition is poor, and that there is no orderly distinction of experimental data from experimental conclusions. In a work which professes a rigid experimental programme, and one with the oft-repeated motto of "systematic experimental introspection", this amounts to a serious error in technique. When the existence of an essentially unobservable, hypothetical entity is being demonstrated by experimental methods, we are entitled to ask for a clearly defined expositional separation of data, deduction, and application.

Argument for Existence and Effects of Determining Tendencies

In view of this confusion, and at the risk of repetition, the following brief summary of the argument is appended for the existence and the effects of the determining tendencies. The experimental facts are, briefly, the sudden appearance in consciousness of the appropriate idea (presentation), when the purpose has not been represented in consciousness; the facts of apperceptive substitution and fusion, and of determined apperception; those of hypnotic suggestion; the fact that an association can be formed between two nonsense syllables that have not been experienced together, and that the same stimulus may give rise to different responses with different purposes. These seem to be the primary experimental data on which is based the hypothesis of a directive influence proceeding from the content of the aim-presentation, although it has been seen that these data are not given when the main experiments are being described. Observation shows that such an influence is not directly represented in consciousness, but its effect may be seen in the Awareness of Determination. Granting the hypothesis of the determining tendency, then determined abstraction seems to follow as an application of the hypothesis though the logical sequence is not made clear. And as a general application, we have the undoubted fact that the course of thought is directed, teleological. Such at least seems to be the argument, though it is difficult to disentangle.

Criticism of the Experimental Work of Watt and Ach

Following the practice already adopted, criticism of *specific* points only in the work of Watt and Ach on the mechanism of thinking will be made at this point. The first, and perhaps the most serious, of such specific criticisms immediately suggests itself from what has just been said. *Ach's method of obtaining the facts in question was not really experimental in any strict sense.* It did not comprise a series of strictly controlled observations, made under standard and therefore reproducible conditions. There were, for example, no standard questions which the experimenter asked the subject. Questions, indeed, there were; that was part of the method. But they varied, apparently, from experiment to experiment and from subject to subject. "In this way there takes place a continual, closely-knit exchange of thoughts between the observing subject and the observer who is recording" (Ach, 1905, p. 8). A set of conditions (questions and remarks on the part of the experimenter) which varies intimately with the nature of what is being observed and recorded is not and cannot be strictly scientific. Neither Watt nor Ach gives any hint of a list of standard questions, for the reason that there was no such list. The point seems not to have occurred to them. Watt gives certain questions incidentally; throughout Ach's monograph there is no mention of specific questions *in situ*, only the general statement quoted above, and similar statements and implications.[39] (see, e.g., p. 14). Ach is indeed cognizant of the relative uncertainty of his method compared with that of the exact sciences, and of the difficulty of obtaining standard conditions (p. 16). When "wide play is allowed for the tact and cleverness of the experimenter" (p. 17), standardization and thereby reproducibility was necessarily ruled out. It was, says Ach, impossible, "beyond any man's strength", to record the questions. One has considerable sympathy for him; yet this impossibility nevertheless touches a grave fault of method. Actually, in the passage where Ach speaks of the possibility of "variation of single conditions of experiment" and the resultant "possibility of establishing lawfulness of behaviour" (p. 21), he has apparently forgotten that not only variation of conditions is necessary for experiment, but standardizing of conditions as well. And this he has himself confessed that he could not obtain.

Thus in one important respect, that of standardization of conditions, Ach's demonstration of the existence of the determining tendencies falls seriously short when judged by rigid experimental canons. But apart from this, it has already been indicated that there is no real attempt to correlate the conclusion with the main body of the experimental results. Thus it has been seen that the determining

[39] A sample of the questions is given in Ach, 1905, p. 17. There is, however, no hint of any regularity in posing them. Questions used in the experiments on hypnosis are recorded on pp. 207–8, footnote, and also on p. 233.

tendency is apparently introduced for the first time almost casually on p. 119, after eighty-eight pages describing the main body of the experiments.[40] There are indeed references to the "set" (*Einstellung*) towards movement (pp. 52–3); but this is no novelty, and is a very different thing from the statement that an entirely new and fundamental principle of mental life must be set up as a result of the previously described experiments. There is further no clear demonstration of the necessity for assuming both purpose and determining tendencies. It is stated, for example, that the "quality of the determined presentation follows in consequence of the activity of a previously given Aim-presentation" (p. 228). Just before, the same effect had been attributed to the D.T.'s (ibid.). Watt, who was working in the same laboratory, would have been well entitled to ask what evidence there is for the necessity of assuming the determining tendency in addition to the *Aufgabe* with which he himself worked. In fact, Ach has not shown experimentally that his multiplication of entities is necessary or desirable. The most he can be said to have done in this direction is to have effected a certain elaboration of Watt's theory. In his introduction (p. vii) Ach states: "Part of the work, including those results which led me to the assertion of the determining tendencies, or of the Realization-Tendencies, as I then called them, . . . was announced in the Summer semester of 1902."[41] In contrast to the experimental exposition of the *Bewusstheit*, one cannot avoid the uneasy feeling when reading the monograph that the writer's mind was already made up on the question of the Determining Tendencies; that they were not really being demonstrated but assumed, or alternatively put in as an afterthought. The contrast with the *Bewusstheit* in this connection is interesting: one does really feel that the *Bewusstheit* is being made the subject of an experimental inquiry, that the word was naturally used at the time to describe what was experimentally observed, and that the section (p. 210) which specifically describes the awareness is a summary of previously reported experimental findings.

[40] The present writer has read carefully through Ach's book with the express purpose of discovering any previous reference to the determining tendencies. If any such are actually present in the book, they are incidental, and not an integral part of the argument at any point.

[41] Questions of priority are always unpleasant. It may be pointed out here that Ach uses the *Aufgabe* several times in the discussion of the difference between sensorial and motor reactions. Watt made exactly the same differentiation, in the same context, in a work published the year before (Ach, 1905, p. 114; Watt, 1904). Külpe made the same fundamental distinction, but with a different terminology, in 1893.

The determining tendency seems, in fact, to have been forced upon Ach not by experimental data but by psychological dogma. His endeavour is apparently to describe the facts of purpose or motive in terms of the presentational psychology. This may be illustrated by various statements throughout the book. The determining tendencies are influences which proceed from peculiar presentation-contents of the aim-presentation (p. 187); the tendencies set in readiness by the aim-presentation facilitate relevant reproductive tendencies proceeding from the aim-presentation (p. 192); these sets, working in the unconscious, proceeding from the meaning of the aim-presentation, directed towards the coming stimulus-presentation, . . . we designate as D.T.'s (p. 228). Clearly the problem is here, then, considered in terms of the influence of presentations upon one another. In order to understand how the experimenter's instructions cause a specific response to a later stimulus, the assumption is that we must consider the presentation of the purpose and the presentation of the stimulus, and show how the one can influence the other.

There is no need at this date to flog the ancient and dead horse of presentationism. For a complete and subtle demolition of this doctrine, the reader is referred to Ward's *Psychological Principles*. It is enough to mention the fallacy, already discussed in the particular case of the judgment, of assuming that the thought and action of a man in his environment can—indeed must—be explained by manipulation of presentations—perceptions or images—of that environment. Specifically, the question must be asked of Ach—why does action follow when what he calls the determined presentation has been fashioned under the influence of the determining tendencies? Specifically, a subject is instructed to add: the figures 6 and 5 are shown. We know that they may appear bent towards each other, or with the plus sign between them, or in some other modified form. What then? The reproductive tendencies corresponding to the process of addition are favoured by the D.T.'s, and there is "spontaneous appearance of the determined *presentation*" (p. 228). "The movement-*presentation* is, as we say, set in readiness, or determining tendencies are founded by the purpose to move, so that immediately after the appearance of the stimulus the appropriate movement follows" (p. 119; italics are the present writer's in both quotations). Ach's experimental account contains no hint of a "movement-presentation", as separate from the actual movement. On the contrary, Ach's own words here deny the existence of any such intermediate step. But even if a movement-presentation did occur, there is no justification for stating that actual movement will necessarily follow it. He is working in a closed world of presentations, and has neglected to show how to escape from it into the outside world of objective fact and objective action. Throughout the treatment there is the implicit assumption that once given the determined presentation, action will follow by itself. The more closely Ach's schema is examined, the more cumbrous and essentially inconsistent it appears. In his latest book Ach adds a further stipulation: Not every perception or presentation leads to a voluntary movement . . . rather is there necessary in addition a further event called a Will Impulse or Fiat" (*Analyse des Willens*, Berlin, 1935, p. 121). Will Impulse is defined in the first book as *Bewusstheit* that movement must follow (1905, p. 104). Disregarding the implied assumption that what finally causes action is the imageless awareness that action will follow, we then have as Ach's final statement something like this. The words of the experimenter who repeats the instruction cause an aim-presentation to arise in the subject's mind. This disappears as such, but from it proceed unconsciously functioning determining tendencies, which when the stimulus-presentation appears, cause the determined presentation, the "end product" of determination, to arise. This relational process is the establishment of a purpose. With the determined presentation is associated the movement-presentation (that is the idea of *saying* "eleven", as contrasted with the idea or presentation of the word "eleven"), but the manner of this association is not made clear. After the movement-presentation must come a "will-impulse or Fiat" before movement actually takes place. That is to say, a second set of determining tendencies is postulated to cause movement. In reality Ach has set out to show how the will operates; he concludes that it is through a "Will-impulse or Fiat".

One of the difficulties Ach had to contend with was the implicit assumption inherent in the presentational psychology that action is *through* the determined presentation *to* the perceived card. Such an implication is of course psychologically untenable. Action is *directly to the perceived card*. No determined presentation is necessary as an intermediate step between perception of the card and response. This is not to deny the extreme complexity of the relation between perception of the world and action in the world. But any discussion of this difficult question must start with the fact that we do react directly to our environment, not indirectly through a presentation. It was partly, perhaps largely, because his thinking was cast along presentational lines that Ach found himself forced to postulate unconsciously working determining tendencies, by means of which the aim-presentation, after it had, as a matter of experimental fact, disappeared from consciousness, could influence the stimulus-presentation. Without the necessity of explaining what happens in presentational terms, the necessity for postulating separate determining tendencies disappears, and one is left with the simpler statement that the purpose or task exercises a directive influence over the course of thought and perception. To speak of *influences* or *tendencies* seems to come very near to the scholastic "properties"—as when salt was said to have the property of melting ice. The relation of the purpose or task to the perceived words or sentences by which that task is communicated; the relation of these to the perceived "stimulus"; the relation of both to the action that follows, these constitute difficult problems. Ach's attempted solution in terms of determining tendencies by which, in his words, the "presentation of aim" works on the "presentation of stimulus" solves neither the general nor the particular problem. A detailed solution would show what is meant by the statement that purpose or motive can unify and incidentally modify the whole course of perception, thought, and action consequent upon a later situation. This Ach is far from giving.[42]

One final defence is possible. It may be said that Ach has solved his specific problem which is to show how thought is determined. Action, the objectors might say, is a different problem, and may properly be left for later consideration. Two answers may be given. First of all, thought *cannot* thus be divorced from action. The two form an inseparable unity—psychologically inseparable, that is to say. Any theory which tears thought from its natural matrix must at least be one-sided, and will almost inevitably be false. This is even more obviously true of will, in terms of which Ach cast his problem. Clearly, will cannot be separated from action. Secondly, even as a

---

[42] Certain readers will still argue thus: "Purpose, as gained through auditory perceptions of the instructions, must nevertheless have an effect on reaction to the perceived stimulus. But purpose is not conscious when the stimulus appears. Therefore there exist unconscious effects of the purpose, which is what Ach meant when he used the term D.T.'s." But once more, the answer is that as soon as science begins to hypostasize *effects* of X, as separate from X itself, a mythology springs up. The data at present are that a purpose or if it be preferred motive can unconsciously influence action or, to be more exact, that human beings, when activated by what is known as purpose or motive modify their perceptions and actions accordingly, without being at every moment necessarily "conscious" of the purpose in question. To bring in determining tendencies complicates rather than simplifies the problem.

theory of thought *in vacuo*, if such were possible, Ach's Determining Tendencies do not help us. For once again, the data are that purpose (motive or task) at one time conscious, may, after its original conscious representation has disappeared, affect thought and perception. Again, why put in determining tendencies, of which neither Ach nor anybody else knows anything? They are, once more, an unnecessary piece of machinery, and their apparent explanatory value is spurious. Actually, then, Ach's solution is not valid even in the restricted field which he might be said to have marked out for himself. And when one begins to inquire into the mechanism and nature of the determining tendencies, another flock of difficult problems arises. The D.T.'s spring from the "presentational content of the aim-presentation" (Ach, 1905, p. 187). How and when do they achieve unconsciousness? Or are they ever conscious at all? If not, the notion of intrinsically unconscious *tendencies* proceeding from conscious presentations seems very difficult and complicated, especially when they must work on other, qualitatively different and equally unconscious, reproductive *tendencies*. And is the determining tendency qualitatively different from the reproductive tendency? If so, how is it different? Watt assumes in general such a qualitative difference, but has not experimentally demonstrated it. One has the right to ask for an answer to these and many other questions, even though Ach has explicitly disclaimed knowledge of the nature of the determining tendencies.

Watt's simpler statement is apparently preferable to Ach's because it dispenses with the elaborate superstructure which Ach has built up upon observed fact. Ach's fundamental contribution, which he no doubt owed at least indirectly to Külpe, was the proposal, or at least the experimental verification of the dichotomy (task)-(reproductive-tendency). As Watt states it, this is a dichotomy separating the mechanical from the non-mechanical factors in thinking.[43] Concerning this fundamental dichotomy and its relation to other proposed dichotomies, more will be said later in this book. It should here be pointed out, however, that the dichotomy is made by both Watt and Ach, Watt's statement of it being preferable for reasons already given. There remains to discuss Watt's particular presentation of this part of the theory that is common to both.

Watt assumes as a groundwork the conventional associational theory that if experience A has occurred together with experience B, then if either A or B occurs later, there is a tendency for the other to

[43] Watt, 1905, p. 187.

recur. This theory Watt has overlaid with the stipulation that before this tendency can be realized, there must be a task present, which will itself contribute energy that may reinforce or inhibit any particular association. It is necessary to examine this more closely.

The fundamental question is this: whence comes the dynamic power, the energizing force which causes an "event in our mental experience", to use Watt's phrase? Starting from Watt's theory, there are four main possibilities. The energy might conceivably originate either in (1) the reproductive tendency; that is, from the bond between one experience and another. This is in essence the theory that was upheld by Thorndike under the title of "connectionism",[44] though Thorndike added certain embroideries of his own. It is, we have seen, the conventional associational theory. The energy may, however, conceivably originate in (2) the task or motive. This is apparently the root idea behind the modern theory of drive or motive. Or, thirdly, both task and associative bond may be powerless in themselves to induce a mental event, having this result only when they interact, to form, so to speak, a dynamized unity. This may be called the unitary theory. Or, finally, associative bond and task may, each of them, possess dynamic force, which is, however, manifested only when the two occur together. In any particular case they may work in the same or opposite directions. This may be called the contributory theory. It is apparently that of Watt.

I have been wondering, for example, how to afford a certain ocean trip. I think of the sea, and the thought of a tossing ship follows. According to the first, the "connectionist" theory, this sequence is due to the associative bonds which exist between ship and sea. According to the second theory, the driving force is the task of finding ways and means for the trip; this task causes the thought of the ship to arise. This demands, of course, that the task shall have the requisite material to work upon; but it also demands that the material of past experience is *simply* material, to be used by the energizing task and without the dynamic power of itself to cause a mental event. This seems to be the fundamental idea behind the "wish" psychology of Freud, the hormic psychology of MacDougall, and the motivational theory of Lewin. Again, the third theory would demand that both the task of finding ways and means and the thought ("visual presentation") of the sea are of themselves powerless to induce a further mental event. Specifically, that the fact that sea and ship have been experienced together in the past,

[44] See Thorndike, 1932.

under whatever circumstances and with whatever result, whether pleasant or unpleasant, does not produce a connection through which, if the thought of sea occurs, the thought of ship will follow. Instead, when the thought of sea comes up and meets with the task in question, a new dynamic unity is formed, from which proceeds the next term, ship. Here the energy is provided by the union. This is the earlier theory of Selz and would perhaps be allowed as a possibility by the Gestalt group. Finally, the task and the thought of "sea" may each of them be unable in itself to determine a further mental event. But when the two occur together, they may each contribute determining energy as the result of which the thought of the ship follows. This, then, seems to be Watt's theory.

Quotations may readily be found in illustration. First, the task cannot of itself determine a mental event. "The task may find no reproductions, in which case no reaction can occur" (1906, p. 261). "An association must be presupposed before the task working with the stimulus could produce any reaction" (ibid., p. 259). And "The tendency to reproduction, which realizes itself *ceteris paribus*, is that one which, by reason of more frequent actualization, possesses a greater speed of reproduction. The task which is no doubt itself a wider and stronger tendency to reproduction has been sketched in detail as an operative force. . . . Over against any tendency to reproduction the task can only overcome a limited power of force." And further, "The influences which determine every event in our mental experience fall into two large groups, the operating task and the individual strength of the reproductions which come thereby into question.[45] That is to say, both task and reproductive tendencies must be present, and each is represented as exciting psychic "force".

This raises difficult problems. If a reproductive tendency has power to cause reproduction *against* the prevailing task, one may ask why it cannot do so when there is no task present at all. That is to say, why is the task necessary? Further, the conception of a task which does not energize the reproductive tendency, but which by its presence enables the latter to function, seems very difficult. It is not as though we are dealing with a release function, at least of the usual kind, such as that of the biological stimulus in determining the biological response. For when the task appears it directly contributes energy to succeeding events, while the biological stimulus, for example, essentially contributes no energy to the nerve impulse. Whether it could be possible for the task to effect some kind of

[45] Already quoted.

release, and at the same time to contribute to the energy of succeeding events, it is difficult to say. At least such a theory would require experimental proof such as Watt has not provided.

Closer examination of Watt's account reveals further difficulties. The account of judgment as involving a task, and as contrasting with those mental events in which "the reaction which constituted the judgment was determined by the overwhelming strength of the tendency to reproduction" (ibid., p. 264), really presupposes the existence of mental events which are determined without the operation of a task. The apology may be made that such recalcitrant reproductions are determined by other, conflicting tasks. But this, if taken to its logical conclusion, would imply the reference of all mental action to tasks alone ; that is, to a hormic principle working on inert memory-material. It would imply, that is, a scheme of the second, task-dynamic type, mentioned before. As a defence of Watt's scheme, it would not be of service. Watt apparently saw the difficulty of classifying "free association" in the interval between writing the first and second paper. In the first paper he writes, "Everything which happens solely by virtue of the inherent force of the reproductive tendencies is not yet a judgment. This can be clearly seen in all investigations on memory and the like" (1905, p. 411). In the second paper he is apparently careful not to say that "an absolutely fixed and rigid system of reproductions" ever operates in practice; instead, he says that it "gives no judgments". Nevertheless, the implication of the taskless reproduction is clearly present in the second paper, and it is contrary to his statement in the first paper that every mental event is doubly determined.[46]

When further we come to action, as contrasted with thinking, there is again inconsistency. Here a reproductionless theory is implied. He explains "reactions which through frequent repetition are held by many to become *unconscious* or *mechanical*" by the statement that "a task is always necessarily presupposed for the accomplishment of such a reaction. The task may not have been given before each experiment but it must at least have become operative. The stimulus is given and the reaction follows without any conscious links intervening whatever. There is no need to appeal to the unconscious when everything else falls away except the essentials, task and stimulus" (1906, p. 263). The stimulus itself contains no motive power for action. There is no mention of the reproductive tendencies. The meaning of the passage, which, like

[46] For other difficulties, see Titchener, loc. cit., p. 260.

all others taken for criticism of Watt's theory, is from the second abstracted paper, and thus represents the writer's mature opinion, must be that the task is the motor, to use a term of Lewin's. That is to say, that the reaction experiment, after practice, becomes task-dynamic. Once again, an apology is possible. It may be said that by frequent association with the action in question the stimulus has acquired reproductive tendencies, that is to say, reproductive of action, not thought, and that the learned, automatic reaction is the product of the particular task and the reproductive tendencies in question. This was certainly not in Watt's mind. The whole passage is intended to show that in such reactions everything falls away but the task and the perceived signal for action. But apart from what he intended, it is doubtful whether the apology would hold good. For the essence of the reaction experiment is that an originally indifferent stimulus—that is, one with no adherent reproductive tendencies acquired by sheer association—does, by virtue of a specific task, come to set off a reaction. That is to say, it is not necessary that the task shall find appropriate reproductive tendencies in order that it shall function for the first time at least. It is abusing the concept of the reproductive tendency to maintain that, on the first occasion of reaction, the stimulus acquires adherent reproductive tendencies to action when the instructions are given, and before the experience of its perception has ever occurred together with the action. The only way in which on the conventional theory reproductive tendencies to action can be acquired by the stimulus as perceived is for the action to occur simultaneously with the mental event of perceiving the stimulus. Association by contrast or similarity is not admitted by Watt (ibid., p. 261). But actually it should not be necessary once more to apologize for the fictitious apology which we have put into Watt's mind, and which was obviously not there when he made an abstract of his argument in 1906. The passage is obviously a plea for the task-dynamic nature of mechanized motor reactions. Rather than attempt to patch up Watt's avowed theory by questionable emendations, which certainly did not occur to him at the time, it seems better to pay him the compliment of assuming that he was a good enough man of science momentarily to forget his theory in the face of what seemed to be fact. The doctrine of presentations, at least in the form in which Watt assumed it, must come up against difficulties when action is to be explained. Once more, it is a doctrine of mental action in a closed system, and contains no provision within itself for reaching out beyond its confines into action and the objective world. This we have already seen illustrated in our criticism of the Würzburg theory of judgment and of Ach's determining tendencies. Watt's theory would explain why, on perception of the stimulus, the thought of action might come into the subject's mind; it does not explain why action takes place. For that some fresh principle is necessary.[47]

Thus Watt professes to hold what we have called a contributory theory of mental energetics, one which derives motive power in the kind of experiment which he performed, and for all mental events, summatively from task and reproductive tendency, with the possibility that these may function in opposite senses. Actually, his explanations of specific points imply that some mental events are task-dynamic, while others are bond-dynamic, each of which possibilities is irreconcilable with the contributory theory. Whether the contributory theory, in its simplest form or modified in some way, can be made to fit all facts of mental life, is not here discussed. The point will be elaborated later in this book. At least Watt has not succeeded in showing experimentally that this theory is a necessary and adequate explanation for the motivation of all mental events.

There is no doubt that Watt was handicapped, as was Ach, by an uncritical acceptance of current presentational psychology and all that this implied. Accepting this theory as axiomatic, and finding a residue which it did not explain, he equated the latter with the task. This appears to be the ultimate argument. It can be seen clearly exhibited in Watt's own summary, from which have been taken most of the quotations of the last few pages. He states first that the task is found to have an influence on the nature of each subject's experiences, whether, for example, they are predominantly visual or not; the same influence is exerted on the duration of the reactions, but the percentage of complex reproductions, those with intervening mental events, is independent of the task's nature. And as quoted before: "The number of tendencies to reproduction which diverge from any one stimulus must depend on the number of ideas with which the stimulus is associated. It is impossible to conceive how the task should change these, as an association must be presupposed before the task working with the stimulus could produce any reaction. The occurrence of a complex representation would depend then on the nature of the stimulus word given and not on the task. The influence of the *task* has therefore to be carefully distinguished from that of the *stimulus*" (1906, p. 259. Watt's italics). Here it is first stated that

[47] As e.g. the now discredited ideo-motor theory.

association must be presupposed before the "task working on the stimulus could produce any reaction". That is to say, the distinction of task and reproductive tendencies is first laid down as axiomatic. Then it is argued that *therefore* we must distinguish the task from the reproductive tendencies. The question is begged. This, it should be noted, is the first of the two critical points of his argument, the point that is, where he explicitly attempts to show that his experimental results demand the separation of reproductive tendency from task.

Estimate of the Würzburg Experiments on Motive

It cannot be said, then, that either Ach or Watt has succeeded in giving experimental proof of either the necessity or the adequacy of the summative combination of task or purpose and the reproductive tendency as an explanation of the mechanics of mental life. Nevertheless, their contribution is great, both historically and for present-day psychology. They have shown alike the inadequacy of the presentationism current in their day, and the great importance for mental life of factors of which we are not conscious. They showed, or at least Ach did so, that non-associational factors can influence perception. Most important of all, they brought into the laboratory the fact that the process of thinking was directed, controlled, "determined" by machinery of the working of which we are largely unconscious. All this was no doubt known before. But Watt and Ach demonstrated it under experimental conditions which, if they fall short when judged by modern standards, are at least very much better controlled than anything hitherto attempted. Their enthusiasm, their patient work and their hard thinking have shown that it is possible to employ the experimental method in the investigation of the mechanism of thought. Most important of all, they introduced into experimental psychology the problem of "motive." There is nobody who reads the accounts of their detailed and laborious investigations but will come away with a very high respect for the quality of these two men, and a conviction of the importance of their work for today's psychology, fifty years later. It seems probable that they saw the problem in terms at once too complex and too simple—too complex because of the machinery of reproductive tendencies and presentations with which they encumbered it, too simple because of the abstract nature of the experimental situations they employed. But they were the first to examine motive in the laboratory: Watt was the first actually to relate the nature of the thought-process with the nature of the motive, he and Ach the first to adopt the experimental hypothesis of unconscious motivation, Ach the first to sketch an experimental hypothesis of the integrative nature of thinking, a hypothesis which bore fruit in the later work of Selz, Maier, and the Gestalt group. This is achievement of a high order.[48]

NOTE ON THE USE OF THE WORD "SET"

J. J. Gibson, in his excellent article "A Critical Review of the Concept of Set in Contemporary Experimental Psychology", *Psychological Bulletin*, 1941, has mentioned some forty ways in which the word "set" has been employed in relatively modern psychology. Many more could be added by a sufficiently patient reader, especially one who collected the ways in which the word *Einstellung* has been used in German and English literature. Gibson claims that no common meaning can be discerned in all these usages. For this reason, when the accepted term motive is to hand, I feel that to call the Determining Tendencies or the Task a "set" as Woodworth does (1938, p. 790), makes confusion worse confounded. No clear line of distinction has yet been drawn between what Ach and Watt were describing and the "Motive" of more modern usage. One of Ach's subjects said, "I had the *need* to add". Murphy defines Motivation as the process by which *needs* give rise to behaviour (1935, p. 15). There is no hard-and-fast line where a set to action becomes a motive to action. If it be said that Motive is specific, e.g. hunger motive, while set is more general, e.g. set to add different pairs of figures, it should be pointed out that a man can properly be said to be motivated by hunger to steal, to "work", or to ask for a second helping. This is not to deny that there are contexts in which the word set is properly used, but only that Watt's *Aufgabe* is one of them. Finally, to say as Young does that the *task* produces a *set* to performance seems once more to add an unnecessary *tertium quid* between task and performance. This is not to decry the excellence of Young's experiments. (Reported with references in Young, 1948.)

[48] Mention should be made here of the work of May (1917) and Jersild (1927), both working at Columbia University, who verified and somewhat expanded Watt's work. Since these papers are well reported by Woodworth (1938, pp. 791–4), further details will not be given here.

CHAPTER IV

CRITIQUE OF THE WÜRZBURG WORK

(1) Wundt's polemic. These are bogus experiments. Everything that takes place in a laboratory is not necessarily a scientific experiment. Answer to Wundt: He is really indicting the introspective method, as he himself practised it. The criticism that "suggestion" was probably at work is perhaps justified.

(2) The Würzburg contention of imageless thought was corroborated by many, including Binet ("it should be called the method of Paris"), Woodworth, Bovet, Selz, Willwoll.

(3) Many experiments have contradicted those of Würzburg, in particular those of Titchener's school at Cornell.

(4) The Cornell hypothesis was that the so-called imageless processes were faint kinæsthetic images. Hence the translation "conscious attitude". Conscious experience was made up of sensory material in the form of sensations (the product of the analysis of perceptions), and images, also of sensory nature, plus *Affekt*. So that the meaning of an image may be another image. In this way, by the road of kinæsthesis, Titchener, the apostle of "introspection", became a minor prophet of reaction psychology.

(5) Since the Würzburgers claimed that some mental content other than that admitted in section (4) (Bsl., *Gedanken*, both imageless) gave the meaning of an image, Titchener was forced to claim that they were not describing "contents of experience" at all, but independent objects, objects of thought, stimuli, i.e. they were committing the "stimulus error" of describing not experience but the stimulus giving rise to experience.

(6) In essence, the imageless-thought contention maintained that just as you perceive the external world directly, without the intervention of any "idea" or "presentation", so you may imagine or *think* the world directly, part of the process often being imagery. I.e. part of this process may involve sense-resembling processes of a particular modality, and this is the cart, not the horse. The primary "work " when one thinks a proposition such as "Russia is East of Britain" is imageless: but there may also be sense-like processes in the form of verbal or other imagery.

I T WAS PERHAPS to be expected that a method so revolutionary as that of the Würzburgers would meet with strong opposition, particularly since the experimental results were radically opposed to prevailing theory. Chief among the critics were Wundt, who since 1875 had held the chair of philosophy at Leipzig; and in the United States Titchener, of Cornell University. The criticisms of these two men will be considered in detail.

Wundt's Criticism of the Würzburg Work

It was in 1907 that Wundt published his polemic entitled "On the *Ausfrage* Experiments and on the Methods of the Psychology of Thinking". Apart from its importance as a criticism of the Würzburg work, the paper is a significant discussion of the experimental method in its relation to psychology. For that reason it is here considered in some detail. The paper is sixty pages long. It begins by formulating four rules which must be followed by any experimental investigation.

(1) The observer must, as far as possible, be in the position to determine, of himself, the occurrence of the event to be observed.

(2) The observer must be in a state of the utmost concentration of attention to observe the phenomena and to follow them in their course.

(3) In order to safeguard the results, every observation must be capable of being repeated a number of times under similar circumstances.

(4) The conditions under which the phenomenon occurs must be ascertained by variation of the accompanying circumstances, and, when they are ascertained, they must be regularly changed in the appropriately varied experiments. That is to say, in the different experiments they must be on the one hand completely isolated, on the other graded in their intensity or quality.

These four rules, he says, are ideal only. In practice they can be followed only imperfectly even by the physical sciences.[1] He gives examples of psychological experiments, some of which are complete, others incomplete, according to the criteria which he has laid down.

On the twenty-seventh page of the paper the critique proper begins. The Würzburg experiments, Wundt says, are "experiments without instruments".[2] This does not constitute an argument against them; but it does mean that the work must be judged by the four above-mentioned criteria alone. Taking each of these in turn he finds that they are none of them satisfied by the Würzburg work.

The observer cannot himself observe the relevant event. In these experiments the real observer is not the experimenter, but the subject, who has to observe what is happening in his mind. The subject, however, does not know the content of the question about to be put to him; the question is then, for him, an unexpected event, which constituted the most unfavourable condition for scientific observation.

[1] Loc. cit., p. 308.
[2] Ibid., p. 329. His criticisms here, as well as elsewhere, are confined chiefly to Bühler's work, who seemed especially to have roused his anger.

Under such circumstances observation may be possible of simple psychic events, as in the association experiments, but hardly of such complicated ones as those investigated by Bühler. Here the psychic processes involved are so complex that the combined difficulty of solving and at the same time observing is insurmountable. In addition, the factor of surprise itself exercises a severely disturbing influence on the process of thinking. The usual introspective difficulty, namely that the process of observation modifies the event which is being observed, is, in the *Ausfrage* method, intensified at the outset by this element of surprise.

Further, *the observer cannot devote his attention to the events to be observed*. Every psychologist would agree, says Wundt, that we cannot at the same time both engage in an activity which requires our utmost attention, and attend to the mental events which are simultaneously occurring. This would require an impossible cleavage of the personality. To solve a difficult problem, and simultaneously to give an account of our mental processes to an observer with watch in hand, is then a psychological impossibility.

Thirdly, *the criterion of repeatability is not fulfilled*. There is, indeed, repetition in a general way, in that a similar method is used for a number of trials, with the same observer and the same class of questions. But this does not constitute real repetition where the experiment is repeated with similar content in order to rule out irrelevancies. Such repetition is precluded by the nature of the *Ausfrage* experiments. Thus one of the most important features of the experimental method is lost.

Lastly, *the criterion of variability of conditions* is not fulfilled. There is, and can be, no systematic variation of the questions put to the subject; for this would turn the experiments into memory and recognition experiments.[3]

The result is then unequivocal. The *Ausfrage* experiments are not experiments at all in the sense of a scientific methodology, but they are sham experiments, which have the appearance of being systematic only because they take place, as a rule, in a psychological laboratory, and because a *soi-disant* experimenter and subject participate in them. In reality they have no scientific value, because they fall short when judged by all the criteria which distinguish the self-observations of experimental psychology from those of ordinary life. They are even inferior to ordinary self-observation, where the observer at least waits until the favourable moment for the mental

Loc. cit., p. 333–4.

event appears; while in these experiments the subject's attention is under the strain of solving difficult problems. Further, the "division of labour" of which the experimenters speak is no real division of labour. On the contrary, the presence of the observer puts the subject in the position of a student in an examination room. Experience has shown that the presence of another person in the experimental room acts as a strong distracting influence; thus once more the *Ausfrage* experiment is at a disadvantage as compared with the old method of self-observation.

Similar considerations apply to Ach's method, whereby questions are asked after the experiment is finished. "There is no doubt that the quick forgetting of many events that hasten only fleetingly over consciousness . . . reduces all reports upon that which is experienced in consciousness to fragments of reality, which in addition are falsified in many cases by illusions of memory." Thus questioning after the event cannot elicit the truth. The only result can be a suggestive effect on the subject's answers. The suggestion may easily impose the theoretical views of the experimenter upon the subject, so that he thinks he has observed what was never in his consciousness at all. Ach's experiments have, however, at least the merit that they deal with relatively simple mental events, and in addition provide the control of exact time-measurement.

Thus the *Ausfrage* experiments are in no sense correct self-observations, but "self-observations under conditions of difficulty, conditions which favour self-deception rather than self-observation" (p. 343). In addition to these methodological errors, they contain, one and all of them, what may be called a psychological error. They attempt to treat the problem of thinking as an isolated one, without consideration of its relation to the general facts of consciousness, of attention, of the progress of the psychic events in question, and so on. These psychological complications are of the highest importance, but they are entirely neglected. To this point we shall return later.

Apart from the general logical reflections of the subject and the experimenter, which have nothing to do with the psychological problem, the upshot of this mass of work is that "the observers observed nothing at all".[4] "The thought certainly stood as a whole clearly before consciousness. But this thought was bodiless. It lacked the substrate of sensations, feelings, presentations, or any other conceivable content of consciousness. These contents did indeed at

[4] Loc. cit., p. 344.

times swirl through consciousness, but so casually, and in most cases probably so out of relation with the thoughts themselves that they could with perfect right be treated as chance accompaniments. What is then, finally, the thought itself? It is . . . a content of consciousness *sui generis,* different from everything else which we include among experiences of consciousness (*Bewusstseinserlebnissen*) and, in particular, different from its sensory component parts".[5] We find ourselves back to the "actus purus", the *pure act* of the scholastics, who came to this result not by means of *Ausfrage* experiments but as a theoretical deduction from the "creative mind"[6] of Aristotle. According to the scholastics this active, contentless spirit could bring about only that which was itself contentless. Thus psychology has reverted to a dualistic spiritualism which has been consistently rejected by experimental psychology. According to the Würzburg doctrine, thought is then definable only in terms of itself. How one thought differs from another, and how this thought, existing like a thing-in-itself, can ever clothe itself in presentations or words—such questions are left unanswered.

One chief reason, Wundt says, for this negative result of these writers has already been mentioned: they confuse consciousness and attention. They have concluded that because they observed no sensory elements in consciousness when they experienced a thought process, therefore thought is essentially non-sensory in character. Such a conclusion rests on the presupposition that everything in consciousness must be immediately given in self-observation. This in its turn presupposes that consciousness and attention are identical. This conclusion has been shown to be false by common observation and psychological experiment alike.[7]

As a matter of fact, he continues, the problem of thinking cannot be treated, in the manner of the *Ausfrage* experiments, as though it were divorced from the rest of psychology. Not only does it require all available psychological information, but also every available psychological method. Of the latter, one of the most important methods is to be found in the psychology of speech. By his own observations Wundt has made it clear that "a thought is not first formed while one speaks the sentence, but that it already stands as a whole in our consciousness before we begin to fit words to it. With this whole there is, nevertheless, present at the focus of consciousness none of the verbal or other representations which form during the

[5] Loc. cit., p. 345.   [6] νοῦς ποιητικός.
[7] The point is repeated by Wundt, ibid., p. 352.

development and the linguistic expression of the thought; but only at the moment when we develop the thoughts are their separate parts successively lifted to clear consciousness".[8] This, Wundt continues, is not the "actus purus" of the *Ausfrage* results; it is parallel to the feeling-effect (*Gefühlswirkung*), which may be observed when a total presentation is in consciousness with certain details missing, and which adequately covers the character of the thought, including the missing details. Such feeling effects may be seen when poetical and ethical thoughts come to our mind.[9] Such a feeling is able to carry a rhythm; we are able to identify a rhythmically repeated series of taps "because this beat-form creates a peculiar rhythmic feeling which is characteristically different from any other beat-form". The logical form of the thought is parallel to this beat-form.

For Wundt thought is, then, a logical total presentation which appears as a totality in consciousness. "As such it is constituted of the same nexus of single presentations as that into which discursive thought articulates it afterwards in successive apperception of the single elements. But it is, with all these parts, dimly apprehended[10]; and only because this is so can it be given at all as a simultaneous whole, which enters the forms of consciousness in discrete presentational elements by means of the total feeling peculiar to it. This also not seldom happens when the process of thought-articulation is inhibited. The real development, or, as we could better call it here, unfolding of the thought, is constituted in the successive grasping of the separate constituent elements of the total presentation standing in the background of consciousness."[11] This far we can go, says Wundt, and no farther.

In summary, Wundt divides his criticism into four headings. (1) The *Ausfrage* experiments are not real experiments, but self-observations with obstructions. They do not satisfy a single one of the criteria of a real experiment. (2) They represent the worst type of the old method of self-observation. "They employ the attention of the observer on an unexpected, more or less difficult, intellectual problem, and in addition require him to observe the behaviour of his own consciousness." (3) The *Ausfrage* method is to be rejected in both its forms. When employed to question the subject before the experiment, it exposes the subject to the unfavourable influence of cross-examination. When employed to question him after the experiment, it opens the door wide to suggestion. In both forms it

---

[8] The point is repeated by Wundt, ibid., p. 349.   [9] Loc. cit., p. 351.
[10] *dunkel bewusst*.   [11] Ibid., p. 356; cf. Wundt, 1912, p. 248.

influences self-observation to an excessive degree in that it exposes the subject, who should observe himself, to the simultaneous observation of another person. (4) The method violates the rule that when related problems are to be solved, those should first be attacked which are simpler and are presupposed by the others. "As a result, the users of the method confuse attention with consciousness, and fall into the popular error of believing that every event in consciousness can without more ado be followed up in self-observation." This last error is enough to vitiate the whole method.

Examination of Wundt's Criticism

These criticisms of Wundt will be considered *seriatim*.

Begin with the four rules for experiment laid down early in the paper! When Wundt denies that the observer—that is, the subject—is in the position to observe the relevant event, he is of course using an argument which has been directed against the whole introspective method. The problem whether the mind can be set to observe itself without disturbing the data of observation is an old one: it was old in Wundt's day. What Wundt has here said in effect to the Würzburgers is: "The stock objections to the introspective method apply to the kind of experiment you are making, but not to those which I have made." There is, of course, no *a priori* reason why this statement should not be true. But definite reasons must be given. These, of course, Wundt does give. The element of surprise enters into the experiments under consideration. The data are too complicated. It is impossible to take the first of these objections seriously. It is out of the question that a professor of a German university in the early nineteen hundreds, and one of the calibre of Külpe, should have been so surprised when an undergraduate asked him to solve a problem—which, after all, he was expecting—that his mental processes were seriously disturbed. That he should have been reduced to "examination-flurry"[12] is ludicrous. As a serious objection, the element of surprise may be dismissed. Nor need the charge of complexity *per se* be taken any more seriously. There is no *a priori* reason why complexity of data should in itself vitiate introspection. Once the introspective method has been admitted as methodologically sound, then it must be assumed to be applicable to all mental events, unless special reasons are shown to the contrary. That is to say, the important thing to demonstrate is why a particular mental

---

[12] *Examenspresse*, p. 358 and *passim*.

event is not amenable to the introspective method; such terms as "complexity" and "difficulty" confuse the issue. Wundt reproaches the Würzburgers with not knowing the psychology of attention. It is perhaps no accident that in 1913, six years later,[13] Watson was to direct an attack on the whole introspective method, using the concept of attention as an example of the untrustworthy nature of introspective evidence in general. In his charge that the Würzburg data were too complex, Wundt is then really voicing the stock objections to introspective psychology.

Wundt's second rule for scientific experiment requires that the observer shall be able to give his directed attention[14] to the event to be observed. Here again, his criticism, namely that in these experiments full attention is impossible for the problem at hand, cannot be sustained. As Bühler pointed out,[15] the Würzburgers insisted throughout that their introspections were recollections obtained by examination of the perseverative memory of the event in question. It is true that Wundt replied that such a procedure inevitably gave a distorted picture of the original mental event.[16] But this is a different criticism. Conceivably some such distortion may have taken place, but Wundt presents no evidence that it was serious enough to invalidate the fundamental Würzburg theses. At no time in their work did the Würzburgers maintain that they were simultaneously attending to the problem and to the mental process of solving the problem.

Nor is the charge justified that the Würzburg experiments are essentially unrepeatable. To begin with, as Wundt admits by implication, the term repetition, as applied to an event of nature, is clearly ideal and non-realizable in any concrete case, like the term equality and the term circle. No two concrete objects in nature were ever ideally equal in every respect. No two experiments on any event of nature were ever ideal repetitions, because nature never repeats herself. When, however, he comes to use the third rule in criticism of the Würzburgers, he insists on the necessity of repetition "with similar observed content".[17] The word *similar* is disingenuous. Wundt realizes, of course, that identity of content cannot be demanded on successive occasions, and that anything short of it implies

[13] Watson, J. B., 1913.
[14] *Gespannte Aufmerksamkeit.*
[15] Bühler, K., 1908 (*b*).
[16] Wundt, 1908. Müller (1911, p. 137 ff.) criticizes Ach on the ground that the perseverative image is not necessarily reliable.
[17] *bei gleichem beobachteten Inhalt.*

abstraction of identical features in successive experiments. Every psychological, as well as every physical, experiment demands such abstraction when it is repeated. Now it is true that an experiment on thought cannot be twice used with the same problem on account of what is now known as the practice effect. But it is possible to abstract identical features from experiments on different thought problems, and with reference to these identical features there is repetition of the experiment. To maintain that the mental processes involved in solving different problems have nothing in common would be pure scepticism, and would deny any meaning to the general term thought or thinking. And once more, if there is something common to such different mental processes, then solution of different problems involves repetition with reference to the common factor in question. Actually, it was of course precisely such a factor common, for example, to different reaction experiments that Ach professed to find in his *Bewusstheit*, or awareness. Bühler's "Consciousness of a rule" is similarly an abstraction from the mental processes involved in solving many different problems. If the generalizations of Ach and Bühler are correct, then any reaction experiment which involves the appearance of a *Bewusstheit* is an adequate repetition of the original experiment, no matter what the nature of the reaction situation; and any experiment which involves consciousness of a rule adequately repeats the original problem situation no matter what the specific problem. If the generalizations leading to the concepts of *Bewusstheit* and of consciousness of rule are incorrect, they should be specifically disputed. To question them on the score of the impossibility of repeating the experiments is disingenuous.

The answer to the third criticism carries with it the answer to the fourth, which concerns variation of conditions. It has been shown that, from the methodological point of view, the Würzburg experiments did fulfil the experimental criterion of repetition with variation. All in all, it is therefore not possible to take very seriously Wundt's statement that these are "sham experiments which have the appearance of being systematic only because they take place in a psychological laboratory". In the preceding chapter of this book certain methodological defects in the experiments were, however, indicated. In particular it was pointed out that the conditions of Ach's experiments were not standardized, in that the questions were not published in full and no regular order of questions is hinted at. These defects did, we say, constitute a serious objection to the method, as did the fact mentioned later by Wundt that the use of questions must have exercised a suggestive effect. We shall, then, in the main reject Wundt's general criticisms of method, but will consider these two objections as established.

To proceed with the more specific part of Wundt's critique, to reproach the Würzburgers with "observing nothing", and with going back to the "actus purus" of the scholastics is, of course, to say merely, "I do not agree with you". He asks: "How can one such thought differ from another?" The answer is obviously just as one sensation or one feeling differs from another; that is, by the attributes peculiar to its category. The fact that a mental category is *sui generis* does not mean that mental events belonging to that category are indistinguishable; it means only that it rests for science to discover the attributes by which such distinction may be made. It is impossible to believe that Wundt overlooked this elementary fact; once more, one cannot believe he is entirely disingenuous either here, or when, in the same context, he accuses the Würzburgers of Locke's fallacy of the *tabula rasa*.

It remains to consider the general objection that the Würzburg approach considered the problem of thought as though it were isolated, independent of other psychological problems, and specifically that the factor of attention was neglected. The criticism that conventional distinctions are overlooked has, of course, been brought against many scientific innovations. Actually, a characteristic feature of the Würzburg doctrine, namely the theory of the determining tendency and of the *Aufgabe*, involves the distinction in question. For it is of the essence of these that they represent directive factors which are not ordinarily observed, but which may be observed if attention is specifically directed towards them. These factors form an exact parallel to the tachistoscopic experiments to which Wundt appeals, and which show "how much attention and consciousness differ not merely in the manner of apprehension of what is given . . ., but also in the range of the regions which they control".[18] But apart from the doctrine of the determination of thought, which is apparently overlooked by Wundt, the same answer must be made as before. Wundt's criticism applies to the introspective method in general, not merely to the Würzburg results. It is generally easy to object to an introspective finding on the ground that it would have been different had attention been differently directed. This constitutes a major source of uncertainty in the introspective method; and it was the difficulty involving the psychology of attention, among

[18] Wundt, W., 1907, p. 352.

others, which, as already indicated, caused Watson five years later to reject the whole method as unscientific and unreliable.

Specifically, Wundt's criticism amounts to saying that images were present in experience to the Würzburgers during the so-called image-less processes, but that attention was not directed towards these images; just as the red light of a traffic signal may be present in the experience of a motorist who is "staring straight at it", but the motorist may not be aware of the signal until his attention is drawn to it by the traffic officer. To accuse Külpe, as Wundt actually did, of ignorance of what was at that time a conventional psychological distinction is ridiculous. And actually the reports of hundreds of Würzburg experiments show that Wundt's accusation simply is not true. The subjects were obviously on the alert to observe imagery, and imagery was reported in hundreds of cases. But there were also many cases where, although they were on the watch for imagery, they observed none. To assert that if the attention of these observers had been properly directed they would have observed images in these cases is sheer dogmatism. Wundt's criticism cannot be admitted.[19]

Finally, when he comes to his alternative proposal for a psychology of thinking, Wundt is really restating the Würzburg position in his own words. The pre-linguistic thought-whole, which is in consciousness, and which unfolds itself by means of speech; the feeling-effect which adequately covers the character of the thought, and which is able to carry a complicated rhythm—these are surely none other than Ach's *Bewusstheit*. To use the term "feeling-effect" is surely to play with words and to confuse the issue.

In summary: The only one of Wundt's criticisms which is justified, as specially directed against the Würzburgers, is that concerning suggestion. Much of this long polemic is given up to objections which really criticize the introspective technique in general, and which, in fact, have since been used against that technique. Little of it is characterized by that dispassionateness which we feel we have a right to expect from one who held, and whose name still holds, an eminent position in the world of science. This is one of the notable critiques in the history of psychology, both from the effect it had on contemporary prejudice and opinion, and for the indirect influence it has accordingly exerted on the direction of psychological thought up to the present day. Yet to one who rereads it a generation later it seems in many places shallow and preten-tious, and to have employed the authority of a great name unworthily.

[19] The special case of kinæsthetic imagery will be considered later.

Other Experimental Confirmations of the Würzburg Conclusions

Wundt was an experimentalist. Though it was not supported by actual experiment his criticism of the Würzburg work was based on experimental presuppositions and supported by experimental findings. Nevertheless, Bühler was justified in reproaching Wundt with not having himself performed *Ausfrage* experiments. Other workers did, in fact, employ much the same methods as those of the Würzburgers. In spite of Wundt's diatribe, they actually did arrive at similar conclusions. This corroborative work is additionally impressive, in that it was apparently independently executed. It is fair to say that the discovery of imageless thought was independently reported from laboratories in three countries, from the Würzburgers in Germany, Binet in France, and Woodworth in America.

Binet (1903, 1903a, 1909, 1910), working with his two little girls, aged fourteen and thirteen, found evidence of thought without imagery. He observed cases where image did not correspond to thought, and where only part of thought was covered by the imagery. In aphasics and imbeciles, also, he found thought without verbal imagery, from which again he concluded the presence of imageless thought. Here, as Ogden points out (1911, p. 188), he apparently left out of account the possibility of kinæsthesis. So closely did Binet's result agree, both in method and in general conclusion, with the German work, that he claimed that the method should properly be called not the Würzburg method but the method of Paris. In the same way, Woodworth maintained from experimental evidence that "in many cases the imagery present in consciousness did not exhaust the content of consciousness. Sometimes the subject, though clearly aware of the movement he was about to make, denied that he had any visual, kinæsthetic, verbal or other imagery of it" (1906, p. 702). Woodworth's experiments were carried out upon voluntary movement and upon perceptual material of visual and auditory modality (1907). There are, he claimed, non-sensorial components in sense perception (1907). When I hear a horse galloping past, there is more in my consciousness than the sheer auditory sensations (1915). I can be conscious of the horse with my mind free of sensory material other than the auditory sensations in question. The results of the Würzburg investigators were, in general, confirmed also by Bovet, in Switzerland, in a paper published in 1908.

Later we find Pratt summarizing the experimental work for the five years 1922–6 as follows: ". . . there emerge three rather definite and generally accepted conclusions regarding the nature of thought".

The first of these he labels "*Rejection of Associationism*"; the third "*The Steering Principles of Thought*". The second concerns us more directly in this context. It is headed "*Impalpable Character of the Contents of Thought*". Pratt's summary of the experimental evidence on this point is as follows: "Some of the ideas which accompany the act of thinking present sensory aspects. These ideas may or may not be relevant to the purpose of the act. But there are persistent contents of thought which reveal no sensory stuff whatever. A goodly proportion of thought is imageless" (1928 p. 551). Pratt instanced the work of Selz, who, as we shall see later, maintained the existence of "impalpable awarenesses of relations and directions". "T. Weiss," he says, "emphasizes the actualization of the second term in an impalpable knowledge-relation as the most important operation in controlled associations" (Pratt, 1928, p. 552). It will be noted that each of these authors maintains that the general principle of imageless thought-contents is upheld by his own experimental results. Rösgen's observers noted the general presence of impalpable knowledge which functions as an anticipatory framework (Rösgen, 1925). Dunn employed legal cases and geometrical problems, and concluded that the fundamental processes employed in reasoning are free of sensory content (Dunn, 1926). Other observers mentioned by Pratt as reporting imageless contents in thinking are Weinhandl, Simonheit, Willwoll, and Clarke.[20]

Gibson and McGarvey (1937), in their survey ten years later, again noted that nobody then questioned the directive nature of the thinking processes; although, since the time of the Würzburgers, there has been a certain development of opinion as to the nature of this direction. This development will be considered later in the appropriate context. In the matter of imageless thought, two studies only are noted, both confirmatory of the Würzburg conclusions. Bowers (1935) used an ingenious method of determining the rôle of imagery in thought. He argued that if thought is primarily the manipulation of images, then those problems which are more easily imaged will be more easily solved; and those persons who have the power to form stable, vivid imagery would have an advantage in solving problems. The weight of his experimental evidence was uniformly against the sensory theory.[21] It should be noted that this experiment does not show that imagery has no function in thinking;

[20] See Pratt's bibliography for the references.
[21] He did find that imagery was apparently of use in verbal recall. See note 12, in Chapter 10. See also the chapter on "Generalization".

it shows only that reasoning is not synonymous with the formation of images. In any case, the experiment is not wholly decisive. The advocate of the sensory theory will still maintain that ability in reasoning depends not on ability to form images but on ability to use them; the advocate of the non-sensory theory, that if the ultimate *medium* of reasoning is imagery, then the more exactly the problem concerned can be represented in terms of images, the better the problem must be understood and the better will be the reasoning about it. The other study mentioned by Gibson and McGarvey in their résumé, viz. that of Peillaube, was of a more conventional nature, and came by methods similar to those of the Würzburgers to similar conclusions.

Experimental Findings Contrary to Würzburg

In contrast to this confirmatory work, there were important dissentients. First of all, Titchener adopted a thoroughgoing sensationalistic position. Theoretically, for Titchener conscious mental processes are reducible to either sensations, images, or feelings (affections). "If we can trace an attitude [Bsl.] back, within the same mind, to an imaginal source; if it thus appears not as original endowment but as residuum, not as primule but as vestige, then I should protest against its ranking as a mental element." By this theory, then, the constituent elements of mental life are processes of an ultimately sensory nature and their affections. Consider now the visual image of the printed letters CAT. What is the difference between the mental processes of the Englishman when he forms this visual picture, and those of a Japanese who cannot read English but can presumably form exactly the same visual image? Many answers have been given. Ach's is that the one has a *Bewusstheit*, an awareness of meaning, which the other lacks. This Titchener cannot accept. Clearly he must find another image. "An idea means another idea . . . if it is that idea's context! Meaning is originally kinæsthesis; the organism faces the situation by some bodily attitude, and the characteristic sensations which the attitude involves give meaning to the process." Later in the evolutionary scale, the kinæsthetic sensations are replaced by images. The upshot is that we must expect to find what the Würzburgers and others called imageless thoughts dissolving into imagery, much of the more obscure being of the kinæsthetic and verbal type; for words were at first kinæsthetic contexts.

Thus we have an entirely "pure" psychology, one which confines its description entirely to mental states. When, says Titchener, Bühler's observers describe their *Thoughts of something*, or the *Thought that something is the case*, e.g. "the thought that the end of altruism is not attained" (1907, p. 311); when, presumably, Ach speaks of an awareness as an imageless knowing that something is so; then the observers in question are not describing consciousness but "formulating the reference of consciousness to things", not describing thought but reporting after the event what the thought is about. They are committing the "stimulus error", as when the inexperienced student reports not the mental event but the external event (fact) that is the occasion of the mental event.[22] Psychology must confine itself strictly to facts of consciousness; it must not allow itself to digress into inference concerning the objective occasion of the primary psychological datum.

To test this hypothesis four experimental studies were undertaken in the Cornell laboratory, those of Pyle, on Expectation; of Okabe, on Belief; of Clarke, on "Conscious Attitudes", and of Jacobson on Meaning and Understanding. Pyle confronted his observers with series of stimuli, two or more in each. Thus a coloured disc might follow an auditory stimulus; a visual stimulus might be repeated; and the blow by which a pendulum was released might be followed by the sound of one or more balls falling, and so on. The observers reported on their experiences between the first stimulus and the following stimuli. "The psychophysical organism 'sets' to meet an imminent situation; and on the conscious side, this 'set' is expectation. On the physical side are: bodily attitude, strained muscles, inhibited breathing, fixed sense organs. The image of the coming impression may sometimes be present, but is not an essential factor, not a characteristic element" (Pyle, 1909, p. 569). Here, it will be noted, conscious expectation *is* kinæsthetic sensation. Okabe confronted his observers with sentences expressed visually or orally, or with pairs of such sentences. The observers were requested to note whether the single sentences aroused belief or disbelief, and after this practice to report introspectively upon the belief- and disbelief-consciousness. There were four observers. At the end of the experiment a summary of each observer's reports was read to him, and he was asked whether he concurred. These reports differed, of course,

---

[22] The same criticism was voiced by von Aster, who claimed that Bühler's observers practised *Kundgabe*, rather than *Beschreibung*, of conscious experiences, *intimation* (that their experiences related to certain objective facts) rather than *description* (of mental events).—Von Aster, 1908; cf. Dürr, 1908.

from observer to observer. The relevant section of the author's final summary is as follows: "The belief-disbelief consciousness may be a straightforward experience, given, e.g., in terms of a general kinæsthetic attitude or of internal speech and localized kinæsthesis, or of the mutual relations of visual images; or it may be bound up with, incorporated in, a particular consciousness, verbal or visual. In the former case the contents come to the observer as being specifically belief; in the latter case they come to him as the vehicle of belief" (Okabe 1910, p. 594). Three of these four observers were asked after the main series of experiments whether they found any trace of imageless content; none was found. The exception was observer G, whose analysis made the question unnecessary.

Clarke investigated the *Bewusstseinslage* specifically, taking over Titchener's translation, "*Conscious Attitude*". The experiments required the observer to form a tactual perception of letters and words written in the blind point-alphabet. Reaction time of recognition was measured by a Vernier chronoscope. Sample analyses are appended.

Awfulness: Once analysed as a strong unpleasantness and frowning, and again as the same with the addition of inhibition of breathing.

Caution: Verbal idea, be careful.

Comparison (Two observers): The two things were side by side, visually.

I ought to know that: Organic sensation and disagreeable feeling.

Injustice: Gasping for breath. I started back and threw my head back.

Pride: Slight tendency to straighten up my neck and smile. Pleasant feeling.

Surprise: At not feeling the better. Something moving along inside the body, a dull pressure going upward from the stomach to the back of the mouth.

"There is no doubt that the reports were intended at the time to represent the attitudes themselves, and not merely incidental or concomitant occurrences."[23] The introspections "show that imagery does not need to be specific and elaborate in order to carry thought . . . the mere setting of the mouth, or the right mode of exhalation, serves as well as the complete word". Stages in clearness of visual imagery are noted, and also the fact that the *Aufgabe* is shortened and modified by repetition and tends to disappear. Experiments were also performed on Understanding. Here again it was found that the understanding of words and sentences is mediated by

[23] Clarke, 1911, pp. 218, 219, 220, 221, 225.

images, verbal or object-visual. However, there are noted observations where the imagery is inadequate, contradictory, and even irrelevant. The summary contains the statement that "The cases in which thought-elements or imageless thoughts or attitudes are reported as the "consciousness that", etc., are cases not of psychological description, but the translation into words of the meaning of a conscious state" (*Kundgabe*).[24] "Imageless Thought" really stands at the end of a graded series of decreasingly clear images, and is thus generically sensory, according to Titchener's postulate (see above p. 50, for a similar description by Ach who argues that it thus passes out of the sensory category altogether).

Jacobson's paper (1911) reaches much the same conclusion. Letters, words, and sentences were shown visually to the subjects, who were instructed to give as precise and minute an account as possible of everything that occurred in consciousness. "The meaning of the stimulus words were . . . thus carried by visual, auditory and kinæsthetic processes; or to speak more precisely, the meanings which these processes bore were the meanings of the stimulus words, in so far as the latter were consciously realized."[25] The introspection of one subject will be quoted. In this case: "The visual and auditory images and sensations from reading [were] the sole processes present in consciousness, while yet the sentence had meaning."

"*The affair was bewildering.* (One sec.) White and black sensations (from paper and background) in background of consciousness. Simultaneous with the visual clearing of each word, auditory images. The meaning of the sentence was in the auditory images and visual sentences themselves. *No other context to carry the meaning that I can find.*"[26] Thus the general conclusion of the Cornell experiments is unanimously in favour of Titchener's hypothesis.

Assessment of the Contradictory Experiments

We are then faced with two flatly contradictory sets of experimental findings. Certain experimenters, headed by the Würzburg group, Binet, and Woodworth, claimed to have found non-sensory components of thinking. Others, chief and representative of whom were the Cornell group, failed to find such components. The latter claimed that on careful experimental examination the so-called imageless experiences were analysable into sensory elements, prominent among which were kinæsthetic sensations; that further a very elementary sensory process could carry very elaborate

[24] Loc. cit., p. 248.   [25] Ibid., p. 564.   [26] Ibid., p. 572.

meaning; and that the error of the opposing group had been in disregarding the lesser degrees of kinæsthesis, and in including in their psychological account the *thing* meant, which is of an essentially non-psychological nature. The question cannot be decided by majority vote, nor by repetition of the experiments, which would do no more than add another vote to one or the other side. The only way of settling the experimental question is to examine the experiments themselves. For this purpose, the two technically best groups will suffice.

Careful examination of the experiments of Würzburg on the one hand and of Cornell on the other can lead to only one conclusion. The Cornell experiments failed to reach their avowed objective which was to "describe in analytical terms" certain kinds of experience. This failure was masked by an unjustified use of the metaphor "vehicle of meaning". In addition, the attempt to give a sensationalist account of the mental processes under examination forced the workers to the use of descriptive terms which are only explainable on the hypothesis that either the abjured stimulus error has been committed, or alternatively that, as a matter of fact, imageless processes were being described. Finally, it will appear that the stimulus error itself, with which the Würzburgers had been reproached, cannot be committed at all if the sensationalist hypothesis is true. If the Cornell theory is correct, the error with which the Cornell workers tax their opponents is impossible.

For substantiation of the first statement, it is only necessary to glance over any one of the four papers just discussed. Except where ordinary terms are used, it would generally be impossible to recognize from the "description" the kind of experience that is being "described". E.g.: "Visual image of adult and then of child; reference to my own experience. That was a line representing the time from the present to the past; there was nothing more that I can tell. ... Memory of child was very plain but scattered and disarranged; a visual pattern made up of bits which were very clear, and which I could see very plainly; clear-cut and separate from one another. Memory of adult was like a spider's web, all united. All this fitted in, in some way, with the reference to past experience; ... the two things fitted together; but I can't say whether at this stage there was any representation of past experience."[27] One thing that is certain about this is that it is not a "description", analytical or otherwise, of *belief*. It is quoted unchanged and in its entirety except that the words

[27] Okabe, 1910, p. 584.

"Belief in both cases" and "I believed" are omitted. And to speak of "visual imagery of adult and then of child" is illegitimate on the sensationalist hypothesis. What was present in consciousness was of course certain experiences, of, let us say, a quasi-visual character; to call these "visual image of an adult" is to describe not the sheer sensory experience but something else in addition. Either the stimulus error is being committed or non-sensory components of consciousness are being described. For since the total sensory material has been reported, the phrase "visual image of an adult" must either refer to the adult in question (stimulus error) or to a non-sensory component in the consciousness of the subject. The same thing is true of the following "description". "Visual representation of the two sentences at opposite ends of a line; this meant: They are contradictory." Once more either the disavowed "stimulus-error" is present, both in the statement concerning the sentences at opposite ends of a line and in the sentence: "this meant, they are contradictory"; or, again, the subject is describing an imageless process. And once more, without being told, it would be impossible to guess that this was a "description, in analytical terms, of the experience of belief . . . There was, of course, a good deal of *Kundgabe* [verbal statement of meaning][28] in the records at large, and we were content to let it stand as such; only as regards the consciousness of Belief proper were we at pains to translate [it] into *Beschreibung*"[29] (=description of the conscious process). Actually it was necessary to specify that the images were of an adult and a child in order to describe them in recognizable terms. Description was impossible without either *Kundgabe* or description of imageless processes. To say that the image was made up of bits which were very clear is not to describe it. That is to say, again, an analytic description of *Belief* was not given in the terms proposed. The experiment failed to solve the problem set by the worker, and *ipso facto* it failed to fulfil its critical purpose. The same points may be illustrated by Shimberg's later experiments on the Rôle of Kinæsthesis in Meaning. Shimberg confronted her observers with Esperanto words, together with the request to "understand the meaning it [the word] assumes". One observer was shown the word Lerteco; The Response was *Lateral*. Report: "Conscious attitude (Bsl.) 'Think of Something'. Feeling of

[28] Literally *communication*, i.e. of the *nature* of the experience (as opposed to description of it) identified by Titchener with a statement of meaning, or the commission of the "stimulus error".
[29] Loc. cit., p. 567–8.

anxiety. Strain in eyes and throat. Awareness kinæsthetically of position of body. IS (Internal speech) *lateral,* simultaneously muscular relaxation and a feeling of pleasantness".[30] This is given as an analysis of the "conscious attitude". But once again, "Strain in eyes and throat", together with "awareness of the position of the body", is not an adequate description of the mental state, "Think of something". It would be possible to experience these sensations without having the experience corresponding to the words. The imagery is surely the accompaniment of another, unrecorded, mental event. And when "a catch of the breath and a contraction of the stomach . . . symbolized", for another subject, the feeling of assertion, it cannot be said that the feeling of assertion has been described. When further, a third subject reports on *"Boats"*, the following, viz: *Boat, boats,*[31] *image of rowboat,*[32] is the subject not either committing the stimulus- or *Kundgabe*-error, or else describing some imageless process? Shimberg's paper was not intended to add material to the discussion on imageless thought. She does, however, imply that complete description of the mental processes was given in terms of the imagery recorded.

In Jacobson's paper there is recognition of the fact that description of imagery has its own difficulties, and the observer was instructed to parenthesize "meanings, objects, stimuli and physiological occurrences".[33] Omitting the parentheses, we have then for the meaning of a sentence the following description: "Then vague visual and kinæsthetic image, . . . i.e. blue visual image . . . and very vague, featureless image, flesh coloured. . . ."[34] These images with others are said to "bear", "carry", or "be the vehicle of" the meaning of the written sentence "She came in secretly". We are then to understand that apart from certain processes corresponding to the colour of the ink and paper and kinæsthetic-auditory images corresponding to the words, the result in consciousness of reading this sentence was the appearance of a vague visual and kinæsthetic image in a certain projection, together with kinæsthetic images relating to the upper right leg and the muscles of the right side, *and nothing more*. How then is the observer in a position to say as he does, "The sentence meant: Miss X came in over there, through the door secretly?" (ibid.). The only datum he has for making this statement is his own

[30] 1924, p. 176.
[31] Visual and verbal imagery.
[32] Visual and concrete imagery.
[33] Loc. cit., p. 555.
[34] Explanatory words between parentheses are omitted; e.g. for the second parenthesis, "upper left part of skirt".

(conscious) experience, which by his own account is limited to the very meagre imagery indicated. It will be remembered that Bühler met exactly this case with his imageless *Wasbestimmtheiten des Meinens*, qualitative determinations of consciousness corresponding to meaning. In order, Bühler would say, that the observer may be able to state the meaning of this written sentence, there must be some specific conscious experience corresponding to the meaning. For, once more, the observer's conscious experience is all he has to go upon.

Returning to the Würzburg-Cornell controversy, it is now clear that the assertions of page 123 were justified, in that the sensational-istic hypothesis finds itself in the following triple dilemma: either it must commit "the stimulus error", the "error of *Kundgabe*", whereby the "thing meant" is described, a procedure which is illegitimate and outside the province of psychology. In this case, the Cornell group is committing the very fault for which it had called its opponents so elaborately to task. Or secondly, the sensationalist account must, while avoiding description of the thing meant, spirit into the descrip-tion some statement really concerning an imageless modification corresponding to the thing meant (=*Wasbestimmtheit des Mein-ens*), a procedure which does, indeed, rationalize the whole descrip-tion, but which is *ex ipsa hypothesi* illegitimate. Or lastly, it must confine itself to a description of image and sensation which does not correspond to, is clearly not a description of, the conscious experi-ences allegedly being described, and from which meaning cannot be derived.[35]

Actually the rigorous acceptance of the sensationist doctrine would make the commission of the "stimulus error" not merely illegitimate but impossible. For the sensationist position endeavours in effect to analyse all experience (save affect) into pure sense datum. But such sense datum can, of itself, give no indication concerning its occasion (stimulus, as Titchener uses the word). To take a single example: Nobody experiencing simply "blue visual image . . . vague kinæsthetic image", etc., would be in the position to commit the stimulus-error of maintaining that he thought about a woman coming in secretly. How does he know to what these "pure" images refer unless there is something present in consciousness to tell him, and something which is of necessity of a non-sensory nature, since a complete inventory of sensory process has already been made? The *reductio ad absurdum* of the sensationist position is

[35] If I understand him aright, I mean much the same thing as Dr. Boring, both in his invaluable *History* and in his article *Titchener on Meaning* (1938).

surely given in the following quotation from Titchener: "I was not at all astonished to observe that the recognition of a gray might consist of a quiver of the stomach."[36] What is there *in this particular* "*quiver*" to indicate that it is a recognition "quiver", or even to allow the stimulus error to be made from it? The sensationist hypothesis is in the position of precluding the error with which it taxes its opponent.

Lastly, as to the metaphor "vehicle of meaning". It does at first seem to make the sensationistic hypothesis more adequate if one says: the meaning is not the images but it is carried, borne by sensations or images. When, however, the metaphor as thus used is examined, it may easily be seen to be invalid. The critical question is: What is the difference between an image that carries and one that does not carry a meaning, or, what is the effect on consciousness of the fact that an image A carries a meaning X? If there is no effect, how then can the observer know the meaning, as he clearly must be able to do under the hypothesis? (Differences in conscious experience are clearly necessary in spite of Titchener's half-hearted defence of unconscious factors; see note 36).[37] If there is an effect, this must, on the sensationistic hypothesis, result in some difference of a sensory nature. That is to say, the image which is a vehicle is a different one from the image which is not a vehicle. But since meaning has now been directly expressed in terms of image, there is now nothing left for the image to carry. The term "vehicle" has lost its significance. If, on the other hand, the term is to be used as it logically must be used with the implication that meaning is something extrinsic to image, then the meaning must be represented either by unconscious mental processes, which really do not help in a psychology dealing with "experience" (see note 36), or by imageless ones. A sensationalist cannot logically use the metaphor at all. It will be remembered that Ach discusses the imageless awareness of meaning, which is however accompanied by an image. There seems here to be no objection to the use of the term vehicle. In fact, the metaphor "vehicle of thought" or "of meaning" really implies an imageless component of consciousness. Some have even gone so far as to maintain that every image has its imageless component.[38]

We find, then, the Würzburg experiments giving an intelligible

---

[36] 1909, p. 179. See note at the end of the chapter.

[37] The argument applies equally to Titchener's more explicitly developed statement that meaning *is* sensory context. For this statement provides no criteria by which we may tell which images are meaningful and which not. What sort of context is a *meaningful* context?

[38] Ogden, 1913, p. 410; Koffka, 1912, p. 356.

account of certain events, an account which, while it uses descriptive terms inadmissible in the sensationalistic scheme, does at least describe. We find, on the other hand, the sensationalist experiments often completely failing in their descriptive object, because of the inability of the theory on which they were based to distinguish between the psychologically admissible[39] "conscious modification of meaning" and the inadmissible "thing meant". So that their descriptions in an often unsuccessful attempt to avoid the "stimulus error" regularly missed an essential descriptive element.[40] We find the Cornell group consequently forced to employ a metaphor which is only allowable if their opponents' contentions be granted. We find, further, that the fundamental Würzburg thesis was maintained, alike by the majority of the strictly experimental workers, including Binet in France and Woodworth in the United States, and by theorists of the rank of Herbert Spencer, James, Stumpf, Stout, and Calkins,[41] to choose a few names at random. "It thus appears that the introspection of a score of psychologists, of different periods, prepossessions and training, speaks unequivocally in favour of the occurrence of elements neither sensational nor affective.[42] These are psycho-

[39] I.e. admissible, on general grounds, as part of a psychological description in contrast to *Kundgabe*.

[40] If the point is not already overworked, the following descriptions of Miss Clarke's are worth examining:
Consciousness that the letter was too small: Muscular strain and organic sensations.
The I-consciousness: Was a kinæsthetic sensation in the back of the mouth.
Conviction that I was right: Reappearance of the verbal image of the letter to which I should have reacted.
Here it is clear that the descriptions do not describe. Also that what Titchener would call the "stimulus error" is used in the last description. But unless the words "of the letter to which I should have reacted" are inserted after "verbal image", even the image is not described. The only piece of recognizable description comes from the employment of the so-called "stimulus error", or, alternatively, from description of non-sensory processes (Clarke, 1909). Really, the two methods here confront each other. Würzburg description, "the consciousness that", etc. (equals Ach's *Bewusstheit*), really does describe a certain kind of experience. Cornell description (equals muscular strain, etc.) does not describe the experience. There seems to be no doubt at all that the method advocated by the Würzburg group proved itself in practice superior. The Cornell experiments really added evidence on the side of the Würzburgers. They were a concrete demonstration of the fact that certain experiences could not be described in sensory terms; specifically, that when the attempt is made to describe, in such terms, experiences called by the Würzburgers "the consciousness that", the attempt fails. This is, of course, exactly the Würzburg contention.

[41] Spencer, 1855, p. 285; James, 1890, p. 247; Stumpf, 1917, pp. 7 ff., 29 ff.; Calkins, 1909.

[42] Calkins, 1909, p. 276.

logists. Of the great names in philosophy, it would be hard to find one, save that of Hume, who states unequivocally that thinking can be described without residue in terms of images. Kant explicitly avows his belief in imageless thought.[43] That the Würzburg description of the class of events termed in these pages "imageless thought-processes" is final, nobody is at present in the position to maintain. That the conscientious, able, and massive experimental attack of the Würzburgers resulted in a real step forwards in psychology is undeniable.

In conclusion, the following statement is tentatively offered. *We perceive objects directly, not through the intermediary of "presentations", "ideas", or "sensations".* Similarly, *we imagine objects directly,* not through the intermediary of images, though images are present as an important part of the whole activity. In each of these two cases, we may assign an important part, though not all, of the activity to one or other of the sensory modalities. *We may, however, think a proposition, or (draw) an inference* (and an inference is of no use to even the starkest logician unless somebody does draw it!) *in such a way that the activity in question falls within none of the sensory* modalities; though in general such activity is accompanied by either perception or imagination. This would be a fair conclusion, stated in more modern terms, from the experiments of which those of the Würzburg school are typical.

Whether of course the "Thought Elements" of Bühler should be considered as experimentally established is doubtful. For a generation, attention has been directed less and less to the general problem of mental elements. For example, R. M. Ogden wrote in the early days of Gestalt psychology: "By a bold declaration that there are no elemental conscious contents gathered together in 'bundles' through the agency of association, the investigation of mind has been turned to concrete common sense experience as the only truly empirical point of departure. . . . We do not find 'sensations', 'images' or 'affections', or even 'imageless thoughts', either singly or in combinations. We do, indeed, find sensory aspects of experience and others which we may call imaginal, affective and cognitive. . . ."[44] Many would not care to subscribe to the Gestalt doctrine in its entirety, but the quotation from Ogden may be taken as typical of the growing belief that the psychological description of the later nineteenth

[43] Aristotle maintains that images are *necessary* for thought, but for him the thinking process is psychologically not the same thing as the images.

[44] Ogden, 1923.

T.—9

century was cast in too rigid a mould. The "thought-element" of Bühler was a product of the pulverizing tendency and technique of the times. That it will survive, as a descriptive concept, at least in the form in which Bühler left it, seems to the writer to be doubtful. On the other hand, it seems probable that the psychology of the future will include among its descriptive concepts something very close to the *Bewusstheit*, the non-sensory "awareness". This much we may take as progressively and experimentally established, or perhaps confirmed, by the experimentalists of Würzburg.

Concerning the Würzburg doctrine of the mechanism of thought, little has been said in this critique. Little opposition was raised to it at the time. The *Aufgabe* and the *Determining Tendencies* have been more or less carelessly absorbed into psychological tradition. But here again it is improbable that the last word has been said. It has been intimated in the last chapter that these two concepts are subject to serious criticism. More will be said on this point later. Here also the Würzburg psychologists must be given their due. Before their time it had long been recognized that thought was controlled; but to them belongs the credit of giving this recognition experimental status. They have given us laboratory demonstration of the fact that thought is directive. The fundamental fact will stand, however much its description may be modified in the future.

Thus ends the discussion of the Würzburgers as such. Under both fundamental headings, that of the material and the mechanism of thought, they effected a significant and indeed a profound contribution and clarification. Their work is truly a milestone in the history of experimental psychology.

NOTE ON UNCONSCIOUS RECOGNITION, AND UNCONSCIOUS MEANING
(see note 36 of this Chapter)

There are two points that should be noted. First, Titchener maintains here that after repetition, apparently, recognition may be effected or meaning "carried" in a "purely physiological way"; that is, without consciousness. This seems today a misuse of words, especially for one who professed that psychology is the study of experience, considered as depending on the subject. It would imply, I think, that when I go home tonight and shut the door, I "recognize" the door as well as react to it. The man in the street would say that I don't have to "recognize" the door but simply open it, and he would be right. There is certainly no conscious recognition. Nor when I glance down as I type is there conscious recognition of the keys. To assert that there is *unconscious* recognition, or physiological recognition, seems completely formalistic. Surely there was either conscious recognition, "unanalysed", or else recognition (together with many other conscious processes) had disappeared through repetition.

Secondly, in this as in the further case which Titchener discusses where there is no conscious correlate at all of meaning, not even such a "quiver of the stomach", we should probably say nowadays that Titchener had acquired a discriminated conditioned reflex. (He automatically wrote "yes", when confronted with a grey he had seen before.) The fact that a response is included in an experiment on recognition, does not mean that such response necessarily involves recognition. When Titchener claims that "a word you understand is experienced otherwise than a nonsense word" because of a *plus* that "lies on the side of the unrecognized, the unknown", he is simply changing the co-ordinates of the problem; we now have to discuss the psychology of the *unrecognized* (p. 179). Titchener himself did, in fact, seem uneasy about all this (p. 180). One who has in early days fallen under his spell feels uneasy at thus criticizing him when he cannot reply!

CHAPTER V

THE WORK OF SELZ

THE WORK OF the Würzburg group may be considered as a reaction against the associational hypothesis and its correlative sensational thesis. It has been seen that the attempt was made to replace sensationism by an empirically grounded doctrine of imageless thought, while at the same time, on the side of mechanism, Watt and Ach supplemented the classical hypothesis of Reproductive Tendencies by the Task and the Determining Tendency. Bühler's theory made necessary the rejection of associationism, since for him the constituent elements of thought were, somewhat dramatically, not associative reproductions. Indeed, none of the Würzburgers made any attempt to explain the mechanism by which imageless thought appeared. Association, "reproductive tendencies", were precluded; and in common with the others of the school, Bühler failed to provide an alternative mechanism. In general, it may be said that the Würzburg school accepted associationism and explicitly denied its adequacy to explain the facts without the assumption of the supplementary mechanisms of Task and Determining Tendency. Implicitly, also, the doctrine of imageless thought contradicted associationism.

Experimental Method of Selz

Selz's experiments were avowedly a continuation of the Würzburg work, and, indeed, Külpe and Bühler were among his subjects. His general aim was to provide a completely non-associational theory of thinking,[1] and thus, in fact, to remedy the gap which the Würzburg doctrine of imageless thought had left. While the Würzburgers had maintained that the associational mechanism was necessary but inadequate, he rejected it altogether as the fundamental mechanism of thinking.

Nine subjects were used. The method of partially constrained association was taken over from Watt and Messer, but with the modification that the *Aufgabe* was varied from experiment to experi-

[1] By this is not meant that Selz does not admit association; he does, but not as the fundamental mechanism of thinking. See, e.g., Selz, 1913, pp. 51, 98.

ment. It will be remembered that in Watt's and Messer's experiments repetition of the same *Aufgabe* with different stimulus words had resulted in the gradual disappearance of the *Aufgabe* from consciousness. Selz's aim, on the contrary, was to bring the *Aufgabe* and the processes associated with it under the closest possible introspective examination, and the variation of *Aufgabe* was planned to this end. For the same reason unusual tasks were set, with the object of inducing genuine and protracted thought. Sometimes the same *Aufgabe* was used a number of times on the same stimulus-word. Time was taken with a stop-watch, and subjects warned not to hurry their responses but to take care to give a good response. *Aufgabe* and Stimulus-word were presented in the form of cards with typewritten words on them, the *Aufgabe* being given in the form of a question, such as: Co-ordinate? Hunt; Superordinate? Burial.[2] The subjects were asked for careful description of any palpable experiences, and were specifically questioned concerning the appearance of these during designated stages of the whole process. All subjects but one were ignorant of the purpose of the investigation, and the single exception had only a general idea of what was being done. Care was taken to avoid leading questions, especially concerning the relation between the *Aufgabe* and Stimulus-word. Twenty-eight *Aufgaben* were used in the main series, giving 748 trials on seven of the subjects, the experimental procedure being slightly varied with the other two.

General Results

Selz starts where Watt and Ach left off. He considers as established the existence of Ach's *Bewusstheit*, the imageless awareness that something or other is the case. By means of the conceptions of the philosopher Meinong, this was developed into the doctrine of the imageless *Wissen*, the knowledge or knowing which is the consciousness of a relational fact.[3] A relational fact is defined as "the fact that certain objects stand in a certain relation". It must be distinguished from the objects on the one side and the relation on the other, for it includes both the objects and the relation. For example, *Frank Smith is the father of John Smith* would be the relational fact. It is to be distinguished both from the objects, Frank and John Smith,

[2] Other examples of *Aufgaben* given by Selz are: Whole? Part? Subordinate? Description! Definition! Ibid., pp. 12, 13.

[3] *Sachverhältnis* (=*das in einer bestimmten Beziehung Stehen bestimmter Gegenstände*) ; 1913, p. 34. The word *Sachverhalt* has been translated as "atomic fact". See Wittgenstein, 1922, p. 31.

which stand in the relation, and from the relation (father-son relationship) in which they stand. The *consciousness* of the fact that
Frank and John stand in the relation is the *Wissen*, or knowing.
The term object is taken over from the philosopher Meinong. It is
used in a very wide sense, as equivalent to any object of the mind,
and may thus be an abstract or general term, or even a relation itself
(object of higher order[4]). According to Selz, we possess many such
knowings. They may be actual, as when we are actually conscious of
the relational fact in question; or they may be potential. I may
potentially have the knowledge that Frank is the father of John; but
the knowledge may not be in my consciousness at any particular
moment, as when I am thinking of some other topic. In the same way,
my driver's licence certifies to my potential ability to drive a car,
which, however, I am not doing at this moment. When I start my
car and drive down the street, I may be said to practise my ability;
Selz would say I actualize my potential ability. When I am asked by
my garage man how many pounds' pressure I wish in the tyres and
answer "thirty-five", Selz says, correspondingly, that I actualize a
potential *Wissen*.[5]

According to Selz, his experimental results prove that reproductive
thinking, the kind mainly investigated by Watt and Ach, consists
largely[6] in the actualization of such a potential *Wissen*, and is not
produced by reproductive tendencies working together with an
Aufgabe or *Determining Tendency*. An example of an introspection
will illustrate the point:

"Parson—Co-ordinate? Chaplain." (2·4 secs.)

"I read the words successively with understanding. Immediately
came the consciousness that something co-ordinate was very
familiar. Then came the word Chaplain, internally spoken. It is
certain that the consciousness of the familiarity of a solution preceded the, as yet, uneffected appearance of the word Chaplain."[7]
The subject, says Selz, had the potential "*Wissen*" (imageless), that
Chaplain is co-ordinate to Parson. The existence of this *Wissen* was
shown by the vague "consciousness that something co-ordinate was
very familiar", but it still remains at a relatively potential level until
the appearance of the word Chaplain. When this appears, it is fully
actualized.

[4] *Gegenstand höherer Ordnung.*
[5] I.e. of a *Sachverhältnis* (= there is usually thirty-five pounds' pressure in my
tyres).
[6] 1913, p. 83.			[7] Ibid., p. 32.

It should be noticed that the *Wissen* is a unitary consciousness of the unitary, indissoluble fact that *Chaplain is co-ordinate with Parson*. It cannot be split up into knowledge of Parson, knowledge of Chaplain, and knowledge of the relationship between them. It is an organic complex involving all three, namely the *consciousness that Chaplain is co-ordinate, etc.* Further, the word Chaplain does not appear as the result of reproductive tendencies belonging to Parson; it appears as the result of the actualization of the unitary *Wissen*, the existence of which is shown by its effect on consciousness before the word appears. In reproductive thinking, then, a relational whole is reproduced, not a conglomerate of individual images or "presentations". Thus a subject was asked: "Ballot—two chief varieties." He answers (quoted in part): "Immediate appeal to memory. This search for something known already in experience is totally different from the cases where I seek an original solution of the *Aufgabe*. In this case, it comes over me that I *know something*[8] and I seek to ascertain what I know. . . . There was a complete absence of presentations . . . a vague consciousness that these two magnitudes, i.e. classes containing the two kinds of ballot, secret and direct, divide into some other kinds of groups. . . . No presentations (subjectively sure!)." The "answer" given was "direct and secret" (i.e. ballot). Selz comments: This "illustrates particularly clearly the occurrence of reproductions which cannot be derived from the recall, by presentations or complexes of such, of other presentations which were formerly present with them in consciousness. It was not the case that the word-presentations 'direct' and 'secret' or the discrete meanings corresponding to them, viz. 'direct and secret ballot', lead to the reproduction of the presentational complex 'direct and indirect'; but the relational totality attained by the trial-and-error[9] solution, viz. 'the direct and secret ballot are two principal varieties of ballot', actualizes the *Wissen* that these two kinds of ballot are members of different classes of ballot. So that it was not presentations but relational wholes that were . . . reproduced." And "it comes over them first of all that they *know* something and they then seek to ascertain *what it is they know*"[10] (present writer's italics).

Thus Selz's answer to the associational theory of thought as taken over and supplemented by the Würzburgers was this. Experiment shows that so far from consisting of the recall of an elementary presentation, or discrete group of such, by means of reproductive tendencies adherent to the stimulus-word, reproduction consists essentially in the bringing into consciousness of a total unitary and latently present relational fact. Experience of such a relational fact is imageless.

What causes the potential *Wissen* to become actual? Selz has rejected the idea of a reproductive tendency residing in the stimulus-word, so he must look elsewhere for a moving or energizing force. He finds it first of all in the tendency of a complex towards completion. A complex, he claims, tends to be completed if a part of it is given, or if a scheme or pattern anticipating the complex is given.[11] Thus a candidate in an oral examination is trying to remember the name Melanchthon. A kindly examiner gives the first letter *M*, then the second *e*, and the third *l*. As a result of this assistance the whole word is remembered. At this point we shall omit Selz's polemic against association, and proceed to his explanation. By the presentation of the syllable *Mel*, "The consciousness of the word sought is changed from the consciousness of a not more closely defined word to the consciousness of a word beginning with *Mel*. . . . We must think of it as though the empty scheme of a concrete word is partly filled out by the insertion at its beginning of the sounds spoken in anticipation. . . ."[12]

The presentation of a part of the complex or of an "anticipatory scheme" is not, however, enough to bring about the completion of a complex in the manner demanded by reproductive thinking. These are ordinarily *determined*, the phrase being taken with a slight alteration from the "Determining Tendencies" of Ach. The determination, to use Selz's phrase, comes from the *Aufgabe*. Thus Selz lays down three laws of complex-completion.

(1) A complex-part, given as a unitarily working whole, has the tendency to bring about the reproduction of the whole complex.

(2) A scheme anticipating a complex in all its constituents has the tendency to bring about the reproduction of the whole complex.

(3) The determination directed towards the completion of a schematically anticipated complex causes [13] the tendency to completion of the whole complex.[14]

The *Wissen* is of course impalpable, imageless. Nevertheless, these laws apply to relational wholes as well, and in particular to the *Wissen* as a unitary relational complex. In fact, without the influence of the unitary underlying *Wissen*, the completions involved in the conventional *Aufgabe* experiments would not take place.

[11] 1913, p. 128.   [12] 1913, p. 114.
[13] *begründet*,   [14] 1913, p. 128,

The Total Aufgabe

It is perhaps in his treatment of the *Aufgabe* that Selz has made his greatest contribution. Selz's rejection of the associational scheme implies a corresponding rejection of the dual action of *Aufgabe* and reproductive tendencies, with the former exercising a directive influence over the latter. Instead he must find a basis for his unitarily functioning *Wissen*. This he finds in the notion of a unitary *Aufgabe*, compounded from the *Aufgabe* proper of Watt, and the stimulus-word. He first proceeds to show how such a unitary *Aufgabe* is formed. An example may be given: "Co-ordinate? Hunt. *Rowing*.[15] (12·8″). I read both words in succession, understood *Aufgabe* and stimulus-word. I remember we have spoken of the meaning of the word co-ordinate. I related the *Aufgabe* to the stimulus-word, remembering the preceding conversation. Then I directed my attention upon the meaning of the word hunt; I knew what hunt is [that is, in general] as soon as I understood the stimulus-word. I then sought a superordinate idea to hunt, so that I might thence find a co-ordinate. I sought for a long time; then I suddenly found the superordinate idea *Sport*." Selz says: the *Aufgabe* and stimulus-word are each of them understood in general. Then the subject forms the unitary consciousness of the total *Aufgabe*, "that a co-ordinate is to be found to hunt" by relating the stimulus-word hunt and the general task, to find a co-ordinate. Thereafter follows a narrower determination of the stimulus-word. It is not, says Selz, a matter of replacing the task *co-ordinate* by the abstract task *superordinate*, and allowing the reproductive tendencies attaching to the stimulus-word *hunt* to function; but rather "the application of the solution method, of determining a co-ordinate by a superordinate follows from the formation of a total sub-*Aufgabe*".

Another example:

"Poem—Superordinate? *Work of Art*. (2.4 secs.)

Once more, immediately a full understanding of the *full Aufgabe*.[16] Then again an intensive glance, the symbolic fixation of that which is sought; then at once the flitting memory of Art, Poetry, etc., appeared. The word *Art*, I think in auditory-motor terms. Then the thought that I cannot subsume poetry under art but only under artistic production. With this, I am certain, no words and images; then I said, 'work of Art' ".[17] On this Selz comments: "It is not the understanding of the stimulus-word nor the understanding of the

Aufgabe in the narrower sense [i.e. the sense in which Watt used the term], alone, nor both of these taken together in isolation, but the understanding of the total *Aufgabe* to which is here attached the characteristic search, which is often accompanied, in B's case, by a symbolic fixation of the goal, a 'setting of the eyes upon Infinity'."[18]

A third example:

"Bite: Cause? *Dog*. (No time given.)

Only a general understanding with bite. Then, *as soon as* I had read the *Aufgabe the search was on*. I had also a picture of a leg with a wound on it, and saw nothing else. Then 'dog' came to me in the form of an idea, with the consciousness: *dogs bite*." "The stimulus word alone has no effect beyond a general understanding. But as soon as the *Aufgabe* is read, there begins the search to which, as with another subject, a special consciousness of meaning directly attaches itself, accompanied by images. This shows the bite in the light of something caused,[19] namely a wound (thus not the preliminary to the bite), and thereby makes ready for the actualization of the *Wissen* of something which causes such bite-wounds. The actualization of the *Wissen* comes out very clearly from the fact that it is not the word 'Dog' alone which enters consciousness but the *Wissen* of the whole relational fact, that dogs bite." Thus the *Aufgabe* in the narrower sense has a "blanket quality", which is made more specific only when the stimulus-word is understood.

The formation of the total *Aufgabe* is demonstrated partly by the subjects' direct description, partly indirectly from the same descriptions. Among the relevant facts are (*a*) the subject's indifference to the stimulus-word before the *Aufgabe* is understood, and heightened interest thereafter; (*b*) appearance of images only after the *Aufgabe* is understood, such images being then relevant to the *Aufgabe*, (*c*) the "blanket" nature of the *Aufgabe* when it precedes the stimulus-word, (*d*) the appearance of an "aim-consciousness" with an object corresponding to the total *Aufgabe*.

That the total *Aufgabe* is a new creation, so to speak, is shown by the fact that the meaning of both the stimulus-word and the Task may have to be modified to suit the new totality in which they are to function. Thus one observer, confronted with *Krebs*[20]: *cause or effect*, reported that he understood the word at first in a zoological sense, with a visual image. "I said to myself, . . . *Krebs* must have another

[18] 1913, p. 198.
[19] *Stellt den Biss unter den Gesichtspunkt eines verursachten*, 1913, p. 199.
[20] Either "crab" or "cancer".

meaning"; and finally the meaning *cancer* came to him. In the same way, the Task may be modified to suit the stimulus-word, although on account of the material used these cases were not so frequent or clear-cut as the others.

The total *Aufgabe* was, of course, foreshadowed by Ach's *purpose*, which is brought about by the establishment of relations between aim- and object-presentations, and which creates "sets" otherwise termed the determining tendencies.[21] It is, however, Selz's great merit that by ridding the description of the presentational terminology, he has expressed the fundamental fact of synthesis in terms acceptable to modern psychology. He has, further, taken the germ-idea and developed it into a doctrine firmly established on experimental fact. It is one of Selz's great achievements to have brought out clearly the integrative nature of thinking. The doctrine of the integrative total *Aufgabe* is one instance of this general treatment.

Summary of Selz's Treatment of Reproductive Thinking

Thus Selz directly rejects the atomistic hypothesis whereby, through the clash of discrete associative bonds (reproductive tendencies) and directive agencies (determining tendencies, *Aufgaben*), a response (idea) is caused to rise. In its place he substitutes the hypothesis that the "stimulus-word" and the "*Aufgabe*", in Watt's sense, are integrated into a unitary total *Aufgabe*. As the result of (*a*) the determination and (*b*) the schematic consciousness of the relational fact, both of which it brings, the total *Aufgabe* initiates the general intellectual operation of complex completion. The result is the actualization of a unitary *Wissen*, or consciousness of a relational fact.

Productive Thought

The same general rule holds for productive thinking, whereby new mental products are achieved by contrast with the sheer reproduction of past experience. In productive thinking "the actualization of mental operations or solution methods, that is to say . . . processes of a reproductive nature can give rise to productive mental work" (Selz 1924, p. 16; 1922, pp. xi and 528, 529). The *Aufgabe* with the determination (determining tendencies) which it contains, initiates certain special mental operations, already in the repertoire, which lead to the solution of the problem. These operations he calls Means (i.e. means to the end of the solution), and an important part of the process of solution is accordingly that of the Finding of Means. "All general operations of the Finding of Means have this in

[21] Ach, 1905, pp. 217 ff., 224.

common, that they are introduced by the schematic anticipation of operations which lead to a determinate result. . . . The special operations which are being sought are indirectly determined in this anticipation by their consequence, which constitutes the goal; that is to say, they are indirectly determined as means to this end" (ibid., pp. 528, 529).[22] We may say, then, that for Selz a problem is a "schematically anticipated complex". The final solution is, of course, not given explicitly in the data, or there would be no problem. But there is a sense in which it is given implicitly, in that it is known to stand in certain "general and expressly given" relations to the data.

Thus the problem is a set of data with a gap; and the effect of the determination is to initiate previously applied methods to fill the gap. So that the newness of productive thinking consists essentially in the application of such previously applied means to new material.

The three chief cases of the Finding of Means are named by Selz the methods of *routine actualization* of (already known) means, of *abstraction of means*, and *productive utilization* of previously established Abstractions,[23] respectively. The discussion will be confined to a consideration of the second—the operation of the Abstraction of a Means.

"In this case," says Selz, "those subsidiary intellectual operations are installed which lead to the discovery of new methods of solution [in contrast to the utilization of previously used methods, as in case 1]. These operations all end by the springing into consciousness of the means-end relation between the aim and a determinate method of solution. This [relation] emerges from a totality, is abstracted from this totality. For this reason the process receives its name, viz. that of the *Abstraction of Means*. As with all determined operations of abstraction, in the operation of abstraction of means the direction of the abstractive process is determined by a corresponding schematic anticipation of the result of the abstraction. In the case of Abstraction of Means the result of abstraction is schematically anticipated as an, as yet unknown, solution-method which will effect a known aim, viz. to bring about a determinate partial result."[24]

This he illustrates by the method which Franklin used to "bring down the lightning from the clouds". Here the aim was to bring the thunderstorm electricity to earth. To do this, he must make a con-

---

[22] The above use of "determined", "determination", must not be confused with the use of the same words in relation to "determining tendencies".
[23] The last case is an abbreviation of Selz's own statement (1924, p. 27).
[24] 1924, p. 21.

nection between the cloud and the earth. That is to say, he must find X, the result of which will be that such a connection is established. X is not included in the data,[25] otherwise, as we have seen, there would be no problem. The data[26] do include the general aim, viz. to bring down electricity, and also the partial result of effecting the physical cloud-earth connection. The data also include the relation in which X stands to the aim (X is a means towards attaining the aim), and the relation in which X stands to the partial results (X will have the result of making the earth-cloud connection). Thus we have the following data: Aim, to bring down thunder-cloud electricity to earth; partial result, R_1, to make a connection between earth and cloud. *Wanted:* something, X, with the following relations also given: (*a*) X will bring about the Aim, (*b*) X will bring about the partial result. (See figures 1 and 2.) So that the combined data, Aim, partial result, relations form a schematic anticipation of the whole complex, a set of data with a gap. The gap is filled by finding X the kite, which fulfils these conditions. The process is then one of determined complex completion, the *Aufgabe* supplying the necessary determining tendencies.

The operation by which the gap is filled is called one of determined abstraction, because the fact that a kite may form a connection between earth and cloud must be abstracted from the observable facts connected with the flying of kites. (See figures 1 and 2.) Thus "the direction of the abstractive process is determined by a corresponding schematic anticipation of the result of the abstraction" (*vide supra*).

SELZ

Figure 1

Schematic anticipation in the operation of abstraction of means.

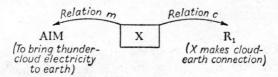

Franklin's aim was to bring thunderstorm electricity to earth. (AIM.) He knew that he needed to make a connection between the cloud and the earth, i.e. that he needed something (X) *the result of which would be that*

[25] At least, it is not included in the data in the sense of being recognized as being in the requisite relation of connection between the cloud and the earth.

[26] The term is used by a slight extension to include those factors in his possession after the partial result has been seen.

such a connection was made. (R_1 or partial result.) This *something*, X, is not explicitly given in the data; but it is known (*a*) that it is a means towards the aim (relation *m* to the aim), (*b*) that it will cause (*c*) the partial result of making the connection, etc. (relation *c* to R_1). Thus the data include Aim and R_1 explicitly, together with the relations *m* and *c* in which the missing X stands to these. The solution is found when this complex is completed by filling in X.

Figure 2

Figure 1 completed by "kite".

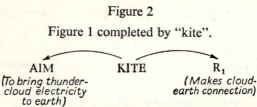

AIM   KITE R_1
(To bring thunder-
cloud electricity
to earth)   (Makes cloud-
earth connection)

The determining tendencies inherent in the *Aufgabe* bring a tendency towards the completion of the schematically anticipated complex ("complex with a gap") of figure 1. This is effected by the operation of *Abstraction of Means* (abstraction, from the sight of kites flying, of the fact that they may serve as a link from earth to the cloud). Thus this operation is effected as the result of the process of the determined completion of a complex. The "solution" (kite) may, as often happens, follow from a chance sight of a flying kite after the incompleted complex is set up.

The other two main cases are explained on similar principles.

Selz gives two other illustrations, apart from the experimental data from which he claims this general scheme to be an induction, and apart from the analysis of Köhler's experiments on apes, which, he maintains, exemplify his theory. The first concerns Faraday's discovery of the induction current. Here the aim was to produce electricity from a magnet. The partial result was presumably, though this is not so stated, to cause a deflection of a galvanometer needle. Happening one day to be moving a magnetic core in and out of a coil connected with a galvanometer, the scientist observed a deflection in the attached galvanometer. The abstraction of means was made: "a *moving magnet* produces a current in a closed circuit". Similarly, Darwin's discovery of the origin of species was effected by the abstraction of the idea of struggle from Malthus's book on population.

Criticism of Selz's Theory

Selz's theory, of which the foregoing is a brief statement, is worked out in greater detail than any other experimentally grounded theory of thinking. His general thesis that an associatory scheme, even one as modified by the Würzburgers, is not adequate to explain all the facts, seems to be established beyond question. Apart from this negative, critical contribution, however, his general hypothesis does not seem to bear detailed examination. This is particularly true of his theory of productive thinking.

The main criticism can be briefly stated thus. Productive thinking is said to be ultimately brought about by the completion of a schematically anticipated complex. But if the word "productive" is to have any meaning, the essence of productive thought must be that the complex, which is the end result of that thought, is not in existence at the beginning of the process of solution and *has never been in existence*. For if it had been, the process would not be productive but reproductive. It will be remembered that we are dealing with complexes of experience. Thus the term completion of a complex, on which the whole argument depends, is really a false description. For productive thinking results not in complex-*completion* but in complex-formation; that is to say, in the *formation* of a *new complex*. To take his own example, Franklin's final solution consisted in the formation of the experienced complex *thunder-cloud electricity may be conducted to earth by a kite*. Before the solution came, that unitary judgment did not exist in Franklin's mind, nor, as far as we know, in anybody else's. The terms: "thunder-cloud electricity", "earth-connection", did exist but, on Selz's own showing, as disconnected elements. Adding the *desire* to connect the two does not make the two essentially discrete terms or factors into a complex or unity. It is as false to speak here of the completion of the unity as it would be to speak of the completion of a bridge by joining the two sides of a stream with a plank. The bridge is created, not completed. The complex is created, not completed.

The use of the term "complex-completion" is justified in the case of what Selz calls reproductive thinking; for here the experiential unity has existed, and has, according to Selz's theory, left its imprint, so to speak, in the possession of a potential *Wissen*, which, as a unity again, is actualized in the process of thinking. Here is no creation of a unity, but the reproduction of one.

If it be said, as Selz actually does say, that the operation is reproduced, while the material on which it works is novel,[27] the answer is that to use a known method does not produce novel results unless the method is used in a new context; that is, in new relations. To use a thermometer in order to measure the temperature of a record-making heat spell would not be considered by anybody to be an act of

[27] See, e.g., Selz, 1927.

productive thinking. On the other hand, the use of a thermometer for the first time, in relation to the temperature of the human organism, in the clinical relation, so to speak, would be so considered, because the familiar instrument is here used in a new context. That is to say, unless the old method is used to form part of a novel unity, the ensuing thought is not productive.[28] Of course Selz's theory does not admit of the old methods being related in a new way to the total complex, for its essence is that the schematically anticipated complex consists of known terms and known relations, with only one gap, namely an already known operation, to fill in. One has the uneasy feeling also that Selz has confused the two meanings of the word "anticipation", which can signify (a) mere priority in time, (b) psychological expectancy.

Further, Selz's scheme, comprising aim and partial result, together with cause-effect and means-end relations, does not provide such an already known but incomplete complex. These relations are much too general to have the particular psychological function which the theory demands. They simply pose the problem, and in a highly artificial way. In fact, Selz's diagrams really do no more than state the problem. They do not give any basis for understanding the psychology of its solution. Admittedly Franklin wished to find some method by which the earth and the cloud could be connected. Such a statement of the general problem of thinking was made by William James in 1890.[29] As an analysis, in general terms, of the form assumed by the process of thought at a certain stage, it is valuable. As a schema showing the working of particular acts of thought, it is as valueless as was the general statement of the problem of medicine —given the disease, problem, to find the remedy—actually proposed by a French physician—in showing the means by which a particular disease is healed. There is some divergence of opinion as to the nature of the distinction between logic and psychology. At least, however, it will probably be admitted universally that logic deals with the process of thought by the use of a greater degree of abstraction—abstraction from the judging person, abstraction at times almost entirely from formal content, as is the case with symbolic logic. From the standpoint of the degree of abstraction involved, then, it may be said that Selz's theory approaches the logical rather than the psychological method of description. This distinction is not to be stressed. What is desirable to stress is that to say that a problem

[28] I think I owe this point to Dr. N. R. F. Maier.
[29] James, 1890, Chapter XXII.

is solved by filling in an intermediate, which is connected with the data by the cause-effect relation, is of too great generality to provide any particular psychological understanding of the processes involved.

Reflexoidal Co-ordination

Thus Selz's theory does not succeed in solving the psychological problem which asks: what are the conditions, relating to the thinking individual, under which certain propositions, relatively independent of the thinker, are established for the first time, certain novel courses of action initiated? He has failed to solve it because his whole hypothesis is ultimately one of the reinstatement of the past as contrasted with the creation of the new.[30] His is one more endeavour to show how novelty can be created by manipulation of standardized, pre-existing units. One immediately thinks of the *reflex, conditioned-reflex* hypothesis as an objective counterpart. In fact, Selz insisted on the parallel between his description of the thinking process and the physiological reflex. The whole process, by which the determination contained in the *Aufgabe* initiates mental operations such as that of "determined abstraction of means", is said to be of a reflex-like or "reflexoidal" nature. The two chief passages are quoted.

"Physiology has for a long time been exploring a system of specific reactions in the reflexes; for it is exactly characteristic of these that there is a constant, unique co-ordination with a specific releasing stimulus. Thus the effect of a corrosive fluid on a definite spot on the skin of a decapitated spinal frog forms the specific stimulus for the wiping reflex. The entry of light in the human eye automatically causes the narrowing of the pupil (pupillary reflex). In diametrical opposition to the play of associations which varies according to the constellation present, and which the theory of diffuse reproductions has in mind, we find everywhere fixed, undisplaceable co-ordinations, which assure a biologically useful, conservative response to stimulation, and turn out to be a constant regulative factor in the vital processes. Using the reflexes as an instance, we may call the kind of co-ordination which occurs with specific reactions *reflexoidal co-ordinations*" (1924, p. 10). And in a little more detail:

"We have in the reflexes phylogenetically established co-ordinations between sensory stimuli of a determined kind and motor operations, which are mediated by the central nervous system and,

[30] Selz, 1924, p. 30.

moreover, without concomitant events of consciousness. On account of their relationship with the reflexes the aforesaid co-ordinations, which also comprise co-ordinations between stimuli and intellectual operations, may be termed reflexoid or reflexoidal (reflex-like). We shall understand by reflexoidal co-ordination every co-ordination between a stimulus (that is to say, any occasion for reaction) and a motor or intellectual operation, which has for its result that the stimulus effects the release of the operation.[31] The reflexes are thus special cases of reflexoidal co-ordinations. Reflexoidal co-ordinations differ from associations (in the usual, narrower sense), in that the co-ordination is not established by the experienced succession of stimulus and operation, but can precede it. From the preceding deductions[32] there follows the following law of the determined origination of reflexoidal co-ordinations: as the result of the experienced relation between a fixed stimulus and a fixed operation which is established in a determination, there arise reflexoidal co-ordinations, in that an already established operation is co-ordinated with another stimulus (first case); or in that (a) by anticipation, a fundamental operation experiences a new specialization, or (b) operations already to hand are joined to make a combined operation, and the operation newly constituted in this manner is co-ordinated with a fixed stimulus."[33]

There have been many attempts to reduce the higher types of psychic and behavioural process to a unit of fixed co-ordination with external stimulation. Such an attempt was, indeed, part of the original behaviourist programme, where thinking was claimed to be largely the manipulation of verbal symbols, with an admixture of visceral and implicit manual reactions, words were said to be acquired, like all other learned reactions, by the mechanism of the conditioned reflex, and a situation said to be "analysable into a complex group of stimuli" which can be "added to or subtracted from".[34] In another context I have shown the inadequacy of a behavioural psychology that is based on the reflex and conditioned-reflex formula; and, indeed, modern psychological theory is fast

[31] *der Reiz die Operation zur Auslösung bringt.*
[32] *Ausführungen.*
[33] 1922, pp. 569-70.
[34] Watson, 1931, Chapter X; 1919, p. 8; 1920. Bechterew, 1926, Chapter XXII, gives an analysis of the "creative process from the reflexological standpoint", and so claims that Bühler's results can be brought into agreement with his system, which bases all mental events on reflexes and conditioned reflexes (ibid., p. 385-86).

being forced by the experimental evidence to re-examine the pre-suppositions of such a simplified formula. Here it is only necessary to point out that the simple reflex, where a completely defined single re-action follows inevitably from a stimulus that is qualitatively and quantitatively defined, only occurs under very special, and indeed limiting, conditions,[35] and that Sherrington the greatest living authority, has referred to the simple reflex as a "convenient abstrac-tion."[36] If a behaviouristic system based on units with a one-to-one co-ordination of response and stimulus is unworkable, one which is based on such a co-ordination of psychic process and stimulus is preposterous. The conditions which in Selz's term "release" the mental operation of thinking the syllogism "All men are mortal, Socrates is a man, therefore, etc.," may be the presentation of the first two sentences in the form of print, of typescript, of hand-writing in pen and ink, or in chalk or a blackboard; it may further be an auditory stimulus, spoken either in a woman's or a man's voice. Conceivably it may not be of a linguistic nature at all. One could easily find many "equivalent" stimuli other than those men-tioned, all of which would set off the same mental process. The fixed, undisplaceable co-ordination between the intellectual operation and the stimulus simply does not exist. If it be answered that these are alternative stimuli or occasions for reaction, and that for each of these alternatives there is a co-ordination between the intellectual operation and this particular stimulus, then Selz's statement means no more than that an intellectual operation will be released on cer-tain occasions, and will not be released by others. This is possibly true but not very illuminating. And serious objections should prob-ably be brought, even against this relatively modest statement. Can an external event truly be said to *release* an intellectual operation? Is this not to cause the environmental tail to wag the psychological dog? Is there any rational sense in which it may be said that the sight of certain events in the physical world *released* the opera-tions by which Lord Maxwell obtained the famous Maxwell's equations?

Selz's reflexoidal theory of mental operations is in the same class with the conditioned-reflex theory of Watson and the reflexological theory of Bechterew. The trend of psychological research during the last twenty-five years[37] has brought to many psychologists the

---

[35] Humphrey, 1933, Chapter IX and, in particular, pp. 229–30.
[36] Sherrington, 1906, Chapter VIII.
[37] Written in 1950.

progressively growing conviction that such mechanistic hypotheses cannot explain the facts.[38]

So much for the Selzian theory of intellectual operations. To the correlative problem, namely that of the determination of thinking, Selz has contributed little. Having rejected the associational theory of the mechanism of thinking, according to which the elements of a process of thought are caused to arise by virtue of the reproductive tendencies, it has already been seen that Selz must look elsewhere for an energizing principle. This he has been seen to find in the determining tendency of Ach and the *Aufgabe* of Watt. The results of these investigators he assumes without more ado. He assumes that the energizing principle is "determining tendencies" or a "determination", which is Selz's own derivative, springing somehow from the *Aufgabe*. But for Ach the ultimate energizing principle is the reproductive tendency, which Selz has rejected together with the rest of the associational scheme. Consequently Selz is not justified in taking over without more ado the term determining tendencies, which, in its original context, denotes a purely regulative function; regulative, that is, of an energizing source which he has rejected. Further, it has been seen that according to Watt's theory the task and the reproductive tendency both contribute energy. With the energy of the reproductive tendency gone, the sole moving principle of mental processes must reside in the task. This is apparently what Selz has in mind. His theory is, in fact, apparently what has been already named a "task-dynamic" one, though he never examines the point. For example, he equates the determination with a modification of the will but without further discussion. This hardly seems satisfactory today. It is nowadays not enough to speak of Will or Determination as though the terms of themselves provide sufficient explanation. In fact, Selz has not given any reason why the mental events which he so carefully describes should ever take place, except to say that they are determined or "released". If he wished to provide a task-dynamic theory, he should have elaborated such a theory instead of assuming it, especially when he was attacking another theory which did provide an explanation of the facts. The non-explanatory nature of his statements is, of course, obscured by the fact that he made over the term determination from a context in

[38] Lashley, e.g., has expressed himself as being against the strict conditioned reflex theory. "In the study of cerebral functions we seem to have reached a point where the reflex theory is no longer profitable either for the formulation of problems or for an understanding of the phenomena of integration" (1930, p. 12). The dispute over the "continuity" of learning is of course a sequel.

which a definite meaning had been assigned to it, a meaning which, however, he must reject together with the rest of the associational theory. Throughout Selz's account there is great confusion between the Determining Tendency of Ach, which is inadmissible on his theory, and the Task of Watt which, without the reproductive tendency with which it works, is equally inadmissible, at least without explicit treatment such as Selz does not give.

The Contribution of Selz

This account may seem to constitute rather a step-motherly treatment of what is, after all, a notable research. The two major works, published in 1913 and 1922 respectively, together constitute just over a thousand pages of closely reasoned and carefully written exposition. The experimental method was an ingenious modification of that bequeathed to Selz by his acknowledged predecessors, the Würzburgers. The positive contribution is great. It lies first of all in the confirmation of the thesis of the Würzburgers that thinking may proceed independently of images. The second contribution, of more importance, perhaps, because it was largely original, is the emphasis which his experimental results laid on the idea of total integration in the process of thinking. After the masterly exposition of the formation and function of the *Gesamtaufgabe* contained in the volume of 1913, it is impossible for any serious psychology of thinking to proceed on the assumption that thought is the clash of discrete elements. It is problematic whether the rather rarified doctrine of the Relational Fact, with the other implications belonging to the Austrian school, will remain as a permanent part of the psychological picture. This is a set of distinctions and a terminology which are primarily the product of the speculative rather than the experimental method, and psychologists are not likely to accept them until they have been subjected to further experimental verification. In the opinion of the writer, it is for his positive doctrine of the *Aufgabe* and his critically experimental attack on associationism that Selz is most likely to be remembered. He is the first psychologist to incorporate an explicitly non-associational doctrine into an experimentally induced psychology of thinking.

CHAPTER VI

THE GESTALT THEORY OF THOUGHT

General Characteristics of the Gestalt Theory

AT THE PRESENT TIME, the Gestalt theory of thinking consti- tutes a programme rather than a fulfilment. Nevertheless, the programme is sufficiently suggestive, sufficiently developed, and, in part at least, in sufficiently clear outline to merit somewhat detailed consideration. It is well known that the Gestalt theory re- jects many of the conventional concepts which were assumed by those whose work was described in previous chapters of this book. Thus the terms sensation and association are rejected (Koffka, 1922), mainly on the ground that they imply atomistic collocations of mental states which are essentially unchanged by the co-existence of other mental states with which they are experienced (associated), just as the chemical atom of hydrogen is regarded as essentially un- changed by the fact that it is associated with other atoms to form water or ammonia. Psychological analysis which proceeds on the assumption of such self-subsistent mental entities as sensations is held to be false and to lead to false conclusions. They are artifacts of the psychological laboratory, and their use leads to false descriptions and false conclusions. It is well known that in their place a larger unit is proposed, namely the organized whole or *Gestalt*. The same criticism is directed against the analysis of behaviour into the units ordinarily called reflexes.

Thus we find Köhler stating (1929, p. 193): "This indeed is the most general concept of *gestalttheorie*: wherever a process dynami- cally distributes and regulates itself, determined by the actual situ- ation in a whole field, this process is said to follow principles of *gestalttheorie*. In all cases of this type, the process will have some characteristic which exists in an extended area only, so that a con- sideration of local points or local factors as such will not give us full insight into the nature of the process. . . . According to the most general definition of *Gestalt*, the processes of learning, of reproduc- tion, of striving, of emotional attitude, of thinking, acting and so forth, may be included as subject-matter of *gestalttheorie* in so far as they do not consist of independent elements, but are determined in a situation as a whole."

At the outset it should be pointed out that these wholes, which are to serve as psychological units, may be, and in fact characteristically are, extended in time. To borrow a phrase from the physicists they are four dimensional. As Köhler puts it, they are *processes*. Thus the "phi-phenomenon" of Wertheimer, which may be called the experimental starting-point of the theory, is the experience of spatial motion over a certain period of time. For example, if two spots of light are thrown on a screen with suitable lengths of exposure and at suitable intervals of time and spatial distance, the observer sees not two stationary spots but one moving spot. This latter experience, according to the theory, cannot be analysed into two discrete experiences corresponding to the patches of physical light on the screen. It is the experience of a single patch of light moving from this point in space to that. The experience corresponding to each stationary spot of light taken separately has been modified, and an entirely new kind of experience has been created, namely the phenomenal *Gestalt* of motion from one point to the other. This "Gestalt of motion" is then "four dimensional". The same thing is true of musical notes. The experience corresponding to each such note is different according to the melody of which it forms part and to its place in the melody. The musical note B natural has a different effect according as it occurs as the tonic note of the scale, B major, or as the leading note in the scale of C major. The whole gives the meaning to the "elements", and cannot be analysed into them; for such analysis neglects the fact that when originally separate experiences are juxtaposed, with the result that a new *Gestalt* is formed, those original experiences lose their original character and acquire a fresh character from their membership in the new whole. Physically, a melody can of course be analysed into so many discrete notes; psychologically it cannot. The melody-*Gestalt*[1] is, again four dimensional; it takes place in space and time. It is, for example, the melody "God Save the King" roughly localized in space as sung by the singer on the platform and lasting about thirty seconds. True, the visual-perceptual unities, which Gestalt psychology has often used in illustration, are treated as though they are spatial only and lacking a time dimension. But this is, of course, only by a process of abstraction. Such figures can be abstracted from the time dimension because they are relatively independent of it. Nevertheless, the

[1] Von Ehrenfels, 1890.

experience of looking at a geometrical figure is clearly time-extended. An observer cannot simply observe such a figure; he must do so for a certain period of time. Actually, of course, the geometrical figures are subject to a still further process of abstraction, in that they are considered as being two dimensional only. But, as a matter of fact, every such figure is actually experienced as being at a certain distance, that is, in a three-dimensional framework. In many figures the time factor obtrudes itself, as in the case of "illusions" of reversible perspective, where the phenomenal *Gestalt* changes with the time dimension.

Newness

From the elementary statement foregoing several points emerge. The *Gestalt* is new. Under the proper conditions, a new kind of experience is born out of the *disjecta membra* of relatively discrete experiences. The spots of light are experienced as two discrete spots, if the interval is properly chosen. Wertheimer states that an interval of about 0·03 sec. gave two simultaneous lines in perception, one of 0·2 sec. two successive lines, while one of about 0·06 sec. gave motion[2] (Wertheimer, 1925, p. 73). The individual notes of "God Save the King" are experienced as separate notes if the intervals between them are sufficiently long. But under the proper conditions the melody experience arises, which is new.

Isomorphism

Further, it is claimed that between the experience and the physiological processes directly underlying it there is a specific relationship, of congruence or isomorphism, to use Köhler's term. Actual motion of a spot of light in the field of vision is presumably accompanied by some kind of neural displacement in the visual area of the brain. Wertheimer's hypothesis is that in the case of apparent movement, there is a similar shift of excitation from one centre to another in the brain, a physiological short-circuit.[3] Apparent motion and real motion thus have similar physiological correlates, namely actual neural displacement. This is generalized by Köhler into the state-

[2] Korte lays down other conditions for phenomenal movement. These relate to spatial separation, temporal separation, and intensity. (See Korte, 1915.) Later work has thrown some doubt on the rather rigid specifications of Korte and Wertheimer. See, e.g., Neuhaus, W., 1930. Neff, W. S., 1936, gives a good summary of work on the phi-phenomenon.

[3] 1925, p. 88.

ment that "experienced order in space is always structurally identical with a functional order in distribution of underlying brain processes", and similarly for time.[4] The same principle applies to the experience of totality, wholeness. An experienced whole, according to the theory, implies wholeness, totality in the underlying physiological process. If the melody is to be perceived as a unity, there must be unity in the correlative physiological processes. And in general, "units in experience go with functional units in the underlying physiological processes". Indeed, Köhler is prepared to extend the notion of isomorphism still further. Language, he points out, is the direct outcome of physiological processes in the organism. Hence, "It does not matter very much whether my words are taken as messages about experience or about these physiological facts."[5] Thus an introspective method in psychology is equally a method of describing unobservable pieces of behaviour, and indeed it does not much matter whether the language used in introspection is taken as a symbol of experience or of such unobservable behaviour.

Unification

The process by which this unification takes place may be represented as one of interaction. Thus, the local excitation caused by luminous spot A interacts with that of spot B, with the result that a stream of nervous energy passes from the one neural locus to another.[6] Or again, the several local excitations caused by different notes of the melody may be said to interact with each other so as to produce a unity composite of actual excitation and mnemonic traces. Gestalt theory demands that this process of interaction, once again, shall be self-regulating; that is to say, that once sensory excitation has taken place, the outcome both in the neural field and in experience shall be a series of events determined as a whole by the mutual relationships of the total segregated field.

The last three notes of the national anthem are differently experienced from the first three notes of the tune "Three Blind Mice", although from the purely physical point of view the notes are the same in each case. Clearly, also, the neural events initiated by the three notes must be different in each case; otherwise the notes would not

---

[4] Köhler, 1947, pp. 61–3.
[5] Ibid., p. 64.
[6] Presumably theory would demand that the corresponding experiences interact also.

sound different. Further, this difference in the neural effects of identical stimulation in the two cases is due to the fact that the primary nervous impulses consequent upon stimulation interact with the mnemonic traces left by the playing of "God Save the King" in the one case but not in the other.

General Statement of the Gestalt Theory of Thinking. Structural Reorganization. Resolution of Intrinsic Stresses. Insight

In conformity with the general principles briefly outlined above, the Gestalt theory of thinking may be summarily stated as follows. There is first stimulation by the situation. This gives rise to a nexus of perceptual processes of a psycho-neural nature, which by dynamic interaction, with each other and with the mnemonic traces present, results in a re-ordering of the first perceptual processes, in the way which we call "seeing the problem",[7] or "formulating the problem". At this stage, the psycho-neural process remains mainly at the perceptual level. Because of the dynamic interaction of the processes leading to it there has been a certain amount of transformation of the original perceptual material; but the stage is still provisional. Seeing the problem is only "a step towards solution". From the psycho-neural processes which we describe subjectively as "seeing the problem" springs a series of events which we call the thinking proper. They are called into being by the mutual interaction (*a*) of factors inherent in the problem as seen and (*b*) of mnemonic traces[8]; they lead from the seen problem to the solution. Thus through the thought-processes the solution springs from stresses inherent in the seen-problem, in a manner comparable to the way in which perception of "a spot in motion" springs from the stresses inherent in the psycho-neural *ensemble* of the phi-phenomenon experiment. The whole series of events, from seen-problem to solution, is then unitary. It is the series of events leading from one state to another of a self-regulating system under stress. This series is comparable to the total

---

[7] "*Denkvorgänge, Vorgänge bei originärer Lösung eines Problems.* . . . *Vorgänge beim Sehen eines Problems . . . erweisen sich . . . als konkret-charakteristische, bestimmt geartete Gestaltsprozesse*" (Wertheimer, 1921, p. 56). In many cases the stage of "seeing the problem" is merged indistinguishably with other processes of solution. However, in view of the statement here expressly made by Wertheimer, it seems better to incorporate the distinction in the exposition of Gestalt theory.

[8] "This raises the question whether the stress of the present problem can directly produce a reorganization of the trace system, a question which I dare not answer" (Koffka, 1935, p. 644).

series of swings of a pendulum coming to rest, which is likewise of a unitary nature. We are here speaking of a successful, even-flowing train of thought. The question of errors will be considered later. It will be noticed that no attempt has been made to segregate neural events from those of experience. This omission is deliberate, and is in accordance with the principle of isomorphism. Very briefly stated, then, the thought-process is, by this theory, the unitary process whereby the problem-as-seen is resolved, by the action of its own intrinsic stresses, into the solution. Perception and thinking are ruled by principles which are fundamentally the same, the chief difference being that in thinking these principles have freer play because there is less interference from the relatively intractable outside world. Our sensory perception must be regulated more or less strictly by what we are perceiving. Our thinking can and, as in modern physical science, characteristically does operate in relative independence of the rigid framework of external stimulation.[9]

Examples may be given. The first is a simple form of the now well-known detour experiment. A little girl of one year and three months, able to walk alone for a few weeks, is brought into a blind alley, set up *ad hoc* (two metres long and one and a half wide), and on the other side of the partition some attractive object is put in front of her eyes; first she pushes towards the object, i.e. against the partitions, then looks round slowly, lets her eyes run along the blind alley, suddenly laughs joyfully, and in one movement is off on a trot round the corner to the objective.[10] Köhler gave at the time no analysis of this experiment. According to Gestalt principles, what happened would be described about as follows.

First the little girl pushes towards the object, i.e. against the partition. Within the child, there is set up a perceptual-motor system which is such that its component factors engender mutual stress.[11] We describe the situation by saying that the child *wants* the object, BUT the barrier stands in the way. To this psychic conflict there must, according to the principle of isomorphism, correspond mutually stressful neural processes. The process whereby the stressful system comes into being is known as "seeing the problem". Subsequent events, perceptual and motor, are stages in the resolution of this stress. First comes the slow turning away from the unwelcome barrier, a natural first outcome of the neuro-psychic conflict. Then

[9] Koffka, 1935, p. 614; 1925, pp. 574–5.
[10] Köhler, 1925, p. 14.
[11] Remembering the principle of isomorphism!

"she lets her eyes run along the blind alley, [and] suddenly laughs joyfully". Here there is presumably "alteration in structure" (*Umstruktuirung, Umzentrierung*) of the perceptual field. This alteration is achieved as the result of the stress in the total motor-perceptual field. It takes place *in conformity with* the existing texture of stresses, and in such a way that the total stress is lessened; just such changes occur, according to Wertheimer's hypothesis, as will relieve the total neuro-perceptual stress. Again, the change in perceptual structure results in, or possibly is the same as, the relating of hitherto unrelated factors or elements. The passage is now seen in relation to the desired object. It is now not simply a passage but a means to obtain the object. The new light in which it is seen is determined by its relation to the desired object. This relating of hitherto independent aspects of a phenomenal[12] field is known as *Insight*. It figures largely in Gestalt accounts of the process of thinking. Insight is: "Our experience of definite determination in a context, an event or development of the total field; and in the actual cases there need be nothing like an invention, or a new intelligent achievement, or so forth. A total field would be experienced without insight if all its several states, wholes, attitudes, etc., were simply given as a pattern in which none was felt directly to depend on any other, and none to determine any other" (Köhler, 1929, p. 373).[13]

A second example. The geometrical problem is given: the sides DA, BC of the square ABCD are produced so that AP equals CQ. Find the sum of the areas APCQ and ABCD.[14]

According, again, to the hypothesis outlined, the reading of these lines by a geometrically informed reader will set up a system of neuro-perceptual stress. If it does not do so, then, as far as the reader is concerned, there is no problem. The reasons why one reader will accept the problem and another not depend on questions of individual psychology which are here irrelevant. But for Gestalt psychology, the fact that any reader has accepted the geometrical problem is synonymous with the statement that a system of neuro-perceptual stress has been established. The process of solving this problem is the process by which this stress resolves itself.

---

[12] Or possibly a more extensive psycho-neural field.

[13] In a later volume (1947) he has defined insight simply as the direct awareness of determination (p. 371).

[14] The problem is given by Wertheimer, 1925, p. 176. Certain changes of terminology have been made, and the alternative solution added.

The first "step" is to draw the figure (see Figure 3)   (1)

Then: area required = area of △ PDC + Area of △ ABQ   (2)

= PD.DC = DA.DP   (3)

Alternatively, the construction in dotted lines may be drawn.   (2a)

Then: area required = area of ABCD + Area of CDXQ   (3a)

= area of ABQX   (4a)

= PD.DC   (5a)

Figure 3

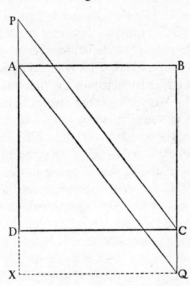

The stage called "seeing the problem" is not fully achieved until the first construction is made as in line (1). When this is done, the system of neuro-perceptual stress already set up is more clearly defined. A transformation has already occurred, the new system still being under stress. Under the influence of that stress the further transformation takes place by which the total area ABCD APCQ is seen to be the sum of the areas of the triangles ABQ and PDC. The way in which figure 3 is seen suffers alteration. From this follows line (3). It will be remembered that according to the theory resolution of the stresses present must take place under the conditions established by the mnemonic traces. It is these traces that give at least the final stage of line (3). If the alternative method is adopted, then the mnemonic traces enter into the successive neuro-psychic events objectively signified by lines (2a), (3a), (4a), (5a). In this case, the actual course by which the stress is resolved is determined, again, jointly by the original system-in-stress and the mnemonic traces present; though here the influence of the traces is more obtrusive.

What Wertheimer calls "*Umzentrierung*" or Recentering comes out very clearly in this example. The triangles ABQ and PDC must be seen as areas. The figure as originally drawn contained them implicitly, indeed; but they are not explicitly present as phenomenal areas. Otherwise the problem would be immediately solved by everyone to whom it is presented. This is far from being the case. Still less are the steps (2a), (3a), and so on explicitly contained in the original phenomenal figure. In order that the construction (2a) may be drawn, the parallelogram APCQ must be seen in a fresh light, by means of the mnemonic traces, namely as equal to a rectangle on the base CQ and between the same parallels. That is to say, once again the factor of newness is stressed, particularly in the first solution which is the original one given by Wertheimer, but also, though perhaps to a less degree, in the second solution.

At the same time, the concept of Insight is likewise illustrated. To take the first solution. When it is "seen" that the area of the parallelogram plus the area of the square is equal to the area of the overlapping triangles PDC and ABQ, then follows the solution, namely that the area required is DA.DP, again through the trace systems. As the proof might be stated formally, *because* the area required equals the sum of, etc., *therefore*, etc. In Köhler's terms, there is an experience of "determination" in a context. The fact that the required sum of areas is seen in the new way "leads", as we say, to the solution. Thus Insight and structural reorganization (*Umzentrierung*) are closely related to each other, as indeed they should be according to theory. For the structural change is the product of the stresses inherent in the problem-as-perceived. There is complete insight, because the whole process is experienced as sequentially determined. Incomplete insight occurs when this experience of determination is confined to part only of the whole process. This might be the case if somebody had made the construction CDXQ as above simply because he realized that the area of the parallelogram equals that of any parallelogram between the same parallels and on the same base, and had then "discovered" that the problem was solved. Whenever there is any degree of "blundering into" the situation, there is *at first only* a varying degree of partial insight. A parallel instance for the example of the cul-de-sac would be the experience of the child who runs away from the barrier because "I'll have to get out of this", and then *finds* that access to the desired object is now unimpeded. In these cases, says Koffka, "the result, although it follows necessarily, contains an element of surprise, that is, the final solution is not entirely free of stress" (1935, p. 641). The same kind of thing is involved in many "chance solutions", and in the story of Newton and the apple.

The Mechanism and the Material of Thinking in Gestalt Psychology. Köhler's fundamental work

The programme outlined proposes modifications in the theory both of the mechanism and of the material of thinking. The material used in the thinking process is necessarily new, as contrasted with the material assumed by the older theories. Previous theories have held it as axiomatic that the material of thinking is the product of past experience which is incorporated into the thought-process in an unaltered form. The combination may be new, but that which is brought into combination (the empirical data) is essentially old. This is clearly true of the associational psychology, which in its classical form assumes that the material of thought consists of ideas whose appearances and combinations are manipulated by associatory bonds. It is true also of that modified form of the associational theory sponsored by Watt and Ach, according to which, in addition to the bonds of association, the task or the determining tendency controls and directs the reproductive tendencies like a dog directing a flock of sheep. It is likewise true of that part of the Würzburg theory which has to do specifically with the material of thinking, namely the theory of imageless thought. Here, it will be remembered, the fundamental concept is that of the *Wissen*, the *knowing*, which is "impalpably given". Now the point is not explicitly raised, but the assumption throughout is that the *Wissen* essentially preserves unchanged, though perhaps in a sublimated form, the experience of the past. How this can be so, when past experience has primarily occurred, according to the theory, in sensory terms, is one of the difficulties which the Würzburg construction has to face. It has been seen that Ach's solution was that the *Bewusstheit*, or awareness, is a watered-down image, a conception which it was found necessary to reject.

The Gestalt theory introduces a profound modification. For it, the material of thinking is essentially new because thinking only occurs when a fresh Gestalt is formed, and the process produces an essential modification of those originally disconnected experiences the bringing of which into combination results in the formation of the new Gestalt. That is to say, even though we were to start originally with disconnected experiences which as such are identical with previous ones, yet the act of bringing these into combination during the process of thinking would modify them. So that an experience of a blind alley, to use the example already given, if it occurs during the process of thinking, is fundamentally coloured by the total new context. It is experienced as "the alley by which I cannot get the desired object", and as such differs from a sheer reproductive memory. Many examples more favourable to this fundamental conception of Gestalt psychology might be given. It may then be said that the Gestalt psychology essentially stresses the creative side of thought. For the members of this school, true thinking is productive as distinguished from reproductive. Any theory which is based on association of fundamentally unchanged experimental data may, if this distinction be justified, account for reproductive, but can never account for productive thought. Real thinking necessarily implies novelty of material.

In the theory of the mechanism of thinking Gestalt psychology proposes an equally important change. Pre-Würzburg theory held that the fundamental mechanism of thinking is association, "reproductive tendencies". Thinking is essentially the clash of associations. A psychic event is "the centre of a system of associations which diverge in every direction. . . . Each associated idea becomes again the centre of a system of diverging associations."[15] Thus the fundamental mechanism of thinking is a "system of diffuse reproductions", to use Selz's term. The Würzburg theory supplemented this by the conception of the *Aufgabe* or Determining Tendency, by which it was hoped to bring order out of the chaos of the diffuse system. But this, we saw, introduced a dichotomy into the whole process, namely that between the reproductive tendencies and the favouring or inhibiting determining tendencies. Nevertheless, the introduction of the *Aufgabe* did mark the recognition of the fact of direction in thinking. Once this fact had been pointed out, psychology could not go back to the "diffuse" directionless hypothesis of the classical association theory.

Gestalt psychology proposes to retain the concept of Direction without recognizing the Würzburg dichotomy, which was grounded on the principle of association. Direction is to be given to the process of thinking not by determining tendencies acting upon reproduction, but by the self-adjustment of a system in stress. Once more we may quote from Köhler. He is speaking of the displacements of physical systems: "Not only movement or process as such, *but also the direc-*

[15] Selz, 1924, p. 6.

tion and distribution of process, is determined dynamically by inter-action" (1929, p. 134). Similarly: "In all these systems we have one resulting force at each point at each instant of time. All the resultant forces together form a single texture of stresses. [Therefore] . . . the immediate effect of those forces will have one definite direction" (ibid., p. 139). And once again, "So we are led to a more complete application of the theory of direct dynamical determination. There is no mere sequence of indifferent events connected indirectly. Each phase of what happens grows out of its predecessors, depending on their concrete nature. And the subject, whose experiences are an expression of this one developing context in the brain field (principle of isomorphism) will experience the development, along with its "referring to", "depending upon", "away from" and so forth—that is, with *insight*" (ibid., p. 391). Köhler is here speaking of an act of behaviour, but the general principle is the same. In fact, the problem of direction is the same in the fields of behaviour and thinking, involving as it does the selection of the "right" and the "suppression" of the "wrong" in each case. Thus, we may say, the intrinsic properties of the system under stress—that is to say, of the perceived problem—give Direction to the ensuing train of thought and action. Movements and thoughts which will increase the psychophysical tension will be avoided, and only such movements and thoughts will occur as will decrease the tension. According to this view, thinking is then the process by which a state of initial disequilibrium comes to one of equilibrium.

The experimental evidence for these views will now be examined.

The most fundamental experiments were performed, not on human beings but on animals, by Professor Köhler. Although the discussion of the animal mind is only incidentally germane to the general problem of this book, nevertheless these now classical investigations made such a fundamental contribution that at least a summary and partial account of them is indispensable in any account of the Gestalt theory of thought. In all, Köhler employed sixteen situations to each of which a number of chimpanzees was subjected. The whole set formed a series of progressively increasing difficulty, and the animals were started at the easy end and gradually worked up to the more difficult situations. In a preliminary experiment a basket with fruit was hung in such a way that the fruit could be obtained by loosening from a tree the end of the rope suspending it. This was solved by *pulling* at the rope so that it broke in the end.[16] It will be seen that

---

[16] I follow Koffka's numerical classification of these experiments (1924) with explanatory quotations from Köhler, 1925.

"the nub of the situation, i.e. the rope connection, is grasped as a matter of course" (Köhler, 1925, p. 9), but it is not certain whether the animal could have solved the problem in the best way by loosing the rope from the tree. In the first of the graded series of experiments that followed, the basket is inaccessible from the ground. When it is swung, however, it can be reached from a platform, but only for a few moments (p. 18).[17] Three chimpanzees are let in, one makes a dash for the basket and misses. Another, however, goes to the platform and waits for the basket "with outstretched arms".

In the next experiment, number 2 (p. 26), the fruit must be pulled into the cage by a string. The experiment in this form was easily solved. But when the complication was introduced of laying other, irrelevant strings across the attached one, the cleverest of the apes pulls helter-skelter until he gets the right one (p. 29). In experiments 3 (p. 31) and 4, the goal must be reached either by pulling it into the cage by a stick or by climbing on to a box. In number 5 the animal must swing up on a rope attached to the roof.

In these experiments "the stick has now acquired a certain *functional* or *instrumental* value in relation to the field of action under certain conditions, and . . . this value is extended to all other objects that resemble the stick, however remotely, in *outline* and *consistency* —whatever their other qualities may be. . . . Hats and shoes are certainly not visually identical with the stick and therefore interchangeable in the course of the test experiments; *only in certain circumstances are they functionally* sticks", that is after the animals have already used a stick correctly (ibid., p. 37). A very important factor in all these experiments was the "*location of the implements* both in relation to the animals themselves and to the objective". If the animal could not see the stick and the goal at the same time, the task is immeasurably harder. That is to say, what may be called the topography of the problem-situation as seen visually is of importance.

"If one *single part* of the solutions . . . be considered by itself and without any relation to the remaining parts, it represents behaviour . . . which seems to be either quite irrelevant or else to lead in the opposite direction. It is only when the whole course of the experiment be considered that . . . each of the sections takes on meaning as a part of *this whole*. . . . When a man or an animal takes a roundabout way . . . to his objective, the beginning—considered by itself only and regardless of the further course of the experiments—con-

[17] The references are to Köhler, 1925.

tains at least one component which must seem *irrelevant; in very indirect routes there are usually some parts of the way which when considered alone, seem in contradiction to the purpose of the task* because they lead from the goal. If the subdivision in thought is dropped the whole detour and each part of it considered separately becomes full of meaning in *that* experiment." The next series of experiments illustrates in greater clearness the existence of sections which, when *taken separately, are meaningless in relation to the task,* but which become *significant again* when they are considered *as a part of the whole*" (ibid., p. 105). One group of these experiments was called "making of implements".

Thus in experiments 13 and 14, the principle of the "meaning-less of partial activity" was developed by making it necessary for the animal to obtain the tool by the intermediate use of a second tool. Thus in number 13 a long stick must be obtained by a shorter stick, which was in itself inadequate to obtain the goal. In number 14 a box, with or without stones in it, had to be dragged up to obtain the stick. Here the secondary tool (the short stick or the box) is useful only in connection with the tool, which is itself useful only *as a means* to the goal.

In number 15 the goal was placed outside the cage in a blind alley turned *away* from the animal. The chimpanzee must poke the food away from itself towards the mouth of the blind alley, round the end, and then back on the outside of the alley to the cage. In number 16 a stick is tied to a rope, the other end of which is secured to a ring which is slipped over a nail sticking out vertically about ten centimetres from a heavy case. In order to secure the goal, the animals must be able to grasp the arrangement "ring over nail" (p. 245). In the final experiment, a stick is secured to a tree, with barriers arranged that the only solution is to use the stick to push the object to a position where it can be reached with an arm from the other side.

In both experiments 15 and 17 it may be noted that the goal-object must be pushed away from the animal with a tool. All the tests were performed by the animals, except number 9, which involved fastening a rope to a hook on the ceiling. This was beyond the capacity of every animal tested. There were great individual differences, as might have been expected from the observations of all who have worked with animal subjects. The distinguishing mark of these experiments is that the solution, when achieved, is fully comprehensible to the chimpanzees. Therein they differ from those of

Thorndike with puzzle boxes, where there is indeed the sequence *activity-success*, but where the nature of this sequence is, in many cases at least, meaningless to the animal. For example, it will be remembered that a cat might be released after it had made certain motions with its paw.

Actually Köhler did observe much behaviour of the type which Thorndike would call "trial and error". Thus, when the goal is to be drawn in by a string (experiment 2), and unattached cross strings are laid over it, "Sultan is led to the bars, glances out, and then pulls in rapid succession two of the wrong strings and then the right one. His mistakes can scarcely be fortuitous", for he pulls the string which leads by the shortest route from the goal to himself, regardless of whether it is attached to the goal (p. 28). In the stick experiment, number 3, "Tschego first tries to reach the fruit with her hand; of course in vain. . . . Then she makes another attempt, only to give it up again. This goes on for more than half an hour. Finally she lies down for good, and takes no further interest in the object. The sticks might be non-existent as far as she is concerned, although they can hardly escape her attention, as they are in her immediate neighbourhood." Other animals approach. "Suddenly Tschego leaps to her feet, seizes a stick and quite adroitly pulls the bananas until they are within reach. . . . She uses first the left arm and then the right, and frequently changes from one to the other" (p. 32). In the same way, "Koko suddenly seized the stick"—after some useless attempts to take it with his hand—". . . gazed at his objective then again let fall the stick". He then tried unavailingly with his foot. "Then he suddenly took the stick and drew the objective towards himself though very clumsily" (p. 34). Such "trial and error" is copiously illustrated throughout the book.

The Gestalt interpretation of this extended series of experiments would, I believe, today be something as follows. The animal finds himself confronted with a desired object, in a setting to which he is indifferent. Neurologically, this implies that one part, factor, "moment", aspect, of the receptor-cortical field[18] is differentiated from the rest in some way not at present known. Owing to this polarity, movement is initiated in the direction of the object. At some point or other, external conditions check this progress (in the box test (p. 39), "all six apes vainly endeavoured to reach their objective by leaping up from the ground"). Thereafter, as the result

---

[18] Or possibly one part of the total activity pattern of the same, recent researches seeming to indicate that the whole waking cortex may be active all the time.

of some process not at present known, there occurs a reorganization in the whole receptor-to-cortical "sector" such that the strictly delimited polarity, corresponding in experience to the contrast of goal vs. background, is broken up. In its place appears a new polarity, corresponding experientially to goal-tool background, and such that activity is initiated which results first in the dragging of the box towards the goal, and secondly in such subsequent activities as lead thence to the objective. This reorganization in the neuro-receptoral "sector" is accompanied by insight, which is the counterpart in experience of the new neural relations that have come into being between those parts of the total activity pattern which were at first relatively independent. That part of the environment which is thus singled out for special relationship with the goal is said to have acquired "functional or instrumental" value (Köhler, 1925, p. 36). The experienced transformation is thus described by Köhler. "In consequence of my anxious expectancy, a transformation takes place in my own field of view, so that longish and movable objects no longer are seen as though they were mere things of indifference, static in their respective positions; instead, they begin to appear as if in a 'vector', and as if under pressure they were being drawn toward the critical position."

The reason why this transformation takes place, according to the hypothesis, lies in the intrinsic nature of the total pattern of excitation at the time when the animal's progress towards the goal is checked; that is to say, at the time when the problem is perceived as such. It is at this time that, in a nervous system of the requisite calibre, there is established a neuro-perceptual pattern in a delicate state of imbalance which can be resolved through appropriate reorganization. In any given case this reorganization may be beyond the powers of a given nervous system. For instance, a bitch showed no interest in the string attached to the goal, although she was interested in the goal itself. Thus "Dogs, and probably, for instance, horses as well, unless they made sudden lucky movements or received indications from outside themselves, might easily starve to death in these circumstances which offer hardly any difficulty to human beings —or to chimpanzees" (Köhler, 1925, p. 27). Presumably in the case of the dog the same, or a very similar, neuro-perceptual pattern would be established as in the case of the chimpanzee, the difference being that in this case the structure would be more rigid, and would not admit of resolution by reorganization. On the other hand, the chimpanzee would of course be powerless in the face of problems that would offer no difficulties to a human being (Köhler, 1925, p. 37).

If one asks what determines the nature of such cortical reorganization, the first answer is the general nature of the whole activated field. Köhler's experiments seem to indicate certain ways in which this general statement could be made more exact. For example, there is apparently a general factor which may be called topographical. Thus the animal will always pull the attached string when it visibly touches the object. When the string and the object are wide apart, the string will generally not be pulled. When the distance between is moderately wide, the string may or may not be pulled (Köhler, 1925, pp. 30–1). In the same way, there is apparently what might be called a segregation factor. The box will not be used as a tool if it is fitted into the corner of the room. There is apparently an intensity factor. Actions may only take place if the animal is very hungry. But these are details which it is not necessary to fill out in order to apprehend the general sense of the hypothesis.

The statement given above endeavours to give the Gestalt hypothesis in its lowest terms. That is to say, it attempts to explain the experiments in terms of the Gestalt theory of Thinking, without the inclusion of other hypotheses which are indeed characteristic for the general theory, but which are not necessary for our present purpose. Thus, for example, the question of the effect of experience is to a large extent left uncanvassed. It is indifferent, for instance, whether or not the string has actually been used before by the animal as a means by which to pull in objects. The main point is that the psychoneural field is structured as it is at the time of the experiment, no matter what the cause; that the structure is in a disequilibrium which can resolve itself by transformation of the field as the result of the inherent stresses.

The work of Köhler is perhaps the most elaborate attempt to give an experimental demonstration of Gestalt principles in reasoning. One cannot fail to be impressed by this massive, yet acute, piece of work. It still stands as the most important contribution to the Gestalt theory of thinking. There are other experimental sources where certain implications of the same results come out more explicitly.

Duncker's Experiments on Reorganization

The most thoroughgoing treatment of the concept of reorganization during thinking, both from the experimental and the theoretical point of view, is that of Duncker. His two published researches include various kinds of problems. A selection follows.[19]

The Ball Problem: "Suppose this to be a metal ball one drops upon a metal surface. We know it jumps up again after having struck and what makes it rebound is the fact that the ball gets a flattening where it touches the surface. The elastic forces of the ball, however, make it regain its former shape, and this process causes the rebounding (think of a rubber ball!). Your task is to prove the occurrence of the flattening, to find a method which not only shows that a flattening actually takes place but also the shape and size of the ball's flattening."

The X-ray Problem: "Your problem is to find out how to apply a certain kind of X-ray, high intensities of which destroy organic tissues, in order to cure a man of a tumour within his body (for instance in his stomach)."

A sample protocol is given for the latter.

4(*a*) Apply plates to protect the neighbouring parts from being destroyed ("that is not the trouble").

(*b*) Send rays through a tube in œsophagus. (Hints: "Draw a cross-section of the body; the intensities must be different.")

(*c*) Make the tumour more susceptible by some kind of injection. (Hint: "Treat good and bad tissues differently".)

(*d*) Send weaker rays from two opposite sides so they will meet each other in the centre. (He saw that this would not help, that the trouble was not yet fully removed. "Why do you let the two radiations go the same path?")

(*e*) Aha! (He sees the solution, which is to converge a number of pencils of relatively weak rays from different directions on to the tumour.)

The Pendulum Problem: This involved the construction of a pendulum which would preserve the same length in spite of changes of temperature and consequent expansion.

These problems are selected from Duncker's paper of 1926. Duncker's first argument is directed against the associative theory of thinking, as advanced either in its original, more primitive form, or in its more sophisticated form by Müller on the one hand and the Würzburgers on the other. Duncker's argument is that his problems cannot be solved by the use of past associations, for there were no

[19] Duncker, 1926, 1935. Duncker has published also an English version of his book (*Psychol. Mon.*, 58, 1945). The references (and translations) in this chapter are from the German edition.

such associations to use. In fact, the subject had to *make* the means of solution out of the original situation by reorganization of the original data (1926, p. 650).

In his second publication (1935) Duncker uses the problems of the first paper, together with others. Such, for example, are:

The "13" task. How far is it true that all numbers of six digits in the form 276 276, 591 591, 112 112 are divisible by 13? A single protocol is given "which, not counting several typical but useless divergencies, included the most direct solution."

(1) Are the triple numbers themselves divisible by 13?

(2) Are there perhaps any rules involving cross summation, as for divisibility by 9?

(3) The conclusion must follow from some common principle of structure that is hidden. The first triple number is ten times the second, 591 591 is 591 times 11, no: times 101 (*experimenter:* is that so?) no: times 1001. Is 1001 divisible by 13?

A second problem in the same book is as follows.

The "Perpendiculars" Problem: If the feet[20] of the perpendiculars from the three angles of a triangle are joined, the so-called pedal triangle is formed. Why do the perpendiculars bisect the angles of this pedal triangle?"

These problems are given as samples of the kind of material which Duncker employed. Others will be given as occasion makes this necessary.

For Duncker, the process of finding a solution is a development of the problem. "*The final form of the individual solution-stroke is in general not reached by a single step from the original problem situation*, but the principle typically appears first, the functional value of the solution; the final *Gestalt* of the corresponding solution only comes by successive concretization[21] [embodiment] of this principle. In other words, the general, essential, peculiarities of a solution proceed genetically from its special peculiarities. The former organize themselves from the latter."[22]

The finding of a general solution-property is always synonymous with a reorganization of the original problem. For example, a subject in the X-ray Problem said: "The intensity of radiation would have to be diminished *en route*." This, says Duncker, is the decisive

---

[20] This statement has been found confusing. "If the points of intersection with the sides of a triangle of perpendiculars drawn from the angles are joined, etc."

[21] *Konkretizierung.*

[22] Loc. cit., p. 9. Italics as in original, except for the German word *Gestalt*.

transformation of the problem. The subject no longer seeks for a method of raying without destroying the tissue, but for a method of diminishing the intensity of the rays *en route*. "The problem has now sharpened, specialized", and from this transformed problem comes the final solution. The solution-properties, functional values, which are discovered, regularly play their part as productive transformations of the original problem-situation.

A stage in the process of solution[23] can be described equally well as a development of the solution or as a development of the problem. The final form of a solution is typically reached by means of intermediate phases which possess the character of a solution when seen from behind, and that of a problem when seen from in front.[24] Further, a solution has two roots, one in what is given, the other in what is demanded. "A solution arises from the demands of what is given through what is demanded."[25] These two components play a variable part according to the nature of the material. In other words, the process of reaching the solution is effected by the mutual interaction of the two parts of the problem—the data and the goal. These two conflict, or else there would be no problem. This process of interaction *is* the process of thinking, which is thus essentially the resolution of a conflict by means of a series of progressive reorganizations. These are effected by general "heuristic methods"[26] such as analysis of the goal and of the situation. Of the process of Reorganization in general, Duncker writes as follows: "Every solution rests on some kind of change of the given situation. This is a change not only of this or that feature of the situation, but, in addition, there is a change in the psychological total-structure of the situation (or of certain special partial regions)." Such changes are called Reorganization.

While the process of solution (conceived broadly) is taking place, such reorganization is occurring, for example, in the "Emphasis-pattern"[27] of the situation (its figure-ground pattern). Situational parts and moments, which psychologically existed hardly at all before or existed only in the background, "unthematically", spring forward immediately, gain a leading place, becoming a theme, a figure; and contrariwise.

Apart from emphasis, there is alteration in the material part-properties, or "Functions". The newly emerging parts of the

---

[23] *Lösungsprozess.*   [24] Loc. cit., p. 13.
[25] *aus der Beanspruchung der gegebenen durch das gefordete* (loc. cit., p. 13).
[26] P. 28, and Chapter III.   [27] *Betontheitsrelief* (op. cit., p. 35).

situation owe their prominence to certain (relatively general) functions. "That thing there" becomes a "hindrance!", a "point of attack" a feature of the conflict; another thing becomes a "Means"; and so on. At the same time, there is alteration in the more special functions. (For example, the pipe becomes "a passage for X-rays", or a triangle made of matches the "surface of a tetrahedron".)

"Particularly radical reorganizations are wont to occur in relationships of totality or connectedness. Parts of situations, which before —as parts of different wholes—were separated from each other, or— although parts of the same whole—still had no special relation to each other, join up together in *one* new whole. For example, in certain 'solutions' of the pendulum problem the place of suspension suddenly comes to have a connection with the length of the pendulum, although there was no previous connection between these two moments."[28]

Duncker's account of the process of Reorganization in thinking is illustrated by a wealth of experimental illustration which makes it especially valuable and interesting. Considerations of space unfortunately preclude a more extended account of this very condensed discussion. The philosopher will find especially interesting the account of the psychology of "synthetic" insight in the Kantian sense (loc. cit., pp. 62 ff.), which is derived from Husserl's premises as contrasted with those of Kant.[29] Duncker has also an interesting experimental investigation of what he calls constraint (*Gebundenheit*) of the materials of problem solution. The difficulty with which an object could be given a new "functional value" by what we have termed reorganization was found to be much greater if the object had already been used in the experiment for another purpose. "Under the conditions of our experiments the unbound (i.e. previously unused) object is discovered nearly twice as easily as the bound one" (loc. cit., p. 105). The same principle is used in the discussion of geometrical proofs, where it is shown that considerable difficulty is often caused by the fact that, in the reorganization necessary for thinking, a transformation must be made of a fact already perceived in some sense opposed to the solution (loc. cit., p. 131). Duncker's book is of first importance to the psychology of thinking. It is especially valuable on account of the strict contact

---

[28] Loc. cit., pp. 34–5.
[29] "We reduce the synthetic *a priori* not to rules (*Verordnungen*) of Reason invested in the object but consider them as grounded in the peculiarities of the object itself" (loc. cit., p. 65).

which it preserves at every point with experiment—often of a novel type.

Ruger; Claparède

There is some confirmation of the theory of reorganization in thinking in Ruger's work, published in 1910 and reissued in 1926. Ruger, working under the influence of Thorndike, gave his subjects a series of mechanical puzzles to solve, the same puzzles being repeated up to a maximum of 1,440 times, the standard number of repetitions being 50. Time was taken with a split-second cumulative stop-watch. The general statement of results first draws attention to the contrast, then fashionable, of "human" and "animal" methods of learning. "The latter has been represented as a process of mechanical stamping in of those random or instinctively determined movements which have brought success, and the stamping out of those which have failed. The 'human' method has been described as one of understanding of principles and the consequent learning of a single successful experience. These designations, human and animal, have been used as equivalents of 'trial and success' and 'reasoning' respectively. . . ."[30] The general conclusions are:

(1) That even when the task . . . is essentially that of "learning by understanding", there are important differences in human methods of learning.

(2) That some of these methods show objective points of similarity to animal methods.

(3) That the "human" and "animal" methods should not be considered as exhaustive of the forms of learning, but as two out of a larger and at present undetermined number.

(4) That the "human" and "animal" methods should be considered as limiting members of a series of methods in which different types of analysis play an important if not the determining rôle.

(5) That these distinctions as to analysis do not correspond merely to that between percept and image, but are also found within the perceptual field itself.

It is interesting to observe that in Professor Lashley's term, used in another context, these experiments prove too much. They prove, that is to say, not that animals do not "reason", which was strongly maintained at the time by Professor Thorndike, but that human beings often do not reason either. The net result of these much-quoted experiments is to lessen the gap between the animal and the human method of attacking a difficult situation.

[30] Ruger, 1926, p. 8.

With reference to the question of what is called in this chapter reorganization, Ruger has this to say. He first divides analysis into sensory or perceptual analysis, and "image or ideational analysis". "The process of perceptual analysis does not seem to consist in plastering an image on to a percept, but it seems to be a direct transformation within the perceptual field itself. The experience seems to correspond to what some writers have spoken of as a 'movement of attention'. The experience of the analysis is distinct from that of ordinary perception on the one hand, and from that of a motor impulse on the other. It is oftentimes a striking experience and seems to come with a rush or as a flash. These suggestions are based directly on the writer's introspections, but are supported by occasional remarks of subjects to the effect that they seemed to see the relations involved in solution directly and without the use of imagery" (Ruger, 1926, p. 13).

And again: "the process of analysis, of 'seeing through a thing', is a very distinct experience. In many cases it came as an extremely sudden transformation, a 'flash' experience . . . The element of novelty is just as striking as that of its revived character in the cases where the latter can be detected. The process of analysis in the percept and in the image seem introspectively to the writer to be of the same sort. The process in the case of perception seems to be a change taking place immediately in the perceptual stuff, not the addition of imagery to it" (loc. cit., p. 33). Ruger quotes Woodworth as experiencing the same perceptual change in the well-known staircase figure.

These rather lengthy quotations have been made both because of their inherent importance in support of the Gestalt doctrine of reorganization, and because Ruger's study is often adduced as in experimental support of a trial-and-error theory of human thinking; that is to say, one which is diametrically opposed to the fundamental principle of the Gestalt theory. It will be seen that, so far from affording an experimental disproof of the Gestalt theory, Ruger's work offers a rather striking anticipation of one of its chief tenets.

Such an important concept as that of perceptual reorganization is undoubtedly in need of still further experimental verification and analysis. Nevertheless, the hypothesis does seem, at the present time, to be justified by such experimental evidence as we have.

Claparède, in reviewing the Gestaltist position, refers to the hypothesis of reorganization, and gives one or two excellent examples. It occurs, he points out, in puzzle pictures. When we are told to "find the cat", and succeed in doing so, we "destructure the tree in order to structure the cat", he says. When we need a riding-whip, again we may "destructure" a tree for the purpose. He finds this statement, however, one of description only, not of explanation. "The problem which interests us is that of knowing how this useful centering is accomplished" (1934, p. 53); "how, in a word, this adequate organization of the elements of the problem field is realized." The Gestalt theorists reply, he says, by a word: Insight. This again, he says, does not explain, but only invokes a *deus ex machina*. This hardly seems a fair criticism. It is not, according to contemporary Gestalt theory, that insight effects the reorganization of the problem-as-seen. It is, rather, that the reorganization is effected under stress of the contradictions, opposing features, intrinsic in the problem, and that Insight is the name given to the characteristic experience, such characteristic experience being noted also by Ruger, as already stated. It is perhaps worthy of note that Claparède's own subjects reported perceptual transformation during the solution of a problem. "The whole situation was instantaneously illuminated, everything took on another meaning. In the light of this new element, the physiognomy of the old elements sometimes changed. These facts of metamorphosis agree with the descriptions of the Gestalt theorists" (loc. cit., p. 145).

The concept of insight has come in for a certain amount of criticism.[31] The most extended is that of Bulbrook, who made an experimental investigation upon processes occurring during the solution of various kinds of problems. Samples are: to make a regular out of an irregular pattern in a string of beads without restringing the beads. (Solution, crush certain of the beads with a pair of pliers or, in a second use of the problem, dye some with ink.) Trace continuously round a geometrical figure. Construct four equilateral triangles out of six matches. Recognize phonetically scrambled passages of verse. (The passages were printed *vertically*.) The general conclusion was that: "In the examination of our descriptive material we have found no characteristic process, operation, form of conditioning or mode of discovery which we could with propriety distinguish as 'insight'" (Bulbrook, 1932, p. 453). The difficulties inherent in this kind of investigation may be seen from the fact that certain of the reports would undoubtedly be claimed by Gestalt psychologists as evidence for reorganization in the sense previously defined. Thus:

[31] It is maintained by Meili, 1936, that the theories of Duncker (as expressed in the earlier paper) and of Claparède are really in substantial agreement. I must confess that I cannot see the agreement.

"The pipe stem was apprehended no longer as a pipe stem with its specific application but was generalized into a tube" (loc. cit., p. 436). "The procedure consisted of action under self-instruction followed first by a period of search for the cause for failure under the first trial and then by a reapprehension of the experimental conditions with a consequent new self-instruction followed by action" (ibid., p. 437). Similarly: "The solution here consisted in a recognition of the three-dimensional alternative. Perceptive apprehension of a significant condition was prevented by a predisposition to lay figures on a plane. . . . For those who solved the problem the occasion brought about a reapprehension with a consequent recasting of the instruction" (ibid., p. 431). "The procedure in this problem . . . consisted in apprehension of the object, search for a method . . . inspection and comment . . . action under 'self and occasional instructions', and reapprehension due to a further realization of the limiting conditions of the experimental object. The assumption that the word was to be spelled . . . [in the obvious way] . . . was a misleading instruction . . ." (ibid., p. 433). The general method given for "the initial steps of the solving process" are: apprehension, inspection and comment, search for method and procedure under self-instruction until that instruction is perceived as inapplicable, reapprehension and search for another method (ibid., p. 416). It seems to the present writer that the general results of this study are, in substance, approximately in agreement with those of modern Gestalt theorists, and that the main quarrel is one of terminology. For it will be remembered that insight, which goes with the adequate reorganization of the problem-situation, need not arise suddenly, but that according to the more modern theory there may be partial or gradual insight which may or may not be succeeded by full insight. It should also be remembered that Duncker devotes an entire section of his book (op. cit., pp. 102–133) to a discussion of the "constraint of thought-material",[32] referring, that is to say, to the degree of difficulty with which material may be utilized for the process of thinking. This problem will be recognized as one raised by Bulbrook's paper. Both the Gestalt school and the paper of Bulbrook recognize some kind of change of the manner in which the problem-situation is regarded as an important feature of the process of thinking. The Gestalt school goes farther, and describes the concomitant and (? or) ensuing experiential events as insight. This, I believe, is the modern view of Gestalt theory. However, Bulbrook's paper does seem to have

[32] *Gebundenheit des Denkmaterials.* Heading of Part III.

performed the valuable function of calling attention to the fact that the term insight has been used rather vaguely in the past, a fact which Köhler himself admits, and one which has been rightly stressed by several critics.[33]

The Direction of Thinking

The Gestalt theory of the determination of thought is thus stated by Harrower. "The Würzburg school brought to light facts for the explanation of which they needed a concept such as the Determining Tendency, and round it all hopes centered. . . . Productive thought *was* something other than mere association, and that something was accounted for by the concept of the Determining Tendency, this was then isolated as an entity, and regarded as a force which could be set against the associative bond, and thus even measured quantitatively. . . . It was not until the work of Duncker and Maier, following out the line of attack suggested by Wertheimer, that we get a recognition of the determining tendency as the vector or tension produced by the structural properties of the problem. For this new point of view, in productive thought or the solving of a problem, the 'gap' . . . possesses an intrinsic relation to what is already given. It is 'needed' by the phenomenal problem situation itself, not merely demanded by the instructions."[34]

Harrower's material consisted of jokes, which were to be completed. "The Prisoner in Court, 'But, your Worship, I wasn't going 50 miles an hour, not 40, nor even 30. . . .'

"The Judge: . . ."

Two answers were given by Harrower's subjects, namely, "Well, you'll be going backwards soon" (three times with ten subjects). And again, "You won't be going at all soon" (also given three times). The other type of answer appears in: "No, you were going faster." She finds two types of solution, one continuing the "original direction", as in the first solution, the other presenting a change of direction, as in the solution: "No, you were going faster." Other jokes admitted of as many as six or seven different answers. Completion might be influenced, as Duncker found, by varying the circumstances in which the material used to effect the completion was presented. The driving, directional force comes, according to Harrower, from the tendency of an incomplete configuration to complete itself, the tendency, that is, towards *closure*. This term, though common in the perceptual psychology of the Gestalt school, does not

[33] See also Harrower, 1932, p. 84.   [34] Harrower, 1932, pp. 68–9.

seem to be used by the modern theorists as a direct explanation of the mechanics of the thought process. Koffka says, in fact, "We possess a good analogy in perceptual organization: the principle of closure. Just as a perceived circle will as a psycho-physical process 'tend' towards completion, so will x^2+ax, once it is seen as an incomplete square, tend to be completed."[35] The principle of closure does not seem, however, to be mentioned in Duncker's work, in which we see the thought process not as the completion of an incomplete *Gestalt*, but rather the formation of a *Gestalt* from relatively formless, chaotic material. It is true that once we have seen x^2+ax as an incomplete square, there is a tendency to complete the square, just as there is a tendency to complete Harrower's jokes. But that all reasoning can be reduced to so simple a scheme seems doubtful. At least this has not yet been proved.

Let us put the argument in this way. The fact that a train of reasoning is undertaken and brought to a finish is evidence that there is something in the total situation for the organism at this particular moment which leads it to effect certain psycho-physical processes which, on the side of experience, are usually designated as reasoning. This may be otherwise described by saying that the psycho-physical organism is originally in a state of equilibrium, that it meets a complex situation raising a disequilibrium, and that finally, by integrative and other processes it comes again to a position of equilibrium. This is the general statement. Closure of a perceptual form seems to be a very specific instance of this general case. Other specific instances are what are ordinarily known as reflexes, where the organism is disturbed, action follows, and equilibrium is restored; and such a response as the hunger-search of an animal, where action goes on *until* food is obtained and equilibrium restored. The perception of a problem, giving rise to the reasoning processes and finally to the solution with its consequent action[36] and reinstated equilibrium, does seem to come under the general canon *disturbed equilibrium*.[37] But it is as clearly wrong to identify the whole process therefore with perceptual closure as it would be to identify it with reflex action, as the stimulus-response psychology tends to do, or with the hunger-search. As Koffka says, closure is an analogy. No doubt it is for reasons such as these that the word closure is

---

[35] 1935, p. 631–2.

[36] In most cases.

[37] Defining this much-misused word in this context as "constant organic state".

receiving less stress in modern Gestalt accounts of reasoning. Considerable doubt has in any case been thrown on the general principle that Nature abhors a psychological vacuum. (See Hebb and Foord, 1945.)

Among the more interesting of the experiments done from the Gestalt point of view are those of N. R. F. Maier. Maier's experiments start from general Gestalt principles, and part of his work was carried out in Berlin. He disagrees, however, in certain important points with the orthodox Gestalt position. "First one has one or no gestalt, then suddenly a new or different gestalt is formed out of the old elements. The sudden appearance of the new gestalt, i.e. the solution, is the process of reasoning. How and why it comes is not explained."[38]

Among other experiments, Maier (1930) gave eighty-four subjects the problem of making two pendulums, with chalk attached, so that two specified spots on the floor would be marked when the pendulums swung. Three different "part-experiences" were given to some of the subjects, viz. A, how to make a long pole out of two short ones by a table clamp; B, how to make a plumb-line with the material provided; C, how to make a horizontal T in a doorway by wedging one stick between the centre of the other stick and the opposite wall. The solution of the problem consisted in combining these three experiences so that a T was made with a lengthened upright (i.e. as in above) and wedged (as in C) against the ceiling with plumb-lines hanging from the arms of the T (made as in B). A, B, and C were given either as possibilities for solution, or ostensibly "in order to get" the subject " acquainted with the solution and the material". In a control group of fifteen A, B, and C were not given. In certain cases a hint was given by holding one of the wires against the ceiling, thus providing "direction". "The solution was very seldom obtained unless many additional suggestions were given" (loc. cit., p. 121). Other "practical" problems were also used.

"The mere conscious presence of the necessary experiences or data is not sufficient to solve certain problems. Some other factor is necessary before the elements can be integrated into a unified whole, the solution of the problem. This factor we have called 'direction'. . . . By giving 'direction' it was intended that the subject should see the problem in a certain way" (loc. cit., p. 133). Just how "direction" can determine which grouping will be formed is not easy to say; ". . . it might be suggested that 'direction' is some kind of field of

[38] 1930, p. 116.

stress in which only certain groupings are possible" (ibid., p. 139). Maier compares his concept of "direction" with Koffka's "latent attitude" which, he says, is a special case.

These excellent experiments illustrate very well what the Gestalt psychologists mean when they stress the newness of a solution. "When the solution of a problem is broken into three parts and given to a subject as three separate experiences, such experiences are not sufficient to bring about the solution of a problem. . . . The parts or experiences must be combined in a certain manner"; and from the psychological point of view this combination into a new unity is the important thing, not the mere presence of the experiences. The mind (the organism) *does* something; it forms a new unity.

In a later study (1931) Maier repeats: experience and its proper selection were not enough to account for the appearance of an original solution. Rather an organizing principle which was called "direction" was necessary (1931, p. 181). And again: "The particular attempt at solution which is adopted may be called the direction of solution, and most problems may be attacked in several directions" (Maier, 1933, p. 144). If I understand Maier aright, "direction" with him does not bear reference to the fact that a train of reasoning is, by and large, relevant; it is considered as a precipitating cause which will initiate a train of relevant thought and action much as a crystal may initiate solidification in a supersaturated solution, or as a catalytic may initiate a chemical reaction. The conception is an interesting one, and deserves further experimental examination. It will be remembered that many of the workers found that a "hint" might very materially help towards solution. This was done, for example, by Ruger (loc. cit., p. 18), by Duncker (*passim*), and by Claparède. Maier finds that the "hint" which gives "direction" in his sense "was not consciously experienced, except in cases where the solution appeared in steps".[39] "The perception of the solution of a problem is like the perceiving of a hidden figure in a puzzle-picture. In both cases (*a*) the perception is sudden, (*b*) there is no conscious intermediate stage; and (*c*) the relationships of the elements in the final perceptions are different from those which preceded, i.e. changes of meaning are involved" (1931, p. 193).

In a further paper (1933) Maier found that giving instructions how to reason increased the number of successes in solving problems

---

[39] 1931, p. 190. Sixty-one subjects were given the problem of tying together two ropes which hung from the ceiling. The best solution consisted in swinging one rope and catching it while holding the other slant-wise.

from 18·6 per cent. to 37·4 per cent. of the subjects.[40] The instructions are of sufficient interest to be printed here :

(1) Locate a difficulty and try to overcome it. If you fail, get it completely out of your mind and seek an entirely different difficulty.

(2) Do not be a creature of habit and stay in a rut. Keep your mind open for new meanings.

(3) The solution pattern appears suddenly. You cannot force it. Keep your mind open for new combinations, and do not waste your time on unsuccessful attempts.

Maier interprets the result as indicating that "when subjects are carefully instructed to guard against habitual activities and persistent directions", but to be on the alert for new points of view, "there is increase in reasoning ability. . . . Reasoning is at least in part the overcoming or inhibiting of habitual responses." By habitual Maier refers primarily to habits formed during the attempted solving of the problem; so that his work affords interesting confirmation of the fact, noted by several of the Gestalt workers, that there may be a difference in the "disposability", for the purposes of solution, of perceptual or memorial material.

Especially in his later work, Maier has broken more or less with Gestalt doctrine. But seeing that his work, as already indicated, started from Gestalt principles, at least on the critical side, this seems the logical place to describe these important experiments.

Problems Left Unanswered

The statement was made at the beginning of this chapter that the Gestalt theory offers at present a programme, rather than a fulfilment. This statement must now be emphasized. On reading through the literature, one has the feeling of a developing doctrine, which has already left behind certain emphases which were to be found twenty years ago. In place of a rather heavy stress on Insight, for example, such as may be found in Köhler's *Mentality of Apes*, now[41] over twenty-five years old, we find Organization the leading note of Koffka's volume. Instead of Closure, we find dynamical interaction characteristically accentuated. Reorganization, restructuring, as first described by Wertheimer in 1922, is playing an increasingly important part, at least in the theory of thinking, with Insight almost as a by-product. In criticizing the Gestalt theory, this

[40] The experiment was carefully controlled. See Maier, 1933, p. 152.
[41] In 1950.

fact of development should be borne in mind. In addition, Gestalt psychologists themselves seem to stress different things. It is clearly a waste of time here to criticize doctrines now superseded or still being debated.

Which way the tide of future experimental research may turn is for the future to decide. However, there are certain problems which, it seems to the present writer, must be faced by any future experimental attack. The first of them is perhaps of a philosophical nature. It concerns the *newness* of the product of thinking, and thus the distinction between productive and reproductive thought. It may thus be stated: from a certain point of view, every action of every human (and sub-human) being is new. The thirty-eighth run of a rat through a maze is different from the thirty-seventh and all preceding runs, if the runs are described by means of fine enough measuring instruments. The thousandth time a child says "seven times eight is fifty-six" is different from all preceding times. We never twice repeat anything with *exactly* the same tone of voice, and so on. For that matter, not only is organic action essentially new at every moment, but according to an influential school of philosophy, inorganic action also; philosophers such as Bergson and relativistic thinkers such as Whitehead have pointed this out. This problem of perpetual newness does not concern the physicist very much, at least for the time being; for he is mainly concerned to find the uniformities and neglect the newness. But it does concern the Gestalt psychologist, who stresses the newness and wishes in certain contexts to neglect the uniformities. For the doctrine of the Gestalt maintains that any psychological element, whether perceptual or actional, is fundamentally modified whenever it enters a fresh Gestalt.

Now an adequate psychological treatment of the facts of learning and thinking must take account of both aspects, not only the aspect of newness, uniqueness, in response, but also that of uniformity. It is true that the associational doctrine overstressed the latter, by maintaining that all thinking, for example, consisted in the association of the previously acquired ideas. On the other hand, it seems equally true that the Gestalt theory, at its outset, gave the impression of neglecting the factor of uniformity with the past as when insistence was laid on the members of the Gestalt being what they are because of their membership-character in the Gestalt, and as when the "sensation" was totally, and the influence of the past largely, neglected for the same reason. Sensations, for example, were not uniform, because they varied according to their Gestalt-membership.

The discussion thus far is theoretical; but the issue for the psychology of thinking is a very practical one. It can be stated in several ways. If every response has an element of newness, as when I enter my room on November 30th, 1949, and open the day's letters (which are different from yesterday's), why is not restructuring present all the time, with the corresponding insight? When I stand on a table for the first time to open a window, why should the name productive be denied to the activity? There is newness here, there is reorganization (I must see the table as a means to step up, not as a table), there is determination,[42] in the sense that Köhler uses it, since I step on the table *because* I want to open the window. Is then life as experienced not synonymous with insight, reorganization, and productive processes? If not, what is the criterion by which it is possible to distinguish between productive and non-productive newness? According to Köhler, indeed, "scarcely a single total field lacks this characteristic [Insight] entirely" (1947, p. 342). Where is then the distinction between productive thinking, of the kind which Duncker and Wertheimer demonstrated so well, and reproductive thinking, such as was exhibited by the associationists and specifically the early Würzburgers?

The problem as it presents itself to Gestalt psychology may perhaps be briefly recast as follows: there are, says the theory, undoubtedly processes to which the term "new" must be applied; these are characteristic of the "best" types of thinking, and it is possible that the term thinking itself should be confined to them. Such "newness" is very probably to be found if we look for it in all action and all experience. On the other hand, "new" processes undoubtedly utilize "old" experience; *something* in the new process is a more or less stereotyped repetition of the past. How can we effect a description that will justly combine each of these aspects? The same problem faces the response psychologists where it is one of reconciling newness with uniformity of *response*. Koffka has seen the difficulty and has attempted to meet it in his interpretation of the trace-theory of Köhler. But he would, one may suspect, have been the last to maintain that he had completely solved the problem.

---

[42] Köhler's later discussion of Insight would seem to tend in the direction of equating experience itself with Insight (1947, Chapter X). On the other hand, Wertheimer entitles his book *Productive Thinking*, and distinguishes such thinking from mechanized or non-productive thinking.

One may perhaps think of experiences as arranged along a continuum leading from the most chaotic to the most highly organized; likewise from the completely "old" to the completely "new"; and also from the most completely senseless to the most completely "understood". At the one end would logically lie pure chaos, dead repetition, pure nonsense; at the other complete organization, complete novelty, and complete understanding. These limits can never be reached in practice; but within them every possible experience may probably be given a place. Whether there is, in fact, only one such continuum, including all three qualities, or two or three, cannot yet be determined. But certainly the Gestalt theorists seem to be justified in claiming that the "best" thinking is apt to lie towards the second limit in each case. "Newness", "insight", and "reorganization" seem to be more or less tacitly equated in Gestalt thinking, and each is stressed by different experimentalists. But the equation seems to be nowhere explicitly stated; nor the relation between the three.

The problem of doing justice to both the new and the old in thinking is, of course, not unique to the Gestalt psychology; it is a special case of a more inclusive problem which is now creeping over from philosophy into science, and which concerns the nature of time itself. That the Gestalt treatment of thought finds itself face to face with this fundamental problem is an earnest of the advance which has been made. How psychology will solve its own section of the problem, and whether or not the solution will come in terms of Gestalt principles as they are now conceived, no man may say.

Certain other problems raised by the Gestalt approach may be mentioned. It has been seen that Gestalt theory rejects the dichotomy between motive (*Aufgabe*, purpose, determining tendencies) and association (reproductive tendencies), as motive forces in thinking. Associations are not motor, to use Lewin's term. For Gestalt theory the motive force in thinking is the dynamics of the perceived problem-situation. Is there then no "motor" in sheer habit? To believe this would seen to contradict everyday experience; as when I leave a box-room in daylight and pull the string turning *on* the electric light. Must I say with the earlier Freudians that I wish that the evening were here? Such experiences, where sheer association seems to bring about action, are common to everyday life. It does not seem that Gestalt theory has explained them, up to the present time. Koffka admits the existence of "ego-forces", corresponding to what would ordinarily be called "motives extraneous to the problem".

Does this not bring in another dichotomy, another principle other than the sheer dynamics of the problem-as-seen? I tell a psychological subject to solve this particular problem. Is it a correct psychological analysis to say that it is the problem-as-seen which provides the motive power for the various stages leading to solution? There seems no question but that certain problems activities are motivated "from without". The Gestalt theory takes no account of them. These are some of the difficulties which seem to be inherent in the attractive theory that the motive power for reasoning proceeds from the dynamics of the perceived-situation.

There is lastly the whole problem of error. For example, according to theory, a stage in thinking recognized as erroneous should consume as much "energy" as one recognized as correct. There should therefore be so much less energy at the disposal of the problem. Is this deficiency made up out of the ego-forces? If not, by making a sufficient number of errors it should be possible to achieve equilibrium. If the deficiency *is* made up, is not this the same as saying that the problem is motivated from without, and not from within the perceived-problem situation?

Summary of the Gestalt Theory of Thinking

The Gestalt theory of thinking has developed over a period of years, and through the work of a number of people apparently holding slightly differing views. Certainly the contributors to the theory have stressed different things both in their theoretical statements and in their experiments. The accounts have not yet hardened into a coherent doctrine. An attempt has been made in this chapter to give a synoptic description of the theory, and a summary is the more necessary as it is difficult to make.

(1) Like the rest of the theory, the Gestalt theory of thinking represents a rebellion from a psychological past that now seems somewhat static and academic. Pre-Gestalt theory concerned itself mainly with verbal problems, and relied largely on Association to supply both (*a*) the material, which was past experience, and (*b*) the mechanism of thinking, primarily the reproductive tendencies. In spite of its radical intentions, the Würzburg revolt still paid lip-service to the dead hand of the past; though the imageless thoughts were not necessarily reproductions. The mechanism of thinking was at least in the earlier work still associational though this was supplemented by motivational factors. Nor did Selz's later rebellion succeed in escaping the spirit of associationism.

(2) The Gestalt theory maintains that the best thinking is not reproductive but productive. That the thought-activity is not energized even in part by the tendency of the present to reproduce the past.

(3) It proposes the hypothesis that when the organism is faced by a problem, stresses are set up which will work themselves out in organic activity, usually known as *Thinking* or *Problem-solving*.

(4) These activities ordinarily include both experience (conscious processes) and action.

(5) Perceptual reorganization (restructuring, recentering), is a constituent part of the total process.

(6) Accompanied by this reorganization is, according to some of the workers, an experience known as Insight. The term is reserved by Köhler for the "experience of determination"; the relation between these two kinds of experience, viz. reorganization and insight, is left undecided in this book.

(7) The general result of the interaction of problem-stresses is a kind of activity (i.e. experience and action) which may be called, at least relatively, "new".

(8) The energizing motivation is thus "internal" to the problem-as-perceived.

NOTE ON DR. LUCHINS' EXPERIMENTS

In these well-known experiments children and adults first traced a series of mazes where the correct path was in the form of a zig-zag. This habit persisted when they were given mazes where the correct path was straight. At first sight the experiments seem to contradict the general Gestalt thesis that habit is not a "motor". However, Dr. Luchins feels that the children were motivated by the desire to get "what teacher wants", and the adults may have been similarly influenced. The experiments are thus difficult to interpret at present. (Luchins, 1942.)

CHAPTER VII

THOUGHT AND MOTOR REACTION

IN CONSIDERING THE motor reactions which occur during the course of thinking, several fundamental questions must be held in mind. There is first of all the general problem of the relation of thought to action; action, that is, of the gross, overt type more properly, perhaps, designated as conduct. Out of this springs logically the problem of the relation of thought to the finer, covert response of the body, including such processes as muscular tensions and eye movements. The special problem of speech comes under each of these headings. The general problem of the relation of speech to thought must be considered, and, in particular, the relation of thought to those implicit movements of the tongue and other vocal apparatus which the observation of the last fifty years has shown to exist during thinking. Consideration of the implicit bodily reaction during thinking leads naturally again to the problem as to whether the primary physiological process during thinking is central or peripheral; that is to say, broadly, whether it is ultimately cerebral or muscular. It will appear in the sequel that each of these views has been held by representative psychologists. An attempt will be made in this chapter to deal with these questions, with the exception of that concerning the general relation of speech to thought, which will be reserved for a chapter of its own.

Thought and Action

The most primitive organisms react directly to simple stimulating agencies, thermic, mechanical, chemical, photic, and so on. With progressive increase in complexity of structure goes a correspondingly progressive increase in complexity of response and of situations to which response is made. One aspect of the evolution of behaviour is a progressive increase in the time which may elapse between stimulus and response. Even a dog, miracle of high organization though he is when compared with the simplest living being, has a "period of delay" that is very short when compared with that of a human being. And if the chimpanzee and the gorilla may be said to "think", as the Gestalt group of psychologists and others would now maintain, yet their thinking is at least much more intimately and immediately bound up with response than is the highest human thought. It was in connection with the relatively immediate action of obtaining food that Köhler claimed to have demonstrated the existence of Insight (1925). In its evolutionary origin, human thinking has been intimately bound up with action. Without begging the question at this stage, it is proper to say that thought and action are aspects of the total response of the human being to certain situations, and that, of the two, action is the more obvious in the earlier stages of evolution. The simple organism, on being confronted with a situation, immediately does something about it. The human being may think-and-do something about it. In its ontogenetic origin adult human thought is likewise bound up closely with action. Experimental studies of children's reasoning on such problems as those involved in block-building show them actually trying out solutions, and at the same time talking. We have seen processes of "trial and error" reported in great profusion in the protocols of the Würzburg group and of Selz. Such processes have been found whenever the activity of thinking has been carefully examined,[1] In the animal and child they are "acted out". In the adult many though not necessarily all of them are "thought". Once more, the intimate relation of thought to action is exhibited.

To many the foregoing statement may seem to stultify the essential nature of human thought. To many, human thought, in its highest form, will seem to be essentially contemplative, and to contrast sharply with the action that precedes and follows it. Thus in the Würzburg experiments the subject who was asked to give an answer to the question "To give everybody his due would be to will justice and to achieve chaos: Is this true?" is surely exhibiting the essential nature of thought as contrasted with action. He is thinking, not doing, and to find out what he is thinking we must rely on introspection of his own subjective mental processes. When the long introspection is finally given, it is, surely, a description of experience rather than action. No observation of his actions, it will be objected, even one accomplished by means of the most elaborate instrumental techniques, can give us the ultimate description of these subjective

[1] See e.g., Snoddy, 1920; Dewey, 1910; Peterson, J. C., 1920; Watson, 1920, for studies maintaining that the process of finding a solution is essentially one of trial and error. It is hardly necessary here to say that such trial and error is an aspect of the whole process, not the process itself. The term is a description, not an explanation. The problem remains: why is this solution proposed and rejected while that one is proposed and accepted?

experiences. The mathematician or the chess player may think for hours, days, or even longer over the solution of a problem. The description of what has been happening may be couched in experiential terms, where, whatever may be said of the meaning of the term experience, at least this much is claimed for certain, that it is primarily not action. This, or an equivalent statement, is the ultimate anti-behaviourist argument.

It is unnecessary here to take sides on the fundamental point of issue between the behaviourist and the introspectionist. The point that is here being emphasized is the intimate relation of thought and action; and on this point both sides are, and historically have been, in agreement. For the behaviourist, the only psychological data are in the nature of reactions; so that his problem is to show how the activities usually described as thinking come under the general rubric. For the introspectionist thought is qualitatively different from action, but thinking must be considered in its genetic context of action. It is not simply thinking, it is the thinking of a reacting organism. Throughout the Würzburg experiments stress is laid on the motor concomitants of thought, those contractions of the brows and other tensions of the voluntary muscles which accompany the activity of thinking. It will be remembered that it was exactly the structuralist critics of the Würzburg work who stressed this incipient motor activity by claiming that what appeared to be imageless thought was in reality consciousness of kinæsthetic sensations. To have demonstrated the ubiquitousness of these vestigial motor responses during the thinking activity is the great positive contribution of the Cornell critics. Whatever the Cornell group did or did not accomplish, it did at least show the very close relation between abstract thinking and muscular response; and this result has been consistently upheld by later work, much of it directly inspired by the Cornell school.

But apart from kinæsthesis, it may easily be seen that the Würzburg protocols, like all other introspective accounts, are inevitably descriptions of a total thought-action complex. For, after all, the subjects cast their introspections in the form of spoken language, and the protocols are nothing but a record of this language response. They are a description of action, of a unique and highly refined nature indeed but still action. And the mathematician, however elaborate his technical thinking may be, generally records his conclusions in some way, characteristically by making the appropriate writing movements. Similarly, the chess player will move a piece or at least "make a note of" the solution of the problem. It is not denied that a train of thought may be concluded without overt consummatory action. The mathematician may not write anything down, the chess player may keep the solution in his head. It is maintained only that thinking is found to exist in a context of acting; that in many cases even where there is no visible response careful studies have shown the existence of vestigial muscular movements and that, even in the highly evolved human organism, thinking is characteristically followed by overt action even though this be of an abbreviated and apparently insignificant nature. It is true that the immense complexity of the human mind and the human nervous system often separates situation from response by processes of such complexity that the intervening thought processes may dwarf all others in significance and interest. But this fact must not be allowed to blind us to the all-important fact that it is an acting organism that is characteristically performing the thinking. Phylogenetically and ontogenetically adult human thinking is born in a matrix of action from which it never wholly escapes.

General Muscular Tension

It has been mentioned that the Würzburg psychologists, and their critics the Cornell group, brought forward evidence that thinking is often, and indeed characteristically, accompanied by tension of the voluntary muscles with resulting kinæsthetic sensation. This evidence has been amply confirmed by several different techniques. An account of some of the relevant studies will now be given.

One approach to the problem would be to instruct the subject to tense one or other group of muscles and to measure the effect on performance of various tasks. This method has been used in a number of experiments. In his review of the relations between muscular tension and performance, Courts (1942) has listed certain performances, such as memorization, pursuit learning, reaction time, adding digits, and naming letters, which have been shown by various means to be facilitated by experimental muscular tension. In others, such as mirror-star tracing, mental arithmetic and tossing tennis balls at a target, performance is depressed; still others show no effect, examples being continuous addition, syllogistic reasoning, and affective judgments. Courts points out that general conclusions cannot be drawn from the above results—except of course the conclusion that tension of varying degrees may affect intellectual and other performance. (See Courts, 1942; and 1939, for references.)

On the introspective side, the most impressive confirmation of the

Würzburg and Cornell reports of the presence of kinæsthesis during thinking comes from E. Jacobson, a member of the original Cornell group, and whose later work must be considered to some extent a continuation of his Cornell programme. As a result of twenty years of investigation, Jacobson has perfected a technique of physical relaxation which appears to be in advance of any previous method (Jacobson, 1929). During a training period which may last for months, practice is given in relaxing each muscle group singly. Thus facility in relaxation of the biceps-brachial muscle group of the left forearm is given by requesting the subject to flex the forearm against the resistance offered by the hand of the experimenter. "After the subject reports that he has recognized the sensation, he is directed to cease what he has been doing, that is to relax" (Jacobson, 1929, p. 49, legend to illustration). The same procedure is followed for extension of left and right forearms, for flexion and extension of right and left hands, of right and left feet, and legs; similar individual practice is given in the relaxation of the abdominal groups of muscles, such as the psoas muscles which lie deep in the abdomen and are involved during forward flexion of the thigh, of the musculature involved in breathing, shrugging the shoulders, moving the head, wrinkling the brows, and so on. Thus it is claimed that the subject is trained to relax, group by group, all the skeletal muscles. In addition, exercises are given for relaxation of the external muscles of the eyes and of the internal muscles of ocular accommodation, and of those muscles concerned with the activities of speech and swallowing. "After the individual has relaxed in the popular sense there remains, as a rule, a certain degree of tension called 'residual tension'. To undo residual tension in a part may proceed quickly or may require as much as 15 minutes" (1929, p. 51). Progress is necessarily slow. "The entire first period may be devoted to the biceps."

As corroborative objective evidence that the tone of the voluntary muscles is diminished, Jacobson notes a diminished knee jerk, diminished flexion reflexes in the arms, and diminished involuntary start, all of which he claims to be due to the relaxation of the muscles in question. Furthermore case histories and Röntgen-ray pictures are given to show that the smooth muscles controlling the œsophagus and the colon are affected in this general relaxation of voluntary tone.

When they have become expert, Jacobson's subjects report that mental activity in general diminishes as muscular relaxation progresses (1929, p. 181). The evidence of eleven laboratory subjects and ten highly experienced patients[2] was used. During advanced relaxation all subjects reported that imagery, of whatever sense modality, was impossible. "With visual imagery, there is a sense as from tenseness in the muscles of the ocular region. Without such faint tenseness, the image fails to appear. With complete ocular relaxation, the image disappears. This may be done by individuals of greatest skill and experience, not alone lying down but also sitting up with eyes open.

"Motor or kinæsthetic imagery likewise may be relaxed away. 'Inner speech', for instance, ceases with progressive relaxation of the muscles of the lips, tongue, larynx, and throat.

"Auditory imagery also is attended by a sense of tenseness, sometimes perhaps felt in the auditory apparatus, but characteristically in the ocular muscles. The individual tends to look towards the imaged source of sound. With the relaxation of such looking or other tension, the auditory image is absent.

"Progressive relaxation is not as a rule perfect or complete save perhaps for brief periods of time. . . . It appears that natural sleep ensues after the imageless state is maintained for a relatively prolonged time.

"With progressive muscular relaxation . . . attention, thought-processes, and emotion gradually diminish" (Jacobson, 1929, p. 188).

"We find, he says, the experience of muscular tenseness a *sine qua non* of imagery, attention and thought-process" (loc. cit., p. 186), and also it may be added, of emotion.

It is, of course, well known that many thinkers, possibly beginning with Plato, have pointed to the intimate relation of thought and movement. It is, however, safe to say that this remarkable work of Jacobson's together with its sequel, the electrographic registration of the muscular tensions in question,[3] is a landmark in the history of the theory of the relation between conscious experience and motor processes in the body. For certain criticisms which suggest themselves we shall wait until the final summing up of the experimental evidence.

Specific Muscular Tension

One important step towards objective registration of the muscular processes introspectively recorded by Jacobson and others was taken by Freeman. He first devised the method of tendon-deformation to

[2] The clinical aspect of Jacobson's work is not here considered.
[3] To be described later.

observe the small muscular changes involved. In this method, a lever presses upon the tendon of the muscle to be observed. To it is attached a concave mirror, which reflects a beam of light on to a scale. By this means a magnification of approximately five hundred is achieved. In Freeman's experiment ten subjects went through elementary mental activities, such as arithmetical addition or subtraction, counting of various kinds, as counting the *a*'s in a printed passage, solving jig-saw puzzles, performing a general information test, and noting absurdities.[4] The initiation of such mental tasks under an incentive to maximal effort "is almost invariably accompanied by an increase in muscular tension" of the *quadriceps femoris* (Freeman, 1930, p. 318). It is at first sight somewhat surprising to find that mental work affects the muscles of the leg. The result, which confirmed the preliminary observation of Golla[5] (1921), gives objective confirmation of the existence of widespread changes in muscular tonus during thinking. Freeman further found that this initial increase in muscular tension decreases as the performance progresses towards completion. During periods of interruption there was regular and notable increase in tension over that obtaining during uninterrupted work.

In a further paper Freeman has developed the method by recording the tension in the flexor muscles of the fingers of both hands and of the quadriceps muscles of both legs. Photographic registration was here made of the shadow of a three-foot lever resting on the belly of the muscle. The magnification obtained was about 500 diameters. Records were taken showing the change in muscle tonus during the period of anticipation of auditory clicks of greater and less intensity. It was found that there is greater spread of neuromuscular activity during preparation for a stimulus near the auditory threshold. Anticipation of difficulty increases the tension. This general result was confirmed by similar work on finger flexion. That is to say, there are "recognizable differences in the postural preparation for two degrees of difficulty in performance". Comparison of attitudes during the traditional motor and sensory reaction sets shows that during the former the spread of neuromuscular excitation is much less extensive than during the latter. In a further set of experiments the subject was instructed to flex his right index finger for a white light

---

[4] For the full list, see Freeman, 1930, p. 315.
[5] Golla shows the existence of thoracic movements in imagined singing, and on a much smaller scale than those accompanying actual singing. He also shows that the tonic contraction of the *quadriceps femoris* is affected by thinking, and that the amplitude of the knee jerk is increased.

(Instruction 1), and his left for a red light (Instruction 2). If now during preparation under Instruction 1 the subject is told "I've changed my mind, flex your toes instead", startling change of tonus occurs in the legs before the actual stimulus is given for flexion. Again, during expectancy of electric shock to the right index finger changes in tonus occur which are as great, if not as sudden, as those following the actual shock. Comparison with records taken without a period of expectancy shows that preparation increased anticipatory tension but decreased the amount of actual reaction. Records taken during mental arithmetic show an extremely variable pattern of muscular response, enough to indicate that "the supporting (peripheral) pattern of neuromuscular activity is in almost constant flux". Records taken at the beginning and at the end of a period of learning to follow with the hand a visual object in sine-wave motion show widespread muscular activity at the beginning of the training period. After training, this tends to narrow down to the muscles actually required for the movement. The latter result was confirmed by a study of muscular tension during the learning of nonsense syllables, when it was found that as the learning proceeds there is a decrease of supporting muscular activity. There is a tendency for the spread of neuromuscular excitation to be inversely related to the learning score.

From Freeman's work we obtain the conception of two kinds of tonic contraction. There is the general tonic contraction which normally accompanies mental work and conscious experience in general. Freeman reports that this shows a diurnal rhythm, corresponding to a similar rhythm for efficiency of the thinking process, quoting the results of Johnson and Swan who found that work done just before sleep was 6·5 per cent. superior to that performed immediately on waking. Other workers have reported a relationship between the *amount* of such general muscular tension and efficiency of mental work. Thus Bills found that the efficiency of thinking was improved by squeezing a dynamometer (1927). Miller, on the other hand, reports decreased reaction to electric shocks during extreme relaxation, with apparent diminution in the intensity of the stimulus (1926). A certain amount of tension is apparently necessary if thinking is to take place; though common observation and experiment alike seem to show that too great tension impedes efficiency. "Cortical action is reinforced and sustained by a continuous stream of proprioceptive impulses . . . muscular contraction . . . sustains experiential processes in general; the pattern of postural tonus may actually favour the execution of selected acts. . . . Habituation reduces the amount of supporting action; relative fatigue increases it" (Freeman, 1931b).

Secondly, in addition to the general facilitative tonus of the entire body, Freeman recognizes the probable existence of patterns specifically facilitative of special mental tasks. These, though related to definitive mental activities, may be unrelated to them as regards bodily location. Thus mental arithmetic may be favoured by a postural pattern involving the leg muscles.

Muscular Changes Locally Related to the Content of the Thought-process

A further step towards the understanding of the muscular changes occurring during mental work has been taken by the study of the electrical changes in the muscles in question, the so-called action potentials. The most elaborate of the experiments in question are those of Jacobson. Jacobson's work was intended to provide an objective confirmation of the results previously obtained by him through the use of the introspective method. In order to register the minute changes involved, the string galvanometer was used with thermionic amplification. Special electrodes were used, those in the later experiments making possible a fluid contact with the skin over the muscle (1930a, pp. 573–8; p. 594).[7] Potentials of the order of a microvolt were registered. The subjects were trained to relax by the method before indicated. "During a period of general relaxation, when the galvanometer string, with one lead attached to the right biceps, is vibrating slightly and uniformly, recording a fairly steady line, the signal is given for the subject to imagine something—for instance, to imagine that he is steadily flexing the right forearm. Generally within a fraction of a second the string ceases its steady course and engages continually or intermittently in a less frequent series of relatively large vibrations which cease soon after the signal is given to relax any muscular tensions present" (Jacobson, 1930a,

[6] Increase in muscular tension during mental work was first demonstrated by means of increased tension in the knee jerk. (See Bills, 1927, for a summary of confirmatory literature.) Henley (1935) reports decrease of tension for some subjects during mental work, increase in others, the change being greater in each case for the more difficult tasks. These variations could not be correlated with "personality types", psychopathic or otherwise. Henley gives an excellent bibliography. An excellent survey of the methods of measuring muscular tension is given by Davis, 1942.

[7] Jacobson's accounts are taken as given. It is difficult from the published descriptions (e.g. 1939) to assess the technical efficiency of the apparatus.

p. 580). If it has been previously agreed that the signal is to mean, "Imagine bending the left foot", the string generally continues unaltered in its course. A relaxed subject during two specimen records showed 950 linear deflections per second corresponding to a microvoltage of from 0·3 to 9·04 microvolts, with an average of 3·6 microvolts. During imagination there were about 374 deflection lines per second, ranging from 4·6 to 73·9 microvolts, with an average of 18·6 microvolts. For three subjects, with a total of seventy-one "imagining" tests, "the large deflections following the signal to imagine are markedly increased in all cases, having a value of 340 to 530 per cent. of that during complete relaxation" (loc. cit., p. 584–5). No increase occurs in the control tests, with instructions such as "When the signal comes, do not bother to imagine anything, just continue to relax"; or "When the signal comes, imagine bending the left forearm" (the electrode is on the right forearm); or "When the signal comes, imagine that the right arm is perfectly relaxed". "The signal to relax muscularly is followed by the subsidence of the large linear deflections for all the trained subjects" (loc. cit., p. 590). Certain exceptions are explained as being due to the failure of the untrained subject to relax. The earlier introspectively recorded finding was confirmed, that it is impossible to experience a motor imagination of bending the right arm during complete relaxation of this arm. The "reaction time" for the tonal changes in the arm was from about 0·2 to 0·6 ($\pm$0·1) second. The large deflections begin to diminish within 0·2 to 0·5 second after the signal with trained subjects, and complete disappearance of these deflections generally occurs within 1·5 seconds, though these figures did not hold for two out of three of the untrained subjects.

The general conclusion of this study is that the "total physiological activity present when there is imagination of voluntary movement includes neuromuscular processes in the locale comprised in the imaginary act" (1930*a*, p. 607).

These results are extended in a second article (1930*b*) which describes imagination and memory of various specific actions. When the subject imagines, for instance, that he is lifting a ten-pound weight with the right arm, electrical fluctuations were observed in the biceps region of that arm, with string deflections of approximately 186 to 550 per cent. of those observed during relaxation. For all subjects averaged, the deflection value during imagination shows a ratio of 450 per cent. to that during relaxation, this being the equivalent of a voltage ratio of 41/9 microvolts. This may be compared with a corresponding voltage ratio of 37/10 microvolts obtained for imaging the flexing of the arm. Similar records were made for recollection of various actions, such as lifting a glass or a cup of tea at dinner, reading a paper, removing a shirt, putting on a coat or rubbers, rowing, landing a fish. For six subjects the microvoltage recorded from the right arm was a little under 21, about 350 per cent. of that during relaxation. For two subjects who reported experiences of a predominantly visual nature, action potentials were recorded in only 12 of 54 tests. "A relative diminution of electrical response with all types is noted in the present tests on recollection as compared with imagination of bending the arm or lifting a weight. This is in harmony with reports from the subjects that recollection as an experience is more fleeting and vague than imagining steadily bending the right arm or lifting a ten-pound weight" (loc. cit., p. 32). The microvoltage reported was about the same, the difference lying in the length of time during which the electrical change persists (p. 30).

A third paper describes electrical activities during visual imagination and recollection. The electrodes in these experiments were placed above the medial portion of the right orbital ridge and over the right mastoid bone respectively (Jacobson, 1930c). It is claimed that eye movement in any direction is recorded as a photographic pattern clearly distinctive from the patterns recorded from looking in any other direction. During actual eye movements the typical microvoltage recorded is 400 or 500 per cent. of that during relaxation. Reaction time for eye movements is 0·5 second, being under a second for all but 1 of 49 instances. Instructions were for example to "imagine the Eiffel Tower in Paris", to imagine a sky rocket shooting up, the Statue of Liberty, a lake. When during a period of general relaxation the signal is given which will incite the subject to visual imagination, "*generally within a fraction of a second the string shoots forth and back or alternately for fractions of a second or more, producing deviations from the horizontal on the photograph. These deviations cease soon after the signal is given to relax any muscular tensions present*" (loc. cit., pp. 700–1). A slight convergence of the eyes was reported during visual imagination. This was observed with the naked eye when the room was light enough. Photographically, during visual imagination deviations of the galvanometer string are produced of a pattern similar to those produced by actual movement of the eyes. Reaction time is generally under one second (83 of 96 instances), with an average of 0·53 second. In 71 of 93 cases relaxation is fairly complete within 3·8 to 5·8 seconds. Similar tests were made for visual recollection, with positive results in over 97 per cent. of the cases. As in the case of brachial recollection, microvoltages were here somewhat less than for imagination. Both here and in the previous articles objective confirmation is reported of the general thesis that mental activity is accompanied by, and is dependent on, specific change of muscular tonus.

A control series of experiments was made to check whether the electrical currents recorded came from actual contractions of the muscles. By a system of levers this contraction was actually found to be present in the muscles of the arms at the time when electrical changes were registered (Jacobson, 1930d). This check is made to exclude the possibility that the electrical changes previously recorded were due to the psycho-galvanic reflex.

Two further papers (Jacobson, 1931a, 1931b) complete the picture. The first investigates the action currents during the instructions: "Visualize bending the right arm". When the instructions were to imagine bending the arm, action currents were registered from the arm as before (trained subjects). When instructions were to visualize bending the arm, currents were registered from the ocular region but not from the arm. Simultaneous registration from eye and arm (mechanical registration), during general instructions to imagine bending the arm, showed action in the right arm in all instances, and movement of the eyes in many but not all instances. The objective tests harmonize with the subjective reports that "they imagine bending the right arm either through a muscular experience as of bending the right arm or through visual images of the arm performing the act . . . frequently (on instruction to imagine) they engage in both of the above experiences" (loc. cit., p. 120–1).

Taken at their face value, the experiments of Jacobson seem then to have shown that there exists during thinking a third type of muscular activity. The work of Freeman and others has demonstrated the existence of tonic changes which serve to reinforce mental activity in general. Freeman has, in addition, given evidence for specific patterns of muscular tonus, which facilitate specific mental activities, but are not locally related to the activity in question. Jacobson has completed the picture by apparently showing that there are specific patterns the locale of which corresponds to the content of the thought-process.

The relation between the three types is at present obscure. For instance, if during the activity of mental arithmetic one were suddenly to form a mental picture of oneself writing on a blackboard, it is to be concluded either that the general tonic activity disappears, to have its place taken by the specific tonus of the ocular muscles, or of the arm muscles, or of both ocular and arm muscles; or that the latter tonic pattern occurs as a specific, additional local disturbance in addition to the tonic patterns of one or both of the first two types, much as the water on a lake in fairly calm weather will show a general wave pattern, and, in addition, specific "cat's-paws" corresponding to local breezes. The experimental evidence will not at present enable us to decide between these two possibilities. For Jacobson's subjects were specifically trained to relax away any tensions. Thus any general tensional background would have disappeared before the experiment started. Consequently *it is not possible to tell whether the specificity of his results was the normal state of affairs or an artifact induced by the conditions of experiment.*

We have now to discuss the specific muscular tensions found by Jacobson to exist in the locus of recollection and imagination. Several possibilities offer themselves for their function. (1) They might be an overflow from the central nervous activity, a by-product, so to speak, of the real process of thinking. This would give what may be called an "overflow" theory. Such a theory is apparently held by Lashley. (2) They might provide a necessary nervous substratum for the particular thought-process in question; just as, according to Freeman, the general tonus provides general nervous reinforcement for the central processes, and, in addition, specific mental tasks may be reinforced by specific tonic patterns. If this is so, then it is not unreasonable to believe that such specificity may be further delimited by localization in an arm or leg during its imagined movement. This gives what may be called the local reinforcement theory, according to which the constitutive central changes occurring during thinking require the facilitation of appropriate proprioceptive impulses before they can go into action. (3) The latter alternative would make the Jacobson processes a necessary but not a sufficient condition of thinking.

The Peripheral Theory of Thought

It is, however, possible that, together with the perceptual changes to which they give rise, they form a necessary and sufficient condition for thought. It is possible that the changes in the muscles intimately correspond with the nature of the thought, conscious thinking being the perception of these changes. This would give a peripheral theory of thinking, which, like the James Lange theory of emotion, places what may be called the constitutive bodily changes of a mental process at some locus external to the central nervous system. It would mean that the essential work of the thinking process is muscular work, of very small amplitude indeed, but still essentially muscular. Our thinking consciousness would be ultimately derived from the sense organs in the muscles and possibly the joints and tendons. According to this hypothesis, when we meet a problem situation, one that calls forth the activity of thinking, we take up a postural attitude towards it, corresponding to the gross attitude towards external events assumed by our earlier evolutionary forbears.[8] According to the hypothesis, the attitude in a modern human being tends to be of an implicit, rather than an explicit, nature; although in his *Expression of the Emotions in Man and Animals*, Darwin has shown that we still retain many such attitudes in a relatively explicit form. Thus when mentally searching for something we often gaze round the room; on seeing an unpleasant sight we may shut the eyes and so on. The peculiar states of consciousness engendered by the assumption of the *total series* of attitudes, including the preliminary, trial and error, attitudes as well as the final one, would, by the motor hypothesis, *be* the process of thinking subjectively considered. Objectively the changes in tonus and attitude would constitute that process. Sensory perception would always contain a kinæsthetic component. The thinking-experience would be fundamentally a perceptual one; perceptual, that is, of the fundamental peripheral processes, though, it should here be said, not necessarily of these processes as such.

Two Possibilities for a Peripheral Theory of Thinking. (a) *The Pure Motor Theory*, (b) *the Motor-meaning Theory*

For a peripheral theory of thought there are once more two possibilities. (*a*) The characteristic peripheral changes in question, together with the afferent and efferent nervous impulses associated with them, may constitute the somatic basis of thought without remainder. That is, the thought-processes in question may be completely describable in terms of the experience directly associated with these bodily processes. This will be recognized as the motor theory of consciousness, apparently as it is advocated by Dunlap, Washburn, and others.

[8] This would seem to be closely allied to Titchener's treatment. See, e.g., 1909, p. 185. Jacobson was, of course, associated with Titchener at Cornell.

Thus Miss Washburn (1916) writes: "Beaunis has said 'Muscular sensations enter not only into our sensations but into perceptions, ideas, emotions, sentiments, in a word, into the whole psychic life; and from this point of view it may be said with truth that the sense of movement is the simplest and the most universal of psychic elements'. This fact, which is apparent to everyone, is one of the bases of our theory, according to which the whole play of conscious processes depends on the interaction of movement systems, and the connections between ideas are based on the connections between kinæsthetic pathways and motor pathways" (loc. cit., pp. 196–7). And again, consciousness "utilizes, as actual causal mechanisms, certain motor processes. . . . The most important . . . are the slight actual muscular contractions which accompany all attentive consciousness and are the basis, I believe, of all associative activity"— the cortex being the "organ" for such movements. Similarly, Dunlap (in 1914): "Consciousness, whether perceptual or ideational, depends upon reaction, which is primarily a discharge from receptors, through the central nervous system, to effectors, and terminating in specific activity of those effectors. The route over which the discharge travels is designated a reaction arc. . . . No consciousness occurs without a complete reaction. . . . Having regard to the termini of the arcs, we can distinguish three types of reactions: striped muscular, smooth muscular, and glandular. . . . Arcs which connect dissimilar structures . . . [may be called] heterodetic. . . . Homeodetic arcs are perhaps of the muscular types only, since there have been no afferent terminals discovered in glands. . . . The peculiarity of the homeodetic reaction is that the effect of one reaction initiates another. The heterodetic striped muscle arc conditions perception, and the homeodetic arc conditions thought".[9]

Of the two writers quoted, Miss Washburn stresses the perception of implicit movements as the basis of consciousness. For her, the meaning of an idea is an associated movement system. Dunlap, on the other hand, stresses rather the total reaction-arc, including both afferent and efferent neural impulses. For both writers consciousness in general and thought in particular is conditioned by reaction. It is the reaction-process that makes consciousness what it is. Other kinds of experience than such reaction-conditioned

---

[9] This, and the second passage from Miss Washburn, are given as quoted in Max's statement (1934, p. 113). I quote this passage from Dunlap as an admirable statement of the view, not as necessarily expressing Dr. Dunlap's latest treatment.

events of consciousness are not admitted. Thought processes, in particular, correspond intimately with changes in muscle-tone.

On the other hand (b), it is possible *in addition* to experience thus derived, to admit experience of a different sense organ. In particular the sensed peripheral changes may be symbolic, in that they carry a meaning of such different mode; so that the resulting experiential data are perceived not *per se* but as charged with such meaning. This would imply that the interplay of muscular tonus in "movement systems" is symbolic like the movements of the pieces in a game of chess. For Titchener, it will be remembered, recognition of a shade of grey consisted of a quiver in the stomach. Thinking might then consist of an interplay of sensory experience derived indeed from peripheral changes of tonus, but symbolic of experience not so derived.

These alternatives may be called the pure motor theory of thinking and the motor-meaning theory of thinking respectively. They do not necessarily exclude other theories of the somatic basis of thinking and in particular they are not necessarily mutually exclusive. They do, however, imply a sensationalistic theory.[10] Miss Washburn's attempt to reconcile a peripheral theory with a doctrine of imageless thought cannot be allowed. "It is," she says, "only when we localize a kinæsthetic process that we call it a sensation, and since we have seldom been interested in localizing our kinæsthetic processes, it is not surprising that many processes which are based on kinæsthetic excitations do not reveal themselves to consciousness as sensational" (loc. cit., p. 197). Once more, it must be insisted that the fundamental contention of the imageless-thought theory is that thought-experiences exist which are definitely not complexes of sensations, whether these be analysed or unanalysed. Ach's claim is to have discovered experiences describable as "the knowledge that . . . ". If the claim is justified, then this experience is not and cannot be of a sensory nature.

To return to the alternatives. It will be recognized that the sensationalistic hypothesis advocated by Titchener and the Cornell school calls in both hypotheses (a) and (b) at different times. Reference may be permitted back to p. 120. "The psychophysical organism 'sets' to meet an imminent situation; and on the conscious side this 'set' *is* expectation. On the physical side are bodily attitude, strained muscles, inhibited breathing, fixed sense organs. The image of the

---

[10] It will be realized that the motor-meaning theory of thought has already been declared in essence to be untenable.

coming impression may sometimes be present, but it is not an essential factor, not a characteristic element." (Italics are the present writer's.) Here the experience known as expectation is a sensory complex originating in the muscles. The description fits what has been called the pure motor theory. On the other hand, it has been seen that, on Titchener's hypothesis, kinæsthetic sensation may carry meaning. In addition, of course, he admits processes of non-kinæsthetic origin as constitutive of thought. Thus Titchener's hypothesis which exhibits the sensationalistic scheme *par excellence*, incorporates both pure motor and meaning-motor components, as well as non-motor ones.

Thus the opposition between the sensationalistic and the non-sensory hypotheses has, to a certain extent, been transferred to the physiological sphere. Sensationalism is, broadly speaking, peripheralism; it maintains that the constituent elements of the thinking experience are sensations; that is to say, data which are closely correlated with peripheral change in the body. Of these peripheral changes an important part originates in muscular movement. From Titchener's insistence on the importance of kinæsthesis to his pupil Jacobson's insistence that relaxation renders thinking impossible there is but a short step.

The question of sensationalism has already been discussed in the light of the introspective evidence. It now remains to examine the objective evidence for the peripheral hypothesis.

Criticism of the Peripheral Theory of Thinking. Anticipatory Set. Speech Muscles

Jacobson has shown that muscular tension, and the electrical accompaniments thereof, always accompanied thinking in his subjects. He has further shown that when muscular tension ceased, thinking ceased. *Cessante causa, cessat effectus.* Does it follow that thinking *is* muscular process, overt or covert? Examination of the experimental results, those of Jacobson and of others to be mentioned, does not lead to this conclusion. The evidence for this statement will be given.

There is first the evidence from animal psychology. It is realized that this is not conclusive for human thinking. Nevertheless, it must be admitted as at least bearing strongly on the human problem. If there is evidence that a peripheral theory is inadequate to explain the most complex activities of the higher animals, and must be replaced by a hypothesis which places the constitutive physical changes, during more elaborate reactions, in a pattern of excitation of the central nervous system, which pattern may remain constant while peripheral activities vary, then the burden of proof will lie on those who maintain that the human being has suddenly developed a peripheral method of thinking. It is not difficult to find such results in the literature of comparative psychology. Watson, indeed, did attempt to show that maze-running in rats is kinæsthetic in its nature, consisting of the acquisition of stereotyped *ad hoc* motion-systems. But experiment has since completely disproved his hypothesis. Lashley's work in particular is decisive for the existence of a pattern of excitation in the rat's brain which, once acquired, is prior to the *ad hoc* kinæsthetic activity which results when the animal is placed in specific environmental conditions. Admirers of Dr. Lashley's work will hardly need to be reminded of the following passage. He is reporting on animals which have been trained to run mazes by the ordinary method, and have thereafter been subjected to various operations. "One drags himself through with his forepaws; another falls at every step but gets through by a series of lunges; a third rolls over completely in making each turn, yet manages to avoid rolling into a cul-de-sac and makes an errorless run. . . . If the customary sequence of movements employed in reaching the food is rendered impossible, another set, not previously used in the habit, and constituting an entirely different motor pattern, may be directly and efficiently substituted without any random activity" (Lashley, 1929, p. 137). Here it is impossible to avoid this conclusion that we have to do with a central pattern which, to repeat, is prior to the particular kinæsthetic pattern which it engenders in a particular situation in that different motor patterns may be the result of the same central neural pattern. The important thing in this complex activity was the master central process, not the kinæsthetic pattern. The use in this connection of data from comparative psychology is, of course, an *argumentum ad hominem*; for it was the advocates of the motor theory who first employed the evolutionary argument, by maintaining that human thinking exhibits in a rudimentary form the original method of immediate, explicit action characteristic of lower forms of life. The play of motor attitudes is by hypothesis abbreviated action; and action is here shown to depend on a central pattern prior to it.[11]

By prior is, of course, understood what Aristotle called "logically prior", not temporally prior. In the case in question, this would

[11] For further evidence against the motor-pattern theory, see, e.g., Woodworth, 1938, p. 133; Tolman, 1932, *passim*.

imply that different peripheral patterns may ultimately be innervated by the same central pattern. The results on animal learning lead unequivocally to the conception of cerebral activities which are thus prior to muscular patterns, so that, as Woodworth puts it in another context, "the core of the act corresponds to the cerebral mechanism and not to the muscles or receptors employed" (1938, p. 189). In the comparative field, one need only mention the daily variation of the rat in the maze (Dennis, 1929), Krechevsky's demonstration that rats may take different paths in a "checkerboard" maze (first shown by Dashiell), and that those with brain lesions varied less in their paths than normal ones (Krechevsky, 1937), and Macfarlane's demonstration that rats could swim a maze after learning to run it, and vice versa, with little disturbance (1930). As Woodworth remarks, "The evidence, all in all, is fully convincing that something different from a motor pattern is learned" (p. 134).

The Psychophysiology of Anticipatory Set

In human beings, one of the most carefully examined processes is known as Anticipation, Expectancy, or Preparatory Set, specifically during the period immediately preceding movement in the reaction-time experiment. The experiments of Ach have shown the great complexity of this period on the side of experience. Modern work has largely confined itself to the physiological, and mainly muscular, changes involved. Perhaps the most striking of the results was obtained by Hathaway, who made an extensive investigation of muscular tonus during the anticipatory period. Twenty subjects were used and over 150 reactions photographed. The study seems to have been conducted with exceptional care. Hathaway found no preparatory "tension" in the arm due to react, nor in general in the other arm, although choice reactions sometimes showed a slight contra-lateral reaction. It was claimed that sensitivity "approached the utmost . . . possible at present (1935) with electron-tube amplification where the base line is to remain steady". Records taken when the subject was at rest and relaxed showed a quiet base line.

Hathaway's study is only one of many which have been made. For instance, Katzell (1948) investigated preparatory pressures for simple tasks involving grip pressures and leg-extension pressures. The task might be, for instance, to exert enough pressure with the grip so that the meter would give a reading of 30. Tensions in nine different muscle groups were measured simultaneously. Sometimes, though by no means always, preliminary pressures were recorded during the anticipatory period from the group of muscles due to react. There was a characteristic pattern activity among the nine muscles for each of the tasks. Earlier studies show a bewildering variety of reactions in the reaction-finger during the fore-period. (See, e.g., Woodworth, 1938, p. 329.) The hypothesis has been proposed that the preliminary movements are "essentially covert diminished replicas" of the patterns of muscular activity to follow (Davis, quoted in Katzell, p. 408). This general conclusion is disputed by Freeman (1939), who claims that it is not true for more complex movements. According to Freeman (1940), Davis has detected action currents contrary to Hathaway's conclusion.

In general, experiment has shown that during Anticipation of the signal for reaction, there may be in the muscles concerned no muscular activity at all, variable activity, increasing activity, or decreasing activity. What relation these patterns of muscular reaction bear to conscious experience is not known, nor whether they bear any such relation. It can only be said that the most elaborate introspections of this waiting period, namely those of Ach, reported kinæsthetic experience from the hand, together with *a good deal more*. Quoting from Chapter II, observer H. of Ach said that during the anticipatory time "a known relation was given, in the sense that reaction would take place to a change (that is, the appearance of the card) which had to do with the object of regard. . . . There occurs an unequivocal *knowing* that reaction should take place as quickly as possible, as soon as the familiar change comes on the plate. In this complex the most prominent place is taken by the sensation of tension of the hand, which represents the most expedited possible entrance of the movement to be carried out. In addition, it is also given that this movement shall take place in a very short time". Again "the subject knew that the white card would appear over there".

Mowrer claims to have demonstrated a central locus for preparatory set (1940). In spite of the controversy he aroused (Freeman, 1940), the general trend of experimental result seems to bear him out. Davis again claims that the "condition of set is an active process in the organism involving sensory neural and muscular levels". He adds: "To seek the 'essence' of set either in the periphery or in a central locus would therefore be a misdirected endeavour" (1946, p. 402). That "set", whether experienced or behaviouristic, includes proprioceptive components seems highly probable from Davis's discussion, as well as from the above introspection of Ach's subject. (Davis is referring to physiological facilitation only in the simple reaction and the judgment of lifted weights, each of them relatively simple and stereotyped.) It is probably safe to say that in this much-examined field it has been shown that muscular, sensory, and central components are involved on the physiological side, with the preponderance of importance at the central locus; but that present experimental resources are inadequate to relate the total *experience* during the physiological set to the physiological findings.

The Speech Muscles

Another much-examined field is that of language. Language obviously presents that kind of reaction which, above all others, is likely to be intimately involved with the activity of thinking. The general question of the relation of speech and language to thought will be considered in a later chapter. Here the discussion will be confined to the problem of the activities of the speech muscles during thinking and "internal speech".

At least since the time of Bain it has been noticed that when we think in words and sentences there occurs a certain motion of the organs of speech. In 1880 Stricker claimed to have detected during silent speech certain feelings in the organs of articulation.[12] These feelings, he claimed, have their seat in the muscles, and resemble those accompanying the incipient articulation of the words in question. They are inseparably bound up with vocal imagery. Imagination of words in series, and verbalized thought, are conducted in terms of these incipient sounds, Initials, as he calls them.

The next step is said to have been taken by Dodge (1896). According to Schilling, Dodge cocained his own lips and tongue, thus removing the feeling of motion of the lips and the feeling of position of the tongue. He found that neither speech nor inner speech was impaired in the least. His conclusion was that motor word-images were essentially independent of peripheral elements. Schilling's judgment on this work is that by this assumption that verbal images are motor in nature, the progress of research was impeded. Nevertheless, the work seems to the present writer to be of considerable importance as a pioneer study.

In 1895 Hansen and Lehman detected involuntary whispering during concentrated thinking. This whispering could actually be heard by an observer. By means of a tambour placed on the larynx, Curtis (1899) found movements of the larynx in fifteen out of twenty subjects during recitation or whispering of familiar verses,

[12] I take my account of Stricker's work from the paper of Schilling (1929).

and during reading from a book. The other five subjects showed no movements even during whispering. Courten and Wyzoikowski in separate studies, using the same technique, found movements of the tongue invariably present during thinking. Thus experiment has objectively detected actual articulatory movements, of a minor character, during the process of thinking.[13] Of particular interest is the work of Jacobson (op. cit., 1929 and 1931). Jacobson's trained subjects reported introspectively that "Inner speech" ceases with progressive relaxation of the muscles of the lips, tongue, larynx, and throat (1929, p. 188). Another group agreed that during mental activities involving words or numbers they generally felt tenseness in the tongue and lips as in saying those words or numbers (1931, p. 209). The latter group included three subjects who, as part of their training to relax, specially observed the muscle sense in the speech apparatus during thinking. The fact that movements of the tongue or lips occurred during mental activity was, in general, confirmed by Jacobson's electrical technique, though some exceptions were noted (1931, p. 208). Such instructions were given as "Imagine counting", "Think of Ohm's Law", "Meaning of everlasting", "Meaning of incongruous", "Think of infinity", "Multiply 11 by 19" (loc. cit., p. 203). "*When the electrodes are connected in the speech musculature of the trained subject, the string shadow is practically quiet during relaxation. But promptly after the signal is sounded to engage in mental activity involving words or numbers, marked vibrations appear, indicating action potentials. Soon after the subject hears the signal to relax any muscular tensions present, the vibrations cease and the string returns to rest*" (loc. cit., p. 205. Italics as in original).

Thus there is at first sight a certain basis of experimental fact for such a theory as that propounded by Watson in 1914, which reduces thinking to the incipient action of language mechanisms.[14] However, the experimental evidence is by no means unanimous. Dodge's and Curtis's negative results have already been mentioned. Pintner also found that, with practice, silent reading could be carried on even while articulatory movements were inhibited by the overt articulation

---

[13] For references and a fuller account of these experiments, and for an account of other relevant studies, see Thorson, 1925, who also criticizes the various techniques.

[14] Watson's later theory (1931) somewhat develops his first contention, by adding the possibility of visceral and manual components; but the hypothesis is still essentially a peripheral one. See also Watson, 1920, where a symposium was devoted to the consideration of the problem "Is thinking merely the action of language mechanisms?".

of the syllables *la*, *la*, *la* (1913). Rizzolo[15] was able to solve problems while keeping the whole speech-apparatus active by pronouncing the vowel *e* in a monotone. In Jacobson's electrical-registration experiment, two out of five subjects showed one negative result, one showed two negative results, there being seventeen different forms of instruction. Further, the resemblances which Jacobson claims to exist between actual speech and imagined speech are not very striking. They consist, for example, in interruptions of the string shadow, three such interruptions showed themselves when "one, two, three" is whispered and also when the same words are imagined. Although it is stated that "when verbal matters are imagined, or recalled, such as a poem, records . . . are secured resembling those from actual faint speech but of considerably less voltage", such records are not given.

What still seems to be the most thoroughgoing experimental attack on the problem of the action of speech musculature during thinking was made by Thorson in 1925. She proposed four questions:

"1. Do movements of the tongue occur constantly or with any significant frequency during internal speech?

"2. Are the movements which occur identical in their form to those of the corresponding overt speech?

"3. If so, are they an essential element of internal speech, or only an incidental consequence of it?

"4. If they do not occur regularly, what is the significance of the occasional movements which have been reported?" (Thorson, 1925, p. 6).

It will be noticed that the original problem is strictly delimited to the subject of internal speech, or, as it is sometimes called, verbal imagery. The relation of such imagery to thought itself is not mentioned in the programme, though the term "thought" is used later in the paper.

The registration used in this experiment was mechanical, the apparatus consisting of a modification by Lashley of Sommer's "Movement analyser". The magnification was from 3·6 to 4·5, and the apparatus was not affected by respiration or swallowing, except when these directly affected the tongue. Two distinct curves, recording vertical and horizontal movements separately, were marked on a long paper kymograph. Timing was with a Jacquet stop-watch.

The results were clear-cut. It was found that movements of the

[15] Rizzolo, 1931.

tongue were "not universal in internal speech or verbal thought. When they do occur they correspond to movements in overt speech of the same words only in 4·4 per cent. of the cases. Repetition of the same verbal thought is accompanied by repetition of similar tongue movements in only 10 per cent. of the cases where movement occurs" (Thorson, 1925, p. 27). This seems conclusive against a peripheral theory of internal speech, or, as Thorson puts it, "verbal thought". For that theory demands that if two "verbal thoughts" are the same, they are so because of identical peripheral processes.

Thorson's technique of experimental registration has been attacked by Max (1934) on the ground that the sensitivity of the receiver was insufficient to record finer movements, and further that the frequency of the recording system was not great enough. Thorson's records must therefore, he says, be distorted. This, says Max, would account for the divergence Thorson found between records of "thought" and "spoken" material. The faster, "thought", material would be more distorted than the slower, "whispered", material. This criticism does not seem to be justified as against Thorson's actual results and in consideration of her method of scoring. For if there was distortion, it would equally affect all tongue movements of the same speed and amplitude. A distorting mechanism can give a false but not a variable record of that which it registers. But for repeated internal speech, *no two records* of tongue movements were *identical* in ten subjects. Of the total trials for all subjects, 13 per cent. show *similarity*, 87 per cent. exhibited no possible pattern relationship. Three subjects showed no cases at all of similar pattern for repeated internal speech. Max's criticism must then assume that in all these cases of internal speech there were, from repetition to repetition, differences in speed or amplitude sufficient to cause unequal distortion of sufficient magnitude to transform the record. This seems highly improbable in view of the fact that successive repetition of the same whispered words and phrases showed a pattern relationship in 89 per cent. of the cases with 25 per cent. identical patterns. There is no reason why variation in speed sufficient to cause complete distortion should occur in 87 per cent. of the "verbal thought" trials and in a maximum of 10·6 per cent. of the whispered trials. Thus it must be concluded that the lack of similarity shown by the records for verbal thought corresponds, in all probability, to a lack of similarity in the movements themselves. It is probable that Max's criticism is justified to the extent that the discrepancy between records of internal speech and whispering may be due in part, at least, to difference of distortion between movements of greater and less amplitude. But this cannot invalidate Thorson's conclusion that there was no consistency of peripheral pattern between repetitions of the same "verbal thoughts".

Thorson concludes her paper with the statement that "there is no indication of a correspondence between movements of the tongue and verbal formulations in thought. This leaves only the hypothesis that the activities are intra-neural, and do not necessarily involve complete motor expression at each stage of the process" (op cit., p. 27).

Thus the general results of animal psychology, as typified by the experiments of Lashley and others, who show that different peripheral movements may be initiated by what seems to be the same central neural lattern, and also the work on speech muscles, seem to weigh against the peripheral theory. The work on "set" inclines the same way, though it waits a more developed experimental technique. Many would dispute the last sentence.

The Function of Incipient Speech Movements

What, then, is the function of such movements of the speech musculature as have been shown to exist during thinking of the verbal type? It will be remembered that three alternatives were given, on page 197 corresponding to what may be called the overflow, the reinforcement, and the constitutive theories. Thorson claims to have disproved the last of these, and we have agreed with her contention. She is, then, left with the alternative that tongue movements have either an overflow or a reinforcing function, and tends towards the former hypothesis. That is to say, she is inclined to believe that such overt movements as do occur are neuromuscular by-products, the chance results of neural irradiation rather than integral factors in the thought process. This conclusion was based on the fact that the amount of implicit movement was roughly proportional to the distraction, to the amount of other bodily activity involved, and to the general tension. The more difficult tasks involved more movement, this being interpreted by her as meaning that there is more neural irradiation during the greater tension employed while performing tasks of greater difficulty. However, it is at least possible that alternative two may be the correct one, namely that the muscular changes found to be present are local reinforcements of the central process. That is to say, it is possible to interpret her data as meaning that the more difficult mental task is aided by more intense local neuro-muscular reinforcement.

Such an interpretation fits in with what is known of the general, as contrasted with the specific, muscular responses during thinking. It will be remembered that Freeman found that mental work involves an initial increase in muscular tension which decreases as the performance progresses towards completion. Interrupted work showed "regular and notable increase in tension" (1930, p. 332). He further found that the spread of neuromuscular activity is much more pronounced when the auditory stimulus for which the subject is waiting is near his auditory threshold, and that practised, and therefore, presumably, easier, performance is accompanied by decreases in spread of activity (1931, p. 492). Stroud (1931) showed a correlation between tension of jaw and hand tension on the stylus maze. Bills (1927), we have seen, showed that increase of pressure on a dynamometer facilitated thinking. These and other similar results were taken as demonstrating that general muscular tension may have a facilitative effect on the process of thinking. "It seems a conservative method", says Freeman, "to treat the known facts of *specific* facilitation, by way of muscular sets, as existing upon the background of general facilitation" (1931*b*, p. 443. Italics by present writer). He is referring to specific sets of the larger skeletal muscles. But the statement applies also to the activities of specific muscles of the body which are closely related to the process of image-formation in thinking, and particularly to the speech-muscles.

There is, in fact, some *ad hoc* evidence that the process of thinking in words may be facilitated by movements of the vocal apparatus. Schilling describes experiments done on normal children at his request by Karn, a teacher of deaf and dumb children.[16] Eleven boys and eighty-nine girls, from 9 to 11 years old, served as subjects. The children were instructed to read silently, and they were questioned and invited to relate what they had read in order to find out how much they had understood. They were watched for external speech movements. Twenty-seven per cent. showed no externally visible speech movements; in 73 per cent. such movements were visible. The children were graded into five degrees of intelligence, the grades being obtained by using a combination of teachers' judgments and school reports. The results were as follows:

---

[16] Since Karn's monographs are inaccessible to me, I take Schilling's own account (Schilling, 1929). The experiment is not well known and raises some interesting points. For that reason, it is reported in some detail.

TABLE 1

SILENT READING

Intelligence Grade	With Speech Movements	Without Speech Movements
	%	%
1	47·66	53·34
2	68·18	31·82
3	75·00	25·00
4	92·85	7·15
5	100·00	0·00

Of the most intelligent children, not quite half showed externally visible speech movements. As intelligence falls, the proportion of children showing such movements increases, until at the lowest grade of intelligence such movements were universal. The question now arises as to whether "the motor activity is a help in the understanding of what is read, a help of which the pupil makes more use, the lower his intelligence is" (Schilling, loc. cit., p. 222). On examination of the children's understanding of what they had read, it was found that 37 per cent. had read quite mechanically and without any understanding. Others related things which were only remotely associated with what had been read. Three stages were distinguished —that of complete understanding, part understanding, and complete lack of understanding. Children showing these were divided for each grade of intelligence into those who exhibited and those who did not exhibit movements. Thus the following table was obtained:

TABLE 2

SILENT READING

Intelligence Grade	Understanding with Speech Movements	Understanding without Speech Movements	Part Understanding with Speech Movements	Part Understanding without Speech Movements	No Understanding with Speech Movements	No Understanding without Speech Movements
	%	%	%	%	%	%
1	88·89	60·00	11·11	40·00	—	—
2	60·00	42·86	33·33	28·57	6·67	28·57
3	70·83	37·50	25·00	37·50	4·17	25·00
4	38·46	—	30·77	—	30·77*	100·00
5	7·69	—	61·54	—	30·77	—

* As the result of correspondence with Dr. Schilling, this figure was changed from the published value of 61·54 which was a misprint.

Fifty-four per cent. with speech movements read with under-standing, 32 per cent. with part understanding, 14 per cent. with no understanding. Of those without such movements, 46 per cent. read with understanding, 38 per cent. with part understanding, 16 per cent. with no understanding. Thus, for all grades of intelligence taken together those with speech movements apparently are at an advantage, over those without, in understanding. This is not due to the fact that those with speech movements are the more intelligent. For Table 2 shows that, within the same intelligence group, move-ment and understanding go together. At each stage of intelligence, understanding is better for those who move their lips. Thus for the highest grade of intelligence, of those showing speech movements 88·89 per cent. show understanding of what has been read, 11·11 per cent. show part understanding; in the same intelligence grade, of those without speech movements only 60 per cent. show under-standing, 40 per cent. show part understanding, and so on for grades 2, 3, 4, and 5. Thus Schilling concludes: "Motor expression of speech movements favours the understanding of what is read. Suppression inhibits the understanding of what is read" (loc. cit., p. 223).

Karn also reports (Schilling, 1929, p. 234) a difference in two classes dependent on the teachers in charge, one of whom laid con-siderable, the other little, stress on articulation in reading. In the former class, the percentage of children showing articulatory move-ments during reading was greater than that in the latter, and at every stage of intelligence the understanding was better also. Thus Schilling is inclined to the idea that the more intelligent child may prematurely drop articulatory movements, at a sacrifice to understanding of what is being read.

These ingenious experiments lack, of course, exact, objective classification, both of the children's intelligences and of their under-standing of the printed passage. They lack also statistical treatment. Schilling is careful not to claim too much for them. They may, however, be taken as at least initial and rough evidence that move-ments of the order of those registered by Thorson and others may, at least in children, assist verbal thinking. They should obviously be repeated.

Schilling claims supporting evidence for his hypothesis in the results of his experiments with deaf mutes. Here again he claims that during the less automatized, more productive processes of thinking the breathing curve is more like that of the speech-breathing curve.

The more difficult the thought process is, the greater this resemblance becomes. That is to say, the speech-breathing is treated as part of the total complex of speech movement. Movements of articulation were always present, except in the case of two female subjects. One subject could go through the required process of thought either with finger movements or with movements of articulation, and volunteered the information that it was much easier with articulatory movements. He claims that all the deaf mutes whom he had asked report unanimously that inner speech with movements of the lips is of great assistance in their thinking.

In the normal person Schilling thinks of speech as being present in all stages, from explicit speech through whispering and movement of the lips to verbal ideas with no subjective motor sensations. Whether these last would in every case show changes of tonus if objective registration of sufficient delicacy were employed, it is of course impossible to say. He is inclined to believe that not all adults succeed in eliminating movements to the point where they are below the threshold of sensation. Conceivably they are not intelligent enough to do their routine thinking without this aid. Jacobson's work would, of course, tend to the conclusion that complete elimination of all movement is impossible although his results show a few exceptions. Other workers have found a considerable number of cases where thinking was accompanied by no recorded movement. This difference may, of course, have been due to inadequate technique on the part of the earlier workers.[17]

Thus, Schilling's work tends to the conclusion that *just as the grosser patterns of muscular tonus assist the process of thinking, so may the incipient speech movements* observed in a comparatively crude form by himself and Karn *be a definite help to the thinking process, especially when the thought is of a verbal type*. If these movements were a mere by-product of thinking, then they might have been expected, for economical reasons, to vary inversely with the intelligence of a child. This is apparently the case. But by the same token, it would hardly be expected that of children of the same intelligence those showing more movement would show also greater understanding. The reinforcement theory also fits the data of Jacobson, Thorson, and the other workers who have by instrumental means

[17] Schilling makes the interesting point that parents, at meal and other times, and also teachers, may cause neurotic trouble by suppressing loud-thinking or other motor accompaniments of thinking among children. He recommends that children be encouraged to move their lips during silent reading.

recorded movements of the same order but of smaller extent. There is, in fact, no experimental evidence whatever which would lead us to believe that speech movements must be put into a different class from those grosser fluxes of muscular tone whose function is admittedly one of reinforcement. Jacobson nowhere explicitly states his belief in the correspondence theory (but seems to imply it throughout his work). Except for the fact that counting one, two, three mentally and overtly both result in interruptions of the record in three places, the records he obtained from the speech muscles give no support to this theory, nor is it easy to see how such evidence could be obtained by the method he used. On the other hand, all his published results fit the reinforcement theory equally well.

Schilling's theory is interestingly confirmed by an experiment of Barlow. Barlow (1928) instructed groups of children, 278 in all, to learn lists of twenty nonsense syllables. Group A made normal speech responses, group B were required to restrict articulation by holding a pencil between their teeth. At every grade, from the second primary grade at school upwards through eight years to the ninth grade, more syllables were reproduced by those who were allowed free use of their speech muscles than by those whose articulation was restricted.[18] There is a clear though small superiority at all ages. The same difference was found to exist between similar groups (fifty-one in all) of college students. Strictly speaking, Barlow's experiment did not test the relation of thought to articulation. Nevertheless, the process of memorization is sufficiently closely allied to that of thinking for the experiment to be considered on the whole a confirmation of Schilling's hypothesis.

General Picture of Muscular Reaction during Thinking

It is fair to say that the picture is not yet clear. But from the mass of experiment which has been done to date on the relation of muscular activity to thinking, something like the following picture emerges. At the beginning of mental effort, there is in most people a widespread increase of muscular tension which rapidly drops to a level above that of rest. The resulting proprioceptive impulses serve the function of general reinforcement to an increased cerebral activity. This function, as Freeman suggested, is perhaps accomplished by the lowering of certain cerebroneural thresholds. During tasks which are difficult either *per se* or because of distraction, or during interruption of an accepted task, this tension is increased, thus providing

---

[18] It has been suggested that this result was due to distraction.

the additional reinforcement necessary. This reinforcement apparently has an optimal range which varies from task to task and from individual to individual: if it rises above a certain stage, cerebral activity begins to be impeded by some mechanism as yet unknown. On the other hand, when the general bodily tonus falls below a certain stage, sleep may ensue (Jacobson), although even during sleep there may apparently remain an irreducible minimum of general tonus. This occurred in 69 per cent. of the deaf mutes examined by Max (1935). During sleep, also, the general, minimal tonus is from time to time interrupted by sudden visible and widespread changes in motility, which are described by Max (loc. cit., p. 475), Johnson and Wiegand (1927), Tomi Wada (1922), and others. According to Davis (1939) the general excitation is focused for a particular psychological process at some region constant from subject to subject, and exhibits a gradient to other parts of the body.

Superimposed upon it are more or less widespread tonic patterns, such as Freeman found during mental arithmetic, counting a's and so on (1930). Such patterns may gradually become crystallized by practice. They appear to have the effect of reinforcing the particular mental activities in question (Freeman, 1931).

Finally, there are conceivably still more specific changes of muscular tone, located in a part of the body specifically related to a particular thinking process. Possible examples are the changes observed by Jacobson during imagination or recollection of a manual activity; and also the changes occurring in the speech-musculature during verbal thinking which have been reported from many quarters. These, we have shown reason to believe, are probably facilitative in character also. It is possible that they are normally superimposed upon the first, and possibly also on the second type of postural pattern; although Jacobson's reports from his trained observers seem to imply that, in these cases, verbal thinking went on without general tension, i.e. with only local tension. That they do not occur during all thinking seems to be abundantly proved by Hathaway's study; and Jacobson's results also exhibit exceptions. They must be thought of as corresponding only in a very general way with the process of thinking (Thorson). The relation of Davis's focus of activity to the second and third type of pattern has yet to be worked out. And in any case, the existence of the third type, *as a separate type*, is perhaps under doubt.

That peripheral muscular changes *ad locum* are not necessarily involved in thinking about a particular part of the body is, finally, shown by the control records of Jacobson. When his subjects were instructed to imagine bending the arm, pumping up a bicycle tyre, and so on, action currents are recorded from the arm in question, corresponding in time and rhythm to the imagined movements. When the instruction was "Do not bother to imagine", no localized flexion is recorded. But the understanding of these instructions is just as much a mental process as the understanding of the former instructions. One is therefore entitled to ask, where then is the peripheral process corresponding to the understanding of this instruction? According to the theory implied by Jacobson, it must lie somewhere in the muscles. If it is not located *ad locum*, argument for the necessity of local contractions during thinking about parts of the body is vitiated. Similarly, when the instruction is "Upon hearing the first signal, do not bother to think", one must conclude that the signal was not indifferent to the subject, but that it "meant" to her, "Do not bother to think". But no muscular reaction is recorded, and specifically, the record shows "no evidence of action potentials in the tongue" (1931, p. 207). Here, once again, according to the peripheral theory there should have been some peripheral action corresponding to the content of the instructions. The peripheral theory as implied by Jacobson's experiments is in these cases inadequate to explain the facts.

The discussion leads naturally to a consideration of the relation of thought and language in general. This topic will be treated in the next chapter.

CHAPTER VIII

¹ LANGUAGE AND THOUGHT

THE LAST CHAPTER dealt with the general relation of thought to physical activity or response. This will consider the relation of thinking to the specific, and roughly speaking, uniquely human activity of language.[1]

Language as Behaviour

Spoken language is of course behaviour of a highly complex kind. It is customary to consider it under three aspects. There is the primary activity or behaviour of the person engaged in producing the sound. There is the activity or response of the person to whom the spoken language is addressed. And finally, there is the fact of "meaning", which is common to the two persons, the one speaking and the one spoken to, the word "meaning" being used at this stage without any implications. Some meaning must be common to speaker and hearer in order that communication may take place. These three aspects will be termed those of Utterance, Evocation, and Reference, respectively.[2]

Gardiner[3] has an amusing diagram in which these general distinctions are brought out. Six pictures show Mary and James together in a room. Picture 1 is entitled "The rain falls" (statement of a fact unrelated to Mary or James). In picture number 2 "James perceives the rain". In 3, James says "Rain!" (with reference to the falling rain). In 4, Mary pays attention. In 5, Mary sees what is meant (4 and 5 together perhaps constitute the phase of evocation). And in the last picture Mary replies, "What a bore!" (utterance on Mary's part). Here the situation to which James is responding is a complex one, including as predominant factors Mary and the water falling outside. The total context of course plays its part. James would speak differently if he were out of doors in his silk hat.

---

[1] For discussion of the speech of animals, see Esper, 1935; Delacroix, 1930.

[2] McGranahan (1936) styles them Expression, Evocation, and Representation. Cf. Bühler's triple classification of *Ausdruck*, *Appel*, and *Darstellung* (1934). These he calls "abstractive moments" in reference to the fact of the unity of the whole process. See McGranahan, *ad loc.*

[3] Gardiner, 1932.

The distinctions and implications involved in each of the three phases of *utterance*, *evocation*, and *reference* will be discussed in the light of the experimental evidence. In order to avoid misunderstanding emphasis is laid at the outset on the fact that they are three phases of one activity.

Utterance

The sounds produced by a speaking human being are continuous, with no break save at relatively infrequent pauses. This fact of continuity has been noted for many years by linguists, and experimental records made of the speaking voice have confirmed it. The records further show that there is continuous variation in expression. "No two records are alike."[4] The fact of variation in speech-behaviour has likewise been noted by linguists, who have pointed to differences in stress, pitch, intensity, duration, and so on. It has been the task of linguists to analyse this continuum-in-flux into units; that is to say, to show what constant[5] factors participate in the variable flow. The smallest of these constants is the *phoneme*. "Among the gross features of any utterance, then, certain ones are distinctive, recurring in recognizable and relatively constant shape in successive utterances. These distinctive features occur in lumps or bundles, each one of which we call a phoneme." . . . Symbols are assigned to the phonemes, and "all we need is a few dozen symbols, enough to supply one for each phoneme of whatever language we are recording. . . . The number of *simple primary phonemes* in different languages runs from about fifteen to about fifty. Standard English, as spoken in Chicago, has about thirty-two."[6] That is to say, leaving out secondary factors, such as stress, about thirty-two constant units of sheer sound may be recognized in the variable flux of human speech as there spoken. There are also "secondary phonemes", such as stress, which complicate the problem somewhat. The existence of such phonemes was not recognized until a few years ago. Throughout the largest part of the history of linguistics the ultimate unit of analysis was the linguistic form, which it is now recognized can be built up out of the newer and smaller unit, the phoneme.

A combination of phonemes actually used in speaking is known linguistically as the morpheme, which is defined as a phonetic form

[4] Scripture, 1935.
[5] The fact of the constancy of the units is well stressed by Esper, 1935.
[6] Bloomfield, 1933, pp. 79, 87, 90.

with a constant meaning.[7] The *morpheme* is then a constant unit of a higher order than the phoneme. For example, the sentence *Poor John ran away* "contains five morphemes; *poor, John, ran, a-* (a bound form recurring for instance in *aground, ashore, aloft, around*), and *way*".[8] "The total stock of morphemes in a language is its *lexicon*," and the meaningful arrangements of forms in a language constitute its grammar. According to the rules and devices of grammar, which themselves consist of intricately modulated behaviour-constants, still larger units are built up which are known as sentences. Thence come paragraphs, and the even larger unities of literary compositions.

Linguistic science has then analysed speech into a hierarchy of reactions, the larger units being composed of smaller sub-units, the smaller into still smaller and so on, until, from the unity, for instance, of an hour's speech by a polished orator we come down to the smaller unities of the paragraph, the sentence, the morpheme, and finally reach the handful of relatively invariant phonemes, which is the foundation of all linguistic activity. Here we have the most exact and the most scientifically conceived analysis that has yet been made of any aspect of behaviour. Out of a small number of relatively invariant behaviour units, higher and yet higher structures are built by an intricate mingling of invariant and *ad hoc*, adaptive, modes of action, until there appears the most complex behaviour structure of all, the highly unified, immensely complicated, and sensitive activity of human speech.

The integration of elementary "atomic units" of speech into a hierarchy of higher and yet higher units is excellently illustrated by the results of experiment in the telegraphic language.[9] "All the facts point to the conclusion that the telegrapher must acquire, beside letter syllable and word habits, an array of higher language habits associated with the combination of words in connected discourse. Mastery of the telegraphic language involves mastery of the habits of all orders. In a word, *learning to receive the telegraphic language consists in acquiring a hierarchy of psychophysical habits*."[10] The facts were picturesquely stated by the operators questioned by Bryan and Harter. "At the outset one 'hustles for the letters'. Later one is 'after words'. The fair operator is not held so closely to words. He

---

[7] That is to say the "reference function" is added, the morpheme thus being the smallest unit of speech with "reference". See the next section.

[8] Ibid., p. 161.

[9] Bryan, W. L., and Harter, N., 1897 and 1899.

[10] Ibid., 1899, p. 356. Original italics.

can take in several words at a mouthful, a phrase or even a short sentence. The real expert has all the details of the language with such automatic perfection that he gives them practically no attention. ... He can often transcribe while his mind is running on things wholly apart."[11] It will be remembered that the ultimate unit, out of which the complex structure of the telegraphic language is built, is a click, made or heard; and although there is unintentional variation according to the mood or the temperament of the sender, which would probably add what the linguist calls secondary phonemes, yet the number of ultimate units will still remain far fewer than the fifty or so necessary for the analysis of spoken language. The complexity of the feat performed when a telegrapher is receiving may be seen from the statement that the expert prefers to keep six to ten or twelve words behind the sending instrument. This means that he must hold from 170 to 303 separate clicks in his mind, giving an average of 237·7 clicks to be retained for ten words—a remarkable performance, and one only to be achieved, as the authors say, by years of practice.

Bryan and Harter develop the theory of the hierarchy of habits necessary for such a performance. Their statements apply to all language, telegraphic or otherwise. They point out three features of such a hierarchy. (a) There are habits which are constituents of all other habits within the hierarchy (i.e. the phonemes). (b) There are habits which embrace the lower ones as elements, and are themselves elements of higher habits and so on (morphemes, words, etc.). (c) Habits of any order represent unities. There may be added the statement that the habits, as the units of analysis, are the constant features in the pulsating continuum of actual speech, constant, that is, in a relative sense. For it has been seen that there is intentional variation in telegraphic spacing; apparently there is also some variation in the phonemes. Nevertheless, both phonemes and the elementary hand movements and click perceptions of telegraphy do represent approximately constant features of a variable flux. In the same way, the higher habit-units, morphemes, words, grammatical usages, etc., of ordinary speech are approximately constant, though not absolutely so.

There has been shown to exist a similar habit-hierarchy in typewriting.[12] Book gives tracings showing the letter by letter performance of a beginner's first trial where "each of the steps required to make a letter . . . was more or less of a problem". In the record of

[11] Bryan, W. L., and Harter, N., 1899, p. 352.
[12] Book, 1908, pp. 85–100.

another subject, showing the third trial, the typing strokes may begin to group themselves, in sequences corresponding to "syllable and word associations". A later record of the same subject shows an increase of this grouping, while a still more advanced ("semi-expert") stage of another learner shows still larger units to be characteristic. These correspond to phrases.[13] These interesting records show in an illuminating way the kind of hierarchical function which is characteristic of language activity. Thus experiment on telegraphy and typewriting has interestingly confirmed the results of linguistic science. It may fairly be said that telegraphy is a language with two primary phonemes.

To return to expressive speech proper. We have no effectors whose purpose it is exclusively to reproduce speech. "The entire peripheral speech mechanism (lips, tongue, teeth, larynx, diaphragm, etc.) may be identified with biologically older and more fundamental vital functions which are seriously altered during speech. . . . There is not a single muscle group which has been developed to serve speech exclusively."[14] Structures must be pressed into special service which ordinarily have other, coarser functions. Certain functions, such as breathing, must be altered. We know from experiment that there is a special breath rhythm for speech.[15] Other functions must be inhibited, such as swallowing. "In so-called normal speaking the entire peripheral speech mechanism functions as a unit, several individual functions having coalesced to form the whole—a part of the nervous system exerts a dynastic influence (dominance) over other parts to ensure concerted but unequivocal action. . . . The complete speech act in its perfect form demands the proper mobilization, in proper sequence, of a series of complex procedures wherein the time relation is of fundamental importance. A lack of chronological exactitude will throw the entire performance into disorder."[16] Thus a whole array of "sub-linguistic" integrations, so to speak, must be superadded on the linguistic integrations already described. The wonder is, as Travis remarks, not that there are so many of us with speech disorders, but so few.

Confronted with a function of such terrifying complexity, and one dependent for its working upon the exact synchronization of such complicated and unitary sub-functions, present-day neurology is, if not entirely powerless, at least nearly so. It is necessary, as Travis points out, to assume a centre of dominance which can influence

[13] Book, ibid., tracings facing page 88.   [14] Travis, 1931, p. 650.
[15] See, e.g., Schilling, 1929.   [16] Travis, loc. cit., p. 651.

certain sub-cortical and possibly cortical centres as units, exciting some and inhibiting others. All the evidence converges towards the location of such a centre of dominance in the left cerebral hemisphere for right-handed persons, and in the right cerebral hemisphere for the left-handed. Since the researches of Head, it has become clear that this centre of dominance is not a speech centre, in the sense that the activities which produce speech are located there, and still less in the sense that "word memories" or "verbal images" are located there, in such a way that such memories or images can be excised by removal of the centres. According to Head, we should think of nervous centres as nodal foci, centres of integration and of other changes. "Speech, reading, and writing are acquired at a period when the central nervous system is structurally complete . . . they employ highly integrated functional arrangements, developed originally for other purposes. These in turn depend on the integrity of a series of arcs or circuits, subserving processes on the most diverse physiological levels, the highest of which are to be found in the cortex."[17] Motor centres, according to Head, are not primarily the source of the initiation of movements, they are rather a source from which we can interfere with already integrated actions. To use his own metaphor, they are to be regarded as shunting centres where already organized activities are resorted, recombined, and redirected. During the activity of speech, it is probable that the whole cortex is highly active, although perhaps one might say that the focus of the most intense activity is in the areas which have been clinically and experimentally assigned to language.[18]

The Reference Function of Language

"Representation is the relation between speech signs in usage and the objects, events or situations for which they stand as substitutes." We touch here on the "problem of meaning". To return to Gardiner's diagram. That James's utterance of the word *Rain!* is different from the fact of water falling from the sky, and that, further, James's utterance somehow bears reference to the fact, all are agreed. Further, most are agreed to express that relation by saying that the verbal utterance "means" the "objective" proposition or fact; though there are many opinions as to the significance to be attached

---

[17] Head, 1926, p. 475.

[18] An old colleague, Dr. D. O. Hebb, has pointed out that certain patients may be able to speak a word but may not be able to do so voluntarily. This does not, I think, impair the subsequent argument, but it does add to the complexity of the whole problem.

to the statement that *Rain!* "means" the fact. Into the controversy concerning the *Meaning of Meaning*, it is not proposed to enter. The reader who is interested is referred to the voluminous literature.[19] It will appear later that in some contexts at least the "problem of meaning" is a spurious one, artificially created by psychologists and others because of a false analysis of the facts. But as a first statement we shall understand by the "meaning" of speech a fact to which speech may be said to "refer" and which may be analysed without reference to the particular speech activity in question. Thus when James says "Rain!" or "It is raining!", the meaning is the meteorological fact that water is falling from the sky outside; this fact may be analysed independently of James's remark. This use of the term meaning is consistent with the distinction which is important for modern logic, and which we owe ultimately to the insight of Husserl and Meinong, between the judgment on one side and the proposition, which can ideally be analysed independently of its psychological origin.[20] It is recognized that this is a statement of the problem only, and some, including for example Titchener, would say a one-sided statement. Into the metaphysical difficulties involved in the statement it is not proposed to enter.

Now it is clear that the words "It is raining" may be repeated meaninglessly. This might be done, for instance, by a child who is in the early stages of learning to talk; and, indeed, every child has gone through this stage, where sounds are made without the background of meaning ordinarily attached to them. Thus the writer as a child was taken to a primary school after term was started, and found the children chanting the words, "The Humber, the Wash, and the Mouth of the Thames; the Humber, the Wash, and the Mouth of the Thames; the Humber . . ." etc. In this chant he joined, without having any idea of its meaning. Not until a long time later did he realize that these were "the principal openings on the east coast". The same "meaningless" repetition is of course performed by parrots, and indeed when performed by human beings is known as parroting. Of course, much "parroting" is not entirely meaningless. The child who repeats what is to him a jargon often places his own meaning upon it to the confusion of his teacher. However, enough has been said to make it clear that the activity of producing the

---

[19] See e.g. Titchener, 1909; Ogden and Richards, 1923; Stern, 1931.

[20] The use of the term "fact" involves certain metaphysical difficulties, for a discussion of which readers are referred, e.g. to Wittgenstein, *Tractatus Logico-Philosophicus*.

sounds of speech and the activity of producing meaningful speech are, psychologically speaking, two different things. The parrot utters the word "rain". The human being utters the word and means it. The human organism is then doing something which the parrot is not doing, in addition to producing the same sounds. Excluding for the time being the activity of Evocation, the *plus* has been termed the *reference function* or the activity of meaning (something).

Utterance and "reference functions" are thus activities of the organism in producing sounds and "referring to meanings" respectively. The reference function may, in fact, be defined as the activity of referring to meaning. It is a psychological activity, whatever connotation be attached to the word psychological. That is to say, the definition is intended to be independent of any particular definition of the subject-matter of psychology. It has been seen that utterance of itself involves the working of a very elaborate mechanism. Utterance, together with reference, which is found in ordinary speech, is clearly more complex. It is not intended here to imply that in ordinary speech the functions or aspects of utterance and reference are distinguishable either in time or introspectively.

Now it further becomes clear that both utterance and reference functions may vary enormously in complexity. When a ten-months'-old child sees his mother and calls her *mama*, utterance and reference functions are both present but in a very simple form. There is no verb in this primitive sentence, if sentence it should be called. It is interesting to find observers of children noting that many "first words" are nouns, or interjections, the nouns often serving as sentences.[21] All these first words are from the psychological point of view comparatively simple, as regards utterance, but when for example the word "ball" means "I want the ball", reference is more complex. If in Bühler's experiment the experimenter asks orally: "When Eucken speaks of a world historical apperception, do you know what he means?" reference and utterance functions are of a still more complex nature. The experimenter has had to learn the language, which means in part that he has learned, with a limited number of phonemes, to utter these words in German. It has been seen that here is a very complex reference function, for the "meaning" of this question is highly involved. Further, when the subject answers "Yes", the utterance function is simple, for most children of two years old can say this word. But when "Yes" is spoken in answer to this question the reference function is very complex.

[21] McCarthy, in Carmichael, 1946, p. 503.

Once more, it should be pointed out that the reference and utterance functions involved when the experimenter asks the question "When Eucken . . ." etc., are psychological abstractions from the total speech-event of asking the question. There are then psychological reference functions involved in the production, during speech, of single words, and also of more complex linguistic constructions.[22]

There is no Problem of Meaning in Language

The foregoing gives what is perhaps the conventional account of meaning, couched in terms which are intended to be acceptable to psychologists of all shades of opinion. Many readers will prefer to leave the account as it has been given. It expresses a way of thinking which has served both linguistics and psychology well, and it does make possible a description of the facts. In the opinion of the writer however, the terms meaning and reference function are dangerous. They are convenient and common-sense words which may lead to serious misunderstanding unless care is exercised. We have spoken of the problem of meaning. Actually, the problem as it now exists is at least in the context of speech a fictitious one, created by psychologists themselves and not inherent in the data when these are properly examined. In order to understand how the confusion has arisen, consider once more the question of images.

Two chapters ago the statement was briefly made that we perceive the world directly, without the intermediary of some *tertium quid* such as "sensations" or "ideas", the latter giving rise to the Lockian fallacy, according to which we can never perceive the world at all; and that similarly we *imagine* the world directly, without the intermediary of images. That is, when we "have an image of a boy dressed in blue", what is happening is that we are imagining the boy directly. We do not first make an image and then bring in some additional process which tells us its meaning, i.e. that this is an image of the boy. If we are asked what colour the boy's coat is, we can say that it is blue, just as though we were actually perceiving the boy and were asked the same question. Thus the "meaning of the image" presents no problem. It only seems to be a problem because the image has been separated by psychologists from the "boy that is imaged". The apparent "problem" consists of putting the two together again. Putting it in another way, the "image" has been

[22] A beginning of an experimental analysis has been made in a paper by Neff, 1937, who shows the stages by which his subjects passed from perception to apprehension of a "symbol" as such, and distinguishes different kinds of reference.

abstracted from the total process of "imagining the boy", and the difficulty has been to replace it in its context.

The same principles apply to speech, where, however, the distinctions emerge more clearly. But first, certain points in the above account must be amplified. When we perceive a boy dressed in blue, we are doing something. To enlarge upon the details of retinal, cortical, or even mental function during this activity has undoubtedly been confusing in certain rather arid chapters of the history of psychology. Nevertheless, there *is* retinal and cortical activity, and there *is* psychophysical activity, however one may believe it to be constituted. The tendency to substantialize the end product of a part of the activity, and to speak for example of engrams, neural imprints, sensation, sense data, and percepts, has proved in practice to be even more confusing. Thus Sully speaks of the "aggregate of actual and revived sensations" as being solidified or integrated into "the form of a percept"[23]; that is, he adds, an "apprehension or cognition". Such a statement is convenient but dangerous. For when once the term percept—and a very good one it is—has been invented, the problem comes up as to the relation of the percept to the boy "out in the world". The same thing is true of imagery. The psychological process of imagining the boy has as one at least of its end products "an image". The language is natural and convenient, but once the term has been invented, psychologists have further invented for themselves the entirely spurious problem; what is the relation of the image to the boy, what is the meaning of the image, or how can an image "stand for a previous experience"?[24] This illusory problem has arisen because it has been forgotten that the original datum is somebody doing something, viz. imagining the boy. Although the false problem seems to have arisen in this way, it must once again be remembered that there *are* end products (equilibria or constant states) involved in the psychophysical process of imagining, and that image or imagery is a perfectly good term for one of them.

Turning once more to speech, the fundamental datum is the fact that a man is *doing something*, namely talking *to* somebody *about* something. He is specifically reacting to a total situation-complex comprising non-social and social or, as Kantor calls them, bi-stimulational features (Kantor, 1936, p. 73). That this is a difficult kind of reaction is shown by the fact that animals can only achieve

---

[23] Quoted by James, 1890, Vol. II, p. 79.
[24] I quote from the glossary of Murphy's textbook, 1935.

it to a limited degree. John says *Rain!* to Mary; but his total reaction is to Mary as a person who will react, behaviourally or experientially, and also to the water falling from the sky. John has had to learn to make the former kind of reaction; it is the "social adjustment" of child psychology. Once again the learning is not easy. Now just as it is possible though dangerous to abstract the activity of *imaging* the boy, so *it is possible though dangerous to abstract the activity of making the noise "Rain", from the particular situation calling it out as the result of learning. As soon as one forgets that this abstraction has been made*, the "problem of meaning" is engendered; that is to say, the problem of determining how the noise "Rain" can "mean" the physical fact that "there is water falling from the sky".

For the case where the "object of reference" is not immediately present the same principles apply, except that the factor of learning is more obtrusive. Suppose, for example, that John does not look out of the window but has noticed that the barometer has fallen. Coming in, he may make the same remark. In the situation to which he now responds, there is now no non-social factor specifically operative, since he cannot perceive the rain.[25] The following points will be noticed: (1) in order to make the speech-response he must have "learned the language"; (2) he must have learned that a falling barometer is followed by rain; (3) he must have integrated the end products of these two processes of learning into a single response, the spoken word "Rain!", such integration being common in everyday learned reaction; (4) he must be motivated to say the words (he wants to go fishing, there are clothes on the clothes-line, etc.). Of these (1) and (4) are the same as before; (2) and (3) are added for this particular case where the object of reference is not under immediate perception. Those who wish to do so may say that in the latter case the object of reference is operative through memory traces. Whatever the mechanism, it is certain that here, as with every product of learning, very many of the roots of the activity stretch out

[25] Of course there is the general physical setting, including the door, the furniture, the pressure of the air, etc., which may be neglected as common to both situations. These background factors in the situation are common to every response (e.g. reading, counting), and it used to be said that "attention was not directed to them". Later psychologists have spoken of "focalized response", James spoke of the "fringe of consciousness". Whatever the explanation, and whatever terminology be used, reaction is primarily directed to some feature or features of the environment, to the neglect of the others (see the next chapter on generalization), and there must be somewhere a mechanism to account for this duality. Modern psychology has not yet quite caught up with the facts described under the term "attention".

into the past. Thus, when some object not present is "meant" we
have once more the problem involved in the fact that past events influence present activity. That is, the problem is one of learning, not
a unique "problem of meaning". The relation of learning to meaning
will be discussed more fully later.

It may perhaps seem as though the issue is being evaded by putting
the problem in another place and then pretending it does not exist.
It is completely true that a problem is not solved by calling attention
to the fact that it is a special case of a more inclusive one; but it is
also true that from a unique and apparently unmanageable enigma
qualitatively different from any other, what has been called the
problem of meaning thus becomes a perfectly ordinary psychological
question, capable of experimental investigation. It is this: When
John says to his wife "It is raining", *what difference is there in experience from the occasion* (which might be set up experimentally) *when
he makes the same noise but is not "talking about" the rain.* Or, translated into behaviouristic co-ordinates, *what difference is there in his
behaviour* on the two occasions? In either form the problem is
amenable to psychological techniques. In its original form as the
"problem of meaning" the question has to be obscured by the invention of new descriptive terms such as *transcendent reference*,
objective reference or *context* in order to satisfy the scientific con-
science; or else metaphors must be used such as "carry the meaning",
"vehicle of meaning", and so on, their result, again, being to spread
a scientific fog.[26] It will be remembered that Humpty-Dumpty was
safe and sound as long as he was in contact with the wall. When he
left it, even a Royal Commission could not do much about him.
The same confusion has often happened in the history of psychology
when a psychological activity is separated from its environmental
occasion.

The psychological activities of sensing (something), imagining
(something), or talking about (something) (i.e. reacting with certain
effectors to a situation comprising another person and something
else), depend on the biological correlates *organism* and *environment*.
The same kind of confusion has been caused in biology by those who
have tried, often unwittingly, to consider an organism apart from its
environment.

The question must now be raised: if terms are dangerous, why use
them? The answer has been indicated. They have been used because

[26] Even so good a psychologist as Cook states, "Any sign can carry any meaning" (1946, p. 220).

they are useful, and their usefulness has obscured their dangers. In the case of speech the immediately perceptible behaviour of the speaker, which is the end-product of a complex organic process, is especially obtrusive and a special term for it even more necessary. We have to learn with great pains to speak, which brings the process and its end-product, the learned activity of speaking a language, into great prominence. People from other cultures often react differently from ourselves when placed in the same situation. We say they are saying the same thing "in another language". And so on. It is not surprising that common sense has focused attention on the organic end-product of speech-utterance. The question of "meaning" has thus become particularly insistent, more especially perhaps because of the existence of other languages than our own. Thus the "problem of meaning" has been almost forced upon philologists, linguists, and the man in the street himself. It is hardly possible to give an intelligible discussion of the activity of speech without employing terms which if not used carefully lead to the same spurious difficulty . . . namely, how can the noise "Rain" *mean* "water falling from the sky". But for all this common usage, *there is no problem of meaning in language.*[27]

By the utterance function of speech is then meant the end-product of speech-mechanics in the body abstracted from the situation to which the response is made. By reference function is meant that aspect of the total activity of experience or behaviour which correlates with the relevant part of the situation to which response is made, excluding the person to whom the speech is addressed. But throughout it must be remembered that the term reference function, which is employed as a correlative to "meaning", is an *abstraction, which may easily cause serious misunderstanding and false problems.* By the same token, "evocation" is that aspect of the total activity which correlates with the person addressed.

Summary

(1) The person who can "speak" a language must possess from fifteen to fifty relatively invariant behaviour-modes of language—the phonemes.

(2) He must be able to combine these hierarchically into higher units—morphemes, words, phrases, and sentences. The general patterns of such combination are relatively invariant, corresponding

[27] I.e. no separate problem, apart from the general problems of learning, perception, and response; for treatments of language as response-adjustment, see Kantor, 1936; Goldstein, 1948, pp. 23, *et seq.*

as they do to the "rules" of grammar and syntax. At the same time, the whole process must be kept on a strictly *ad hoc* or adaptive basis by the use, within the invariant frame, of variation appropriate to the situation.

(3) This implies a corresponding hierarchy of neural pattern, comprising (*a*) relatively invariant and (*b*) plastic features or aspects.

(4) In addition, meaningful speech involves a set of psychological events which have been termed the reference function, and have been further analysed in the text.

(5) The reference function varies in complexity, but not necessarily according to the complexity of the utterance with which it is associated.

(6) It presupposes neural events over and above those involved in utterance.

(7) The whole process, including utterance and reference functions, is unitary; speech activity, of the normal kind, blends the whole complex of processes in such a way that while there is ordinarily no conscious experience corresponding to the utterance function, there is ordinarily conscious experience corresponding to the reference function.

(8) The terms utterance function, reference function, and evocation are useful scientific abstractions which like all abstractions entail serious dangers. Their dangers are (1) that of treating the total speech activity as comprised of three separate activities, (2) that of considering the total activity as taking place *in vacuo*, apart from any situation, instead of as a reaction *to a total situation*, and thus engendering a spurious "problem of meaning". In spite of these dangers, the terms are necessary and useful ones. With the above reservations, they will be employed in the discussion to follow.

The Function of Evocation

"Evocation has been defined as the causal relation between the speech sounds and the hearer" (McGranahan). Experimental work has reported many processes underlying the comprehension or understanding of words. McGranahan lists imagery, feelings of familiarity, acts of thinking, awareness of meaning, awareness of purpose, directional experiences, awareness of sphere.[28] The imageless thought controversy has played its part here as well, Stout, Binet, Watt supporting the imageless doctrine.[29] To the writer there is little doubt that the existence of imageless processes in understand-

---

[28] Op. cit., p. 193. The references are given.
[29] Listed by Cantril (1932). See McGranahan, loc. cit.

ing of words has been experimentally established. For the evidence the reader is referred to Chapters 2 and 4.

In addition to the evocatory process on the part of the hearer, it should be pointed out that speech involves an evocatory function on the part of the speaker. In the early stages of individual language development this is apparently not present. Among the first words are those apparently formed by reduplication—according to a quasi-conditioned pattern.[30] Here of course is no evocatory function, nor in all probability any reference function. The utterance of these words is apparently produced by "play" activity, which uses the speech muscles, just as other muscles and other movements are used for other forms of play. Perhaps it would be more correct to say that these early vocalizations are words to the hearer, but not to the infant. This is a matter of definition. A child may be heard to practise words when by himself, no evocatory function apparently being involved. The evocatory function is here that aspect of the total activity which correlates with the person to whom speech is addressed.

To return to evocation on the side of the hearer. This involves processes corresponding to the reference function on the speaker's side. John would not say "Rain" unless Jane were going to "understand what he meant". That is, Jane must refer the heard word to the same object (rain falling outside) to which John refers the spoken word. Communication, which is often given as the prime function of speech, thus rests on the fact that there is *an object of psychological reference* common to *speaker and hearer*. This fact has already been mentioned in the preliminary statement on p. 217. When the object of reference is not the same for both parties, then there is "misunderstanding". The warning should perhaps here be given that the reference function involved in speech differs in some respects from that involved in comprehension.

It should be noticed that just as there may be utterance without reference, in the same way on the part of the hearer there may apparently be *hearing* of words without reference. There is a stage in learning a language when the sounds produced by the foreigner are "babble", when, so to speak, they are not heard as words at all. Pathologically, a patient who suffers from such a defect is sometimes called word-sound deaf.[31] There is a second stage where the auditory

[30] See, e.g., Allport, 1924. The first explanation of such words on a conditioned-reflex basis was apparently given by W. F. Dearborn.
[31] See Kennedy and Wolf, 1936, p. 142, who quote the distinction but disagree with it. For a good discussion of comprehension in children see McCarthy, 1946.

phenomenon becomes articulated; where, for example, it is recognized what language is being spoken, and where the words can be recognized as words, but the meaning of some of them at least is not understood. Here is a "perceptual" stage, corresponding to utterance without reference. Pathologically the patient is called "word-meaning deaf".[32] Generally, of course, there is understanding of isolated words. The learner in a language reports that he "caught one or two words", while the general tenor of the meaning escaped him. Apparently children pass through this stage. A child of seven, being asked what the conversation of adults sounded like at the meal-table, replied, "Bla-Bla-Bla-Bla-Bla". Here was sheer hearing, auditory stimulation, without word hearing or reference. Later the same child will no doubt hear words, recognized as such, but to which no meaning can be attached. These are "difficult" words, which are still recognized as words, but in connection with which no reference function, or an imperfect one, occurs. The whole question is of course somewhat speculative, and is very much in need of experimental investigation. But there seems no doubt of the existence, in the hearer of a more elementary word-perceptive function, as well as of the reference function, the latter with the same object as that of the speaker.

In order to avoid possible confusion, two aspects of the reference function should then be explicitly distinguished. There is the reference function associated with utterance, already considered. John says "Rain" with reference to the meteorological fact. There is, further, the reference function in evocation. Mary hears "Rain" with reference to the meteorological fact. *Reference thus straddles the utterance and the evocatory aspects of speech. It is this fact that makes communication possible and gives speech its peculiar character.*

Concerning the reference function in comprehension, the same general statement may be made as before, namely that many will prefer to leave the above statements as they stand. It is, however, necessary to repeat that here again "reference to" and "meaning" involve no unique problems. For, once again, consider the simplest example, what Pavlov has called the Conditioned Reflex. After a number of combinations of the two "stimuli" metronome and food, the metronome always beginning before the food, salivation follows when the metronome alone is heard. As Pavlov puts it, "The sound of the metronome is the signal for food."[33] Stated the other way

---

[32] See preceding note.   [33] Pavlov, 1927, p. 22.

round, the meaning of the metronome-tick is food. Now, in every case "the meaning of any such signal has to be learned".[34] This is of course a greatly over-simplified instance. What of a man reading a book? Here the primary problem is also one of learning. One has to "learn to read", that is, learn that these marks on paper "mean" what they do. Once more, to use the language of "meaning" or "reference" is to make an artificial separation between the end-product of a total learning series[35] and the rest of it.[36] But the separation is convenient for everyday use and likewise for scientific analysis. The same thing is true for the psychology of introspection. The collection of letters "doll" look differently to a child who has learned to read and one who has not, and this is because he has learned that the word *means* "a girl's toy-baby" (S.O.E.D.). They look differently because they come at the end of a learning series, of which what may be called the "sophisticated" sight of these letters is one end-product. Again a psychological end-product has been torn out of the total process (learning series) which made it an end-product, and the problem of meaning has been reborn. Thorndike once remarked in a passage now inaccessible to me that visitors were sometimes surprised at the behaviour of his trained animals. Indeed, one might well be surprised to see a cat put into a cage, immediately wash its nose and thereupon be let out for a meal. Certainly such a visitor might well ask the meaning of the performance, and when he had been told that the animal had been put in the cage fifty times, and had always been let out when it washed its nose, the action would be put into its proper setting and the question thereby answered. The visitor had observed only the end-product of a series, and that is why for him the term meaning would be in order.

Thus once again there is no problem of meaning; that is, there is no primary psychological problem. Problem there is, or even problems. But they are derivative from the great problems of the perception of the world, of thinking (or if the reader prefers it, thinking about) the world, imagining the world, and learning. The so-called

---

[34] I quote from Woodworth and Marquis, 1947, p. 311.

[35] Humphrey, 1933, Chapter V. The learning series is, again, four dimensional.

[36] The meaning is not, of course, the whole learning series (i.e. all the successive presentations of the word doll). But, as Bartlett says, the meaning may be found in the series. There are many irrelevant details, such as the colour of the word, that have nothing to do with its "meaning of doll" (Bartlett, 1932, p. 230). It is for this, among other reasons, that the redintegration theory of Hollingworth (1926, *passim*) will not explain meaning. Many of the arguments brought against associationism may also be brought against redintegration.

problem of meaning is secondary to these—and they are themselves by no means all separate problems themselves.[37]

Thus when Titchener and Boring speak of *context* and others of *transcendent reference*, one may agree with each statement. Certainly the meaning of a word as read involves context, namely *all* the preceding situations in which the word is read; from these the meaning may be abstracted, as every learning "situation" is abstracted from the varying forms in which it appears. (See the next chapter.) But in order to complete the statement one must here add that context must be organically integrated in the way ordinarily called learning. Certainly again the same word involves "transcendent reference", if one likes to use that kind of language to describe the fact that the "learned" word "points to something else", i.e. appears with the effect of previous situations upon it, and so on.

If then the question is asked again how communication takes place, the final answer seems something like this. As a first approximation it may be said that the meaning of the spoken is the same as that of the perceived word. Or that the spoken word and the perceived word "refer" to the same fact or event. Or better, when two people are talking, learning has taken place on both sides, and that the (generally repeated) situations involved have had something in common for each learner.[38] This something in common, which is in each case the constant situational core discussed in the next chapter, is the common "meaning", which makes communication possible.[39] That this is the fundamental fact there seems no doubt. Still in even the most elementary conversation the process of acquiring and using language is overlaid by integrative and other learning processes of enormous complexity. But while it is true that in the present stage of science we hardly begin to understand the complications which we can see to exist, there is no reason to think that they present problems uniquely different from those of perception and learning hitherto studied.

[37] The reader is referred to Hollingworth, 1926, pp. 212 *et seq.*, for an excellent brief account of traditional theories. Morris, 1946, p. 295, also discusses certain theories of meaning. I believe I am fundamentally in agreement with Bartlett, 1932, Chapter XII.

[38] It will be remembered that neither here nor anywhere else does learning involve pure repetition of an exactly similar situation. There is always variation from time to time as one learns; in learning to speak there is much variation both of situation and of response.

[39] The implication is that "meaning" is general, which once more ties up with the nominalistic theory of generality.

Modes of Utterance

In addition to the mode of utterance already dealt with, and which has been called by various writers objective, rational, symbolic,[40] other modes have been distinguished. There is what has been called the emotional mode, best represented by swearing. Here "the appearance of particular linguistic forms is determined chiefly by emotions, feelings, and attitudes" (McGranahan). In Gardiner's diagram Jane responds to the whole situation by saying, "What a bore!" The reference function is not nearly so prominent here as in John's response "Rain!" or "It is raining." McGranahan distinguishes a third mode which he calls "material", as contrasted with the formal and conventional utterance. An angry tone of voice "has certain effects on the hearer . . . but is not formal and representational". Animal language is apparently entirely material and emotional. Although, for example, birds have a large repertoire of sounds which they can produce, there is no reference function.[41] The vocalizations of chimpanzees are apparently "primarily innate vocal expressions" (Yerkes). How far something approaching reference function may be present in an animal who *hears* human speech and has been specially trained is difficult to say.[42]

Comprehension in Animals

In this latter connection Warden and Warner[43] investigated a highly trained dog, which had been talked to constantly almost since birth in much the same way as a child, and which the owner of the animal believed to understand four hundred or more words something as a child would. The following items are selected from the list of "successful reactions" of this animal, under the heading "No special orientation to object or position required". *Sit* (on haunches); *Stand up high* (against some near object, as wall, etc.); *lay down* (*sic*; sits on haunches); *lay down all the way* (prostrate); *put your foot on the chair* (in front of him); *the other foot* (puts other foot on chair); *no, the other chair* (or object or person nearby); *go outside and wait for me* (dog leaves room and waits outside); *do that once more* (repeats act just done). These, and all the others of the fifty-three commands listed under this type were correctly performed. It is

[40] McGranahan, loc. cit., pp. 180–1.

[41] See, however, de Laguna, 1927, for certain conceivable though simple exceptions.

[42] Yerkes, 1932, concludes that chimpanzees can communicate, but "they have no system . . . of sounds which may properly be termed speech" (p. 190).

[43] Warden and Warner, 1928.

impossible to resist the conclusion that the "reference function" is involved in a simple way.

These performances were shown to take place independently of gesture on the master's part; for the latter "gave commands from an adjoining room with the door closed", and when the master and both experimenters were behind screens. However, when the master and dog stood outside the room and the dog was ordered to retrieve objects in the room, there was less success, though a greater success than would be accounted for by chance. For example, the dog might be told to bring a glove from the adjoining room. He had then to enter the room, find the glove and bring it to his master. The statistical summary for the latter type of response with master outside the room was as follows:

Total number of responses	.	36		
Failures	. . .	15 (24 according to chance)		
Successes (certain).	. .	16 (12	„	„ „)
Successes (doubtful)	. .	5		

Seeing that three out of the five doubtful cases should probably be counted successes, it looks as though in the reference function where the object of reference is not present in perception, we have approximately reached the limit of the animal's powers, where the task, though very difficult, is sometimes accomplished.[43a]

Of course, this excellent but difficult investigation shows merely what may be done by an animal under special circumstances of training. To learn such simple language functions under special coaching is far removed from the feat that has been performed by the human race, phylogenetically, in inventing language—for no tribe of people even the most primitive has yet been found without language—and ontogenetically in "picking it up" without any special instructions.

The Problem of Aphasia

For various reasons the amount of experimental work directly performed on the fundamental problems of adult language functions is very small. There is, however, a large body of what may be called quasi-experimental evidence of a clinical nature. Chief among the sources of such is the literature on aphasia, which has now grown to large proportions. It is regrettable that in the past psychology has not been in a position to lend much assistance to clinicians engaged in

[43a] The problem of *reference to things absent* in children's speech is briefly mentioned by McCarthy, 1946, and references given.

this study. In fact, where psychological principles were adopted from the tradition of the day, they apparently did more harm than good. Thus the doctrine that speech is necessarily preceded by an idea or image is an obvious outgrowth of the presentational psychology and the ideo-motor theory, now both abandoned. The fallacy has, however, persisted until quite recent time in the form of the hypothesis that verbal images of various types are stored in the different speech areas, with the result that when the area is damaged, there occurs a loss of the image which must precede action. The interested reader is referred to volume one of Head's monumental work.[44] The problem will later be considered in detail.

Head classifies aphasia under four types, as follows:

(1) *Verbal Defects.*—This type is chiefly characterized by "defective power of forming words, whether for external or internal use". . . . The patient's utterance may be reduced to "yes" and "no", and even these words cannot always be produced at will. In the course of recovery "his vocabulary increases, but his enunciation is slow and halting. Any word he is able to recall can, however, be used for naming an object. . When he attempts to repeat what has been said to him the articulatory sounds are imperfect, but he can usually utter more words than are possible spontaneously. It is characteristic of this form of aphasia that words are evoked with difficulty and tend to be abnormal in structure".[45]

After the initial shock "the power of choosing an object to oral or printed commands becomes perfect, and even orders necessitating choice can be carried out correctly if given in print or in words spoken aloud".[46] With increase of spoken vocabulary in the course of recovery, comes increase in power of writing, though there is difficulty in spelling and in the order of the letters. "The verbal aspect of numerals is affected, but not their significance. Thus when looking up the page of a book or scoring at cards the patient may *utter the wrong number but acts as if he had said the right one.* Simple arithmetical operations can be carried out correctly, except in severe cases; then it is not the process of addition and subtraction which is forgotten, but the act fails because of the difficulty in remembering the requisite figures. These patients can draw, play card games, and

<hr/>

[44] Head, 1926, Vol. I. See also Weisenburg and MacBride, 1935, for a somewhat later presentation containing a critical estimate of Head's work. For a brief account, see Head, 1920. For a criticism of Head's tests for Aphasia see Pearson and Alpers, 1928.

[45] Head, 1921, p. 186.

[46] Ibid., p. 186.

enjoy jokes set out in print or in pictures. In fact, the disorder from which they suffer affects mainly verbal structures and words as integral parts of a phrase; their nominal value and significance are perfect."[47]

(2) *Syntactical Defects.*—Here the patient tends to talk jargon, but may retain the power of naming objects, e.g. may be able to write the name correctly, when he cannot utter a comprehensive word. But "any attempt to utter a formulated statement is liable to end in confusion". The disorder is "essentially one of symbolic expression". It is similar to the disorder called by Pick "agrammatism".[48]

(3) *Nominal Defects* entail "essentially a loss of power to use names, and want of comprehension of the nominal value or meaning of words and symbols". The patient cannot name objects placed in front of him, and when asked to point to an object named aloud or in print, the choice, even if correct, is made slowly and with effort. Writing to dictation is imperfect, but direct *viva-voce* expression is not affected. "Games, such as cards, which demand rapid and correct recognition of the names and power to register a score, are impossible, though chess, draughts, and dominoes may be played correctly." Drawing from a model or from memory is easy, but drawing from imagination, such as a picture of an elephant, is unsatisfactory.

(4) *Semantic Defects* consist in "want of recognition of the full significance of words and phrases apart from their verbal meaning. Other functions suffer which have nothing to do with verbalization, for in this form of the disorder there is loss of meaning in thought. The patient may understand a word or short phrase, and can appreciate the various details of a picture, but the ultimate meaning escapes him". He cannot formulate accurately either to himself or to others a general conception of what he has been told, has read to himself, or has seen in a picture, though he can enumerate many of the details of which it is composed. He cannot play card games or put together puzzles, which confuse such patients greatly. "Memory and intelligence", says Head, "may remain on a comparatively high level. He does not forget people or places, he can recall spontaneously events both recent and remote, and may be able to give valuable information concerning his disabilities. Yet he cannot accurately retain some story which he has read or has been told."[49] According to Head, whose thinking was founded on the work of the English

[47] Ibid. (present writer's italics).
[48] Pick, 1913.
[49] The description of these types is taken from Head, 1921.

neurologist Hughlings Jackson, the four types represent different ways in which the primary process of "symbolic formulation and expression" may break down. This process is that to which Hughlings Jackson, working on the foundation of Herbert Spencer's psychology, gave the name of "propositionizing", the formulation of propositions. "Single words are meaningless and so is an unrelated succession of words. The unit of speech is a proposition"[50] such as, e.g., "Gold is yellow". "Loss of speech is therefore the loss of power to propositionize." Thus Hughlings Jackson stressed the integrative action of speech, though he had due regard for the symbolic aspect also. Head preferred to use the phrase "symbolic formulation and expression", which distinguishes within the total (integrative) activity (1) the making of a formula (a) involving the meaning of symbols, and therefore (b) of more or less general validity, from (2) the process of fitting the words to the formula. The two aspects are not to be thought of as psychologically separate, but are combined in a single mental operation.

Head's classification of aphasic cases has given rise to some controversy, into which it is not proposed to enter. It may be added that Weisenburg and MacBride state that the classification has, in fact, not been generally adopted by neurologists. They feel that Head's classification of aphasics is based on sounder theory, but has not proved to be as useful in practice as classifications less ably conceived from the theoretical point of view. Weisenburg and MacBride themselves propose a fourfold classification.

According to these writers, aphasics may be classed *predominantly expressive*, where the most serious disturbances were in expression of speech or writing; the *predominantly receptive*, where receptive processes suffered more than the expressive, and the changes in speech and writing were mostly of a different nature from those of the expressive disorder, and the *expressive receptive* group where all language processes were extremely limited. To this they were obliged to add a class of *amnesic* patients, "whose expression was disturbed not by defects in word formation, but by difficulties in evoking words as names for objects, conditions, or qualities".[51] This is very close to Head's nominal aphasia.

---

[50] Hughlings Jackson, quoted in Head, 1926, Vol. I, p. 41. This use of the term is to be distinguished from that of the logician who contrasts a proposition (=a statement of objective fact) with a judgment (=the psychological process of affirming or denying it).

[51] Weisenburg and MacBride, op. cit., pp. 143–7.

Leaving the question of the classification of aphasia to those most nearly concerned, namely the clinicians, the following observations may be offered. It is clear that those lesions which come under clinical observation are not strictly localized, as experimental lesions would have been. When nature produces a lesion, we must take what we have. When a lesion is produced in the laboratory, it may be experimentally varied and controlled so as to bring out different points in which the experimenter is interested. That is the disadvantage of clinical against more strictly experimental evidence. The former must necessarily suffer in strictness of control by comparison with the latter.

It seems further clear that the group of patients known as aphasics includes a fairly well-marked sub-group of those suffering primarily from disturbances in what we have designated generally as utterance. Here will lie Head's *verbal defects* and Weisenburg's *expressive* type, as well as Head's *syntactical* and Pick's *agrammatic* types, the latter two involving more complex integrations on the level of utterance. It was seen earlier that *utterance* involves integrative activities of a highly complicated order, so that it is not surprising to find disturbances of this function at different levels. It will be noted that Head explicitly points out that "the disorder from which they suffer affects mainly verbal structure and words as integral parts of a phrase; their nominal value and significance are perfect". It will be remembered again "that the patient may utter the wrong number but mean the right one". That is to say, *utterance* is primarily disturbed, while *reference* is left undamaged. It is for that reason that Weisenburg calls these *expressive patients*. Pick implies, and in one passage explicitly makes, the same point in his discussion of *agrammatism*.[52]

A further group of patients suffer primarily from disturbance of what has been called the *reference* function. Two stages of complication have already been distinguished in this function, and it obviously operates in many degrees of complexity. It is found to be correspondingly disturbed at several levels, of which we may mention as the simplest Head's nominal aphasia, where "the patient possesses plenty of words but he cannot apply them exactly". The same writer's *semantic aphasia* is a much more complex affair, where there is

[52] The definition of agrammatism is given as "the form of pathologically disturbed speech in which the effective events in the grammatical and syntactical formation of speech are deranged in different ways, or occur either not at all or incompletely" (loc. cit., p. 124).

"want of recognition of the ultimate significance and intention of words and phrases apart from their direct meaning. . . . There is loss of power to appreciate or to formulate the logical conclusion of a train of thought or action . . . The fault is essentially a want of recognition of relative significance and intention."[53] Everything tends to be *appreciated in detail*, but the *general* significance is lacking.[54] The disorder clearly, then, affects what may be called the higher reference integrations, together, probably, with certain non-verbal functions. The difficulties are due "essentially to want of power to combine mentally into a single act a series of relevant details".[55]

The reader may be reminded that there are reference functions corresponding to the isolated words "gold" and "yellow". The reference functions involved in the use of the sentence "gold is yellow" implies these together with a higher integration, the reference-object of which corresponds in logic to the *proposition* as contrasted with the *terms* (gold and yellow). It is this higher integration that is affected in Head's cases of semantic aphasia.

Thus his case number eight was a young officer struck in the left parieto-occipital region of the brain by a fragment of shell casing. Articulated speech was unaffected. He could name and recognize objects and write their names. He had no difficulty in understanding the meaning of single words or short phrases. But he could not combine details, duly appreciated, into a coherent whole. He could not solve problems in arithmetic. He could carry out even the complex printed commands of the hand, eye, and ear tests without reading them aloud; but he had considerable difficulty in setting the clock to orders given in a mixture of words and figures. He was asked to read the following passage to himself. "The summer day was splendid, and the world, as he looked at it from the terrace, was a vault of airy blue arching over a lap of solid green. The wide still trees in the park appeared to be waiting for some daily inspection, and the rich fields with their frill of hedges to rejoice in the light." When asked what it meant he said, "It doesn't convey much; it seems to go out of my mind; he is looking out from a terrace on to a park." He read these words aloud with little hesitation and then reported as to the meaning. "It conveys to me a man looking out on to a park with a fringe of beautiful trees, and then I can't remember the rest"; adding, "I had to letter these words out as I read it.

[53] Head, 1926, Vol. I, p. 267.   [54] Ibid. (italics by present writer).
[55] Ibid., p. 261.

The meaning did not come to me at once. I had to read it very carefully before I could read it, so to speak."[56]

Here *utterance* is clearly almost unaffected, and likewise simpler forms of the reference function; for the patient could comprehend simple phrases. It is the higher integrations that are affected, including the more complex reference integrations. That other higher synthetic functions are clearly involved as well as the reference functions is clear, e.g. from his difficulty with jig-saw puzzles. But at the moment we are primarily interested in the effect of his disability on his use of words.

Weisenburg and MacBride's *amnesic* type plainly involves the lower reference integrations (not . . . defects in word formation, but . . . difficulties in invoking words as names . . .). In their classification they have borne in mind the reference function on the side of utterance, but they state that logically these patients belong to the predominantly expressive group. The same writers' account of *receptive* aphasia brings out very clearly the fact of the different levels at which the reference function may operate on the side of evocation. "Cases . . . show different degrees of limitation in the understanding of spoken language, differences extending from failure to appreciate the full significance of the verbal formulation down to a faulty understanding of single words or short sentences, with some difficulty in perceiving the word sound" (verbal word-deafness).[57] Head's classification of nominal aphasia has in mind the simpler levels of the reference function on both sides, utterance and evocatory. Once more, it is not the function of this volume to decide on the question of clinical classification; we leave it to the clinicians to determine whether or not it is clinically more useful to group together patients with these two closely related disturbances of reference-function. The authority of Head is sufficient for the statement that there do occur patients in whom the reference function is deranged on both sides, that of utterance and that of evocation.

As a final example may be taken Head's case number two, that of a highly intelligent staff officer . . . a case of nominal aphasia due to severe and extensive fracture of the left half of the skull, produced by the kick of a horse. "He had no lack of words, but suffered from want of capacity to find one which exactly corresponded to the meaning which he wished to express or was an appropriate name for some definite object. At the same time, he failed to understand the

[56] Head, 1926, Vol. II, pp. 108 *et seq.*   [57] Loc. cit., p. 214.

significance of words presented to him orally or in print."[58] This
officer succeeded after considerable hesitation in choosing the common objects named by Head, but frequently failed to select a colour
to oral command. In ordinary conversation he often became confused because certain words were unintelligible on first hearing.
He could grasp what he heard if enunciation was slow, and words
not understood were immediately repeated. "When a command was
given to him in print he failed entirely to carry it out, and tried in
vain to spell the words of which it was composed. Single words were
read aloud badly, and he failed to reproduce single phrases." The
words, however, as utterance units were not lacking, for he would
sometimes use them in the wrong order.[59] Thus he read "the man
and the cat" as "the dog and the cat". "It might be anything. I have
to think." Here the reference function is impaired on the side of
evocation, for he had difficulty in choosing colours and objects to
command. At the same time, this patient exhibited the amnesic
symptoms mentioned by Weisenburg ("not defects in word formation, but difficulties in invoking the use of the words as names").
Most of the words in ordinary conversation were well pronounced
and intonation normal. But when he had difficulty in finding a
name or some nominal expression he would try out various combinations of sound more or less related to the word he was seeking.
Thus blue was called "ber-loo", orange "or-ridge"; but this seems
to be due to difficulty in finding the significant expression rather than
to lack of verbal aptitude. E.g. to show that he recognized black he
said, "I remember that now, because people who are dead . . . the
other people who are not dead they usually have this colour". The syntax of this patient was unaffected, except in so far that his perpetual
loss for names forced him to recast sentences before finishing them.
Being shown a two-shilling piece, he said: "Two shillings. I call it a
plozens; it's another name I can't remember" (florin). Shown a half-
crown piece he said: "Two and a half; the name I couldn't tell you."

Here then utterance is apparently intact, while reference is impaired on the utterance side, since although he can say words he
often cannot say them as *names*; that is, with reference to a particular
object. We have seen that it is impaired also on the side of evocation.
In this patient there is then impairment of reference on both sides.[60]

[58] Head, loc. cit., Vol. II, pp. 15 *et seq.*
[59] Such patients frequently cannot utter the words voluntarily. This indicates
the great complexity underlying the apparently simple function of "utterance".
[60] See Head, loc. cit., Vol II, pp. 14 *et seq*; also p. 232.

The following table will make clear *some* of the ways in which the utterance and reference functions may be deranged, with the classification adopted by the authors mentioned.

ROUGH SCHEME FOR DERANGEMENTS OF SPEECH FUNCTIONS

ON THE SIDE OF THE SPEAKER

Utterance	Derangement (Conventional) "Motor aphasia".
	Head's { Verbal (simpler). / Syntactical* (more complex).
	Weisenburg and MacBride's Expressive aphasia.
	Pick's Agrammatism.
	Dysarthria.
Reference	Head's { Nominal (simpler). / Semantic (more complex).
	Weisenburg and MacBride's Amnesic.
Evocation	Talking to oneself in senile states, also in children before speech is properly developed.

ON THE SIDE OF THE HEARER

Reception	Deafness (peripheral), functional deafness, word deafness. "Sensory aphasia."
	Receptive aphasia.
Reference	Nominal aphasia.
	Semantic aphasia.
	? Amnesic aphasia.
Evocation	Auditory hallucination.

*Ascribed by Weisenburg and MacBride to the receptive side, since they feel that it is due to the fact that the patient cannot properly hear himself talk.

Can Thought be Identified with Language?

It is now time to consider a question which has engaged the interest of philosophers for perhaps two thousand years, and in addition of linguists and psychologists for perhaps fifty. Plato's *Cratylus* and *Theætetus* are sometimes quoted as asserting the identity of thought and speech. In mediæval times the nominalists made somewhat the same assertion, though of course from a different point of view.[61] In modern times, Max Müller is the most eminent among the linguists to assert the identity doctrine. Since the name of

[61] For a discussion of the history of the theory, see Pick, 1913, Chapter IV; Müller, 1887, Vol. I, Chapter I.

this scholar is often mentioned in this connection while the book in which he expressed this opinion is now long out of print and rapidly becoming scarce, it is perhaps worth while to note what Max Müller did say. The volumes were entitled *The Science of Thought*. As a subtitle appear the lines "No Reason without Language: No Language without Reason." On page thirty of the first volume he heads a paragraph "Language and Thought Inseparable". This paragraph deals with the question of conceptual thinking. "It is curious to observe", he says, "how unwilling people are to admit that concepts without words are impossible, though at the same time they are quite willing to concede that words are impossible without concepts. . . . Why are words to be called miserable crutches? They are the very limbs, aye, they may become the very wings of thought. We do not complain that we cannot move without our legs. Why then should it be thought humiliating that we cannot think without words?"[62] Further, "we do not mean by thought mere suffering of sensations, or willing of actions, nor do we mean by words mere sounds. We mean by language what the Greeks called Logos, word and meaning in one, or rather, something of which word and meaning are only, as it were, the two sides. . . . *Cogitamus sed verba cogitamus*". And again, "All I maintain is that, not only to a considerable extent but always and altogether we think by means of names and that things are not more to us than what we mean by their names".[62] And lastly, "What we have been in the habit of calling thought is but the reverse of a coin of which the obverse is articulate sound, while the current coin is one and indivisible, neither thought nor sound, but word".[63] These quotations fairly express Müller's argument, which is maintained of course in non-experimental terms. As a matter of fact, the statement that concepts are impossible without words was very unfortunate, since recent experiment has shown quite clearly that in Müller's own terms, "concepts are possible without words". These experiments will later be considered in detail,[64] and the general argument now examined.

Inspired by the behaviourists one group of advocates of what may be called the "identity theory" has stressed the importance of the so-called implicit speech movements which occur during thinking. It has been seen in the preceding chapter that the theory that thought consists of such implicit speech is untenable. There do exist during

[62] Müller, loc. cit., pp. 28–34. The first quotation is from p. 30.
[63] Ibid., Vol. II, p. 543.
[64] See Smoke, 1932; Willwoll, 1926.

thought movements of the general nature demanded, but the most careful technique has shown that they cannot serve the function demanded by the theory. Internal speech is not an essentially peripheral, but subaudible, activity. We are then left with the question: are the most complex psychological activities of which the human being is capable fundamentally speech activities, in the sense that they may be described as verbal formulations without remainder, whatever may be the nature of internal speech? There is a further question arising from the answer to the first. If thought is not to be identified with speech, what is the relation of the two?

The answer to the first question seems unequivocal. Whatever the nature of "internal speech", every kind of evidence that we have tends against the proposition that thought should be identified with language. There is first the great mass of the experimental evidence for imageless thought. This evidence has already been reviewed in some detail, perhaps in too much detail for many readers, and the conclusion was reached that the existence of imageless thought had been established. From this conclusion it follows *a fortiori* that thinking may be independent of any kind of verbal formulation. As a matter of fact, many of the Würzburg protocols explicitly ruled out "speech imagery" or verbal formulation from their accounts of the thought processes observed by them. Those who cannot accept the proposition that imageless thought exists will of course not accept this evidence.

There is secondly the theoretical argument arising from the nature of the speech process itself. It has been seen that language proper involves more than the production or hearing of words. That is to say, it involves in addition to the making or hearing of sounds a psychological activity which has been called the reference function. This may be of such relative simplicity that it is within the powers of an intelligent dog, or, on the other hand, it may be of such complexity that it can be achieved by only a small proportion of mankind, as when a competent physicist writes or says Maxwell's equations aloud or to himself.

Now it is easy to see that thought cannot be equated with language, if by language we mean sheer utterance or production of sound. The implication of such a naïve identification theory would be that when two people's utterance is the same, silent or aloud, their thought is the same.

Here is a child who has been taught to say Maxwell's equations without, as we say, understanding them. He is repeating the equations silently in the same room with a physicist, who is also repeating them silently. The naïve theory of identity would demand that the psychological processes involved in the two cases are the same. Actually, the only reasonable statement seems to be that the verbal imagery or formulation is the same but the thought is different. I can teach a child to say the words "Autis epeita pedonde kulindeto laas anaides"[65] without telling the meaning. Obviously the thought processes of the child are not the same as those of the fifth-century Greek, with whom these words referred to the rolling-stone of Sisyphus. It is not here maintained that the reference function which has been seen to be resolvable into certain aspects of learning is the whole of thought, but only that it forms part of the "higher" processes which are ordinarily called thought. It is true that the reference function has been discussed as an aspect of language. And so it is. The fact is that *language, under ordinary conditions, involves psychological activities of the kind ordinarily classed as thought, and this component may vary without varying utterance, silent or aloud.* Conversely, *language may vary*, while in ordinary terms *thought remains the same.* It would be difficult to maintain that the thought of the boy who calls to his dog, "Ruhig!" or that of the same boy who proves a geometrical proposition in German, is *totally* different from that of his English counterpart. To equate language as utterance with thought is then not justified. The relations between the two are more complex than such an equation would imply. Up to this point Max Müller would heartily agree, for he explicitly states that language is word and meaning in one.

But there is a line of evidence directly against the identification of thought with speech as maintained by Müller. It comes from the clinical observations on aphasics. Clinicians are unanimous that a patient who is almost totally deficient in language activity, in both utterance and comprehension, may nevertheless be able to behave in such a way that in a normal person would be taken as evidence of ability to think. There are, first of all, the observations of Head, with Weisenburg and MacBride, who follow him fairly closely in his general statement of the nature of aphasia. For Head, it has been seen that aphasia is impairment of "symbolic formulation and expression". That is to say, the aphasic is not deficient simply in the ability to put words together, but his thinking is to some extent affected. Head's studies give the picture of certain types of thinking

[65] Will the Greek scholar please forgive the script, which is necessary for the argument.

as being dependent on language formulation, and of others as independent of it.

"Thought," he says, "presupposes the existence of language, but exceeds it widely in range, and there are many forms of behaviour, the result of thinking, which do not require the intervention of a symbol. . . . The tests which I have employed in this research comprise a certain number of intellectual operations, based on correspondence of a sensory order or on similarity and difference of perceptions. Such acts are not directly disturbed in aphasia and kindred disorders of speech. All those, on the contrary, which imply more complex adaptation, the recognition of signs, logical symbols or diagrams, suffer more or less severely."[66] A well-known instance is the test where the patient is required to copy the movements of the examiner, seated face to face with him. The verbal aphasic cannot do this, but he can easily copy movements when the examiner stands behind the patient and both are reflected in a mirror. The reason, says Head, is that "he is compelled to formulate to himself that my right hand is opposite to his left and the same is true for eye or ear. In some instances he attempts to express this fact silently in words by saying to himself 'It is the opposite', or even 'His right is my left'."[67]

Of the semantic type, Head says: "These . . . disorders interfere seriously with the activities of daily life and render the patient useless for any but the simplest employment; and yet his memory and intelligence may remain on a comparatively high general level. He does not forget people or places; he can recall spontaneously events both recent and remote, and may be able to give valuable information with regard to his disabilities. But if he is set the task of retailing accurately some story which he has been told or has read to himself, he is liable to become confused . . . ".[68] In the *verbal* type the patient's utterance may be confined to "Yes" and "No", and even these words may sometimes be unavailable for voluntary use. But "The patients can draw, play cards, and enjoy jokes" in print or pictures. When playing cards the patient *may utter the wrong number, but act as though he had said the right one.*[69] In the *nominal* type we have seen that the patient cannot discover appropriate names or find categorical terms in which to express a situation. The patient possesses verbal reactions, but cannot use them properly. *Internal speech is gravely affected*, and the patient cannot understand what

[66] Loc. cit., Vol. I, p. 517.
[68] Head, 1920, p. 189.
[67] Ibid., p. 518.
[69] Ibid., p. 186.

he reads to himself. Nevertheless, he may be able to play chess or draughts, though not cards, since the latter demands the intermediary of number. He cannot perform simple arithmetical operations. Of one such patient Head relates that "he had little power of spontaneous speech, but when a question were put to him, he answered intelligently as far as his scanty vocabulary permitted. E.g. *Question:* "You used to sing, didn't you?" *Answer:* "Yes . . . yes . . . when I was young . . . about ni . . . about twelve . . . when I was about twelve . . . but then I went to the steel . . . I can't get it".[70] Yet this patient could "play draughts correctly, making the moves necessary to avoid the loss of his pieces; he had little power of playing for position. He cleverly avoided the traps I set him and never missed taking one of my pieces that fell his way although he did not see how to force me to give him two for one".[71]

These examples, together with those already given, illustrate Head's conclusion that certain types of thought require the intermediary of verbal formulæ. These types of thinking are obviously abolished by any lesion that abolishes the use of language, especially internal language. An example is the performance of arithmetical operations. On the other hand, the examples clearly illustrate the further fact that Head's descriptions portray certain types of thinking which do not require the intermediary of language. These types may be relatively unimpaired by a lesion that abolishes spontaneous language, though they may be affected. Examples are draughts and domino playing, or sometimes even chess.[72] It would be gratuitous to deny the name "thinking" or "reasoning" to these activities which are presumably far beyond the capabilities of any but human beings.

The argument is carried on by Weisenburg and MacBride. What they have called the expressive-receptive type is perhaps the most illuminating. These patients were almost totally deficient in language response, in that they could not speak, except for a few "emotional or reactive expressions".[73] Of twelve such patients, one only, number 19, scored above the lowest quartile of normals in the language performance tests. Seven scored above the normal lowest quartile in non-language psychological performances, five above the median for the normal group, four above the upper quartile for the normal group.[74] This evidence is unusually impressive owing to the fact that standardized tests were employed, both of language and

[70] Head, 1926, Vol. II, p. 92.   [71] Ibid., p. 98.   [72] Head, 1962, p. xvi.

[73] E.g. *Oh my!* or *No, sir!*   [74] Op. cit., p. 280, figure.

non-language performances. Thus a patient who can say only "What" and "No" spontaneously, and rarely makes any speech sound but a grunt, makes qualitative scores all above the median on the Shorter Pintner Performance Scale, though he was below the median in time scores. On the Imitation Test of the Pintner Non-language Scale he was above the upper quartile of the normal group. On the Stenquist Mechanical Aptitudes Test his score was the equivalent of the 44th percentile of the army men on whom the norms were established.[75] It is again difficult to deny the term thinking or reasoning to these performances. Weisenburg (1934) argues that the non-language work was not of a standard to be expected before the lesion, however.[76]

Foster Kennedy and Wolf (1936) are even more explicit. "We believe", they say, "that there is a distinction between intellectual defect and aphasia, that thought is possible without speech or words, that defective speech can exist as something apart from intelligence, ideation, attention, memory, and powers of association. There are many examples to prove the truth of this statement. Take for instance the case of S—— (an eminent statesman) who went about his duties for half an hour after his cerebral lesion developed, thinking clearly on various subjects without knowledge of mental defect, only discovered to be aphasic when attempting to speak.[77] There was no intellectual defect in the case of Judge N——, who pled a case in court eloquently and yet proved to be alexic on careful neurological examination."[78] "Although", these authors say in their summary, "thought processes are frequently affected in aphasics, especially in large lesions, it is no more fitting to regard 'Mind' and speech as one than it is to expect every moron to be aphasic."

A classical case of the recovery from aphasia of a patient who was later able to give an account of his experiences is quoted by Franz. It confirms the preceding account. Dr. Saloz, the patient, was totally unable to speak, verbally deaf, and agraphic. He had no paralysis. During the six years between his "stroke" and death from another

[75] Op. cit., p. 288. Here may be mentioned the attack of the factor analysts on this problem. E.g. L. W. Murphy, 1936, found that verbal intelligence tests and mechanical intelligence tests measure different traits. Thurstone's factorial results are strongly confirmatory of the hypothesis that language and thought are not identical. See appendix to this chapter.

[76] Weisenburg, 1934.

[77] This is not evident in the case history as published in the appendix, where the statement is made that "he slept rather late, until 10.30 a.m., dressed, and at eleven o'clock found himself unable to give orders to the maid".

[78] Ibid., p. 138.

cause, he fully recovered ability to speak, write and understand; his autobiography, begun during this period has been preserved. Of his condition immediately after his stroke he says, "At that moment I had no lack of continuity of consciousness or in my thinking, and although things appeared much changed, I knew exactly what I wanted to say; I took account of the fact that my intact sensations had only lost their psychological instruments of expression through the symbols of language".[79] It is possible, of course, that in this, as in other cases, internal speech may have been present, and thinking carried on through its medium. On this point we have little evidence. Such evidence as we have, though, is against the presupposition that the thought process could be described in terms of such imagery. Both in "nominal" and "verbal" aphasia Head reports internal speech to be severely affected. In verbal aphasia "any formula or concept which reduces the amount of internal verbalization materially improves the accuracy of the response",[80] on the imitation test without mirror. Patients may, however, play "an excellent game of bridge", though, as we have seen, saying the numbers wrong while "meaning" them right. In nominal aphasia the patient may play chess or draughts.

The same writer finds that "visual images suffer or escape in aphasia according to the part they play in the processes of language or thinking. They can frequently be evoked spontaneously and used for direct reference, but are employed with difficulty as symbols or substitution signs. Moreover, the closer the disorder approaches want of power to appreciate either the detailed significance or the general meaning of a situation, the less easily can a visual image be summoned at will or to command".[81]

That is to say, even though in every case verbal imagery as such were preserved absolutely intact, an assumption which is certainly not justified, such evidence as we have tends to show that it would probably not suffice for thought. It should, nevertheless, be added that, although the statement of so great a clinician as Head is of immense authority, nevertheless the case histories do not always exhibit the evidence for his statements concerning internal speech. The problem of the internal speech of aphasics is in considerable need of experimentally controlled investigation. Head's published results do not absolutely preclude the possibility that, in the patients described, internal speech was (a) present and (b) available for purposes of thinking where overt speech was impossible. Such a

[79] Franz, 1921, p. 85.   [80] Head, loc. cit., Vol. I, p. 227.
[81] Head, 1926, Vol. I, p. 523.

supposition seems, however, to be excessively improbable from the general nature of the evidence and the course of the general argument. There is, again, need of controlled investigation into the point. It should be mentioned here that there is need for an investigation into the possibility of covert tongue movements in aphasics unable to produce overt speech. While we have no reason to believe that such movements are present, yet there is at the present time no proof that they are not.

In spite of this possible loophole, the general argument from aphasia for the independence of thought and language seems, on reading the evidence, overwhelmingly strong.

Weisenburg and MacBride add an interesting postscript to the argument from aphasia. They point out that non-language performances may be satisfactory where the verbal responses accompanying them are extremely confused. Thus we have seen that a patient playing cards may say nine of hearts when he means seven, and play correctly, nevertheless. One doing a multiplication sum may say seven nines are fifty-six and yet perform the sum correctly, behaving as though he had said sixty-three. And so on. "Analysis of the examples seems to indicate that the confusion is confined to the sphere of language, and that behind the wrong names or the incoherent explanations there is a fairly clear concept of the object or the problem."[82]

There is a fourth line of evidence against the identification of language and thought. Somewhat ironically, it comes from the experiments on conceptual thinking, the function which, it will be remembered, Max Müller was certain could not be carried on without verbal aid. The full discussion of the relevant experiments is deferred to the chapter on generalization and abstraction. Here it will be enough to say that the most striking experiment was performed by Smoke,[83] whose work was carried out in entirely objective terms. Smoke required his subjects to learn the arbitrarily chosen names of geometrical figures, which could be varied while at the

[82] Loc. cit., p. 425. It will be realized that no pretensions have been made in this volume to give a systematic account of aphasia. As an example of important investigations not mentioned should be noted the crucial work of Gelb and Goldstein, for an account of which see the discussion in the chapter following. Gelb (1933) in general confirms the statement that there are certain thought functions which are dependent on language, but that they do not constitute the whole of thought. For a thorough discussion of the whole problem of aphasia, the reader is referred to Head (1926) and Weisenburg and MacBride (1935). If anything, the argument from aphasia is understated in the above.

[83] Smoke, 1932, pp. 20, 26, 36.

same time preserving the general structure. For instance, a *Dax* was a circle of arbitrary colour and size, with two dots, one within and one without, at arbitrary positions and distances. The one thing in common was the circle with two dots, one within and one without. It was found that a subject might be able to recognize the general pattern and name it correctly, without being able to give the definition; that is to say, without being able to verbalize what he had learned. In the same way, Hull found that ability to define was often a very inadequate index of the functional value of a "concept",[84] although, for reasons to be given later, what he termed a concept is probably not the product of generalization but of abstraction alone. Willwoll has independently concluded that concepts are possible without verbalization.[85] Quite recently Edna Heidbreder (1947) states: "It is a very common finding, both in experimental and clinical studies, that a person may fail to define a concept adequately, though he is entirely capable of using it" (p. 124). Her experiments seem to show that this inability was most striking when unconventional and unfamiliar forms were in question. Here less than half of the definitions were correct, while over 80 per cent. were correct for the names of concepts involving numbers, and nearly 100 per cent. where concrete objects were involved. She claims that this difficulty is not due wholly to the lack of conventional terms to start off from (e.g. "tree", "circle"), since one of her tests for the acquisition of a concept was of the multiple-choice variety, which does not involve language. Sara Fisher describes the growth of verbal imagery in her generalization experiments, until "A stage was reached at which the concept appeared almost exclusively in verbal terms". . . . The verbal images themselves become fewer and more telescoped and fragmentary until finally the instructions to recall were followed immediately by a few statements descriptive of the prominent general features.[86] In her definition of the experience of generality she speaks alternatively of the presence in consciousness of *concretely or verbally* imagined essential features. Werner and Romanes are quoted by McGranahan as stressing the reality bestowed by verbalization upon a concept.[87]

It has been shown that animals can generalize.[88] Thus Fields concludes that: "When white rats are given a training period specifically designed to provide a large number of different 'triangle

[84] Hull, 1920.   [85] Willwoll, 1926.   [86] Fisher, 1916.
[87] McGranahan, 1936, p. 204.
[88] Gengerelli, 1930; Fields, 1932. See also Lashley.

experiences', the rats are able to perfect a type of behaviour which is fully described by the implications in our use of the term 'concept' ". This experiment has, it is true, been criticized by Maier, but the general conclusion is supported by Lashley.

Thus the process of generalization or concept formation illustrates the general relation of language to thinking. Generalization is possible without verbalization, but verbalization apparently improves and refines the process. Just as, in general, thinking is possible without verbalization, but verbalization improves and refines it.

A last line of evidence against the identification of language and thought may be said to be of a linguistic nature. It consists of arguments based on the nature of language. Many of these have been collected by Pick in his monograph on *Agrammatism* (1913). Thus the structure of language is said to be different from that of thought. For example, "In language the predicate comes after the subject; in thought they come together".[89] Language may be illogical while the thought behind it is logical. One may say in English, e.g., "the party were assembled", or in German "das Fräulein . . . die . . . ". There is a general feeling among linguists that language performs its function only imperfectly, that it is an imperfect instrument: the implication is that the higher psychological processes, in whatever terms one define them, are *more than* language responses. Different languages have widely different forms. It would be absurd to believe that thought in them was equally variable. The logic of Aristotle, it is said, would have been expressed very differently had he been a Mexican.

Again, the words we use are often less than the thought. When we think aloud, we produce a kind of stenogram of the thought with the salient words only expressed, using the form of sentences rather than their actual expression. That is, we think the thought without its own proper words. Only when actually communicating do we use the full language. In the same way in certain aphasics the expression is clearly not commensurate with the thought. The structure is, in fact, not necessarily that of the thought associated with it. Certain languages have no forms to express common distinctions in thought. Thus there is no difference in Semitic between "on the mountain" and "to the mountain". These are all arguments designed to show the difference between language and thought. Many of them have been illustrated by the aphasic patients already discussed. They may be summarized by the[90] statement which is often made that the

[89] Miller, quoted by Pick, loc. cit., p. 182.   [90] Somewhat dangerous.

language of communication is *expression* of thought, and that it may
be cut down when there is no communication and may vary while
the thought remains unchanged. The particular points mentioned
are all taken from Pick's monograph, which contains much other
valuable discussion and many illustrations from aphasic patients.

The linguistic argument is of secondary importance to the experimental psychologist; it offers, however, interesting corroboration of
the results obtained by other means of inquiry.

As a closing statement for this section, the following account given
by an acknowledged master of experimental physics, who has also
made a great contribution to the theoretical side of his science, is of
sufficient interest to be quoted. "Perhaps one of the best examples of
such non-verbal thought is afforded by what we do when we analyse
the action of a machine or sketch on paper the design for a piece of
apparatus. What I do in designing an apparatus is to reproduce in
imagination what my activities would be in watching the performance of the complete apparatus, and I know that for me such an
experience is almost entirely motor in character. I see one part
pushing another and have a tactile feeling for the forces and kinetic
appreciation of the resulting motion, all without consciously getting
on the verbal level. If I analyse what happens I think that I instinctively recognize that a certain kind of push or pull will be followed
by a certain kind of motion, because I remember past situations
which aroused in me the same reactions and I know what happened
in those cases."[91]

The Function of Language in Thinking

Though language and thought are then not identical, nevertheless
language plays an enormous part in thinking. The study of aphasics
has shown that certain kinds of mental processes are seriously
affected, while others are comparatively untouched by serious
language deficiency. Weisenburg found that his patients were sometimes less affected in arithmetical computation than in other "symbolic" activities. Kennedy and Wolf suggest that "arithmetical
ability belongs to a lower order of genius more akin to the idiot
savant than to the real scholar". At least it appears often to be relatively independent of language.

Language processes apparently permeate all thinking; even some

[91] Bridgman, 1936, p. 25. As a further argument against the identity of Thought
and Language, my colleague, O. L. Zangwill, points out that a patient may
suffer severe mental deterioration without any language impairment.

of the "non-language" performances were found by Weisenburg and MacBride to depend on verbal formulations or cues.[92] Most of the cases of aphasia, they claim, show a certain amount of deterioration of non-language performances beyond that due to loss of speed, but the deterioration is not so pronounced as in language performances. It may be due, they state, to the language disorder or to changes in thinking processes that are independent of language. "The so-called non-language work sometimes suffers directly in relation to its dependence on verbal formulations."[93]

Weisenburg and MacBride suggest that the finer analysis of the problem of language and thinking "is a matter for study in the individual patient and the particular performance". What may be non-language performance for one person may involve language for another. The same individual may use language on a certain problem at one time and not use it on the same problem at another time. These authors decry the possibility of making a general statement, which they say will be either superficial or else subject to many qualifications. The most that can be said is that our thinking is shot through and through with language activities, but that such activities are not essential for thinking. When the language functions are disturbed the mind as a whole is not disturbed, but specific psychical processes are interrupted or rendered difficult. Language is, we saw, a mode of symbolic formulation and expression; the patient can still think except in so far as the affected form of behaviour is necessary for thinking.[94]

Experiments on Verbal Formulation

In the above account the fact of verbal formulation or "cues" was mentioned. Some experimental work has been done on this subject. It is established that learning of the manual maze, stylus, or finger is accomplished most readily when verbal formulation can be used. For example, Warden's[95] subjects used the method of motor adjustment (the "feel" of the movement), visual patterns, and verbal organization. The average number of trials necessary by these three methods was 123·9, 67·9, and 32·2 respectively. That is to say, the specifically human method of verbalization cut down the number of trials by nearly three-quarters (stylus maze). The subject might say, for example, "right forward, left forward, then right forward three

[92] Weisenburg and MacBride, loc. cit., p. 423. [93] Op. cit., p. 423.
[94] Head, 1926, Vol. I, p. 535. [95] Warden, 1924.

times".[96] In the same way, it has been found that verbal instruction improves the scores in stylus-maze running.[97] One great advantage of the verbal method of learning such a maze is the fact that the appropriate words can be repeated in between times, so that what might have been manual learning now becomes verbal learning. An advantage in the other direction comes from the fact that a single verbalization may be adequate to ensure adequate learning of a complex task. Thus the subject may say to himself: "Always go as far as possible and press against each succeeding side which interrupts progress". It may be that the superiority of human beings to animals in many learning activities may be at least in part due to the fact that human learning is often a of different kind from that of the animal. The relatively slight superiority of the human being when placed in a maze under conditions comparable to that of the rat seems to be in favour of this possibility.

As might have been expected from the studies on aphasia, it has been found that there are probably many types of skill "for which there are no communicable language equivalents", and performance is here not expedited by preliminary instruction.[98] Further, there are cases where the verbal method cannot be used, or at least where human subjects prefer not to use it and learn almost, if not quite, as efficiently as by the verbal method.[99] In general, it is found that the maze can be learned without verbalization, but performance is much improved if it is used. This result agrees with that found for generalization.

It has been shown that verbalization has an effect on perception and reproduction of visually perceived form. In an experiment that has now become classic, Carmichael, Hogan, and Walter presented a series of stimulus figures to two groups of subjects. Different labels were assigned to the figures when presented to each of the two groups. Thus the same figure might be labelled *Crescent Moon* for one group, and *Letter "C"* for the other. Another figure was called *Eyeglasses* and *Dumb-bells*. It was found that the label exerted a strong influence on the figures as reproduced immediately after the total series of twelve figures had been exposed. For example, when the figure consisting of two circles joined by a straight line was called

[96] Cf. also Carr, 1930; Husband, 1928.

[97] Lambert and Ewert, 1932.

[98] Renshaw and Postle, 1928. Esper (*q.v.*) has a good discussion of the experiments on verbal formulation in maze learning.

[99] Kellogg and White, 1935.

eyeglasses, the straight line joining the circles was bent into the shape of a nosepiece in the reproduction. When the same figure was called *Dumb-bells* the same straight line was split lengthwise in two, and shaped into the form of the handle of a dumb-bell.

In Gibson's experiment it was found that a change in reproduction might be conditioned by cues from a verbal analysis made during perception. Verbal analysis was apt to be accompanied by weak visual imagery. It is interesting that in only 2 per cent. of Gibson's reproductions was a verbal analysis thus employed, over half of the figures being reproduced without any change at all.[100]

Of special importance for the relation of language and thought is the series of experiments initiated by Hunter's invention of the temporal maze. Here the subject, animal or human, must e.g. go twice round one block and then twice round another before obtaining the reward (Hunter, 1920). It was found that only with special coaching could rats solve this problem, apparently in part at least because the same situation, namely the starting-point, involves opposite sets of movements, namely turning to the right and the left, with further complication due to the "double alternation". The series of experiments which followed Hunter's original paper (1920) showed that human adults and older children solve the problem quickly, using words and counting, e.g. "Go twice to the right and twice to the left." As Woodworth remarks, they use "methods which are probably beyond the rat's capacity" (Woodworth, 1938, p. 135). Hunter and Bartlett (1948) used not the temporal maze but another form of double alternation, namely boxes which must be opened in the same order (RRLL, etc.) with thirty-one children as subjects. Among other interesting results, they found that children under five years old might be able to do the problem, but might not be able to say how they knew which box to open. Samples given of children who were successful and could answer the question: "How do you know which box to open?" were:

"Just do—first in one box twice then the other box twice."

"They go one and then in the same and then in the other."

It is noteworthy that in the second of these reports there is a statement of the method but probably not "counting" in the true sense of the term.

Three children who could not put the solution into words, but had, nevertheless, solved the problem said:

"I don't know. I just figure them out."

[100] See Gibson, 1929.

"I don't know how I know."

"I know how 'cause I do."

Those "who were five years or older could give the principle of double alternation verbally; in fact, most of them did so spontaneously. The younger S's, although able to perform the problem, were not able to verbalize the solution."[101]

From this experiment, and that of Gellerman (1931), it seems fairly clear that human beings *can* solve this problem without language and counting, but that language improves the process of finding a solution, a conclusion which is not surprising in view of the evidence already presented.

Kuenne (1946) adds significantly to this picture. Using children, aged four to six, he found that his subjects could generalize without verbalizing, could verbalize without using this process, that verbalization might be effected only after questioning, and that verbalization could be used spontaneously.

Antecedents of Speech

The controversy as to the antecedents of speech has already been mentioned. It seems to the popular mind reasonable that we should first have an "idea" of what we want to say, and then say it. At this stage of the discussion it is hardly necessary to state that such a conception is directly contrary to experimental fact. There is no more reason why an "idea" should precede speech behaviour than it should precede any kind of behaviour. The belief that it must do so is a remnant of the old ideo-motor fallacy, which has many times been experimentally disproved.[102] Specifically, when the speech process has been examined experimentally, it has been found not to be preceded by an image in the majority of cases. The point has been disputed on another front also, namely that of aphasia. The older theorists maintained that aphasia was due to the loss of verbal images of one kind or another. It is fair to say that the most progressive work of the last two generations has consistently opposed this conception. Hughlings Jackson, for instance, asks why, if aphasia is due to absolute lack of images, does the patient exhibit variation in his performance, such that he is able at one time and in one context to say what he cannot say in another context. The French

---

[101] The whole series of experiments is an interesting example of the use of animal subjects in elucidating a peculiarly human problem, namely the function of language in thinking. See, e.g., Gellerman, 1931.

[102] E.g. Woodworth, 1906.

physiologist Marie also attacked the image theory (1906–8), against strong opposition. Franz asks how, if motor aphasia is due to loss of images, re-education takes place.[103] How can the images be restored? In the volumes of Head, and of Weisenburg and MacBride, the question receives only historical mention. It has now died a natural death, together with the presentational psychology and the ideo-motor theory with which it was closely allied.

Another possible antecedent for speech, of a slightly different kind, has been proposed by Pick and, according to Weisenburg, widely adopted among students of aphasia. According to Pick there is a pre-language stage of thought, which is unarticulated, and which is compared to the Scheme of William James (". . . these rapid premonitory perspective views of a scheme of thought not yet articulate . . . the feeling of what thoughts are next to arise before they have yet arisen. . . . Great thinkers have vast premonitory glimpses of schemes of relations between terms which hardly even as verbal images enter the mind, so rapid is the process"). This pre-stage is further analysed by Pick into the *Bewusstseinslage* of Marbe, an "intuitive" stage, to use the term introduced by Erdmann.[104] Following this relatively unformulated stage of thinking comes a slightly more structured stage, corresponding to Ach's *Bewusstheit*, in which, according to Ach, the "contents are known, but are present without adequate verbal designation". Then comes the sentence-scheme, for the existence of which Pick adduces arguments from many philologists and psychologists. Finally comes the choice of words. So that the "way from thought to language" consists of four steps:

(1) Unformulated, intuitive thought (*Bewusstseinslage*).
(2) Structured thought (*Bewusstheit*). [105]
(3) Sentence schema.
(4) Choice of words.

Pick did not believe that these stages are always temporarily distinct. They are obviously not so. Nor are they always present in any given thought. Even though the "ladder from thought to words", as Pick has expressed it, is not accepted as given by Pick, it must be remembered that the distinction of the two main divisions of thought-formulation and language-expression has been accepted by very

[103] Loc. cit., p. 84.   [104] Erdmann, 1908.
[105] As well as by James and Erdmann, the pre-language stage of thought is insisted upon by Gomperz (total impression), Wundt (total presentation), and Selz (anticipating schema).

many workers. It is apparently presupposed by the phrase of Head's "symbolic formulation and expression". In a slightly different form it was apparently accepted by Hughlings Jackson. "There is general agreement", say Weisenburg and MacBride, "that the typical verbal formulation, whether expressed or not, is preceded[106] by a process where thought becomes ordered and falls into a structure which will admit of verbal expression." Goldstein speaks of the "Grammar of Thought" as contrasted with the syntactical grammar of language (1948).

Certain objective psychologists disagree with the term "expression of thought by language". Thus Kantor, in his very able *Objective Psychology of Grammar*, argues against the "expression theory" which "regards speech as a translation of psychic materials into verbal action, generally stated as the expression of thoughts in words".[107]

It is therefore doubly worth noting that objective psychology has itself been forced to very much the same conclusion, though it has used a very different terminology to describe it. The facts may be briefly summarized as those of the variability or plasticity of learned response, and allusion has already been made to some of them in the discussion of the peripheral theory of thought. "The engram of the maze habit consists of some central organization in which the general direction and succession of turns are so recorded that, once the series is initiated, the essential sequence of movements may be performed in the absence of sensory control *and with considerable variation in the actual movements produced*."[108] This conclusion was reached as the result of experiments which it was claimed showed that the rat could run the maze, once he had started on it, with no external sensory cues and no proprioceptive ones either. The conclusion was contested at the time it was made public, principally by Hunter. Of the fact of variation, however, there is abundant further confirmation.[109] It will be remembered, for example, that with Muezinger's guinea-pigs, trained to depress a latch, "a high degree of plasticity will persist even up to the thousandth trial". The phenomenon is called by Tolman the "multiple track".[110] Some of the abundant literature has already been quoted in the preceding chapter,

---

[106] If this implies temporal precedence, the statement is questionable.
[107] Kantor, 1936, p. 57.
[108] Lashley and Ball, 1929 (italics by present writer).
[109] Muenzinger, *et al.*, 1929.
[110] 1932, p. 170.

where reference was made to the conclusion which Woodworth[111] draws from the training experiments, that we have to do with an acquired cerebral pattern which can avail itself of different motor outlets.

The concept of such a master neural pattern as the result of which action may be initiated towards a goal by various means is thus forced upon us by experiment on animal and human beings. In Woodworth's phrase, already quoted, there is a constant neural core which may be associated with different motor neurones and different effectors. This is then the justification, or rather, perhaps, the objective description of, the phrase that language is the expression of thought. There is in these objective results an exact parallel to the statement that a given thought may be linguistically expressed in different languages; that thought may be logically, if not of necessity temporally, prior to language, to use a somewhat discredited term of Aristotle's. I cannot find, therefore, that there is necessarily any "mysticism" inherent in the statement so often made that language is the expression of thought; or in the implication which it carries of a "central" theory of thinking. By a "central" theory of thought is implied, objectively and neurologically, that the highest psychological activities are most properly described in terms of a central neural pattern, which is independent of the particularity of the motor outlet. So that the central neural core or pattern must be distinguished from, and contrasted with, the diverse neuro-effector systems which it may energize. The subjective psychologist will state the same distinction by contrasting the "thought" with its diverse possibilities of expression.

In order not to beg this question, the use of the term "expression" has been postponed until this point, except where quotation has made it necessary.[112]

Behaviourism and Language

The hypothesis that thinking may be identified with language was given fresh impetus in modern psychology by the behaviouristic school. However, Watson, the founder of the school, made haste to repudiate the statement that "thinking is merely the action of

[111] Woodworth, 1938. For the references to the "transfer" experiments, see the chapter on "Transfer of Training".

[112] Among psychologists of the first rank who have spoken of the expression of thought by language are Pillsbury, 1928, Bartlett and Smith, 1920, Pear, 1920, Head, *passim*; and, of the past generation, Ward and Stout.

language mechanisms".[113] Actually the behaviouristic theory is not so much a *verbal* theory but a *peripheral* theory of thinking. For him implicit activity is thinking, whether it be verbal, manual, or what not. Really he believes that most of such implicit activity is of laryngeal nature, so that "Thinking is largely a verbal process".[114] As might be expected, he disagrees with the distinction between thought and expression of thought. It will be seen therefore that the behaviourist theory of thinking has already been dealt with, and the relevant experimental evidence analysed in this and the preceding chapter.

Summary

The attempt has been made to confine this discussion to results based on experimentally or clinically derived data, and has thus left untouched such admirable analyses as are to be found in the works of Stout, Ward, and Adamson. For it has seemed to the writer that such clinical and experimental evidence is now sufficient in quality and quantity to serve as a foundation for a consistent psychological theory of language. The possible exception to this programme is in the case of meaning, where there is little *ad hoc* experimental evidence available. An account of meaning has been given in terms of the "reference function". This kind of treatment although derived analytically has already proved of great service to the vigorous discipline of symbolic logic; at the same time the account has been seen to be strikingly confirmed by the clinical evidence. It has further been shown that the "problem of meaning", engendered in many cases by too facile a use of the concept of reference, is in many cases, at least, spurious.

The principal conclusions to which, on the basis of such a statement concerning meaning, the experimental evidence leads are as follows:

(1) The utterance-aspect of language may be analysed into a hierarchy of habits, which from a few elementary relatively constant, primary sounds, build up highly complex, delicately adjusted structures. In certain types of aphasia and in ordinary "speech defect" disturbances of this function may occur.

(2) In addition to the sheer mechanics of utterance, speech involves a reference function; that is to say, the spoken word *refers* to some object which may be analysed independently of the speech response in question. The reference function is to be understood as a psychological activity.

[113] Watson, 1920. [114] Ibid., p. 104.

(3) The reference function is of various degrees of complexity and integration. It is found in a simple form in animals. It has been shown clinically to be deranged at different levels in various aphasic patients.

(4) The terms "reference" and "meaning" represent a half-way analysis of the total speech activity. They are of practical use but dangerous.

(5) The function of evocation likewise involves a "reference function" of its own, which may likewise be disturbed in aphasia.

(6) All available experimental and clinical evidence is against the identification of thought with language.

(7) Nevertheless, human thinking is permeated with language. There is some elementary experimental evidence bearing on the way in which human language-technique is utilized in thinking.

(8) Thinking may go on in human beings when the language techniques, of utterance and reception, have been destroyed or have not yet developed.

(9) Ordinary language involves processes which would usually be classed as thinking.

(10) There is no evidence that an image of any kind normally precedes speech. But certain objective experiments offer a parallel which makes it legitimate to speak of language as "expressing" thought.

Appendix on the Results of Factorial Analysis

Sir Cyril Burt in his recent article (1949) has given an authoritative statement reviewing the results of factor analysis. There seems to be a general agreement among the factor analysts that verbal ability is independent of the "higher mental processes", such as generalization, abstraction, judgment, and reasoning. Two word factors are distinguished: (1) that dealing with *words in isolation*, and divided into (*a*) that of recognizing, (*b*) that for finding or selecting the right word. (2) A language factor (dealing with *words in their context*). Sir Cyril Burt states that the findings are on the whole in agreement with Head's classifications. Thurstone (e.g. 1945) claims to have isolated three or four verbal factors of which only two "are at present understood". These include a word fluency factor W in addition to a verbal comprehension factor V. It is, I think, fair to say that the majority of psychologists are not yet convinced that such factors really add anything to our knowledge. Their function seems to be rather that of clarifying existing knowledge.

CHAPTER IX

GENERALIZATION

Abstraction and Generalization

THE TERM ABSTRACTION is given to the psychological process as the result of which behaviour or experience is determined, not by the total psychological situation immediately confronting an organism but by some particular feature or features with the exclusion by the organism of other features. When abstraction is from a group of variable situations, and organic modification towards particular situations is determined by a common feature of the group as such, the process is called generalization. Generalization may then be said to be the process by which an organism comes to effect a constant modification towards an invariable feature (or set of features) which occurs under varying conditions.[1] The process necessarily involves the neglect of irrelevancies; this is impossible without abstraction. The converse is not true; for abstraction of a particular feature from a particular context is clearly possible as a unique event which does not concern other particulars. So that

[1] No attempt will be made in this chapter to discuss the question of the universality or generality of thought as such, nor the question of universality as contrasted with a generality which is limited to a specific group. Adequate discussion of these important questions would require philosophical treatment on a scale which would be out of place in this volume. For brief but illuminating discussions, see Adamson, 1903, Chapters III and VI; Dawes Hicks, 1938, Chapter V. It might seem from the statement in the text that every organic reaction, at least, is the product of abstraction. The amoeba moves away from an intense light, whatever the colour. Does it react to the light-energy and abstract from the wave-length? The patient jerks his knee to a hammer of any shape, provided that the blow is dealt in the proper manner. Does he abstract from the shape? This book, however, confines itself to psychological data and processes; that is, to such as are the product of the organism being studied with the means and material at its disposal. The abstraction is clearly made not by the amoeba but by the experimenter. Similarly the patient could, if he were to look at it, abstract from the shape of the physician's hammer; but ordinarily he does not do so. Külpe's definition of abstraction as that process by which the psychologically effective is separated from the psychologically or logically ineffective does not cover the point. His other definition, "the process by which specific part-contents of consciousness come to be accentuated and others allowed to retreat" would not be allowed today, as based too narrowly on a structural definition of psychology. In addition, it begs the question of the "accentuation" of that which is abstracted. For such accentuation, see the discussion below (Külpe 1904, pp. 67, 56).

abstraction does not necessarily involve generalization. However, an important instance of abstraction is that which occurs during generalization, and which results in the psychic separation of the common or general feature from its variable accompaniments.

Learning, Thinking, Abstraction, and Generalization

The problems of abstraction and generalization are thus closely allied to the wider one of learning. In so far as the learning process brings about the elimination of errors, abstraction is present. The rat which has learned the maze neglects certain passages which he originally traversed. The cricketer learns to "keep his eye on the ball". In each of these examples the "wrong" stimuli are neglected after learning in favour of the "right" ones, leaving what has been called a "constant core". Further, in learning an organism is said to modify its action because of past experience; that is, experience of features common to the present with the past. If the present held nothing in common with past situations learning would clearly be impossible; there would be nothing to learn *from*. In ordinary learning experiments the situations present a minimum of variation; indeed, experimental technique ordinarily endeavours to eliminate them altogether. But it can never do so entirely. The psychological situation will vary slightly from trial to trial though retaining a constant core. When such variation reaches the "limen of change", abstraction and generalization will take place if the psychological feat is within the organism's powers.[2] Thus, learning experiments in which the emphasis is placed on the variability of the learning situation are usually termed experiments in generalization.[3] This may be summed up by saying that if an organism learns to effect a constant modification of behaviour or of experience to each of a group of

[2] Whether this point is reached in the ordinary learning experiments, it is impossible to say. Whether also generalization is psychologically possible without variation, i.e. whether a general response could in fact be achieved to a group of psychologically indistinguishable particulars or to one particular, is a matter for philosophers to decide. Aristotle seems to have believed in the latter possibility. Psychologically it is fair to say that, if these are possible cases they are limiting ones. There seems to be no doubt that generalization ordinarily takes place by the method described, i.e. from variable particulars. It has been maintained that all perception involves certain general features. (Adamson, 1903, p. 285; Dawes Hicks 1938, p. 132.) This point will not be further discussed, but the terms perception and generalization will be given their usual sense in experimental psychology.

[3] For Lashley's experimentally grounded thesis that generalization is one of the primitive basic functions of organized nervous tissue, see Chapter I, and especially note 74. It is doubtful whether the "generalization" of the conditioned

situations which separately (that is, apart from the group) would call for different modifications, generalization has occurred. This gives a behaviouristic criterion by which it may be decided whether, in fact, generalization has taken place on any particular occasion.

However, generalization is not confined to those processes to which the name learning would ordinarily be given. When, as in Willwoll's experiments, a subject assigned a generic idea to the terms *Hermit* and *Eccentric*, he was undoubtedly generalizing.[4] Yet the psychological process involved would not ordinarily be said to be one of learning, but rather one of thinking. The terms learning and thinking, in fact, overlap each other, and are only distinguished for the sake of convenience. Where it is desired to emphasize the relation of psychological process to past experience, we naturally speak of learning. Where it is desired to emphasize the psychological present, we are apt to speak of thinking.[5] Thus there is an intimate relation between (*a*) generalization, the process by which the organism comes to effect a constant response to a feature repeated in a variable context, (*b*) learning, that by which it acquires a response to a repeated feature in a context considered as constant; and (*c*) thinking, that by which it meets a problem-situation through the manipulation and transformation of responses and experiences already at its disposal; or, according to the Gestalt psychologists, through the creation of new responses as a result of the clash of new perceptions and already acquired experience and response.

In order to present the results of psychological experiment—the philosophical question involved has been the subject of discussion for two thousand years; already in the twelfth century a writer complains that the world has grown old treating of it[6]—the chief experimental methods will first be described. The principal results will then be collected.

Experimental Methods

These may be divided according as they primarily stress abstraction or generalization.

reflex should be considered to be the same process as that discussed in the present chapter, for it seems to depend on the absence of psychological activity (i.e. the dog fails to distinguish between the active and inactive notes), whereas the process of relating, e.g., a group of animals called dogs is essentially positive.

[4] Willwoll, 1926, p. 62.

[5] Graham, 1939, treats generalization as a form of learning; Maier, 1937, as a form of thinking. Cf. Maier, 1931.

[6] John of Salisbury. He goes on to say that the world has taken more time for its solution than the Cæsars took to conquer and govern the world.

(*a*) *Studies Primarily Stressing Abstraction.*—Of these, the earliest seems to have been that of Külpe (1904). Four nonsense syllables were presented on a screen for 125 ms. These were coloured differently and arranged so as to form different figures. The figures might be exposed without a special *Aufgabe*, or with instructions to observe (*a*) the number of letters, or (*b*) the colours and their approximate location, or (*c*) the figure formed by the letters, or (*d*) the letters themselves with their approximate location. This is probably the first experiment on the *Aufgabe* as such, since Watt's classical paper did not appear until the next year. The paper insists throughout on the importance of the *Aufgabe*. Positive abstraction, by which certain features are singled out, is distinguished from negative abstraction, in which inessentials, what Aristotle calls *accidents*, are rejected.[7] The chief result was the demonstration of the importance of the *Aufgabe*. For example, with the appropriate task, the subject may be totally unable to report on colour and may deny that colour has been experienced at all.

The results of Külpe's study, as of the other studies later to be considered, will be discussed under the general headings presented later in the chapter.

Grünbaum's work (1908) was done at Würzburg, and it follows the Würzburg tradition. Characteristically for the Würzburg work, very simple experimental methods were used. Grünbaum projected on a screen, 4·25 metres distant, two pairs of grouped figures separated by a diagonal line. Of the grouped figures (four in each group) all were different save two, one on each side of the diagonal. (See figure 4.) Thirteen subjects were used, including Külpe, Dürr, Lillien Martin, Michotte, Bühler, Katz, and Spearman—surely one of the most distinguished groups of subjects that have ever sat for a psychological experiment! The figures used were adapted from Moore's experiment (*q.v.*), and according to Moore a number of improvements were made. About 300 figures were employed altogether. Five series were shown to each subject on any one day, with a constant exposure time of 3 seconds. Exposures were made with groups of 2/2, 3/3, 4/4, 5/5, 6/6 figures successively. Instructions were: to fixate no special point, but if fixation is necessary to direct attention towards the middle of the dividing line, and thence to fulfil the task. The primary task was to discover two like elements. After that had been accomplished, the subject was to observe other

[7] The distinction between positive and negative abstraction is said to go back to Kant.

figures (secondary task). The elements found, and especially the like figures, were to be drawn on the paper provided, on which an appropriate pattern, i.e. presumably a diagonal line, was already drawn. After the drawing, the exposed figures were presented, and the question "What have you noticed besides?" was to be answered. The

Figure 4

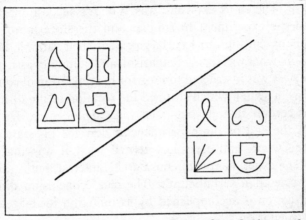

[*From Grünbaum, 1908.*

subject was particularly requested to distinguish the figures really recognized from conjectured ones, those that they "thought" that they recognized. As with Külpe, preliminary experiments of a rather extensive nature were given in order that the subject might accustom himself to the procedure and discover the best method of working.[8] Grünbaum insists on the advantage of meaningless "nonsense" figures for this kind of experiment. In this way he thinks that the effects of memory are minimized, as in the memory experiments. It is doubtful, however, whether here, any more than in the case of nonsense syllables, meaning was entirely eliminated. For example, the upper left-hand figure of the illustration suggests a tooth, etc. Assimilation to known objects is noted by Moore, who used similar figures, and by many other experimenters.

With this elementary material, Grünbaum achieved important results, the chief being the discovery of the process of *accentuation* in perceptual abstraction. His is, indeed, one of the most important experiments to be described in this chapter.

Moore's work was conducted at the Universities of Leipzig and California, between 1905 and 1910. A preliminary report was given

[8] Grünbaum, 1908, pp. 353–5.

at the fifth international congress of psychology at Rome in 1905. Although the study was published two years after Grünbaum's, the general method was admittedly Moore's. Fifteen subjects were used, including Grünbaum and Stratton. A group of five figures was exposed for a quarter of a second, then a blank space for a quarter of a second, and so on, until the series of twenty-five exposures came to an end, or as much of the series was used as was necessary for the experiment. The short exposure was Wundt's suggestion. "It tends to reduce the experiment to simpler and therefore more constant conditions by cutting out to a large extent such variable factors as reflection on what was seen, comparison and voluntary association."[9]

The subject was instructed to look for the repetition of some figure and to turn a switch which stopped the rotation of the disk as soon as it was certain that he had *seen some figure twice*. He was required at the end of the experiment to describe his state of mind during the work, and especially to tell what it was that he first noticed. The experiment is of considerable interest, but is on a much slighter scale than Grünbaum's. The chief conclusion drawn was that abstraction is accomplished by assimilation to imageless (perceptual) categories.

The study of English (1922) was made at Yale. The inspiration for the method came from Aveling, but important changes were made. "The material employed consisted of ten sets of small pictures and ten nonsense syllables of two syllables each. There were five pictures in each set. All in each set were sufficiently alike to be designated by some common name; yet each possessed sufficiently notable characteristics as well, by which it could be singled out from the others."[10] This quotation is given in description of English's group *a*, which was designed to reproduce Aveling's material as closely as possible. Set 1 in English's experiment comprised curvilinear geometrical figures, and the nonsense syllable was *Bekis*. Set 2, musical instruments, *Bojar*; set 3, soldiers, *Hexur*, etc.

The instructions were: "I shall show you a picture and a nonsense word for a short time. Repeat the word aloud once while you regard attentively both word and picture above it."

After seven to nine exposures had been made, the subjects were told: "You will now be shown the nonsense words you saw with the pictures. As soon as the meaning of the word is apparent to you, react by pressing this key. You will be asked to report in what guise

    [9] Moore, 1910, p. 118.
    [10] Aveling, 1912, p. 78 f. Quoted by English, p. 306.

or form the meaning comes to you." The subjects asked for a definition of meaning and were told to give the word its everyday signification. Nonsense words not in the series were occasionally used, as "*Vexierversuchen*".

Group *b* comprised musical elements played on a gramophone, the common feature being the manner of producing the selection. The nonsense words were visually presented at the same time. There were used: baritone solos, duets by male and female voices, mixed vocal quartets, and band selections. "Woolworth" records were used, and also two standard large records.

Group *c* comprised visual presentations similar to those of group *a*, but more complex and more difficult. Beginning with the third or fourth sitting, the subject dictated his introspection into a dictaphone. Group *d* was a control series, in which auditory presentations were substituted for visual ones.

The subjects were not required to give an introspective account of the process of abstraction, but rather to report the train of associations aroused by certain words previously presented together with (*a*) constant material, (*b*) occurring under variable conditions. In this way, however, much light was thrown on the process of abstraction. This study merges with those described in the next section as stressing generalization.

It will be observed that English's study was distinguished from those previously described in that no specific task was assigned.

The chief result was the understanding of the process of analysis involved in abstraction, and the demonstration of the part played by conceptual assimilation.

Weigl, a pupil of Goldstein, worked on the problem of the classification of objects. Patients with cortical lesions and normal subjects were required to group collections of articles. These articles might consist of Holmgren wools (1 group), coloured disks of various shapes (1 group), everyday articles such as a ball, pliers, bicycle-bell, table-knife, toy table-knife (1 group). Patients performed this grouping at a much lower level than normals. Articles might be arranged according to use, but not in other ways which came naturally to normals, such as "spotted colour". The patients found it very difficult to shift from one classification to another (Weigl, 1927). This study has a less "artificial" air than the other studies of abstraction; one feels that it deals with abstractive processes closer to those of everyday life. It also merges with the studies stressing generalization.

Summary of Studies Stressing Abstraction

All four of the reported studies investigated abstraction at a relatively elementary level; three (those of Grünbaum, Moore, English) examined purely perceptual abstraction, while that of Külpe examined processes which were at least of a quasi-perceptual nature. Three of them stressed the *Aufgabe* and its effect, while the fourth, that of English, is unique in attempting to eliminate a specific *Aufgabe* of abstraction. There appears to be need of a programme of investigation which shall investigate abstraction, (*a*) in a more complex, (*b*) in a more natural context. The experiments give the impression of artificiality, which may or may not be avoidable under laboratory conditions.

Experiments in which Generalization is Stressed

Most of these experiments fall roughly into three classes. In Method A, an artificial perceptual class is created and a nonsense syllable attached to it as its name. In Method B, the Multiple Choice Method, a common rule of action must be found for a serial group of situations immediately presented in perception. In Method C, a feature must be found which is common to the meaning of words; i.e. the generalization primarily involves objects not present at all in immediate perception. Methods A, B, and C are of increasing order of difficulty; thus animals have been studied by the first two, but obviously no animal has ever been able to achieve the processes involved in the third. The three methods will be discussed in turn.

Method A: An artificial perceptual class is created, and a nonsense syllable attached to it as its name.—The first and probably the most comprehensive example of this method is that of Fisher (1916), whose study was available to English (1922), already noted as using a similar procedure. The experiments were performed in 1912–13 at Clark University. Five observers were used, including Baird and Fernberger. Four series of drawings were exposed, each series containing ten drawings, 20·5 cm. by 12·5 cm. Each possessed certain characteristics which were common to all the other members of the group, and each also contained certain characteristics peculiar to itself or to only a few others. Each series of ten cards was bound into a booklet, and the exposures were made by hand with the assistance of a stop-watch. Exposure time, 3 seconds. Under each card of each series a nonsense name was printed, the names selected being *Zalof*, *Deral*, *Tefoq*, and *Kareg*. Instructions were: "You are to be shown a series of ten drawings of figures which represent a group or species.

The group name will be shown with every drawing; it is *Zalof* (or *Deral*, etc.). These drawings do not represent real objects; they are to be regarded merely as drawings. Do not attempt to associate them with familiar objects, but confine your definition to what is shown. If such associations occur spontaneously, however, do not inhibit them. Each drawing will be exposed for three seconds, when it will be followed immediately by another. After all have been exposed, you will be given the task of defining the group name *Zalof* (or *Deral*, etc.). You will be asked to furnish detailed introspective accounts not only of your experiences during the examination of the series, but also of the mental processes involved in defining the group name." At a stated interval, usually of one week after the initial exposure, the observer was given the instructions: "Tell me everything you remember about the *Zalofs*, etc.; then give an introspective account of your process of recall." He was afterwards shown the same series for the second time and allowed to continue his examination. On the recompletion of the series of exposures he was asked once more to define the group name, or, if he preferred, to modify his previous definition, adding any new features which he had discovered. This was repeated until no new features were discovered. Thereafter the act of recalling was still continued through a number of sittings. The experiment thus stressed perfection of learning.

Miss Fisher's experiment is distinguished by the fact that it furnishes the most thoroughgoing investigation of generalization of visual material by a structural psychologist. Perhaps the most striking finding is the insistence on the gradual development of the "concept", which was accompanied by a gradual mechanization of the process, with a change in the imagery involved from a predominantly visual to a verbal type, and ultimate disappearance of all imagery in recall. The method was in essence used also by Aveling—four years earlier—and Stevanović.

Hull's able study (1920) dispensed altogether with introspection. One hundred and forty-four Chinese characters were employed as a basis. These were drawn in black ink on cards two inches long and one inch wide. The cards were presented to the subject for five seconds by means of a modification of the Wirth memory apparatus. In the middle of each exposure, during the early part of the experiment, the experimenter pronounced a nonsense syllable, the subject repeating the name immediately after. He was directed to anticipate the experimenter as soon as possible by himself, by speaking the required word during the two and half seconds of the exposure before the prompting. The same nonsense syllable was used for each of a series of characters containing an identical feature (termed by Hull a "concept"), though with varying complications. Thus the task of the subject was to attach the nonsense name to the feature (set of strokes) common to a set of the varying Chinese characters. Twelve common features were employed; each was presented in twelve contexts. A "pack" consisted of twelve cards, each with a different common feature, and six such packs were shown successively. A further series of six packs was used for testing the acquisition of concepts, the test series being graded in order of difficulty. Measures of acquisition were (a) ability to state the "name" of the concept when the learning series was repeated; (b) number of promptings required during learning and while the test series was being run; (c) drawing the "concept". No introspections were taken.

The chief result of this study was the demonstration that there appears to be no advantage in learning a concept by proceeding from a simple to a complex setting, rather than vice versa; and also the quantitative demonstration that such learning is a gradual process. The chief merit of the study was to have provided a more strictly controlled and also a quantitative method of studying the process of generalization. Its defect is the elementary nature of the "concept" studied, which, according to Smoke, makes it rather a study of abstraction than of generalization.

Ach's experiments were performed in 1921. The method will be described in the improved form in which it was used by Hanfmann and Kasanin, which they took from the Russian investigators Sakharof and Vigotsky. The improved form reduces the reliance placed on introspection, and also the duration of the experiment. Twenty-two wooden blocks are used, varying in colour, shape, height, and size. There are five different colours, six different shapes—circles, squares, triangles, trapezoids, hexagons, and half-circles; two heights, and two sizes of top or bottom area. On the invisible underside of each block is written one of the four nonsense words: *lag*, *bik*, *mur*, *cev*. At the beginning of the experiment the blocks are mixed and scattered over the circular part of a square board, the rest of which is divided into four corner spaces. The subject is told that there are four different kinds of blocks, that each has a name, and that his task is to find the four kinds and group them in the four corners. The examiner turns up one of the blocks, shows its name, and puts it into one of the corner spaces. The subject is then told to put into the same corner the blocks which belong there. After the first attempt, another block is turned up and the subject encouraged to continue. This is repeated, the examiner turning up one of the blocks at every false attempt, until the blocks are rightly grouped. The subject is then asked to formulate the principle of the classification. The blocks are then redistributed and the subject re-groups them as a test. Selections made by the subject and corrections made by the examiner are recorded, and the subject encouraged to "think aloud". This method combines the advantages that it is rather less artificial than those previously described; that it involves a real classificatory process, rather than one of memory; and that it does not keep the subject in ignorance of the purpose of the experimenter, as in the method of Hull (used also by Kuo and others) and of Heidbreder, to be described on p. 276.[11]

Two other methods will be mentioned in this section, which deals predominantly with perceptual abstraction-generalization. They are those of Smoke and Heidbreder. Smoke (1932) criticized Hull's method as investigating abstraction rather than generalization. In this he is not wholly justified. Hull's method does require generalization though of a very elementary kind, since the subjects are required to assign an object to a class, and not merely to abstract certain aspects of a particular situation. Smoke's method, however, was an improvement in that in place of identical common elements, which he points out are scarcely ever found in extra-laboratory life as distinguishing class-marks, common *relationships* were used. Ten concepts were employed in the form of geometrical designs. Each type of design was given a nonsense name. Figures illustrating the concept might vary in shape, size or colour, width of line, etc., as long as the fundamental relations were observed. Thus a *pog* is a blue rectangle enclosing a blue circle that touches only the long side of the rectangle, and so on. The cards were three inches square and were mechanically exhibited at a distance from one and a half to two feet from the subject. The subject was told he would see a number of drawings each of which was called, e.g., a *pog*: "Try to find out everything a figure must be if it is to be called a *pog*." Twenty subjects were used, and sixteen figures illustrating one of the concepts were serially exposed. In the main experiment the subjects could substitute another design by pressing a contact key, and raise his hand when he thought he knew what, e.g., a *pog* was. Tests were made by verbal definition, by drawing, and by picking out examples

[11] Hanfmann, 1936; Hanfmann and Kasanin, 1937.

of the correct figure from a series containing "correct" and "incorrect" drawings.

One advantage of Smoke's method has been mentioned, namely that it employed common features of a much more complex kind than Hull had used, and thus investigated a process closer to those of extra-laboratory life. It was strictly objective, as was Hull's. It allowed the subject to work in his own time. All in all, it was thus somewhat less artificial than Hull's method, while retaining the desirable feature of objectivity. However, Hull's method probably admits of closer quantification.

The chief result was the establishment of the fact that a subject can form and utilize a concept without verbalization. The disadvantage here and with Hull's method is that the experimenter is deprived of the information given by the subject's own report of his activities.

Method B: This is essentially the "multiple choice" method; a general rule is arbitrarily predetermined by the experimenter and the subject required to discover the rule.—The perceptual side is thus not emphasized as much as in the methods hitherto described. Heidbreder (1924) used an excellent form of the procedure. By it the subject was presented with geometrical figures which the experimenter had arbitrarily decided were to be marked in a certain way. The marks were assigned to the figure as the result of a preliminary experiment. When each of a number of such figures had been marked correctly, combinations and variations were presented, each in its turn to be marked by an arbitrarily assigned method. By making the conditions more and more complex, very difficult problems could be elaborated. "A problem was considered solved when the subject marked a card correctly, stated a rule which would give successes constantly, and followed his successful reaction with four correct performances" (i.e. in variable contexts). The generalization was here of a *rule*, which had to be applied under variable conditions. Before the problem could be solved, it was necessary not only to meet the individual case, but also to elaborate a general principle which was independent of the particular figure illustrating it. Thus the method is rightly classed by Woodworth as one of examining abstraction and generalization, although the paper is entitled "An Experimental Study of Thinking".

The chief advantage of Heidbreder's method over those previously described is that it studies still more complex processes, and that, in a manner impossible to the other methods, it showed the subject in the process of building up his knowledge step by step. The chief result is the careful analysis of terms commonly used to describe the process of generalization, such as "analysis" and "synthesis", and the demonstration of what Heidbreder calls "spectator behaviour".

Method C: Experiments on Verbal Generalization.—This method was initiated by the Würzburg investigators. Both Watt and Messer used the task "find a superordinate to . . . and . . .". The method was taken over by Selz, and discussed by him in detail.[12] It was used extensively by Willwoll, who employed difficult pairs of words. A selection of Willwoll's material follows.

(1) Pier: stair-landing; (2) motor-goggles: lampshade; (3) scaffold: crutch; (4) Pythia: medium; (5) birdcage: dog-chain; (6) rugged: sudden; (7) unconditioned: complete; (8) invisible: inextended. Thirty-four pairs of words were used in all on twenty-four subjects. The results concerning imagery were of special value.

Discussion of Studies Stressing Generalization

It will be observed that method A, by which a nonsense name is attached to an artificial class, involves two processes: (*a*) the formation of the generalization, (*b*) the attaching of the sign to it. That is, the sign-response is used as a token that the generalization has been formed. It is in a sense an experimental artefact. This use of an arbitrary act of naming gives the method, again, a certain flavour of artificiality; it tends also towards the false implication that naming and generalization are psychologically the same. The impression of artificiality is less pronounced, though not entirely lacking, in method B, as illustrated by Heidbreder's adaptation of the multiple-choice method. Methods A and B involve what may be called the perceptual aspect of generalization; features are sought which are common to sets of objects actually presented in perception. In Method C the emphasis has shifted almost entirely from the perceptual aspect; it is seen that the solution involves finding neither (*a*) common perceptual features in a group of perceptual presentations nor (*b*) a common rule of action for a series of situations immediately presented in perception, but (*c*) a feature common to the *meaning* of two words. Here it will be seen that the common feature which must be found involves objects not perceptually present at all. A perceptual factor is indeed involved, as it must probably be, ultimately, in every act of generalization; but the generalization is much farther removed from it. It is involved rather with the object of reference. So much is this the case that the perceptual material

[12] Selz, 1922, pp. 105 ff.

may be entirely changed, leaving the act of generalization essentially unaltered. Willwoll's experiment may be conducted with the "stimulus-words" in any language known to the subject, without radically changing the generalizing process.

Results of the Experimental Studies

The classical problem in the psychology of generalization concerns the function of images. Two questions may be formulated:

(*a*) Does the process of generalization consist essentially in the formation of a special kind of image?

(*b*) If not, what part does imagery play?

The first question, which relates to the existence of general images, was debated by the philosophers Berkeley and Hume,[13] in the form of the problem of abstract ideas. These two philosophers maintained that general images were impossible. Berkeley's argument still stands today, that a *visual image* is a particular image and must be so.[14] "Whatever hand or eye I imagine, it must have some particular shape and colour." The doctrine of generic images was revived in the last century by Galton and Huxley. Writing on Hume, Huxley says:

"Now when several complex impressions which are more or less different from each other—let us say that out of ten impressions in each, six are the same in all, and four are different from all the rest—are successively presented to the mind, it is easy to see what must be the nature of the result. The repetition of the six similar impressions will strengthen the six corresponding elements of the complex idea which will therefore acquire greater vividness while the four differing impressions of each will not only acquire no greater strength than they had at first, but in accordance with the law of association they will all tend to appear at once and will thus neutralize one another." He goes on to compare Galton's well-known composite photographs, where a number of photographs are superimposed to obtain for example a type-picture of a man suffering from tuberculosis.

"*The generic ideas,*" he continues, "*which are formed from several similar but not identical complex experiences, are what are commonly called abstract or general ideas;* and Berkeley endeavoured to prove that all general ideas are particular ideas annexed to a certain term which gives them a more extensive signification. . . . General ideas,*" Huxley thinks, "of sensible objects may nevertheless be produced in

[13] Berkeley, 1901, pp. 7 ff.; Hume, 1896, pp. 17 ff.
[14] Berkeley, loc. cit., p. 11.

the way indicated, and may exist independently of language."[15] Stout believes that a generic idea may be thus produced, but denies that it is a rudimentary concept.[16] Stout points out that mere vagueness does not give generality: "Imperfection of the sense organs ought on this view to be a great help towards conceptual thinking."

Thus philosophical and quasi-philosophical opinion is divided on the questions of abstract or general ideas, or images: Berkeley and Hume maintaining that images are necessarily particular, Huxley that general images can be fashioned on the manner of Galton's composite photographs, and Stout agreeing with Huxley that such a method of formation is possible, but that it does not bring generality.

What does experiment say on the point?

There are several sources of evidence. Watt's observers reported very indefinite images. Examples may be quoted: "Hide: image of an animal torso thickly covered with hair (very unclear). To what animal it belonged I do not know. Grain: Fleeting image of a rye or wheat field—the species was not clear. Mouth (*Maul*): Beast. Dark image of an utterly indefinable animal. It could have been an ox or a dog with stronger definition of the head and mouth region" (Moore's translation). The last image did function as though it were generic. Watt points out that the fact of generic images does not in itself exclude the possibility of the universal (imageless) idea.[17]

Messer[18] corroborates the observation of Watt that there exist generic images, which stand in consciousness for a whole class. Such an image is often imperfect, so that subjects can only name it by a word describing a class, such as "an animal". Koffka also describes general images such as statues of neither sex, coins of no denomination.[19]

Stevanović (1927, p. 49) found that there might be a schematic image, representing a general type, or a fragmentary image, representing the essential part of the picture, or a verbal representation of such essential part; or the essential character might be known imagelessly.

The weight of evidence is, on the whole, for the existence of the generic image, in the sense of an image that represents a class. But it has been pointed out that generality is not conferred by vagueness. Why then are generic images described as vague? Fisher has here made an important contribution. Her observers did indeed report

[15] Huxley, 1879, pp. 94-6 (italics by present writer).
[16] Stout, 1902, Vol. II, p. 179.
[17] Watt, 1905, p. 364.   [18] Messer, 1906, p. 55.   [19] 1912.

that imagery of generalized features were often vague and schematic in contrast to images of particular features. This, she says, is due to the fact that, owing to repetition, they had become mechanized more rapidly than that of particular features. Images representing particular features might become mechanized equally with those of general features. "Since then imagery of particular features, like that of general ones, began to occur fleetingly, indistinctly, and in isolation as the number of the observers' examinations and recalls of the non-general features increased—or, in other words, since both followed the same course of mechanization under similar conditions—it appears that the difference between the imagery of general and that of particular features is not one of structure. We cannot say that general features inherently tend to be present in vague colourless and attenuated form while particular features are clear, vivid, and detailed . . . there exists no essential structural difference between the two sorts of imagery, provided they are compared at analogous levels . . . Both may be detailed and definite, both may be vague and fleeting. Both tend to evolve from a distinct and complete form to an indistinct form."[20] It would seem that some such process as that described by Huxley may be at work, though, failing specific experiment, the matter is highly speculative. But in any case the function of such a process is not to produce generality.

The conclusion to which the experimental results seem to lead is then that *there are generic images, and in the nature of the case they are apt to be vague and indistinct; but that such vagueness or indistinctness bears no relation to their generality as such. Under certain circumstances a clear-cut, detailed image may be a true generic image, and a vague one may be the image of a particular*. Thus the difference between what is known as a generic image and particular one is not in the images as such and it is ordinarily said that it resides in "what they stand for". One "stands for" a particular object, the other for a general feature. The question concerns the reference function again. The point is ably made by Binet, who states that an image can stand for anything.[21] And in a famous passage James says: "The geometer, with his one definite figure before him, knows perfectly that his thoughts apply to countless other figures as well, and that although he *sees* lines of a certain special bigness, direction, colour, etc., he *means* not one of these details."[22] Again it is usually

[20] Fisher, 1916, p. 180.   [21] Binet, 1903a, Chapter VIII.
[22] 1890, Vol. I, p. 472.

said that the geometer's figure has "general" as contrasted with "particular" reference.

Further Analysis of "Reference"

Once more many will be content to leave this distinction between the particular and the general image in these terms. But it should be repeated that though convenient this is a half-way analysis only, which may easily lead to false psychological conclusions. To begin with the particular. When I "have an image of my cousin Tom", the primary datum is "I imagine my cousin". It has been seen that the image is an end-product of the total activity of imagining which may be included under the visual modality. It is true that there are many general features involved when I imagine my cousin, but the whole process essentially involves a particular person. The term "particular reference" thus indicates that the "image" is part of the process of imagining a particular object. It may, indeed, *be* the sensory part almost without residue; or there may be, and often are, "images" of other modalities, such as muscular tensions (e.g. Jacobson, 1929, p. 173), and so on, associated with it in the total process. Supposing, however, that I imagine a civil servant. Here I may have a particular image, which in the common term "stands for" or "refers to" all the civil servants I have known. I have learned to react to "a civil servant", dropping all irrelevancies, such as colour of eyes, of suit, of complexion; just as a rat in learning a maze has learned to neglect all irrelevancies created by day-to-day variation, or as Pavlov's dogs developed indifference to "external inhibition"; or as a surgeon neglects such irrelevancies as the colour of the patient's skin. In short, this process of learning, like all other learning, is a process among other things of neglecting irrelevancies and connecting up relevancies. Having gone through the process of learning what a "civil servant looks like", or what I think he looks like, I imagine a civil servant, and my image is again that part or end-product of the total process which may be categorized as of the visual modality. Common usage, once more, says I have a general image of a civil servant. The same thing is true for James's geometer, who has learned to neglect the irrelevancies and to connect the relevant features of experienced triangles. That is, he has generalized and really continues the process of abstracting from the unimportant and connecting up the important when he uses his blackboard figure to demonstrate a general proposition. So that the term "general reference" indicates that the image is a learned end-product of a series of experiences. That an "image" can thus be acquired as the end-product of learning, we know in abundance from experimental sources (see, e.g., Fisher). The term is a convenient and harmless one so long as this is remembered.

With the above reservations, other illustrations of general reference will be given. Thus Neff (1937) speaks of reference beyond the perceived figure to *other members* of the group.[23] Again in connection with the sorting of Holmgren wools, Gelb and Goldstein remark: "The normal subject is forced by the instructions into a direction of attention in sorting. He handles the sample by itself *with reference to* the ground colour, independently of the intensity, or purity, with which it occurs. The concrete colour is not taken in its pure, singular, concreteness, but is rather seen as a representative of the 'idea' (Begriff) red, yellow, blue, etc., it is taken only as standing for red, yellow, blue, etc."[24] On the other hand, certain patients examined lacked this "categorial attitude", as Gelb and Goldstein call it. Lack of the categorial attitude in certain patients, and regression to a more primitive method of classification has been demonstrated by several different observers. Thus Weigl (1927) confirmed the original finding of Gelb and Goldstein. Hanfmann's account of a schizophrenic patient is illuminating and typical. "The patient when asked to place together objects of the same kind at first declared that there was only one picture of each kind. She would not group them in any way, but named or described each picture separately. When the examiner pointed out that certain pictures might be grouped together, e.g., because they all represented animals, the patient disagreed and emphasized the individuality of each, saying for instance: "Yes, but they go to different places; the cow goes in the barn, the hare in the fields", etc. (Hanfmann, 1939). That is to say the patient could not see the hare as representative of a class of animals as does a normal person. She is unable to perform the psychological function of reference to this general class. What we have called the function of general reference is impaired. The lack of this psychological ability has been reported in so many instances that it may be taken as fact. It is by means of the "categorial attitude" that James's geometer is able to reason concerning the *class* of triangles; or triangles in

---

[23] "The sort of activity we have called *generalized* also refers beyond the presented figure, but now not to a particular object but to some class of thing of which the apprehended object is a member. The reference is . . . not to 'this chair' but to 'chairs'" (loc. cit., p. 388).

[24] Gelb, A., and Goldstein, K., 1924, p. 152 (italics by present writer).

general, "with his one definite figure before him". It was by means of it that Watt's observer could allow a "dark" (though particular) "image of an utterly indefinable animal" to function as a generic image; once more, it is then not the vagueness or other quality of an image that gives it generality, but the "categorial attitude" or generality of reference—*which means ultimately that it functions as the product of a certain kind of learning.*[25]

Generality is found, *par excellence*, in connection with language. Thus the word "animal" is used *with reference to* the whole class of animals; colour, with reference to the whole class of hues, and so on. It has, indeed, often been doubted whether any thinking in general terms would be possible without language. Experimental results throw doubt on this conclusion. But at least such general thinking would be reduced to a very primitive form were not the tool of language available. The close relationship between language and general thought has in the past given rise to the fallacy of *nominalism*, according to which generality is achieved by giving a name to a class. That this is a fallacy may be seen from the fact that unless the name is used with reference to the class, it cannot "stand for" the class. That is to say, the fact that somebody has learned to attach the word to all kinds of animals irrespective of their singularities is what makes a word into a general term, not the stating of a name.[26]

With this interpretation, the generic image fades from the centre of the picture. Generality being given not by "content" but by "reference" which implies abstractive learning, we may expect that many different kinds of psychological process may have generality; such may be, for example, language, gesture, and other kinds of behaviour. Conversely, it is not surprising to find that such experimenters as Schwiete (1910) find that "ideas" may be very variously represented in consciousness.

The Function of Imagery in Generalizing and other Thinking

Thus generalization cannot be explained as the formation of a special kind of imagery. A concept, which is our way of experiencing

---

[25] The possibility that generalization may take place by the *simultaneous* presentation of a number of objects of course exhibits a limiting case; there is a parallel for learning.

[26] Fisher speaks of "a definite awareness of generalizing, . . . of ascribing the feature to each member of the group" (loc. cit., p. 165). This represents in experience the fact that learning has taken place. See also Dawes Hicks, 1938, p. 123, for an interesting treatment.

or reacting to class features as general,[27] is not definable as an image.

Nevertheless, imagery is constantly associated with it. The question then occurs as to the function of such imagery in generalizing and other thinking. According to Watt, the image appears sometimes to be secondary, accompanying the stimulus like illustrations in a novel. On other occasions it is the starting-point for the solution of the task. It may exert an apparent influence on the way in which the task is performed, whether by inhibition or furtherance or direct suggestion of new ideas. Watt made the interesting observation that a subject's prevalent type of imagery might change with change of the task; which is yet another argument against the now outmoded doctrine of imaginal types.[28] Messer's subjects were able to grade imagery from a very indistinct, "dark" experience, which they called "direction", through the vague imagery usually reported, to vivid imagery. He confirms Watt's conclusion that images may play an important part in the solution of the task, though they are sometimes epiphenomenal; sometimes they make meaning clearer.[29] Thus there is evidence among the Würzburgers and others that images have a function in thought, though the Würzburgers tended on the whole to decry this.

Claire Comstock (1921) claimed that everybody she questioned in or out of the laboratory actually made use of images and that few were irrelevant, a conclusion which is, of course, not at variance with the results of the experiments of imageless thought. Many of her subjects declared that they needed images for thinking. In general, she found that images served as a kind of blueprint for thought, anchoring the problem, providing leads, etc. They might be used as an "escape" from a difficult problem, what Lewin calls "going out of the field".[30]

What of generalizing? Fisher's monograph contains extensive and valuable material on the function of images here also. As the concept evolved, a progressive change in imagery was observed. "Numerous concrete and particular images" appeared at first; their place was gradually taken by visual or kinæsthetic imagery of a more

[27] Cf. G. Dawes Hicks, op. cit., p. 135. A strict behaviourist might prefer to speak in terms of our ability to react to class features as general. The terms "concept" and "Universal" are, of course, to be numbered among the dangerous part-descriptions already discussed.

[28] Op. cit., p. 367.

[29] Messer, op. cit., pp. 52 et seq., 86.

[30] See also Betts, 1909; Fernald, 1912; Galton, 1883; Davis, 1932.

and more schematic form. Meanwhile verbal imagery was assuming a progressively important rôle, until a stage appeared at which the concept appeared almost exclusively in verbal terms. The verbal images themselves became fewer and more telescoped and fragmentary until finally the instructions to recall were followed immediately by a few statements descriptive of the prominent general features. At least ten fairly well-marked stages can be differentiated from the introspective records, though not more than six of these stages can be distinguished in the record of any observer.[31] Throughout the experiment observers reported that the formation of imagery was an integral part of the total process of generalizing. Thus visual images of past figures or of forthcoming figures were sometimes compared with the present perception. Imaginal contents might "function as tentative generalizings". These might be "labelled as intentions, *Aufgaben*, and the like to investigate the focal characteristics". Sometimes the observer, when asked to define, hurriedly reviewed a series of visual images. On reading the accounts of the observers and the summaries of Miss Fisher, the conclusion is inevitable that in this instance at least visual imagery was one of the tools by which generalization was achieved, just as verbal imagery is a tool in other cases. The diminution of imagery as the process proceeds was also noted by Ach.

According to Selz, images served his observers as a basis for *abstraction* and as a point of departure[32] for the solution. In the process of abstraction—that is to say, with the task *superordinate*—there might arise an image of the object corresponding to the stimulus-word which would materially aid in the process of abstraction. According to the careful analysis of this investigator, images are correlated very closely with the *Aufgabe*. Images without *Aufgabe* were practically non-existent, and images contrary to the *Aufgabe*, that is occurring by sheer association, did not occur at all.[33]

Willwoll amplified and filled out the picture. For him it is a question of the function of palpable images in the formation of super-palpable ideas. These images he divides into three classes:

[31] Fisher, 1916, p. 200. It will be observed that Fisher states that the concept appeared "in terms of" the image, a usage which seems to the present writer questionable, but seems to be a necessary consequence of the structural point of view which she adopts.

[32] Bousfield and Barry, 1933, report the same for the imagery of a lightning calculator.

[33] Selz, 1922, pp. 56 ff.; Schwiete, 1910, points out the dependence of imagery on task.

(a) palpable images of objects, (b) symbolical images, i.e. palpable schemata, (c) verbal imagery.

All his observers, he reports, employ palpable images of things to a greater or lesser extent, varying with different Tasks. The more abstract the stimulus-words, the fewer such images were reported. Images are seldom deliberately called up, but appear automatically and are taken for granted.[34]

In contrast to Selz, Willwoll's observers reported a few images contrary to the Task; e.g.:

"With *Einsiedler* [hermit] I immediately had a palpable word-picture, the sound of the word reminded me of the town Einsiedeln in Switzerland."

Six of these purely associative instances are recorded.[35] They are of some theoretical importance as apparently tending against Lewin's hypothesis that sheer association, "couplings", cannot be the "motor" of a mental event. Most images are, however, in the direction of the task.

Willwoll finds a tendency towards mutual co-ordination and integration of images. Images occurring during the solution of a problem may be mutually adjusted; e.g.:

"I thought of roads going steeply upwards, steep mountains . . . then in order to get the ideas similar, I reversed the direction of the first."

This assimilatory process is at times a hindrance to the fulfilment of the task. The need to reconcile the imagery diverts attention from the main problem, so to speak.

In general, Willwoll confirms the finding of Messer and Selz that images often serve as a sheer (epiphenomenal) illustration of the process of thinking, like the illustrations in a book, without exerting any effect on the course of thought. When they do affect thinking they may serve as a permanent check, as a hindrance, or as a guide. One instance of the second case has been given. Another follows:

"With motor-goggles I saw a frightful grimace, an ape-face with motor-goggles. Then I suppressed the monkey-face and a lampshade came, a beautiful light green one, from my mother's room. I clearly saw the light shining through. I would have liked to look at the picture longer, because it was so pretty. . . . But I suppressed it, so as to get on with the job . . ."[36]

Here again the imagery impedes thinking; a number of other instances are given of this, and of the hindrance to thought that comes from the assimilation of imagery, and from picturization or fitting

---

[34] Willwoll, 1926, p. 64.   [35] Ibid., p. 68.   [36] Loc. cit., p. 76.

the images into a consistent picture. *The images which hinder thinking are all of a high degree of clearness. Those which further thinking less clear and less concrete.* It seems as though too strong an organization of images as such may impede their usefulness for the general purposes of thinking, i.e. their incorporation into another unity. It will be remembered that Duncker found that an important consideration in reasoning was the "looseness" (*Lockerheit*) of the material; perceptual material which was too strongly "bound" or organized was not so easily available in the new context presented by the train of reasoning.[37] Willwoll makes the further point that in order that imagery may further thought, it must first be broken up, analysed, so that the organization of the imagery as such may not impede the business of reaching the solution, and the material of the imagery may be made most available to the thought process. This process Willwoll calls the *Intellectualization of the Image*, and gives a number of examples.

Palpable symbolic schemata, the second of Willwoll's divisions, naturally depend on individual differences. Thus one observer had the pattern of a triangle, which was used to represent the task, which it will be remembered was to find a superordinate to two (difficult) words.

(Pythia—medium) ". . . with the coming of the second word I placed both ideas in relation to each other; therewith I had, as always, the Schema of a triangle, which I always have when I wish to form an idea, over a co-ordinate one, to a higher one."

Here the superordinate idea was mentally placed at the apex of the triangle.

Such symbolic schemata in the form of images were fairly frequent; and, as already mentioned, were entirely individual affairs. They are akin to the "number forms" described by Galton and others.

Other symbolic schemata were of a more material nature, as in the case of one observer who saw a "snaky something" bending from side to side and clearing the mental path.

Concerning verbal images, Willwoll finds them often developing simultaneously with thought. Sometimes, however, they precede the thought.

"*Illtreatment, abuse*: 8 seconds. *Inroad on strangers*. With the second word the formulation was already made: both are a kind of abuse. Then I began to discuss by means of ideas."

[37] Cf. Maier's conclusion that reasoning is at least in part the overcoming of habitual responses (1933).

Often the idea has no verbal correlate at all.

Willwoll's material on the behaviour and function of images during the thought process is of very great value, even to a theory that does not accept his basic postulate of imageless thought. It is highly desirable that his experiments should be repeated for confirmation.

Summary

A concept—that is to say, the way we experience or react to general features as such—is not definable as an image of any particular type. A concept may involve imagery, visual or otherwise; in particular it may involve verbal imagery. But the generality of the concept is given not by any characteristic of the image but by the reference function described in connection with language, except that here the reference is always general. This description is given as a first and convenient approximation. A further analysis is offered in the text. Images often, though not always, have a definite function in the formation of the concept. Analysis of the image often forms part of the process of generalization, and when this does not take place the imagery may be a hindrance. There is a tendency for imagery to diminish as the process of generalization proceeds. Imagery should probably be considered as constituting a stage of organization which occurs during the process of generalization *and of other kinds of thinking*. There is great variation from individual to individual and from problem to problem in the extent to which it occurs and is used in thinking, its vividness, and the manner of its use.[38]

The Process by which Generalization is Achieved

(A) *The Process in General.*—There is universal agreement that in the process of generalizing as in other processes of thinking there is a large amount of what is called "trial and error"; or, as it is probably better called by Woodworth, provisional hypothesis. Thus of eight methods of abstraction used by Grünbaum's observers, six employ provisional hypotheses. It will be remembered that the task was here to pick out identical figures on either side of a dividing line.

[38] A group of experimenters have specifically maintained that the concept is of an essentially imageless nature. E.g. Moore speaks of imageless mental categories; Aveling of conceptual overknowledge; Selz, Willwoll, and Ach of an imageless *Wissen*. To correlate these findings would lead too far afield. It should be pointed out that even if the imageless conceptual-content is accepted, there must still be general reference. So that the interpretation given above seems, once again, to be a minimal postulate, whether "imageless thought" is accepted or not; and in either case a necessary postulate.

In Fisher's study of the perceptual generalization of complex visual forms, she continually refers to what she calls "tentative generalizing". "Trial and error" appears throughout the introspective reports of her subjects. In their objective studies with visual forms Hull and Smoke refer explicitly to trial and error, and the same process is found throughout Willwoll's descriptions of verbal generalization, though explicit reference is not made to it.[39] Many other examples could be given.

Heidbreder (1924) has divided trial and error into two classes; viz. (a) participant behaviour, where a hypothesis is adopted and rejected if unsuccessful; (b) spectator behaviour, where a purely random solution is tried.

It will be remembered that Heidbreder used the "multiple-choice" method, by which the subject was induced to formulate successively more and more complicated rules for the marking of geometrical patterns.

Participant behaviour is the usual "provisional hypothesis" type of trial and error, where the subject actively throws himself into the situation, trying out one possibility after another until the solution somehow emerges. It is, in Heidbreder's terms, based on the "tendency to meet a situation with definite enterprise" (p. 35) By contrast, in spectator behaviour the subject marks time, doing something without meaning, waiting like Mr. Micawber, "for something to turn up". "He withdraws from active participation, marking the cards in compliance with the demands of the procedure, but in such a way that the reaction in itself 'means nothing'. At least it represents no hypothesis which is being tried out."

Such spectator behaviour exists in several forms. That already described is the primary one. The subject is not simply idling. "There are usually indications that a general observational activity is occurring—or rather that the organism is set for registering observations not specifically attended to. As a rule, somewhere during the course of a series of spectator responses the subject expresses himself as hoping that they will "bring out something" if he keeps "marking and watching". In a second form of such behaviour, the subject deliberately adopts a hypothesis which he knows is wrong, but usually one which has given some success. Thus a subject said: "I am going to try to mark the lower ones for several times to see if I can get a principle. The lower ones have been right sometimes."

[39] References are: Grünbaum, p. 375; Fisher, p. 165; Hull, p. 85; Smoke, p. 35, in works already cited.

T 10

Of the two forms of behaviour, participant behaviour includes 80 per cent. of all relevant reactions. It occurs in all subjects and all problems; in 9 out of 10 individuals and 16 of 18 problems its frequency is at least twice that of spectator response. Spectator behaviour is apparently an exceptional method of response. It was not used by all individuals nor in all problems. It was never the first method of attacking a problem, and never the sole method. It occurs in long unaided problems, when the subject is having difficulty. Further examples may be quoted:

"I don't know what I meant by that. I couldn't think of anything. My mind was a blank, so I just marked it. I don't think I had anything in mind" (loc. cit., p. 75).

Sometimes the subject was simply "absent-minded", e.g., "I was thinking of something else. I don't know why I did that. . . ." Sometimes subjects "could think of nothing to do". Others thought that random marking might "bring out something"; e.g.:

"I think I'll mark them hit or miss for a while and watch and see what happens. I can't think of anything and I may be able to get something this way."

Hence the name spectator behaviour.

In general, spectator behaviour is, according to Heidbreder, "what is left of participant behaviour when the hypothesis is subtracted from the latter". She suggests that some kind of incidental observational activity always accompanies the participant process, but is usually overlooked. That is to say, in the process of generalizing there may be roughly distinguished a perceptual, observational, aspect and a more central, rational one. These two aspects are normally not distinguished; the processes corresponding to them usually occur in a simultaneous, integrated form, the more rational activity, roughly describable as the formation and checking of hypotheses, obscuring the other. If, however, the latter activity is for some reason inhibited, the usually overlooked perceptual side is exposed.

The division of "trial and error" in thinking into participant and spectator behaviour seems to be of capital importance. It bridges the gap between blind trial and error, and that more rational kind more characteristic of human thinking, at least.

Sudden vs. Gradual Methods.—If the accounts of the experimenters are compared, it becomes evident that generalization and abstraction may be achieved either suddenly or gradually. Grünbaum's subjects used both methods for the recognition of the like figures on each side of the diagonal line. "The suddenness . . . is so surprising that the observer does not trust himself." This was in great contrast to the method employed on other occasions, where the observer laboriously compared one figure with all of those on the other side of the line. Moore found a gradual growth of the recognition that an element had been seen before. Fisher speaks of the common feature in her complex visual figures flashing out in consciousness; in another context she describes a deliberate search, especially when the common feature was obscure. She makes the interesting point that the flashing out of a feature may mark the beginning of a deliberate search to ascertain whether it will occur later. "Insight" here initiates a process of "trial and error". Heidbreder in a second study in 1934 used the objective method of Hull and Kuo (Chinese characters), and noted both sudden and gradual formation of concepts. Smoke found evidences that "insight" may sometimes, though not necessarily always, occur. Hull's subjects acquired their general knowledge very gradually. It seems fairly certain that the different material used by these experimenters accounts in part for the difference of results. For example, Moore's method, by which he exposed "nonsense" figures until the subject recognized that one had been seen before, and likewise Hull's method, by which nonsense figures were exposed until a figure containing a specific element could be named, would seem to conduce towards a gradual learning. It is only gradually that we become acquainted with a totally strange and complicated figure. On the other hand, the fact that abstraction-generalization might be either gradual or sudden with the same experimental material, seems to show that this difference of material is not wholly responsible. The conclusion seems to be that the process of abstraction-generalization may take place suddenly, in the manner described as characteristic of "insight", or more laboriously, possibly in the manner described as characteristic of trial and error, perhaps owing to the necessity of repeating sensory material in order to obtain recognition. Whether there is any difference between the relative frequency of "insight" and "trial and error" procedures as we go from "perceptual" generalization to the more "rational" kind examined by the Würzburgers and Willwoll, we do not know. A valuable line of experiment is suggested.

The Rôle of Analysis.—"Roughly, generalizing may be said to be the process of selecting a mark or feature or combination of marks or features, and liberating it from other marks or features with which it has been presented in perceptive experience . . . every item, thus detached from the perceived content, . . . acquires by this very circumstance a new significance. The mental process to which I have been referring may be rightly described as involving both analysis and synthesis. Some fact is separated out from the mass of detail offered in sense perception, and is then connected with other facts, perhaps widely separate from the given fact in space and time."[40] The general fact that the original perception is broken up is observed in practically all the experimental studies. Thus Fisher's subjects usually ceased at an early stage to perceive the visual figures as whole; after the first two or three exposures "the figures became mutilated in consciousness by an emphasizing of the similarities and a relative ignoring of the non-general features".[41] This well expresses the fact of analysis of perceptual material as reported by numerous observers.

Analysis by Perceptual Accentuation.—There is fairly unanimous agreement that there occurs some sort of perceptual accentuation of the common, repeated figure. This is well brought out by Grünbaum in one of the earlier of the studies. Grünbaum found three varieties of accentuation of the common figure in his simultaneously presented pairs of groups. There was (*a*) accentuation (*Hervorhebung*, literally *lifting out* of the field) without the knowledge that a common figure was involved, a purely perceptual experience. There was (*b*) what he calls accentuation from the point of view of the *Aufgabe*; that is to say, with the knowledge[42] that this is the correct figure, the one that fits, *not* that it is the "like" one. There is (*c*) accentuation with the suspicion of likeness.[43] These forms vary from one subject to another, and from *day to day with the same subject*. Moore, Fisher, and Stevanović confirm the general fact of accentuation. Fisher's subjects regularly reported accentuation in *imagery*. "Whatever the number of images in which the [common] feature appeared, the latter possessed a compelling claim upon attention."[44] This perceptual accentuation is a very striking thing to the observers. Grünbaum's subjects often wondered why such an ordinary figure had so "peculiarly accented" itself when they were shown the sheet of figures after the experiment. They might say: "The figure interested me, I do not know why. . . . It presents itself specially clearly, it strikes the eye by itself," and so on. Fisher's subjects reported accentuation in a feature because of an unexpected change in that feature.

Grünbaum's finding that accentuation may occur without know-

---

[40] Dawes Hicks, loc. cit., p. 125.   [41] Loc. cit., p. 77.
[42] *Bewusstseinslage*.   [43] Loc. cit., p. 376.   [44] Loc. cit., p. 166.

ledge that the accentuated feature is the common one seems to show that the process of generalization is not completed with that of accentuation. It should probably be considered as an early, primitive stage of the process, once more, present unnoticed in most generalizing activities, and only becoming evident when the more rational aspects or processes are rendered less evident by the use of a very primitive problem. It is probably related to the figure-ground distinction of Rubin. It raises interesting questions as to the "Law of Exercise".

Analysis by Assimilation with Known Figures.—This is reported by several observers, among whom may be mentioned Moore, English, and Stevanović. English finds that the whole situation may be assimilated to some familiar category; or the situation may be analysed in such a way that the elements can be so assimilated. Stevanović's subjects "interpreted" the nonsense figures, often by analogy with some concrete object. Thus the figures were called "rabbit-like", "flower-like", "bird on a branch", and so on. Or the figure might be grasped in terms of its relations "three peaks on the left", "two ends alike", etc.[45] Moore gives cases where such association influences recall of his "nonsense" material. Thus, exactly as was the case with nonsense syllables, the nonsense figures used in experiments on abstraction have been found to be not really "nonsense". The observer does not come to them as to a virgin experience, but interprets them in terms of his own categories. Even Stevanović's "relational analysis" is of course ultimately in terms of the observer's experience—e.g. "*three peaks*", "*two ends*". The fact of perceptual predisposition on the part of the observer is one of Huper's chief criticisms of Ach's results. Ach stresses the necessity that the material shall be meaningless; Huper answers that Ach's material was not meaningless; for that matter it may be doubted whether to an adult any material of the visual type could be meaningless.

In any case, the fact of analysis by analogy with concrete objects seems to be sufficiently well established.

Deliberate, Voluntary Analysis.—This is reported by many experimenters. Thus subjects, in one of Grünbaum's "methods", deliberately examine all figures in succession in order to find the like ones. This is really the "trial and error" method on an intellectual plane. No perceptual accentuation is involved, here or in the method by which the subject passes alternately from one *group* to the other, to

---

[45] Loc. cit., pp. 13–15.

find a figure recognized as perceived before. Each of these procedures is a method of analysis, whereby a perceptual mass or field is deliberately broken up in order to find the feature common to it and another. Sometimes the immediate result of such an analysis may be a hypothesis, a wondering whether a particular feature may be the essential one.[46]

Heidbreder gives the most detailed discussion of the process of analysis. She notes seven different processes, which she calls:

(a) Isolation of a particular feature. This is apparently akin to Grünbaum's accentuation.

(b) Perception of a changed feature, the change causing the subject to notice a feature not previously attended to. It has been seen that Fisher reports a similar result.

(c) Location of a difficulty; i.e. certain parts of the situation were distinguished from the rest of the subject's experience because they were associated with failure.

(d) Cleavage responses, where the whole set of data is organized into two or three divisions; e.g.:

"I wonder if there are three rules. Sometimes they are connected so that the point of one touches a side of the other, and sometimes a point touches a point, etc." [47]

(e) Defining response, a verbalizing method of analysis where the subject defines the conditions under which he uses a hypothesis; e.g.:

"Greater number of sides symbol into the other [i.e. the symbol standing for the greater number of sides must be put into the other symbol] when both are curved."

(f) Deliberate analysis, where the subject examined all the information at his disposal. It may use all the six methods previously described. The analysis begins with previously existing concepts. (Cf. the preceding discussion.) It is similar, says Heidbreder, to perceptual analysis, except that it is deliberate rather than automatic. It is not a special form of analysis but rather a comprehensive activity including the other forms.

(g) Use of a hypothesis as an instrument of analysis. Regardless of its chances of success or failure, a hypothesis is employed to isolate a particular fact.

To this list should perhaps be added English's analysis by verbal characterization, where linguistic categories serve as the basis for assimilation, much as do the perceptual categories already discussed.

[46] See, e.g., Fisher, loc. cit., p. 165.   [47] Loc. cit., p. 97.

It is doubtful whether the different analytical processes described represent psychologically different activities. Heidbreder maintains that there is strictly speaking no process of analysis, that the term is only applicable to a result, namely that of breaking up the total data into the relevant (repeated, common, invariant), and non-relevant variable. With the possible exception of the perceptual accentuation found by Grünbaum and others, it seems probable that the process of breaking up should be described in terms of psychological categories more ultimate than that indicated by the term "analysis", though such categories are not at present available. Meanwhile, the descriptions given appear to be the best that are possible at the present stage of psychological science.

The Process by which Generalization is Achieved (ctd.)

(B) *Specific Processes.* (a) *Mutual Effect of Like Figures.*—It has been seen that generalization essentially concerns our behaviour or experience in relation to environmental features which are (a) invariant, but which (b) occur in variable contexts. The process by which generalization is achieved is thus intimately bound up with the psychological effect of invariant or identical features in specific, variable, or particular contexts. There is some experimental evidence that such identical features bring about a direct and specific modification of perception. Thus for the case when two or more identical features are simultaneously presented in the same field, Wertheimer postulates what he calls the "factor of likeness" (1923) which, according to Koffka, may be stated in the form that two parts of the same field will attract each other according to their degree of equality.[48]

Grünbaum's results imply an effect that is somewhat similar. The fact that a figure on one side of the dividing line was like one on the other side affected perception, in that as already described there was accentuation of one of the like figures. Like figures are drawn more frequently than the others (it will be remembered that after the experiment subjects were asked to draw such figures as they could). This was the case even when there was no recognition that the figure drawn was one of a pair of like ones. They "have a special effect, even before the likeness is determined". When two figures that are not identical but similar are both accentuated and reproduced, at least one of them is a repeated figure. When by accident a card was exposed too briefly, and the observer was asked if he had noticed anything, he answered "No, of course not". When later the same card was properly exposed, the observer would correct his previous report and state that he had on the previous occasion noticed the figure now recognized as like. "It is as though one like figure reinforces the other, so that both of them, although they are not given in consciousness, nevertheless stand in a relation which brings about the accentuation of one of them" (loc. cit., p. 434). "One object stands to the other in a relation which need not necessarily be known in order to be effective. In consciousness this relation documents itself as likeness; but if anything prevents consciousness of it occurring, we explain its effect by the support which one of the like figures exerts on the other; this other figure is lost to consciousness" (loc. cit., p. 435). It is probable that in this support of one like figure by another we can see the beginning of the process of abstraction, and possibly of generalization. What, if any, relation such a perceptual process bears to the higher forms of abstraction, it would of course be impossible to say at the present stage of knowledge; speculation would be premature.

(b) *Ach's Hypothesis.*—Ach's extension of Grünbaum's work on the mutual influence of like figures cannot be understood except as part of his general theory. Ach's general theory of abstractive-generalization will therefore be briefly stated at this point (Ach, 1921).

Ach distinguishes between a perceptual and an intellectual phase in generalization, specifically at the stage of determining the correctness or otherwise of the task-solution. The task subdivides itself into minor tasks, approaching what Woodworth and others have called hypotheses or provisional rules of action (cf. Fisher and others), these hypotheses or rules of action not being however of a hard-and-fast nature. Their adoption on any specific occasion depends on a variety of conditions (loc. cit., p. 95). They are seen by Ach as conducing to economy of thought and action, and may be called part of the process of systematization. During this process images, which are at first obtrusive, gradually drop away until they apparently disappear, according to the reports, and their place is taken by imageless knowledge (*Wissen*). This gradual dropping away of images is reported by others, notably Fisher; although of course many will not subscribe to their ultimate disappearance and replacement by the imageless process. The whole of Ach's account here bears close resemblance to that given by Fisher.

Next must be described the process by which the object acquires a name. Here Ach sharply disagrees with Aveling who maintains that naming is accomplished by establishing an association between the name and the object-presentation.[49] The process, says Ach, is more complex than this. The redirection of attention is given a prominent place, as with Fisher. The naming process, by which a name is attached to an object which becomes its meaning, is achieved through the process of *complex formation*, into the theory of which this volume will not enter,[50] except to say that it here involves the process of grouping mentioned by other investigators, notably Smoke, Heidbreder, and Graham.[51] Association enters the process, but is of a more complex nature than the simple association between the name and the object. Ease of grouping, or coherence-grade, is influenced by the degree of similarity of the entities to be grouped. In the limiting case, where such entities are identical, ease of grouping is greatest, and this case is called the *coherence of identicals*.

Thus Ach's analysis to this point agrees with, and amplifies that of, Grünbaum. The concept of the mutual influence of similar figures in a simultaneously presented field (Grünbaum) is expanded by Ach into a theory of the grouping of identicals, whether simultaneously or successively presented, under the influence of the *Aufgabe* and its subsidiary processes. Such grouping has been observed by many workers, but its theory is most highly elaborated in Ach's work. To complete the account of Ach's theory, it may then be said that under the influence of the determining tendencies springing from the *Aufgabe*, the different objects are unified, and these unities (groups) are used as means to fulfil the task. Such a group is handled by means of a mental construct or idea,[52] the purpose of which once more is to effect the economical solution of the task. The formation of the group is accompanied by the striking of a mean between the members composing the group through a process called "convergence". "By convergence we shall understand the alteration undergone by the psychic elements in question, by which such elements approximate a cumulative or a mean value" (loc. cit., p. 128). Once more, the process of convergence is a determined one, and results in economy of task-fulfilment; further, it goes hand in hand with the principle of the coherence of identicals.

Thus we are informed that the method by which Ach's subjects

[49] Aveling, 1912, p. 241.
[50] Ach quotes Müller, 1913, without committing himself to full agreement.
[51] Smoke, loc. cit., pp. 30, 31; Heidbreder, loc. cit., p. 120; Graham, loc. cit., p. 96.
[52] *Objektvorstellung*. It hardly does justice to Ach's analysis to translate this as object-presentation.

effected the process of abstractive-generalization was one of grouping similar objects together, and handling such groups by means of a psychic construct or "idea"; in this process differences, he says, tend to be averaged out, the group idea representing not a single member of the group, but approximating quantitatively to a group-mean.

Ach's research is a notable and powerful one, and gives perhaps the most highly developed hypothesis in the literature of what actually happens when a human being effects a certain kind of generalization. Before it can be accepted in its entirety, there is need of further examination of its main theses. One of the chief merits of the work is that it does suggest further experimental analysis. For example, the principle of convergence should easily prove amenable to quantitative experimental verification. It is worth repeating that in the stress which he places on grouping, on the mutual reinforcement of like elements, on the economical nature of the process, on the importance of the *Aufgabe*, and on the use of the psychic construct to assist the fulfilment of the *Aufgabe* ("hypothesis"), Ach's results are in close agreement with those of later and entirely independent workers.

Generalization and the Task

Mention has already been made of the part which, according to Ach, is played by the *Aufgabe*. According to Külpe (1904), the task determines the abstraction. A report which coincides with the task is better than one which does not do so. For example, if a subject is asked to abstract colour, he gives a better report on colour than when he is asked to abstract form.

Such reports, coinciding with the task, were superior in number, correctness, and definiteness. The more difficult a task is, the more effectively is the rest of the field, i.e. that from which abstraction is made, excluded.

With a "heterogeneous "*Aufgabe*, striking results were obtained on reports concerning colour. Thus one observer who had been asked to give the number of the letters exposed made 14·1 per cent. false reports on colour and 54·7 per cent. indeterminate ones; another gave 8·8 per cent. false and 77·2 per cent. indeterminate reports. Colour might appear as indifferent, or different from that objectively present. Some reported that they had actually experienced no colour at all. In the same way, it was possible for subjects to describe a figure without being able to describe its limiting objects. The exclusion of features from which abstraction is made is termed by

Külpe "negative abstraction", though the term was apparently not first used by him. Külpe's contention here is that negative abstraction is, so to speak, an active, one might say positive, process, by which recall is inhibited of what Aristotle calls the accidents of that from which abstraction is made. *With the material he used*, Külpe has apparently shown that such an actively excluding process is present, as contrasted with a possible negatively operating process of mere neglect of variable features. Moore corroborates this finding. He states that the irrelevant figures in his experiment were "not merely neglected, but . . . positively cast aside and swept more or less completely from the field of consciousness". Owing to the way in which Moore's results are presented, the conclusion does not, however, necessarily follow, although Külpe's results make it probable. Fisher also reported that she had confirmed Moore's finding in this respect, but she does not give further details (Fisher, op. cit., p. 33).

In considering Külpe's results, the reader of today will be reminded of the phenomenon of figure and ground as investigated by Rubin and others of the Gestalt school. The distinction of figure and ground had not been thoroughly examined at the time when Külpe made his experiment, and it is uncertain how far the striking results he obtained were due to figure-ground properties, how far to an actual process of negative abstraction.[53] Further, both Külpe's material and that of Moore, who claimed to have confirmed his results, was of a sensory nature. Whether in the case of a more "intellectual" abstraction such as that examined by Willwoll there is an active process of negative abstraction, we do not know. Only experiment can tell.

Grünbaum's results are of interest in this connection. He gives a table which is intended to show that in his method of successive apprehension there is a tendency for *accentuation* of one figure to impair performance in the secondary task which calls for the reproduction of non-similar figures. The table is, however, not very convincing. There are apparently seven exceptions to the general rule out of twenty-one cases altogether. A second table seems to have proved the further point that completion *of the main task* does impair performance of the secondary task. The result is of great interest in itself; it may possibly indicate the effect of negative abstraction, as Grünbaum assumes; or it may show the effect of

---

[53] The fact that Külpe found negative abstraction had its greatest effect when the task was more difficult, as, e.g., with the task of reporting on irregular figures seems to argue against the identification of negative abstraction with the perception of a feature as part of the ground.

the completion of a task with a consequent release of tension, according to the mechanism which Lewin and his pupils first demonstrated twenty years after Grünbaum's study was made. There is no way of deciding between these possibilities. In fact, both Grünbaum's and Külpe's results may be interpreted as showing the difference between abstraction with and without a task, and this only.

Thus the evidence for negative abstraction, as a special, active process inhibiting irrelevancies, is at present inconclusive. The results of Külpe and of Grünbaum are susceptible of other explanations; those of Moore are not conclusive statistically, and those of Fisher are not available. The existence of such a process has yet to be decided by experiment.

In line with Külpe's emphasis on the *Aufgabe*, Grünbaum stresses the importance of what he calls the *Einstellung*, or set.[54] In our experiments, he says, the set is towards the chief task, "to seek for like figures". He graded the sets of his subjects into four stages: (*a*) the subject might have the total field in consciousness, with the vague consciousness that "likeness might be presented". He directs his attention to the manner of performing the task. (*b*) The subject may sit and wait for the solution to appear, but with the thought, "How am I to do it?" (*c*) There is no consciousness of any means of performing the task, even when the experimenter directs attention to it by questioning. (*d*) There is merely a peculiar consciousness of direction towards a goal. (*e*) One subject could give no account at all of the presence of a goal in consciousness. "I know what I am doing, and wait until something comes of itself." The stages are thus from complete consciousness of the goal to be attained, to complete unconsciousness. The last stage is obviously fairly close to Heidbreder's "spectator behaviour".

Fisher reports the interesting finding that the task may apparently subdivide itself. Her observers reported that once they had noted a general feature, they would often begin thereafter to pay special attention to that feature; so that the original task of finding similarities is now split up into the specific task of watching this or these particular features. In Woodworth's terminology, the noting of an apparently general feature serves to initiate a hypothesis which is thereafter confirmed or rejected. She insists on the fact that if the awareness of similarity is to appear, there must be present a determination for likeness-comparison. See also p. 296 above.

[54] See the end of Chapter III for a discussion of "set".

Finally, English claims that generalization is conditional on the possession of an *Aufgabe* which, however, comes automatically to adults. The subject is conscious of the irrelevant, but only as of something rejected (loc. cit., p. 346).

In summary, the studies show *general agreement that generalization and abstraction are closely related to the task*, or what would now be called the *motive*; though whether the acceptance of a task to abstract a certain feature has an inhibitory effect on the perception or recall of other features cannot yet be said to have been conclusively demonstrated.

Conditions for Efficient Generalization

With the studies dealing with the practical question of the conditions under which a human being best generalizes, we enter a fresh stratum of work, belonging both in time and in temper to the more objective methods of modern psychology. Using the method of Chinese characters, Hull examined the relative desirability of proceeding (*a*) from a simpler context to a more complex one, and (*b*) conversely, from a more complex context to a simpler one. The rule often given to class-room teachers is to begin with the simple and work up to the more complex. After making due allowance for various factors, Hull found that neither of these methods presented any fundamental advantage for the acquisition of the generalization. Further, he demonstrated that in the cases examined by him there was no difference between the "functional efficiency" of generalizations given directly and those only given in a complicating context. Here again a point of pedagogy is touched. Should a child be required to discover his own rules, generalizations, or should he be given the rule first? Other workers have produced material relevant to this problem. Sullivan found that a generalization was better effected if the principle was first illustrated. Demonstration of one instance of the generalization was more effective than the instructions to look for the names of the pictures she employed, or to notice common elements and look for a generalization. Retention was, however, superior by the first method, where the child had to find out first that there was a general principle involved, and then discover this principle for himself. Both children and adults were employed as subjects.

Ewert and Lambert (1932) found that specific instructions helped their subjects to formulate a rule for a disk-transferring game, but that a demonstration did not help. Thus Hull's result is in apparent contradication with those of Sullivan and of Lambert and Ewert. Hull found that to make the general principle explicit before learning did not assist the subject to acquire the ability to recognize the general principle in a complex setting. The other two investigations quoted found that explicit verbal demonstration of instances of the general principle did help. Lambert and Ewert's segregation of the general rule likewise depended on verbal formulation. Thus the experiments tend to show that while segregation of an element common to a number of visual situations may be of little help in forming the generalization that all such situations belong to a class, the use of verbal pre-statements does assist in the formulation of a general rule to deal with different situations. The differences between the material of Hull and the other experimenters are then twofold. Hull's material demanded the abstraction of a concrete, perceptual element, which remained identical in a number of differing contexts. The sameness was of a much simpler sort than in the other two cases, where concrete visual particularity is almost entirely disregarded, and a relational rule must be elaborated. It is not surprising to find that a verbal pre-statement is of help where a visual pre-presentation is of little or no help, since at least one of the functions of language is exactly the precise description of complex relational facts which may be found in very varied contexts. These remarks are intended to indicate the problem for research; experimental avenues are almost totally unexplored in detail.

Negative Instances

Negative instances, in the sense of instances that do not conform to the general rule, and are definitely stated not to fall under the rule, apparently do not help most subjects in speed of generalizing of geometrical figures. There are, however, individual differences. Most subjects claimed to prefer such negative instances, as well as positive ones. They did tend to increase accuracy, apparently by blocking false hypotheses.[55]

Correlation with Intelligence

Several workers have found that ability to generalize correlates with scores made on intelligence tests. For example, among others, Smoke obtained a rank difference correlation of 0.52 ± 0.125 between intelligence and ability to generalize. "Though such a correlation has a high coefficient of alienation, it may be regarded as suggesting a

[55] Smoke, 1932, 1933.

tendency" (1932, p. 41). Graham (1939, p. 101) states that "the ability to generalize was somewhat positively correlated both to higher scholarship and to the intelligence test scores". General scholastic average and percentile ratings on the American Council of Education Psychological Examination were used. Ewert and Lambert similarly found a correlation of from 0·86 to 0·93 between intelligence and ability to generalize. That the ability to generalize is identical with that measured by the "intelligence" tests is in the highest degree improbable. That there is any one ability which can be called ability to generalize is also doubtful; it appears psychologically more probable, especially when the individual differences to be discussed later are taken into account, that some persons may better generalize in one context, others in another. Newton, who effected probably the greatest generalization ever achieved by the human mind in the realm of physical phenomena, might have been unable to formulate general rules for salesmen as well as the average floor-walker. At least, we do not know, and should not assume. Nevertheless, it does seem probable that in any given line of activity, and all other things being equal, there is some correlation between those who are best able to generalize and those who score highly in the "intelligence" tests.

Order of Attainment of Concepts

Special mention should be made of the meticulous series of experiments recently initiated by Edna Heidbreder and her collaborators. Heidbreder was interested in the order in which concepts were attained. She found that this order was—concrete objects, spatial forms, numbers. She interprets these data as supporting the hypothesis that concepts are more or less readily attainable as their attainment requires a slighter or greater departure from the kind of response involved in perceiving a concrete object. The order was statistically well established, and became less marked as conceptualization became more largely perceptual. Conceptual activity, she thinks, is "an extension of the kind of activity involved in the perception of concrete objects", and contrasts it with processes determined by symbolic constructs, such as numbers (paper 6, pp. 193–4). She developed and used the notion of "situational support", corresponding roughly to what the Gestalt group call "external forces". Its amount was directly proportional to the importance which perceptual processes played in generalization. A general trend was found for conceptualization to take place "more or less readily as more or less situational support was provided". However, within the range of activity for which situational support was provided concepts were most readily developed when there was least variation from the kind of activity involved in perceiving concrete objects. Beyond this range, ease of conceptualization was determined "chiefly by the semantic efficiency of the verbal tools". The results are interpreted in terms of a motor theory. This is a notable and sustained research, which fills out many gaps in our knowlege.[56] Welch and Long have also shown an hierarchical order in children's generalizing.[57]

Individual Differences in Generalizing

Practically all investigators remark on the individual differences shown by their subjects. Thus Külpe found that one of his observers was interested in the figure, and reported upon it nearly as well without as with a special *Aufgabe*. One was interested in the figure and colour, but could not report on them without a special *Aufgabe*. Grünbaum reports ubiquitous individual differences; the first of his methods of abstraction was not used at all by two observers, the last was not used by three observers.[58] There is no such thing as a determinate type of observer. Nor do methods belong especially to one particular figure as such. There is even variation from day to day in the predominant method used by subjects. The method employed, says Grünbaum, depends on a certain "constellation" of the subject. Moore reports individual differences in the time required to discover the common element, from five to twenty-five exposures being necessary. Fisher reports that there were many individual differences, both structural and functional. Observers differed in the rate of mechanization of the recalls, and the extent to which non-common features entered into the recalls. They differed structurally

---

[56] Heidbreder, with others, 1946, etc.
[57] Welch and Long, 1940; Welch, 1947.
[58] The eight methods employed by Grünbaum's subjects were: (1) Abstraction by exclusion, where each figure in the one set is examined to see whether it corresponds to a specific figure of the other; (2) successive examination without accentuation; (3) successive with accentuation; (4) successive with accentuation, with reference to the *Aufgabe*; (5) successive, with accentuation and intimation of likeness; (6) successive, with brief interval between one group and another; (7) simultaneous with a pause after the presentation, or immediately after it; (8) "intuitive", where one figure is seen with full knowledge that it is the like one. Later observers have assumed that (8) would have broken down into one or other of the preceding seven methods if more adequate examination had been given.

in the modality of the imagery favoured, and in the rate at which they passed from the concrete imaginal level to the verbal level. "All of the observers failed to reveal various of the ten distinguishable stages" of concept formation. Hull notes individual differences throughout his study. His general results exhibit a composite of several methods of generalization, as do those of the other workers; "seven of the ten subjects show a more or less decided advantage for the simple to complex method". Smoke notes wide individual differences in the number of patterns examined per unit of time, and also individual differences concerning negative instances. Some actually find them a hindrance. Heidbreder, again, notes ubiquitous differences; particularly in the use of spectator and participant responses there are differences "not only in frequency but in the form" in which spectator response is used. Hanfmann and Hull note differences in pathological cases. Truly such differences are everywhere. It may be said that no method of abstraction or generalization has been demonstrated which is constant in rate, general psychological procedure, imaginal content employed, or general conditions; there is a suspicion that this variation obtains not only from person to person, but even in the same person on different occasions and using the same material. Such a supposition would be in line with the results of Grünbaum and also those of Weisenburg and Macbride obtained in another context. Nowhere is the difference between psychology and logic better illustrated. Logic shows the canons by which thought must proceed; granting certain presuppositions these canons are constant from individual to individual. Psychology shows different individuals working according to these constant canons in a bewildering multiplicity of ways.

Summary

The process of abstractive generalization has been studied experimentally by a number of different techniques. The following general conclusions emerge among many others from the mass of results.

(1) Generic images exist but do not play the exclusive part assigned to them by certain philosophers.

(2) When such generic images are found, their generality accrues to them by the process of general reference. A statement concerning this function is given in the text.

(3) Vagueness in an image should not be confused with generality.

(4) Imagery decreases and becomes more mechanized as generalization is perfected.

(5) Trial and error is prominent in the process, although the process is often effected suddenly.

(6) The subject may lapse into a process of semi-meaningless activity, where he watches for "something to turn up" (spectator behaviour).

(7) An early stage in the process is one in which the total perceptual field is broken up, analysed, into like and unlike elements.

(8) This is often marked at the perceptual level by a perceptual accentuation of the common elements. Such primitive "structuring" of the field seems to be akin to the "figure-ground" phenomenon. It is possible that such primitive structuring *is* an early stage of what is called analysis.

(9) A common method by which the original field is structured is by assimilation, in whole or in part, with known objects.

(10) Such primitive analysis must be contrasted with a more intellectualized, voluntary analysis, which may accompany the procedures mentioned in (9) and (8), or may take place independently of them.

(11) A primitive factor probably involved in the process of abstractive generalization in its earlier stages and forms is the effect which perception of an element seems to have upon the subsequent or possibly simultaneous perception of an identical element.

(12) The process of abstractive generalization is intimately connected with the *Aufgabe* which has been accepted, and with the fulfilment of the *Aufgabe*.

(13) It is characteristic of the same process, as apparently of other activities to which the name "thinking " is given, that the aim is accomplished by intermediate, mental constructs, psychic "scaffoldings", "hypotheses", by which the original *Aufgabe* is reoriented.

(14) It has been maintained that there exists an active process of negative abstraction, by which the "accidents" of the total field under consideration are actively excluded from psychological consideration. The experimental evidence is here not yet conclusive.

(15) Verbal pre-statement of a general rule apparently assists in the formulation of such a rule by the subject.

(16) Ability to generalize is probably correlated with ability to score highly on the "intelligence tests".

(17) Relatively little research has been done on abstractive generalization at levels higher than the perceptual. Conclusions (1) to (14) concern experiments done almost entirely on the perceptual level.

(18) All studies agree that there are great individual differences in the methods by which the process of abstractive generalization is accomplished.

Concluding Remarks

Like every other living organism, the human being may be envisaged as struggling ceaselessly to preserve an identity of organic pattern in a chaotic world. In order that this process of self-preservation may be advantageously effected, the organism must be such that it discerns, in a measure gradually increasing as evolution advances, similarities existent under the superficial variations in its environment. Only by such discernment of similarities can the organism survive; without it organic response must be chaotic in a chaotic-seeming world. The ability to discern and act upon similarities hidden beneath divergence is the ability to generalize, discussed in this chapter. It is, at bottom, the ability to learn from experience.

CHAPTER X

SUMMARY AND CONCLUSION

FIFTY YEARS' EXPERIMENT on the psychology of thinking or reasoning have not brought us very far, but they have at least shown the kind of road which must be traversed. Looking over the immense mass of literature which has now accumulated, several persistent problems or perhaps groups of problems seem to obtrude themselves. There is first the problem of the "motor" of thought, as the late Professor Lewin might have called it. Thinking or reasoning does not happen by itself. Some term corresponding to "motivation" is necessary in order to describe what takes place, the word being used without any implication that it corresponds to a separate psychological process, but for experimental and theoretical convenience.[1] Inheriting the doctrine from their predecessors, the earlier experimentalists took it almost for granted that the "law of association" provided the necessary motor, although there were some dissentients; and the classical work of Pavlov enabled the behaviourists to translate association into their own language. It has been seen that the experimental attack on associationism developed in three stages. The first was reached by the Würzburgers, who found the "reproductive tendencies" of the time inadequate to explain thinking, and postulated the determining tendencies and the *Aufgabe* as epicyclic mechanisms. Following their lead, Selz argued with telling effect against the whole associational structure, and experimentally demonstrated the integrative nature of at least one stage of the thought process, thus putting forward a principle basically opposed to that of classical associationism. Finally a concerted attack was made by the Gestalt psychologists, who claimed to have shown experimentally that habit, identified with association, is never the motor of a psychic event, and developed the theory of the unitary

---

[1] By his experimental demonstration of the formation of the *Gesamtaufgabe* Selz has shown that in the type of thinking he is examining there is a recognizable unification of motivational and non-motivational processes. *Thereafter* only, the process of thinking is unitary and motivation is an aspect of it. It is from this unitary stage that the Gestalt psychologists begin. Ach recognizes a similar stage of unification (q.v.). The rapid descent of many maze-learning curves for the rat possibly corresponds to a similar unification also.

system-under-stress.[2] But the theory is by no means dead. Thorndike's theory of "connectionism" was professedly associational. Boring, Langfeld, and Weld's *Foundations of Psychology* (1948) devotes the first six pages of the chapter on *Learning* (Hovland) to what is called a "simple type, associative learning", that is, to conditioned-reflex learning, and ends the section with a formulation of the *law of contiguity*, which, the writer says, must be supplemented by other principles, especially by motivation. There are many other psychologists of the first rank who hold some kind of associational theory today.

The fact is that in spite of many serious criticisms from both the experimental and the analytical side the theory is still of undoubted value in providing a formulation of relatively complex events. At the same time, many feel with Hovland that it must be supplemented, at least by the concept of motive. Using the hypothesis of need-reduction, Clark Hull has made an impressive attempt to combine both principles, that of association and that of motive (1943). There are, however, great difficulties in the equation which he makes of need-reduction with motive.[3] In addition the notion of motive is itself vague, and, as Woodworth once remarked, there are doubts whether it can ever be made scientific. It certainly holds many dangers, of which not the least is that of begetting a new Faculty psychology; but its use by psychologists of the highest competence testifies to its convenience and value. And as giving recognition to what Lewin called the "motor" for physical or mental events and recognizing the part played by the larger integrations of the organism, larger, that is to say, than what might be called the "quick-fire" of associationism, the modern doctrine of motive does seem to have justified itself. But the theory of thinking thus finds itself in the paradoxical position of being forced to employ two concepts or hypotheses one of which experiment seems largely to have refuted, while theory has but uneasily digested, if indeed it has digested, the other.

In addition the psychology of thinking must deal not only with conscious but also with unconscious processes and motivation. It was of course Freud that first taught us to recognize the existence of "wishes" of which we are not conscious, and it has been seen that the *Aufgabe* and the *Determining Tendencies* were claimed to function unconsciously. It has been seen that Messer also postulated an

---

[2] Lewin himself spoke of the "pressure of will or of a need" and apparently approved of this formulation in 1935 (Lewin, 1935, p. 44).

[3] See Hilgard, 1948, pp. 106 ff.

unconscious machinery underlying the conscious process of thought, and that, of the modern experimentalists, Maier showed that what he calls "direction" can be given unconsciously.[4] There is ostensible evidence from other souces that what would ordinarily be called thought-processes may occur without the consciousness of the thinker, who may "lay the problem aside".[5] It appears fairly certain that scientific and artistic invention may be consciously initiated, laid aside for a while and suddenly completed with full consciousness after an interval which may in some cases amount to years. In all probability some form of working that is unconscious must be postulated to explain these cases.[6] The question whether unconscious steps occur analogous to those of conscious reasoning has yet to be decided experimentally. If such unconscious thought processes do occur, we do not know whether they are of the same general nature as ordinary conscious reasoning, or, as Freud claims for the workings of his Unconscious, radically different. The necessary experiments should not be impossible to devise.

There are thus many problems clustering round the concept of the motor of thinking. Only experiment can solve and probably in some cases even formulate them. It seems likely that both problems and their solutions will ultimately be found to belong not to the psychology of thinking alone but to the broad field of Psychology itself.

Another salient group of problems centres on the fact that thinking involves not only "covert" processes, those of experience, of the kind the Würzburgers treated, but also "overt" activities, the existence of which they did indeed notice but only incidentally. The most obvious of these is speech, but clearly other activities are in many cases involved. It is fair to say that in general while a human being thinks his problem out, an animal acts it out, though there are many exceptions

[4] It is conceivable, of course, that the cue was immediately forgotten in Maier's experiment.

[5] Platt and Baker (1931, p. 1977) and Rossman (1931) give many interesting examples; as does Hadamard (1945). Some of these are collected by Humphrey ... 36, reports the same kind of thing for ... necke (1934), who set problems to an ... Again one finds the process of "laying ... who believes that "a large part of our ... ic", has a most interesting and properly ... tion". He traces the notion to Hamilton ... n-experimental examples of what seems ... data.

... ie, fresh stimulation, etc., may account ... ne cases.

to be found. Probably here again there is a continuum from, as far as we know, a complete "acting-out" in the more primitive organisms, to a nearly complete "thinking-out" in human beings engaged in certain problems. It has been seen that one form of action, namely speech, is of great assistance to human thinking, and reason has been given to believe that the elementary activity known as muscular tonus is in all probability of assistance also. We still lack any intimate knowledge of the relationship of the two terms in the Thought-in-Action complex. Except for a very few experiments we do not know the nature of the dazzling advantages conferred on our thinking by language. We do not know exactly what it means to say that different series of activities, verbal and otherwise, may result from processes which in a genuine sense of the word are prior to them. Lashley's and Dashiell's experiments, as well as everyday experience, have shown us the fact beyond doubt. A hundred years of psychologizing have shown only what statements to avoid, such as the "idea results in action", or "the idea (or image) precedes thought".

One other problem seems to be worth noting which does not seem to be related directly to the other two. During the "trial and error" activity which may be found in much thinking and perhaps at every level of psychological activity, nobody has yet asked the question how the thinker recognizes the (correct) solution when it occurs to him. For covert trial and error the question answers itself—at least we assume that it does. That is to say the conventional statement is that the cat in the puzzle makes a number of movements until it obtains food. There is "need-reduction", in Hull's language, and activity stops. But what of a man thinking out a way to earn food? All sorts of solutions come to mind. Some are rejected, but on what principle? We do not know at present. It is, of course, conceivable that "motive" is again involved.

General Statement of the Present Position

After fifty years of experiment the following skeletal account may then be tentatively given. The intention is, in the main to include experimentally derived fact, with only such analytical statement as is necessary to provide a framework for it.

(1) *Thinking as the term is understood in this book may be provisionally defined as what occurs in experience when an organism, human or animal, meets, recognizes, and solves a problem.*[7] (The term

[7] The term *problem* is used with some hesitation. Since problem and non-problem situations shade imperceptibly into each other, the term must

reasoning is preferred by some writers.) It is thus part of the total process of organic interaction with the environment. On the side of the organism this total process includes many levels of organized activity, of which thinking itself should possibly be considered one, as apparently by Bentley and the later Würzburgers. Those considered in this volume generally facilitate the total process, but there is some evidence that they may on occasion be a hindrance to it. (See paragraphs 10, 12, 13 to follow.) One may compare the popular belief that thought itself if over-elaborated may hinder "action". There is probably no hard-and-fast distinction between learning and thinking, though the former term is generally used when there is repetition of the total organism-environment complex, and when certain other conditions are complied with.

(2) *A problem is a situation which for some reason appreciably holds up an organism in its efforts to reach a goal.* In practice the problem often though not always contains contradictory factors, which have to be reconciled.[8] Duncker has drawn attention to what he calls "constraint", which is often found in problem situations.

(3) *The process of thinking involves an active combination of features which as part of the problem situation were originally discrete* (Selz, Maier, Gestalt, Herrick, many philosophers). This process is the culmination of the organic process of integration described and examined minutely by such writers as Sherrington.[9] The delay characteristic of reaction to a problem is often due to the fact that

necessarily be indefinite. It should be noted that there is no qualitative difference between problem and non-problem situations, that "thinking" occurs during, perhaps is "released by", the period of delay, that a given situation will or will not be a problem according to the experience and capacities of the particular organism concerned. To borrow Woodworth's remark about motive, it is perhaps doubtful whether the term problem can ever be made scientific. Nevertheless it has been and still is of value in psychology. For reasons given in Chapter VI, Woodworth's definition in terms of "novelty" cannot be accepted. A first attempt is made in this general statement to combine Woodworth's "Problem solving" with his "Thinking" (1938, Chapters XXIX, XXX). Madison Bentley's excellent article: "Where does Thinking come in?" (1943) discusses with great acumen the definition of thinking. He makes it a single, *distinctive* resource of the organism. When he says that it "integrates . . . simpler and more primitive operations", the conclusion reached here fully confirms and perhaps elaborates on his conclusion. Chrisof, a pupil of Bentley's (1939), collects the more common definitions of thinking.

[8] E.g. Maier's rats were motivated to traverse a certain path, but the path was impassable (Maier, 1938). One of Bühler's problems was: Is this true? The smaller the woman's foot, the larger the bill for the shoes.

[9] Charlotte Bühler, 1918, found that her subjects were unable to apprehend two meaningful words *without* relating them.

the necessary integration begins to approach the limit of organic capacity.

(4) *It involves the use of past experience. The fact is obvious, but the method by which it comes about is still not decided.* The early experimentalists thought that a replica of past experience was produced by association ("reproductive tendencies"). Various alternatives have been proposed, such as the "actualization" of (stereotyped) knowledge (Selz); a (more or less) inert and modifiable "memory-trace" (Gestalt); a Schema (Bartlett, 1932; Chapter X; Oldfield and Zangwill, 1942, 1943), the "conditioned response", and so on. It is possible that more than one of these suggested mechanisms may actually operate.

(5) *Not only the method but also the form of the ingression of the past into the present is under dispute.* One school maintains that the relation between past and present is particular (Hull: the "continuity theory"), an opposing school that it is general (Lashley). This divergence of opinion has had its counterpart among philosophers. Paragraphs (4) and (5) involve problems which are being attacked in the field of learning. The problems belong equally to the field of thinking, as so many others.

(6) *There is ubiquitous "trial and error" during thought-activity, whether animal or human, overt or covert.* This has been noted in verbal (Würzburg, Selz, Willwoll) problems, puzzle-solving by human beings (Ruger), generalization and abstraction, mechanical and practical problem-solving by human beings, and so on.

Such behaviour may be found in the descriptions of the Gestalt experiments. The mechanism by which the "wrong" solutions are rejected in overt learning is obscure; it is doubly obscure in thinking. Trial and error or its counterpart is a general principle of adaptive behaviour, and may be found in organisms of many grades.

(7) *For purposes of psychological analysis, motive (motor) may be distinguished as an aspect of thinking.* This distinction seems to be made necessary by the pioneer work of Watt and Ach, and it was sharpened by the work of Lewin. The motivation of thought has received little experimental attention, though much attention has been paid to motivation in learning. Motive implies a goal. It might thus be said that for the thinker the problem-field becomes polarized towards the goal.[10] The polarization disappears when the problem is solved. Although the present concern with problems of motivation

---

[10] Conceivably this is the process of "seeing the problem". The problem is perhaps a problem because of incomplete polarization.

is a healthy one, it is entirely possible that further developments will render the dichotomy no longer useful.[11]

(8) In addition there must be postulated some principle to account for the "direction" of thinking; that is, to account for the fact that thinking keeps more or less to the point. The fact was long ago noticed, and many explanations have been given for it (Humphrey, 1940). The assumption is generally made that the motive performs this function, but it is not necessarily correct. (Distinguish this use of the term "direction" from Maier's.)

(9) *The Würzburg group, under the direction of Külpe, developed the doctrine that thought-as-experienced is free from sensory content of any kind.* Thus they contradicted the conventional (structural) theory of the time which claimed that experience comprised only sensation, images, and affects. The Würzburg results were confirmed by many, notably by Binet, who indeed claimed priority for them. They were contradicted by the results of the Cornell experiments, which resolved the imageless thoughts into kinæsthetic sensations. It is maintained in this book that the position of the Cornell group is untenable. Since they are stated in demoded terms the Würzburg results are unacceptable in their original form to many modern psychologists. An alternative statement is proposed in the text.

(10) *The Würzburg psychologists were inclined to underestimate the importance of the image. The image is a form of organization which is part of the more inclusive process of response.* It seems undoubtedly to be of value in certain contexts, though there is evidence that it may be valueless at times and even a hindrance to the total process. Individual and group differences may be important here, and also the nature of the problem.[12]

(11) *The Gestalt theorists, and in particular Kohler, Koffka, Wertheimer, and Duncker, have stressed production as against (associative) reproduction in thinking. At the same time they have developed the notion of the organism under stress to account for the motor of thought.* Certain experimentalists allied to this school, such as Luchins and

[11] D. O. Hebb in his recent book *Organization of Behaviour* (Wiley, 1949) has pointed the way in this direction.

[12] Bowers (1931, 1935) found images of use in some tasks but not in others; Willwoll found images generally a help but sometimes a hindrance; Galton gives some anecdotal cases which tend towards the hindrance conclusion; Klüver (1931) states that eidetic images may at times be a hindrance, and believes it is difficult to distinguish them from ordinary memory images, an opinion shared by Morsh and Abbott (1945). Comstock (1921) has already been quoted as finding that images are of value. See Chapter IX.

Maier (1938), seem to admit also a principle akin to association, which according to their experiments may be detrimental to productive thinking. The latter is accompanied by a restructuring of the perceptual field, which gives "insight" into the problem.

(12) *Even when the thinker is overtly still, traces of the matrix of activity in which thought has grown up still remain in the changes of muscular tonus observed by many experimentalists.* There is an optimal range of tonus, above or below which any particular process of thinking is impeded. Thus tonus, like muscular activity in general, may under the right conditions help and under the wrong conditions hinder solution. (Trial and *error*: see also Maier, 1938, p. 41.) "Thinking out" may clearly prevent a disaster that would have been precipitated by "acting out". That is why the "thinking" method has won its evolutionary place.

(13) *A specialized form of activity is speech, which at least in its derivatives, such as writing and mathematics, is peculiar to human beings. Clinical, experimental, and factorial results agree that language cannot be equated with thinking.* Language is ordinarily of great assistance in thinking. It may also be a hindrance, as pointed out by Woodworth ("often we have to get away from speech in order to think clearly"—1938, p. 809) and many others. This is probably because speech, too, is so highly organized an activity.

(14) *Generalization may be defined as the activity whereby an organism comes to effect a constant modification towards an invariable feature or set of features occurring in a variable context.* Since all learning involves a context which is to some extent variable, the process is common to both learning and thinking. Like all kinds of thinking, *generalization does not necessarily involve language, though it is often improved by language.* (Query: Is it ever impeded by language?)

(15) Thus a number of different grades and kinds of organization are involved in the total response to a problem-situation; of these (1) images of various modalities; (2) muscular action, including, in particular, (3) speech, have been mentioned as such; to this list there should perhaps be added (4) concepts. The total process is in general facilitated by these organizations, but, apparently, cases occur where it is hindered by at least (1), (2), and (3).

(16) An artificial problem of "meaning" has been created by treating the *image* and *speech-activity* apart from their total context. (Conceivably the same kind of confusion has been created by treating the "concept" apart from its environmental context, thus invoking the "problem of the Universal".)

REFERENCES

A good bibliography, with 169 titles, will be found at the end of D. M. Johnson's excellent paper entitled: "A Modern Account of Problem Solving", *Psychological Bulletin*, **41**, 1944. See also Gibson and McGarvey, 1937. To certain of these titles specific reference is not made.

Ach, N., 1905, *Über die Willenstätigkeit und das Denken*. Göttingen.

—— 1921, *Über die Begriffsbildung*. Bamberg.

—— 1935, *Analyse des Willens*. Berlin & Wien.

Adams, S., & Powers, F. F., 1929, *Psychol. Bull.*, **26**, 241–60.

Adamson, R., 1884, *Mind*, N.S. **9**, 438.

—— 1903, *The Development of Modern Philosophy*. Edinburgh & London.

Allport, F. H., 1924, *Social Psychology*. Boston.

Allport, G. W., 1937, *Personality*. New York.

Arons, L., 1933, *Amer. J. Psychol.*, **45**, 417–32.

Asch, S. E., 1935, *Psychol. Bull.*, **32**, 718.

Aster, E. A. von, 1908, *Z. Psychol.*, **49**, 56–107.

Aveling, F., 1912, *The Consciousness of the Universal*. London.

Bain, A., 1855, *The Senses and the Intellect*. London.

—— 1887, *Mind*, **12**, 161–82.

Barlow, M. C., 1928, *J. exp. Psychol.*, **11**, 306–12.

Bartlett, F. C., 1932, *Remembering*.

Bartlett, F. C., & Smith, E. M., 1920, *Brit. J. Psychol.*, **11**, 55–62.

Bechterew, W., 1926, *Allgemeine Grundlagen der Reflexologie des Menschen*. Leipzig & Wien.

Bentley, M., 1943, *Amer. J. Psychol.*, **56**, 354–80.

Berkeley, G., 1710, *The Principles of Human Knowledge*. London, 1937.

Betts, G. H., 1909, *The Distribution and Functions of Mental Imagery*.

Bills, A. G., 1927, *Amer. J. Psychol.*, **38**, 227–51.

—— 1937, *Psychol. Bull.*, **34**, 286–307.

Binet, A., 1903, *L'étude Expérimentale de l'Intelligence*. Paris.

—— 1903*a*, *Rev. Phil.*, **1**, 138–52.

—— 1909, *Année Psychol.*, **15**, (*avant-propos*).

—— 1910, *Année Psychol.*, **16**, (*avant-propos*).

Binet, A., & Simon, T., 1908, *Année Psychol.*, **14**, 284–339.

Blanshard, B., 1939, *The Nature of Thought*. London.

Bloomfield, L., 1933, *Language*. New York.

Bolles, M., & Goldstein, K., 1938, *Psychiat. Quart.*, **12**, 42–65.

Book, W. F., 1908, *The Psychology of Skill*. New York.

—— 1912, *Psychol. Bull.*, **9**, 30–4.

Boring, E. G., 1929, *A History of Experimental Psychology*. New York.

—— 1938, *Psychol. Rev.*, **45**, 92–6.

Bousfield, W. A., & Barry, H., Jr., 1933, *Amer. J. Psychol.*, **45**, 353–8.

Bovet, P., 1908, *Arch. de Psychol.*, **8**, 9–48.

Bowers, H., 1931, *Brit. J. Psychol.*, **21**, 271–82.

Bowers, H., 1935. *Brit. J. Psychol.*, **25**, 436–46.

Bradley, F. H., 1887, *Mind*, **12**, 354–81.

—— 1912, *The Principles of Logic*. New York. (Original, 1883.)

Bridgman, P. W., 1936, *The Nature of Physical Theory*. Princeton University.

Bryan, W. L., & Harter, N., 1897, *Psychol. Rev.*, **4**, 27–53.

—— —— 1899, *Psychol. Rev.*, **6**, 345–75.

Bühler, C., 1918, *Z. Psychol.*, **80**, 129.

Bühler, K., 1907, *Arch. ges. Psychol.*, **9**, 297–365.

—— 1908, *Arch. ges. Psychol.*, **12**, 1–23.

—— 1908a, *Arch. ges. Psychol.*, **12**, 24–9, b, 93–122.

—— 1926, *Z. Psychol.*, **99**, 145–59.

—— 1934, *Sprachtheorie*. Jena.

Bulbrook, M. E., 1932, *Amer. J. Psychol.*, **44**, 409–53.

Burnham, W. H., 1921, *Ment. Hyg.*, **5**, 673–706.

Burt, C., 1949, *Brit. J. Educ. Psychol.*, **19**, 176–99.

Burtt, H. E., 1934, *Psychol. Bull.*, **31**, 671–2.

Calkins, M. W., 1896, *Psychol. Monogr.*, **2**.

—— 1909, *Amer. J. Psychol.*, **20**, 268–77.

Cantril, H., 1932, *Psychol. Monogr.*, **42**, 5.

Carmichael, L., 1946, *Manual of Child Psychology*. New York.

Carmichael, L., Hogan, H. P., & Walter, A. A., 1932, *J. exp. Psychol.*, **15**, 73–86.

Carpenter, W. B., 1874, *Mental Physiology*. London.

Carr, H., 1930, *J. genet. Psychol.*, **37**, 189–219.

Cason, H., 1934, *Amer. J. Psychol.*, **46**, 207–28.

Cassirer, E., 1923, *Substance and Function and Einstein's Theory of Relativity*. Chicago.

Chant, S. N. F., 1933, *Amer. J. Psychol.*, **45**, 282–91.

Chapman, D. W., 1932, *Amer. J. Psychol.*, **44**, 163–74.

Chrisof, C., 1939, *Amer. J. Psychol.*, **52**, 161–85.

Claparède, E., 1934, *Arch. Psychol.*, **24**, 1–154.

Clarke, H. M., 1911, *Amer. J. Psychol.*, **22**, 214–49.

Comstock, C., 1921, *Amer. J. Psychol.*, **32**, 196–230.

Cook, T. W., 1946, *Psychol. Rev.*, **53**, 214–24.

Courts, F. A., 1942, *Psychol. Bull.*, **39**, 347–75. Bibliography of 82 references.

—— 1942, *J. exper. Psychol.*, **30**, 504–11.

Curtis, H. S., 1899–1900, *Amer. J. Psychol.*, **11**, 237–9.

Davis, F. C., 1932, *J. exper. Psychol.*, **15**, 630–61.

Davis, R. C., 1939, *J. exper. Psychol.*, **24**, 451–65.

—— 1942, *Psychol. Bull.*, **39**, 329–46.

—— 1946, "The Psychophysiology of Set", *in Twentieth-century Psychology* (Harriman, ed.). New York.

Delacroix, H., 1930, *Le Langage et La Pensée*. Paris.

Dennis, W., 1929, *J. genet. Psychol.*, **36**, 59–90.

Dewey, J., 1910, *How We Think*. Boston.

Dodge, R., 1896, Die Motorische Wortvorstellungen. *Abhandlungen zur Philos. u. ihre Geschichte* (Erdmann.) viii. Halle.

Duffy, E., 1932, *Amer. J. Psychol.*, **44**, 146–62.

Dumas, G., 1932, *Nouveau Traité de Psychologie*. Paris.

Duncker, K., 1926, *Ped. Sem. (J. genet. Psychol.)*, **33**, 642–708.

—— 1935, *Zur Psychologie des Produktiven Denkens*. Berlin.

Dunlap, K., 1936, *Elements of Psychology*. St. Louis.

Dunn, M., 1926, *The Psychology of Reasoning*. Baltimore.

Durkin, H. E., 1937, *Arch. Psychol.*, **210**.

Dürr, E., 1908, *Z. Psychol.*, **49**, 313–40.

Ebbinghaus, H., 1885, *Über das Gedächtnis*. Leipzig.

Ehrenfels, C. von, 1890, *Vierteljahrschrift für Wissensch. Phil.*, **14**.

Eisenson, J., 1938, *The Psychology of Speech*. New York.

English, H. B., 1922, *Amer. J. Psychol.*, **33**, 305–50.

Erdmann, B., 1908, *Umrisse zur Psychologie des Denkens*. 2 Aufl.

Esper, E. A., 1935, " Language ", in *Murchison's Handbook of Social Psychology*. Clark University Press.

Ewert, P. H., & Lambert, J. F., 1932, *J. gen. Psychol.*, **6**, 400–13.

Ewing, A. W. G., 1930, *Aphasia in Children*. Oxford.

Fernald, M. R., 1912, *Psychol. Monogr.*, **14**, 58.

Fields, P. E., 1932, *Comp. Psychol. Monogr.*, **9**, 2.

Fisher, S. C., 1916, *Psychol. Monogr.*, **21**, 90.

—— 1931, *Amer. J. Psychol.*, **43**, 131–6.

Flach, A., 1925, *Arch. ges. Psychol.*, **52**, 369–440.

Ford, A., 1929, *Amer. J. Psychol.*, **41**, 1–32.

Franz, S. I., 1921, *Psychol. Rev.*, **28**, 81–95.

—— 1930, *J. gen. Psychol.*, **3**, 401–11.

Freeman, G. L., 1930a, *Amer. J. Psychol.*, **42**, 173–212.

—— 1930a, *J. gen. Psychol.*, **4**, 309–34.

—— 1931a, *J. gen. Psychol.*, **5**, 479–93.

—— 1931b, *Psychol. Rev.*, **38**, 428–49.

·—— 1933, *Amer. J. Psychol.*, **45**, 17–52.

—— 1938, *Amer. J. Psychol.*, **51**, 146–50.

—— 1939, *Amer. J. Psychol.*, **52**, 16–30.

Frenkel, E., 1931, *Z. Psychol.*, **123**, 193–258.

Galton, F., 1879, *Proc. Roy. Inst. Great Britain*, 161–71.

—— 1883, *Enquiries into Human Faculty*. London.

Gard, W. L., 1907, *Amer. J. Psychol.*, **18**, 490–504.

Gardiner, A. H., 1932, *The Theory of Speech and Language*. Oxford.

Gelb, A., 1933, *J. de Psychol.*, **30**, 403–429.

Gelb, A., & Goldstein, K., 1924, *Psychol. Forsch.*, **6**, 127–86.

Gelfan, S., 1931, *Amer. J. Physiol.*, **96**, 16–20.

Gellerman, L. W., 1931, *J. genet. Psychol.*, **39**, 358–92.

Gengerelli, J. A., 1927, *Amer. J. Psychol.*, **38**, 639–46.

—— 1930, *J. genet. Psychol.*, **38**, 171–202.

Gibson, J. J., 1929, *J. exper. Psychol.*, **12**, 1–39.

—— 1941, *Psychol. Bull.*, **38**, 781–817.

Gibson, E., & McGarvey, H., 1937, *Psychol. Bull.*, **34**, 327–350. Review with 108 references.

Goldstein, K., 1933, *J. de Psychol.*, **30**, 430–96.

—— 1936, *J. Psychol.*, **2**, 301–16.

Goldstein, K., 1948, *Language and Language Disturbances*, New York.

Golla, F. L., 1921, *Lancet*, **2**, 115–22, 215–21, 265–70, 373–79.

Graham, J. L., 1939, Lehigh Univ. studies (reprint from Peterson Memorial Number, *Psychol. Monogr.*, 1938, **50**).

Grice, G. R., 1948, *J. exper. Psychol.*, **38**, 1–16.

Grünbaum, A. A., 1908, *Arch. ges. Psychol.*, **12**, 340–478.

Hadamard, J., 1945, *The Psychology of Invention in the Mathematical Field*. Princeton University.

Hamilton, W., 1846, *Reid's Works*. Edinburgh.

Hanawalt, N. G., & Demarest, I. H., 1939, *J. exper. Psychol.*, **25**, 159–74.

Hanfmann, E., 1936, *Psychol. Bull.*, **33**, 796.

—— 1939, *Arch. Neurol. Psychiat.*, **41**, 568–79.

—— 1939a, *J. abnorm. soc. Psychol.*, **34**, 249–64.

Hanfmann, E., & Kasanin, J., 1937, *J. Psychol.*, **3**, 521–40.

Hansen, K., & Lehmann, A., 1895, *Wundt's Phil. Stud.*, **11**, 471–530.

Harrower, M. R., 1932, *Psychol. Forsch.*, **17**, 56–120.

Hartmann, G., 1931, *Psychol. Rev.*, **38**, 242–53.

—— 1933, *Amer. J. Psychol.*, **45**, 663–77.

Hathaway, S. R., 1935, *J. exper. Psychol.*, **18**, 285–98.

Hazlitt, U., 1930, *Brit. J. Psychol.*, **20**, 354–61.

Head, H., 1921, *Brit. J. Psychol.*, **11**, 179–93.

—— 1926, *Aphasia and Kindred Disorders of Speech*. Cambridge.

Hebb, D. O., & Foord, E. N., 1945, *J. exper. Psychol.*, **35**, 335–348.

Heidbreder, E., 1924, *Arch. Psychol.*, 73.

Heidbreder, E. F., 1934, *Psychol. Bull.*, **31**, 673.

—— 1936, *Psychol. Bull.*, **33**, 724.

—— 1946, *J. gen. Psychol.*, **35**, 173–89.

—— 1946, *J. gen. Psychol.*, **35**, 191–223.

—— 1947, *J. Psychol.*, **24**, 93–138.

—— 1948, *J. Psychol.*, **26**, 193–216.

—— 1949, *J. Psychol.*, **27**, 3–39.

—— 1949, *J. Psychol.*, **27**, 263–309.

Heidbreder, E. F., Bensley, M. L., & Ivy, M., 1948, *J. Psychol.*, **25**, 299–329.

Heidbreder, E. F., & Overstreet, P., 1948, *J. Psychol.*, **26**, 45–69.

Henley, E. H., 1935, *Arch. Psychol.*, 183.

Heron, W. T., 1924, *Comp. Psychol. Monogr.*, **2**, 8.

Herrick, C. J., 1926, *Brains of Rats and Men*. Chicago.

Hicks, G. D., 1938, *Critical Realism*. London.

Hilgard, E. R., 1931, *Psychol. Monogr.*, **41**, 1.

—— 1948, *Theories of Learning*. New York.

Höfler, R., 1927, *Z. Kinderpsychiat.*, **33**, 414–44.

Hollingworth, H. L., 1926, *The Psychology of Thought*. New York & London.

Holt, E. B., 1931, *Animal Drive and the Learning Process*, Vol. I. New York.

Hovland, C. I., 1948, "Learning", in Boring Langfeld and Weld's *Foundations of Psychology*. New York & London.

Hull, C. L., 1920, *Psychol. Monogr.*, **28**, 1, 123.

—— 1934, "Learning: II", in *Murchison's Handbook of General Experimental Psychology*, 382–455. Worcester, U.S.A.

Hull, C. L., 1935, *Psychol. Rev.*, **42,** 219–45.
—— 1943, *Principles of Behavior*. New York.
Hume, D., 1896 (1739–40), *A Treatise of Human Nature*. Oxford.
Humphrey, G., 1933, *The Nature of Learning*. London.
—— 1940, *Brit. J. Psychol.*, **30,** 183–96.
—— 1948, *Directed Thinking*. New York.
Hunter, W. S., 1920, *Psychobiology*, **2,** 1–17.
Hunter, W. S., & Nagge, J. W., 1931, *J. genet. Psychol.*, **39,** 303–19.
Hunter, W. S., & Bartlett, S. C., 1948, *J. exper. Psychol.*, **38,** 558–67.
Hüper, H., 1928, *Arch. ges. Psychol.*, **62,** 315–408.
Husband, R. W., 1928, *J. gen. Psychol.*, **1,** 15–28.
Husserl, E., 1913, *Logische Untersuchungen*. Halle.
Huxley, T. H., 1879, *David Hume*. New York.
Jacobson, E., 1911, *Amer. J. Psychol.*, **22,** 553–77.
—— 1929, *Progressive Relaxation*. Chicago.
—— 1930, *Amer. J. Physiol.*, **91,** 567–608; **94,** 22–34; **95,** 694–712.
—— 1931, *Amer. J. Physiol.*, **96,** 115–25; **97,** 200–9.
—— 1934, *Amer. J. Physiol.*, **108,** 573–80.
—— 1939, *Amer. J. Psychol.*, **52,** 620–4.
James, W., 1890, *Principles of Psychology*. London.
Johnson, H. M., & Weigand, G. E., 1927, *Proc. Penn. Acad. Sci.*, **2,** 43.
Joseph, H. W. B., 1916, *An Introduction to Logic*. Oxford.
Kakise, H., 1911, *Amer. J. Psychol.*, **22,** 14–64.
Kantor, J. R., 1936, *An Objective Psychology of Grammar*. Bloomington.
Katona, G., 1927, *Psychol. Forsch.*, **9,** 159–62.
Kellogg, W. N., & White, R. E., 1935, *J. Comp. Psychol.*, **19,** 119–48.
Kennedy, F., & Wolf, A., 1936, *J. Nerv. Ment. Dis.*, **84,** 125–45, 293–311.
Klein, D. B., 1936, *General Psychology*. New York.
Klüver, H., 1931, Article in Murchison's *Handbook of Child Psychology*.
Koffka, K., 1912, *Zur Analyse der Vorstellungen und ihrer Gesetze*. Leipzig.
—— 1922, *Psychol. Bull.*, **19,** 531–85.
—— 1925, "Psychologie", in *Lehrbuch der Philosophie*, 497–603. Berlin.
—— 1927, *Psychol. Forsch.*, **9,** 163–83.
—— 1935, *Principles of Gestalt Psychology*. London & New York.
Korte, A., 1915, *Z. Psychol.*, **72,** 194–296.
Köhler, W., 1925, *The Mentality of Apes*. New York.
—— 1929, 1947, *Gestalt Psychology*. New York.
—— 1941, *Proc. Amer. Philos. Soc.*, **84,** 4, 489–502.
Krechevsky, I., 1937, *J. comp. Psychol.*, **23,** 121–63, 351–64.
Kuenne, M. R., 1946, *J. exper. Psychol.*, **36,** 471–90.
Külpe, O., 1893, *Grundriss der Psychologie*. Berlin.
—— 1904, *Bericht über den 1st Kongress für experimentelle Psychologie*, 56–68.
—— 1922, *Vorlesungen über Psychologie*. Leipzig.
Kuo, Z. Y., 1923, *J. exper. Psychol.*, **6,** 247–93.
Laguna, G. A. de, 1927, *Speech, its Function and Development*. Yale University.
Lambert, J. F., & Ewert, P. H., 1932, *J. gen. Psychol.*, **6,** 377–99.
Lashley, K. S., 1921, *Brain*, 44.

Lashley, K. S., 1929, *Brain Mechanisms and Intelligence*. Chicago.

—— 1930, *Psychol. Rev.*, **37**, 1–24.

—— 1934, "Learning", in *Murchison's Handbook of General Experimental Psychology*. Worcester, U.S.A.

—— 1942, *J. gen. Psychol.*, **26**, 241–65.

Lashley, K. S., & Ball, J., 1929, *J. comp. Psychol.*, **9**, 71–106.

Leeper, R., 1935, *J. genet. Psychol.*, **46**, 3–40.

Lewin, K., 1926, *Psychol. Forsch.*, **7**, 294–329.

—— 1934, *Psychol. Forsch.*, **19**, 249–99.

—— 1935, *A Dynamic Theory of Personality*. New York & London.

Lindley, E. H., 1897, *Amer. J. Psychol.*, **8**, 431–93.

Long, L., & Welch, L., 1941, *J. Psychol.*, **12**, 21–44.

—— —— 1942, *J. Psychol.*, **13**, 41–59.

Luchins, A. S., 1942, *Psychol. Monogr.*, **54**, 6, 95.

McCarthy, D., 1933, "Language Development", in *Murchison's Handbook of Child Psychology*. Clark Univ. Press.

—— 1946, "Language Development in Children", in *Manual of Child Psychology*. Ed. Carmichael, London & New York.

Macfarlane, D. A., 1930, *Univ. of Calif. Pub. Psychol.*, **4**, 277–305.

Maier, N. R. F., 1930, *J. comp. Psychol.*, **10**, 115–43.

—— 1931, *J. comp. Psychol.*, **12**, 180–94.

—— 1931, *Psychol. Rev.*, **38**, 332–46.

—— 1933, *Brit. J. Psychol.*, **24**, 144–55.

—— 1936, *J. comp. Psychol.*, **21**, 357–66.

—— 1938, *Compar. Psychol. Monogr.*, **15**, 1–43, 44–85.

Maier, N. R. F., & Schneirla, T. C., 1935, *Principles of Animal Psychology*. New York & London.

Maier, N.R.F., & Curtis, Q. F., 1937, *J. comp. Psychol.*, **24**, 1–19.

Maigre, E., 1908, *Année Psychol.*, **14**, 380–9.

Marbe, K., 1901, *Experimentell-psychologische Untersuchungen über das Urteil*. Leipzig.

Max, L. W., 1934, *J. gen. Psychol.*, **11**, 112–25.

—— 1935, *J. comp. Psychol.*, **19**, 469–86.

—— 1937, *J. comp. Psychol.*, **24**, 301–44.

May, M., 1917, *Arch. Psychol.*, 39.

Mayer, A., & Orth, J., 1901, *Z. Psychol. & Physiol. d. Sinnesorg.*, 26.

McGranahan, D. V., 1936, *Psychol. Bull.*, **33**, 178–216.

Meili, R., 1936; *J. de Psychol.*, **33**, 614–28.

Meinecke, G., 1934, *Arch. ges. Psychol.*, **92**, 249–54.

Messer, A., 1906, *Arch. ges. Psychol.*, **8**, 1–224.

—— 1907, *Arch. de Psychol.*, **6**, 421.

Mill, J., 1829, *Analysis of the Phenomena of the Human Mind*. London.

Miller, D. S., 1895, *Psychol. Rev.*, **2**, 535–50.

Miller, M., 1926, *J. exper. Psychol.*, **9**, 26–44.

Mittenzwei, K., 1907, *Psychologische Studien*, **2**, 358–492.

Moore, T. V., 1910, *Univ. of Calif. Pubs. in Psychol.*, **1**, 2.

Morgan, J. J. B., 1916, *Arch. Psychol.*, **5**, 35.

Morris, C., 1946, *Signs Language and Behavior*. New York.

Morsh, J. E., & Abbott, H. D., 1945, *J. comp. Psychol.*, **38**, 47–63.

322 THINKING

Moskievitcz, G., 1910, *Arch. ges. Psychol.*, **18**.

Muenzinger, K., Koerner, L., & Irey, E., 1929, *J. comp. Psychol.*, **9**, 425–36.

Müller, G. E., 1911, *Z. Psychol.*, **5**.

Müller, G. E., & Pilzecker, A., 1900, *Z. Psychol.*, **1**.

Müller Freienfels, R., 1912, *Arch. ges. Psychol.*, **23**, 310–38.

Müller, M., 1887, *The Science of Thought*. 2 vols. New York.

Murphy, G., 1935, *A Briefer General Psychology*. New York & London.

Murphy, L. W., 1936, *J. Psychol.*, **2**, 353–66.

Naville, F., 1918, *Arch. de Psychol.*, **17**, 1–57.

Neff, W. S., 1936, *Amer. J. Psychol.*, **49**, 376–418.

Neuhaus, W., 1930, *Arch. ges. Psychol.*, **75**, 315–458.

Ogden, R. M., 1911, *Psychol. Bull.*, **8**, 183–97.

—— 1913, *Psychol. Rev.*, **20**, 378–410.

—— 1923, *Amer. J. Psychol.*, **34**, 223–30.

—— 1932, *Amer. J. Psychol.*, **44**, 350–6.

Ogden, C. K., & Richards, I. A., 1923, *The Meaning of Meaning*. London & New York.

Okabe T., 1910, *Amer. J. Psychol.*, **21**, 563–96.

Oldfield, R. C., & Zangwill, O. L., 1942, 1943, *Brit. J. Psychol.*, **32**, 267–86; **33**, 58–64.

Orth, J., 1903, *Gefühl und Bewusstseinslage*. Berlin.

Otis, A. S., 1920, *Psychol. Rev.*, **27**, 399–419.

Patrick, C., 1935, *Archiv. Psychol.*, 178.

—— 1937, *J. Psychol.*, **4**, 35–73.

Pavlov, I. P., 1926, *Die Höchste Nerventätigkeit (das Verhalten) von Tieren*. Munich.

—— 1927, *Conditioned Reflexes*. Oxford.

Pear, T. H., 1920, *Brit. J. Psychol.*, **11**, 71–80.

Pearson, G. H. J., & Alpers, B. J., 1928, *Arch. Neurol. & Psychiat.*, **19**, 281–95.

Peterson, J. C., 1920, *Psychol. Monogr.*, **28**, 129.

Pick, A., 1913, *Die agrammatischen Sprachstörungen*. Berlin.

Pintner, R., 1913, *Psychol. Rev.*, **30**, 129–53.

Platt, W., & Baker, B. A., 1931, *J. Chemical Educ.*, **8**, 1969–2002.

Pratt, C. C., 1928, *Psychol. Bull.*, **25**, 550–61.

Pyle, W. H., 1909, *Amer. J. Psychol.*, **20**, 530–569.

Razan, G. H. S., 1939, *J. exper. Psychol.*, **24**, 95–105.

Rees, H. J., & Israel, H. E., 1935, *Psychol. Monogr.*, **46**, 210, 1–26.

Renshaw, S., & Postle, D. K., 1928, *J. gen. Psychol.*, **1**, 360–7.

Rexroad, C. N., 1925, *J. exper. Psychol.*, **8**, 325–36.

—— 1926, *Psychol. Rev.*, **33**, 451–8.

—— 1926, *J. exper. Psychol.*, **9**, 1–18.

Rizzolo, A., 1931, Columbia Ph.d. dissertation (reported in Murphy, 1935, *Briefer General Psychology*, p. 546).

Roberts, K. E., 1933, *Univ. Iowa Stud. in Child Welfare*, **7**, 3, 94.

Robertson, G. C., 1878, *Encyclopædia Britannica*, 9th edition.

Rossmann, J., 1931, *The Psychology of the Inventor*.

Rubin, E., 1921, *Visuell wahrgenommene Figuren*. Copenhagen.

Ruediger, W. C., 1920, *Psychol. Bull.*, **17**, 254.

Ruger, H. A., 1926 (1910), *The Psychology of Efficiency*. New York.

Saint, P., 1909, *Rev. Philos.*, **1**, 106.

Schäfer, R. C., 1934, *Arch. ges. Psychol.*, **92**, 289–314.

Schilling, R., 1929, *Z. Psychol.*, **111**, 204–46.

Schwiete, F., 1910, *Arch. ges. Psychol.*, **19**, 475–544.

Scripture, E. W., 1935, *J. exper. Psychol.*, **18**, 784–91.

Selz, O., 1913, *Arch. ges. Psychol.*, **27**, 367–80.

—— 1913a, *Über die Gesetze des geordneten Denkverlaufs*. Stuttgart.

—— 1920, *Z. Psychol.*, **83**, 211–34.

—— 1922, *Zur Psychologie des produktiven Denkens und des Irrtums. Eine experimentelle Untersuchung*. Bonn.

—— 1924, *Die Gesetze der Produktiven und Reproduktiven Geistestätigkeit. Kurzgefasste Darstellung*. Bonn.

—— 1927, *Kantstudien*, **32**, 273–80.

—— 1926, *Z. Psychol.*, **99**, 160–96.

Sherrington, C. S., 1906, *The Integrative Action of the Nervous System*. Yale University Press.

Shimberg, M., 1924, *Amer. J. Psychol.*, **35**, 167–84.

Shaw, E., *Psychol. Monogr.*, 113.

Skaggs, E. B., 1930, *J. gen. Psychol.*, **3**, 435–42.

Smith, F., 1923, *Brit. J. Psychol.*, **13**, 271–82.

Smoke, K. L., 1932, *Psychol. Monogr.*, **42**, 191.

—— 1933, *J. exper. Psychol.*, **16**, 583–8

—— 1935, *Psychol. Rev.*, **42**, 274–9.

Snoddy, G. S., 1920, *Psychol. Monogr.*, 28.

Spencer, H., 1855, *The Principles of Psychology*. London.

Stern, G., 1931, *Meaning and Change of Meaning*. Göteborg.

Stevanović, B. P., 1927, *Brit. J. Psychol.*, **12**, Monogr. 4.

Stinchfield, S. M., 1933, *Speech Disorders*. London & New York.

Stout, G. F., 1901, "Associationism and Association of Ideas", in Baldwin's *Dictionary of Philosophy and Psychology*.

—— 1902, *Analytic Psychology*. London.

Stroud, J. B., 1931, *J. exper. Psychol.*, **14**, 606–31.

Stumpf, W., 1907, *Abhl. d., Königl. Akad. d. Wissenschaften*.

Sullivan, E. B., 1927, *Psychol. Monogr.*, **36**, 169.

Taylor, C. O., 1905, *Z. Psychol.*, **40**.

Thorndike, E. L., 1932, *The Fundamentals of Learning*. New York.

Thorson, A. M., 1925, *J. exper. Psychol.*, **8**, 1–32.

Thurstone, L. L., 1945, *Theories of Intelligence*. Chicago.

Titchener, E. B., 1909, *Lectures on the Experimental Psychology of the Thought Processes*. London & New York.

Tolman, E. C., 1932, *Purposive Behavior in Animals and Men*. New York.

Travis, L. E., 1931, *Speech Pathology; a Dynamic Neurological Treatment of Normal Speech and Speech Deviations*. New York.

—— 1933, "Speech Pathology", in Murchison's *Handbook of Child Psychology*.

Varendonck, J., 1921, *The Psychology of Day-Dreams*. London.

Wada, T., 1922, *Arch. of Psychol.*, 8.

Ward, J., 1886, "Psychology", in *Encyclopædia Britannica*, 9th Edition.
—— 1893, *Mind*, **2**, 247–62.
—— 1894, *Mind*, **3**, 509–32.
—— 1933, *Psychological Principles*. Cambridge.
Warden, C. J., 1924, *J. exper. Psychol.*, **7**, 243–75.
Warden, C. J., & Warner, L. H., 1928, *Quart. rev. Biolog.*, **3**, 1–28.
Warren, H. C., 1921, *History of the Association Psychology*. New York.
Washburn, M. F., 1916, *Movement and Mental Imagery*. Boston & New York.
Watson, J. B., 1913, *Psychol. Rev.*, **20**, 158–77.
—— 1914, *Behavior: an Introduction to Comparative Psychology*. New York.
—— 1920, *Brit. J. Psychol.*, **11**, 87–104.
—— 1924, *Psychology from the Standpoint of a Behaviorist*. Philadelphia.
—— 1925, *Behaviorism*. New York.
—— 1929, "Behaviourism", *Encyclopædia Britannica*, pp. 327–9.
Watt, H. J., 1905, *Arch. ges. Psychol.*, **4**, 289–436.
—— 1905–6, *J. Anat. Physiol.*, **40**, 257–66.
Weigl, E., 1927, *Z. Psychol.*, **103**, 1–45, 257–322.
Weisenburg, T. H., 1934, *Arch. Neurol. Psychiat.*, **31**, 1–33.
Weisenburg, T. H., & MacBride, K. E., 1935, *Aphasia*. New York.
Welch, L., 1947, *J. genet. Psychol.*, **71**, 201–22
Welch, L., & Long, L., 1940, *J. Psychol.*, **9**, 59–95.
Wendt, G. R., 1930, *Arch. of Psychol.*, **18**, 123.
Wertheimer, M., 1921, *Psychol. Forsch.*, **1**, 47–65.
—— 1923, *Psychol. Forsch.*, **4**, 301–50.
—— 1925, *Drei Abhandlungen zur Gestalttheorie*. Erlangen.
—— 1945, *Productive Thinking*. New York.
White, M. M., 1934, *Psychol. Bull.*, **31**, 700.
Wilcocks, R. W., 1925, *Amer. J. Psychol.*, **36**, 324–41.
Willwoll, A., 1926, *Begriffsbildung*, Psychol. Monogr. von Karl Bühler, Hïrzel, Leipzig.
Wittgenstein, L., 1922, *Tractatus Logico-Philosophicus*. London & New York.
Wolf, A., 1930, *Textbook of Logic*. London.
Wolters, A. W. P., 1933, *Brit. J. Psychol.*, **24**, 133–43.
Woodworth, R. S., 1906, *The Cause of a Voluntary Movement*, Gaerman studies in Philosophy and Psychology. Boston.
—— 1906, *J. Philos. Psychol. & Sci. Method*, **3**, 701–8.
—— 1907, *J. Philos. Psychol. & Sci. Method*, **4**, 169–76.
—— 1915, *Psychol. Rev.*, **22**, 1–27.
—— 1938, *Experimental Psychology*. New York.
Woodworth, R. S., & Sells, S. B., 1935, *J. exper. Psychol.*, **18**, 451–60.
Woodworth, R. S., & Marquis, D. G., 1947, *Psychology*. New York.
Wundt, W., 1901, *Sprachgeschichte und Sprachpsychologie*. Leipzig.
—— 1907, *Psychol. Stud.*, **3**, 301–60.
—— W., 1908, *Arch. ges. Psychol.* **11**, 445–59.
—— 1912, *Völkerpsychologie*, 2 Bd., Die Sprache, 2 Teil, 3 Aufl.
Yerkes, R. M., 1943, *Chimpanzees*. Yale University.
Young, P. T., 1948, Chap. XIII in Andrew's *Methods of Psychology*. New York.
Zartman, E. N., & Cason, H., 1934, *J. exper. Psychol.*, **17**, 671–79.

INDEX